The Ontology of Socratic Questioning
in Plato's Early Dialogues

SUNY series in Contemporary Continental Philosophy
Dennis J. Schmidt, editor

SUNY series in Ancient Greek Philosophy
Anthony Preus, editor

The Ontology of Socratic Questioning in Plato's Early Dialogues

SEAN D. KIRKLAND

Cover photo: Battle of Lapiths and Centaurs, west pediment, Temple of Zeus, Olympia
(Photo: Hirmer Fotoarchiv, München)

Published by State University of New York Press, Albany

© 2012 State University of New York

All rights reserved

Printed in the United States of America

No part of this book may be used or reproduced in any manner whatsoever without written permission. No part of this book may be stored in a retrieval system or transmitted in any form or by any means including electronic, electrostatic, magnetic tape, mechanical, photocopying, recording, or otherwise without the prior permission in writing of the publisher.

For information, contact State University of New York Press, Albany, NY
www.sunypress.edu

Production by Laurie D. Searl
Marketing by Anne M. Valentine

Library of Congress Cataloging-in-Publication Data

Kirkland, Sean D.
 The ontology of Socratic questioning in Plato's early dialogues / Sean D. Kirkland.
   pages cm. — (SUNYseries in contemporary Continental philosophy) (SUNY series in ancient Greek philosophy)
  Includes bibliographical references and index.
  ISBN 978-1-4384-4404-8 (paperback : alk. paper)
  ISBN 978-1-4384-4403-1 (hardcover : alk. paper) 1. Plato. 2. Socrates. 3. Ontology. 4. Questioning. I. Title.
  B398.O5K57 2012
  184—dc23
                                                     2011047982

10 9 8 7 6 5 4 3 2 1

Contents

Acknowledgments ix

List of Abbreviations for Ancient Works Cited xi

Introduction: Socrates and the Hermeneutic of Estrangement xv

PART I. SOCRATIC PHENOMENOLOGY

CHAPTER 1. SETTING ASIDE THE SUBJECT-OBJECT FRAMEWORK IN READING PLATO — 3

Aristotelian Assessments of Plato's Socrates — 3
Construction or Destruction in the Early Dialogues — 8
From Excessive Being to Objective Reality and Back — 12
    Articulating Plato's Anti-Relativism — 13
    Distinguishing Socrates' Search for Definitions from Twentieth-Century Nominalism — 14
    Excavating the Everyday Understanding of Being in Plato — 16
    Consequences of Presupposing an Understanding of Being as Objective — 17

CHAPTER 2. ON *DOXA* AS THE APPEARING OF 'WHAT *IS*' — 23

Doxa versus Opinion — 23
Phainesthai and *Doxa* — 25

PART II. VIRTUE'S ONTOLOGICAL EXCESS AND DISTANCE

CHAPTER 3. THE EXCESSIVE TRUTH OF SOCRATIC DISCOURSE — 35

The Indefensibility of Philosophy in Plato's *Apology of Socrates* — 36
   Socrates' *Muthos* — 38
   Socrates' *Logos* — 41
The *Prooimion* to Socrates' *Apologia* — 43
   The Rhetorical Discourse of Socrates' Accusers — 43
   Socrates' Way of Discourse in His Defense — 46
   Socratic Truth as *Deinos* — 48
   Socrates' Way of Discourse in His Philosophical Activity — 55

CHAPTER 4. THE SHELTERING OF *TECHNĒ* VERSUS THE EXPOSURE OF HUMAN WISDOM — 59

Socrates versus the Sophists — 65
From Shelter to Exposure — 73
   The *Technē-Tuchē* Antithesis — 74
   The Socratic Understanding of *Technē* in Light of *Metaphysics* Alpha — 76
   The Non-Knowing of Virtue as Socrates' Aim — 82
   Socrates and the *Technē*-Model of Virtue — 87

CHAPTER 5. THE TRUTHFUL ELENCTIC *PATHOS* OF PAINFUL CONCERN — 93

Elenctic Pain and Being Concerned by Virtue — 94
Meletē in the *Apology* and *Aporia* throughout the Early Dialogues — 96
A Phenomenological Consideration of *Meletē/Aporia* — 101
Serenity in the Interpretations of Nehamas, Vlastos, and the Stoics — 105
Meletē/Aporia as Itself the *Alētheia* of 'What Virtue Is' — 109
Distance and Excess versus Transcendence or Immanence — 111

PART III. SOCRATIC VIRTUE IN THE FACE OF EXCESSIVE TRUTH

CHAPTER 6. THE COURAGE OF VIRTUE AND THE DISTANT HORIZON OF THE WHOLE IN THE *LACHES* — 119

Finite Transcendence and Socratic "Being With" — 120
Sophistication and the Everyday Attitude in the Introduction of the Two Generals — 123

The Unity of the Question 'What *is* Virtue?'	126
Being Many Everyday	132
Aristotle on Socrates and Definition *Katholou*	133
Meno 71d–73d	136
Euthyphro 5c–7a	138
Socrates' Interlocutors and the Confusion of Appearance and Being	140
Aporia and the Truth of Appearances	144
The Socratic Here and Now	150
CONCLUSION: *APORIA* IN THE MIDDLE DIALOGUES	153
Idea/Eidos as 'Look' and Phenomenal Being in the Middle Dialogues	156
Alētheia as Divine Wandering	159
The Good beyond Being and the Ideas as Excessive Measures	162
Human Monstrosity and Being between One and Many	166
Notes	173
Bibliography	247
Index	261

Acknowledgments

While researching and writing this book, I was fortunate to receive funding from the following sources: the State University of New York at Stony Brook; the Collegium Philosophiae Transatlanticum (CPT), which was funded by both the Deutsche Forschungsgemeinschaft (DFG) and the Kade Foundation; the Latin/Greek Institute of Brooklyn College and the City University of New York Graduate School; the Deutsche Akademische Austauschdienst (DAAD); and the University Research Council (URC) of DePaul University.

As this text is related, however distantly, to my dissertation, I would like to take this opportunity to acknowledge the great debt I owe to all the inspiring teachers I have had during my years at Gustavus Adolphus College, Stony Brook, and the University of Wuppertal, Germany, as well as at the Latin/Greek Institute. I am especially grateful to the two professors who acted as coadvisors for the dissertation, Peter Manchester and Klaus Held, and in addition, I thank the rest of the committee, Professors Clyde Lee Miller, Edward S. Casey, and Francisco Gonzalez, for their helpful questions and comments. Since taking a position in the Department of Philosophy at DePaul University, I have grown as a thinker thanks to the challenge and inspiration provided by my colleagues here; various parts of the following have benefited in particular from the criticisms and suggestions of David Farrell Krell, Richard A. Lee, William McNeil, Michael Naas, Franklin Perkins, and Peter Steeves. Finally, colleagues elsewhere who have substantively improved this work along the way with their comments on and responses to chapters they have read include Sara Brill, Jill Gordon, Heinrich Hüni, Malek Moazzam-Doulat, Andrea Rehberg, and Peter Trawny.

Intellectual stimulation and moral support have come in equal measure from family and friends and I take the opportunity here to express my sincere appreciation to them all *en masse*. Most of all, I must thank my wife,

Lisa Mahoney. Because I adore her she lends a flattering light to everything that appears on my horizon, but this work has benefited from her in substantive ways too, not only from her discerning editorial judgment, but also from her clarifying intelligence and essential questioning.

List of Abbreviations for Ancient Works Cited

All texts in Latin and Greek are taken from the *Oxford Classical Texts* series (Oxford: Clarendon Press) and translated by the author, unless otherwise noted.

AESCHYLUS
- *Ag.* — *Agamemnon*
- *Prom.* — *Prometheus Bound*
- *Suppl.* — *Suppliants*

ARISTOTLE
- *APo.* — *Posterior Analytics*
- *De An.* — *De Anima*
- *De Part.* — *De Partibus Animalis*
- *EE* — *Eudemian Ethics*
- *EN* — *Nicomachean Ethics*
- *MM* — *Magna Moralia*
- *Met.* — *Metaphysics*
- *Phys.* — *Physics*
- *Pol.* — *Politics*
- *Rhet.* — *Rhetoric*
- *SE* — *Sophistici Elenchi*
- *Top.* — *Topics*

Aristophanes
  Brd.   *Birds*
  Cl.   *Clouds*
  Fr.   *Frogs*

Cicero
  Acad.   *Academica*
  Tusc.   *Tusculan Disputations*
  De Off.   *De Officiis*

Diogenes Laertius
  Lives   *Lives of Eminent Philosophers*

Epictetus
  Disc.   *Discourses*
  Ench.   *Encheiridion*

Euripides
  Bacch.   *Bacchae*
  Med.   *Medea*
  Mel.   *Melanippe*

Herodotus
  Hist.   *Histories*

Hesiod
  Op.   *Works and Days*
  Theog.   *Theogony*

Homer
  Il.   *Iliad*
  Od.   *Odyssey*

Hippocrates
  OAM   *On Ancient Medicine*, fr. *Hippocrates*, Vol. I (Cambridge, MA: Harvard University Press, 1923)
  PT   *Peri Technēs*, fr. *Hippocrates*, Vol. II (Cambridge, MA: Harvard University Press, 1923)

HIPPOLYTUS
  Ref.   *Refutatio*

PINDAR
  Ol.   *Olympian Ode*

PLATO
  Alc. I   *Alcibiades I*
  Ap.   *Apology of Socrates*
  Chrm.   *Charmides*
  Cra.   *Cratylus*
  Cri.   *Crito*
  Ep. VII   *Epistle VII*
  Euthd.   *Euthydemus*
  Euthphr.   *Euthyphro*
  Grg.   *Gorgias*
  Hp. Ma.   *Hippias Major*
  Hp. Mi.   *Hippias Minor*
  La.   *Laches*
  Lg.   *Leges* (*Laws*)
  Ly.   *Lysis*
  Mx.   *Menexenus*
  Men.   *Meno*
  Prm.   *Parmenides*
  Phd.   *Phaedo*
  Phdr.   *Phaedrus*
  Phil.   *Philebus*
  Plt.   *Politicus* (*Statesman*)
  Prt.   *Protagoras*
  R.   *Politeia* (*Republic*)
  Sph.   *Sophist*
  Smp.   *Symposium*
  Thg.   *Theages*
  Tht.   *Theaetetus*
  Ti.   *Timaeus*

PLATO (SPURIOUS WORKS)
  Ax.   *Axiochus*
  Hipparch.   *Hipparchus*

PLUTARCH
  Adv. Col.   *Adversus Colotem*

SENECA (LUCIUS ANNAEUS)
  Epist. Mor.   *Epistulae Morales*, fr. Seneca, *Epistles* (Cambridge, MA: Harvard University Press / Loeb Library, 1925)

SEXTUS EMPIRICUS
  Adv. Math.   *Adversus Mathematicos*

SOLON
  Solon   Fragments, fr. *Greek Elegiac Poetry* (Cambridge, MA: Harvard University Press / Loeb Library, 1999)

SOPHOCLES
  OT   *Oedipus Rex*
  Ant.   *Antigone*

XENOPHON
  XAp.   *Apology of Socrates*
  XSmp.   *Symposium*

Introduction:
Socrates and the Hermeneutic of Estrangement

> Evidently Socrates had called something into being long ago which was very explosive. Intellectual dynamite! A moral bomb!
> —Winston S. Churchill, *My Early Life: A Roving Commission*

As is true with every work of interpretation, our subject matter in the following chapters presents itself as hidden. After all, interpretative effort is required of us only when we encounter resistance, and we are then guided in that effort by trace indications of something not yet grasped, not yet fully available. Given that our topic here is Socratic philosophizing in Plato's early dialogues, we might understand ourselves to be addressing texts that are foundational to a tradition we receive as our own. If so, let us acknowledge at the outset that, in reading such tradition-laden texts,[1] we should not look begrudgingly on this hiddenness or view it as a regrettable if inevitable obstacle. Rather, we should welcome just this play of resistance and indication, for it alone provides us with some hope that we are responding to that which most concerns us today.

Indeed, the liminal position in which we find ourselves, our transitional moment at the still undetermined and open end of metaphysics, complicates the historical hermeneutic task facing us. Plato's early Socrates should be fascinating just now not because he represents an established or heroic philosophical ideal, not because we are able to recognize and affirm his approach to thinking and questioning as sound or beneficial, but rather only to the extent that he emerges before us with a radically unfamiliar, even a bizarre philosophical project. That is to say, with a project perhaps not wholly delimited by those fundamental metaphysical principles operating throughout the tradition of thought inaugurated by the Greeks and still joining us to them. This is the Socrates who attracts our attention, for it is only as such a shadowy and confounding figure of our still living philosophical past that he might gesture ahead to our as yet uncharted philosophical future.

To be sure, the Socrates who thus provokes the following reading of Plato's early works, and who emerges into view through that reading, is a figure existing neither in the past nor in the present, neither as a product of Plato's imagination nor as a mere figment of our own. Rather, in his calling forth our interpretive effort, he exists *between* our past and our present, between Plato's text and us, allowing each to disrupt the other's sedimentation and, perhaps, set one another free. In approaching this figure, we ask not simply what Plato's Socrates says, but what he has to say *to us* . . . and we are delighted to hear something disturbing.

In *Socrates, Ironist and Moral Philosopher*, Gregory Vlastos might seem initially to be hearing something quite similar. He describes there his decision not to publish his first book-length manuscript on Socrates because it had failed to do justice to what was truly perplexing about this character, his essential "strangeness." This early failure left the twentieth century's most important Socratic scholar with the conviction that, when approaching the central figure of Plato's early works, "his paradoxes, pushed to the margins in that book, had to be brought into dead center."[2]

Indeed, Vlastos insists that everything be viewed in the obscuring light of what he elsewhere refers to as "*the* paradox of Socrates."[3] That central paradox is as follows. Socrates is, on the one hand, committed to the search for ethical knowledge, and he insists that only in the possession of such knowledge are we able to live well as human beings: "He has an evangel to proclaim, a great truth to teach: Our soul is the only thing in us worth saving, and there is only one way to save it: to acquire knowledge."[4] And yet, on the other hand, in both word and deed, Socrates consistently seems to undermine the very possibility of this knowledge. Throughout the early dialogues, he declares in both general and specific terms that even after a lifetime of exemplary searching he knows nothing. Even worse, his fundamental mode of philosophizing, the elenchus or refutation, seems aimed *exclusively* at exposing the absence of any such saving knowledge in others. Vlastos once summed up the Socratic endeavor in the following terms:

> Socrates' characteristic activity is the *elenchus*, literally, "the refutation." You say A, and he shows you that A implies B, and B implies C, and then asks, "But didn't you say D before? And does C contradict D?" And there he leaves you with your shipwrecked argument,

without so much as telling you what part of it, if any, might be salvaged.⁵

In his central mode of philosophizing, Socrates seems to engage us in an urgent search for knowledge even while relentlessly indicating its unattainability. Again and again, these Socratic conversations do nothing but reveal his interlocutors and himself to be suffering from an intolerable epistemic and ethical inadequacy. Vlastos has drawn our attention to this interpretive dilemma and, in my opinion, rightly demands that we allow it to direct us in our reading of these Platonic texts.⁶

However, there is, I would suggest, a depth of strangeness here that Vlastos and his many adherents fail to recognize. Indeed, it seems that for these interpreters the perplexity generated by the figure of Socrates is merely provisional and, ultimately, even somewhat superficial. That is, in order to cope with this troubling character no fundamental self-scrutiny is required *of us*, no reconsideration of our basic philosophical presuppositions or principles. It might even be said that, in the end, Vlastos effectively excises the malignant paradox, declaring the Socratic elenchus not at all the negative or destructive philosophical method it initially seemed to be. Rather, the elenchus is ultimately redeemed as successful in establishing certain positive Socratic moral precepts. It does so, Vlastos argues, by showing over time that anyone holding an opinion contrary to one of these precepts also holds other inconsistent beliefs and is therefore always in conflict with him- or herself. Thus, the apparently negative but merely circuitous elenchus does indeed secure salvific knowledge; it gives Socrates (and us) good, logical reasons for accepting select propositions about human virtue as sufficiently true and trustworthy, even if not absolutely certain or unassailable.⁷

The Socratic paradox seems for these interpreters a knot tied from familiar strands, strands commonly in use today to weave together a philosophical understanding of our world and ourselves. For even in taking this initially perplexing aspect seriously, a resolution on our own terms is identified and we arrive at a notion of Socratic philosophy that is quite coherent, compelling, and not at all strange from our late modern perspective.

In what follows, I argue for a very different, even a contrary position: a more illuminating and satisfying attitude toward the central Socratic paradox involves the recognition of his profound and fundamental estrangement *from us*, such that resolving the paradox requires a radical transformation on our part. That is, Socrates' philosophical activity is carried out according to a fundamentally anti-modern or, better, ante-modern conception of the relation between human thought and its world. This deeper, epochal difference between the fourth-century Greek philosophical project and our own has not been taken properly into account in the dominant scholarly approaches to the early dialogues. Rather, the great majority of scholars have presupposed that Socrates is engaged in what remains, even for us late moderns despite our sometimes postmodern pretensions, the orthodox philosophical (and scientific) search for knowledge of objective reality. In the readings of the early dialogues presented here, I hope to show that Socratic inquiry into the being of virtue does not operate within the parameters of any such *objective ontology*.

Once freed of this all-determining bias, what emerges in reading the dialogues is *a peculiarly ancient Greek proto-phenomenologist* at work questioning everyday opinions about virtue, which is to say, questioning the ways in which 'what virtue *is*' first *appears*. We come to see Socrates as a student of the initial *phenomena* of virtue, which he understands as *always* in some way the real appearing or self-presentation of 'what virtue is,' even if these appearances prove themselves inadequate and in need of perpetual interrogation or clarification. In what follows, this Socratic phenomenology *avant la lettre* is shown to entail notions of Being and self, as what appears in these initial appearances and the one to whom it appears, which are quite removed from the object and subject that still so often set the terms and establish the aims of our philosophical thinking today. In short, the Socrates of Plato's early works will prove more profoundly strange than we have realized.

Of course, Plato's concepts, arguments, and images have been incomparably influential on later thinkers, even when they have been altered, exaggerated, or degraded through their subsequent appropriation. As distant inheritors of a tradition that still bears his stamp, a certain transmission of Platonic influence is already at work even within our own pre-philosophical worldview. For this reason, Plato's translated texts can seem at first blush quite familiar and accessible, almost self-evidently clear. Indeed, we almost always feel that, even when we disagree with the claims made in the dialogues or reject the arguments offered, we understand Plato perfectly well. We enjoy a vague confidence that we speak roughly the same conceptual language and are engaged in the same philosophical project.

This is the most available of errors. For all the sameness and repetition in the transmission of Plato's thought through the centuries, the differentiation and loss that belong to that process are much more vital, more pertinent to the task of thinking that faces us today. It might be said that, in order to draw nearer to the early Plato's Socrates, we must push him further away.

To this end, I attempt to concentrate attention on those moments where his great distance from us, his foreignness, can become apparent. This allows us to mark and then wrestle with the radical differences between his worldview and that of the modern, metaphysical, subject-object ordered epoch that continues to draw to a close even today. Through this interpretive effort, Socrates comes to present himself as a figure thinking *in excess of* the philosophical project that we ourselves are seeking to work through, or as one who, thinking *at the origin* of that project, can indicate how we might think *in its closure*. Indeed, he becomes an odd kind of contemporary, sharing with us a position at the limit of the tradition that still binds us somehow to him and the Greeks.[8] In the hope of reading Socrates in this manner, these chapters employ what might be called a 'hermeneutic of estrangement.'

Although ultimately naming nothing more than a certain spirit of interpretation, I might here in the introduction point to a few concrete reading practices to be employed in service of this hermeneutic.

1. Non-translation—I refer often to Greek terms and phrases used by Plato, explaining them and considering their usage elsewhere rather than simply replacing them from the outset with a given standard English rendering. Indeed, I often intentionally disrupt the common or orthodox translations, adding available alternative meanings and etymological connections, even if the significance or advantage of these is not immediately apparent. This does not require a reader expert in ancient Greek, but it does require patience, an openness and a willingness to attend to the many and complex valences, echoes, and associations that are often obscured or filtered out by translation.

The vocabulary that emerges from this practice and becomes essential for understanding the Socratic philosophical project in the early works of Plato will no doubt appear odd from the perspective of standard scholarship, perhaps even outlandish. For instance, terms such as 'excess,' 'exposure,' 'distance,' 'suffering,' and 'concern' all come to play central roles in the following interpretation of Socratic ontology. I must insist, however, that these terms are not arbitrarily imposed upon Plato, but always stem ultimately from and are developed by means of a close engagement with the text. The term 'excess' assumes a central role by way of the interpretation, on the one hand, of the *deinos* or 'uncanny, terrific' character of Socratic truth and, on the other hand, of his explicit opposition to something like the transcendence of the sophists' presumed wisdom; 'exposure' becomes important simply by taking seriously Socrates' opposition to the essentially sheltering character of a would-be *technē* of virtue; 'distance' is introduced in order to think the relationality that is indicated by *aporia* or 'waylessness, frustration'; and finally, 'suffering' and 'concern' are direct translations of Plato's *pathos* and *meletē*, which prove vital to understanding the condition provoked by Socratic elenchus. I can only ask for the reader's initial indulgence as we trace together the emergence from the text of this unfamiliar, but, I believe, legitimate and ultimately illuminating conceptual vocabulary.

2. Non-clarification—I often refuse to clarify and even choose to dwell within the obscurity of certain moments in the dialogues, resisting the urge to explain away what might first appear to us as confusion or lack of precision on Plato's part. This does not mean that we are to congratulate ourselves for standing adamantly dumbfounded before the predetermined inaccessibility of Plato's texts. Rather, we must simply acknowledge that what seems to be confused or hopelessly obscure from our perspective might itself reflect an original experience of the world now all but lost to us, constitutive excesses and disruptive moments having been conceptually smoothed over, submerged, and forgotten in that text's transmission. Allowing ourselves to be properly disturbed by this inaccessibility may be the first step toward doing interpretive justice to these works.

3. Non-resolution—Finally, there are certain moments in which Plato's texts present themselves as not just obscure, but as though recommending apparently contrary or even contradictory positions, e.g., the aforementioned 'Socratic paradox' that we will confront in various manifestations throughout the following chapters. We might feel compelled to resolve these moments to one side or the other of the dilemma in question or, where such an interpretive resolution seems impossible, to dismiss them as unfortunate logical blunders or inconsistencies on Plato's part. Instead, I do not insist from the outset on this binary logic of non-contradiction in these instances. Allowing us rather to struggle with and even inhabit these paradoxes and contradictions, I look for the ways in which apparently opposed or contradictory positions might ultimately be understood as existing quite comfortably together in the native context of Plato's thinking.

Such tactics as these allow the early Plato's Socrates to present us with his ancient strangeness and, precisely thereby, to challenge and perhaps push us beyond our own still persistent modern presuppositions about our world, ourselves, and proper philosophical thinking.

The works in which I am interested here are those now generally deemed authentic and more or less unanimously judged by criteria both stylometric and substantive to have been composed earlier in Plato's career—*The Apology of Socrates, Crito, Alcibiades I, Euthyphro, Laches, Charmides, Hippias Major* and *Minor, Lysis, Ion, Theages, Euthydemus, Menexenus, Gorgias, Protagoras*, and *Meno*.[9] These are listed in no particular order, for the chronology within this group is open to debate and utterly inconsequential for the present discussion. Crucial is simply that all of these early works together present us with a more or less uniform portrait of the central activity of Socratic philosophizing—Socrates engages in a conversation about some topic related to human *aretē* or 'excellence, virtue,' a conversation that begins from the *doxai* or 'opinions' of Socrates' interlocutors, asks after a definition of 'what "x" is' with regard to the topic at hand, and ends by exposing the inadequacy of these *doxai* without ever arriving at that sought after definition, which is to say in a more or less dramatic or explicit form of *aporia* or 'frustration, waylessness.'[10] The present study concerns the portrait of *this* philosophical project as presented in *this* group of dialogues *en masse*. I ask here what notion of Being is at stake in the aim of this quintessentially Socratic 'What *is* "x"?' question, and I approach this problem by investigating the proper and truthful human comportment toward or relation to the being of virtue that Socrates seems to believe his philosophizing brings about despite its aporetic character.

Plato's *Apology of Socrates* serves again and again in these chapters as the point of departure, but the analysis is explicitly extended to include the works of Plato's early period all together.[11] This is accomplished by drawing connections between passages in the dialogues based on thematic resonances and shared vocabulary. That is to say, I do not limit myself here to the approach that has become common in books of Plato scholarship, each chapter (and sometimes the entire book) devoted to the adamantly internal, exhaustive, and step-by-step treatment of a single dialogue. I do recognize that such an approach represents a healthy corrective to the still regrettably prevalent scholarly tendency toward handling Plato's writings as ornamented treatises, tearing arguments, statements, or terms from their dramatic contexts, robbing them of their *in situ* depth and complexity, and elevating some of them to the status of Platonic 'doctrine.' Opposing such a tendency myself, I too believe that in order to interpret any given claim or argument in a dialogue, one must consider the speaker and the addressee, as well as the sometimes richly drawn and highly specific dramatic context. For just this reason, when moving from one passage to another I always strive to attend to the dialogue form through which Plato chose to make public his philosophical thought and, thus, to the inescapably situated character of the passage in question.[12] However, even in recognizing the discontinuities and heterogeneities between dialogues, my discussion will often emphasize instead the overarching consistency of Socrates' philosophical aim and the points of illuminating comparison between passages in different early works.

In sum, I would suggest that there is a certain (indeed fundamentally Socratic) notion of *philia* or 'friendship' among the works of Plato here discussed. As we learn in the *Lysis*, human *philia* properly speaking holds *neither* between those who are simply like *nor* between those who are simply unlike one another. After Socrates and his interlocutors have rejected both of these two options, he suggests that the friend might be understood as the one who is *oikeios* or 'akin, kindred' (*Ly.* 222b), but only if this can mean something other than the likeness or sameness previously rejected as the source of friendship. Socrates thereby challenges his interlocutors (and us readers by extension) to imagine what kinship or being akin to one another might mean, if it is not grounded in the possession of, e.g., like names, like blood, or like attributes. Having thus excluded the standard connotations of *oikeios*, we are left to dig down to the word's root, *oikos*, which means 'home, house, dwelling place' and then via synecdoche 'family, kin' (insofar as family members are understood as living together in the same place or structure). The suggestion then is that human *philia* might be understood as the condition of sharing the same dwelling place, perhaps that very aporetic site in which we find ourselves situated at the end of the *Lysis*, and every other early dialogue as well. Being together in a human way would be based upon neither our likeness to nor our difference from one another, strictly speaking, but rather upon our inhabiting together a site *distant from* but nonetheless *toward* the being of virtue. We might think of the relation between the dialogues as just such a peculiar *philia*.

In relating a passage in one dialogue to a passage in another then, we are not to assume that, because Socrates is the speaker or because the same terms are used, the passages articulate the very same position and the terms and arguments are simply identifiable. Doing so would be to overlook their distinct determining contexts. Nor however must we resign ourselves from the outset to passages from different dialogues being so contextually delimited and different as to be utterly incommensurable with one another. Rather, they can be viewed together as sharing in a perplexing and tenuous human community, every dialogue presenting a context-specific appearance of that withdrawn ground toward which Socrates and his interlocutors point in their questioning, but from which they remain aporetically distant. The reader will have to judge for him- or herself whether or not this approach succeeds in uncovering a compelling and vital Socrates at work in the early dialogues.

One last issue. As mentioned earlier, *The Apology of Socrates* and its presentation of Socratic philosophizing will be employed throughout as a lever to open up and interpret the rest of the early dialogues. There is very good reason for this. In the *Apology*, Socrates focuses upon, indeed explains and defends, his own expressly elenctic and aporetic philosophical activity, that very same activity we find repeatedly and more or less consistently portrayed throughout the works with which we are concerned. That is, here and here alone Socrates' questioning and searching way of discourse is *itself* thematized and treated extensively. Moreover, this self-presentation by Socrates is directed toward the *everyday attitude*, i.e., toward that understanding of our world, including ourselves and one another, prior to philosophy's interrogation of our unarticulated principles and values. Plato names this pre-philosophical attitude by reference to those who are largely confined to it, 'the many (*hoi polloi*),' and his term for the mode in which we relate to the world when immersed in our everyday lives (and indistinguishable from 'the many') is '*doxa*.' Thus, we can say that the *Apology* thematizes Socratic philosophizing most centrally in its problematic relation to the everyday attitude and *doxa*, insofar as it is here that Socrates attempts to bring himself to light *qua* philosopher before 'the many,' embodied by a jury of (likely) 501 of his fellow Athenian citizens. This gives the *Apology* a privileged status for us, as the relationship between Socratic philosophizing and *doxa* proves to be crucial throughout the following interpretation, the truth of the former being nothing but the disruption of the latter by which what is already appearing in *doxa* is brought more clearly to light as it is. Thus, although it was likely the first work Plato wrote and although it surely reflects to some unknowable degree Socrates' actual defense oration, the priority of the *Apology* for us is neither historical nor chronological, but substantive.

This book is divided into three parts. Part 1, comprised of chapters 1 and 2, is intended only to open up a space in which to interpret the early Plato otherwise. First, a constitutive ontological presupposition is identified in the orthodox and analytic approaches to Plato by tracing a certain shift or leap in logic evidenced by some seminal works in that mode. That is, there is an unjustified move from, on the one hand, these scholars' acknowledging the fact that 'what *is*' for Plato's Socrates does exceed or is not exhausted by its initial everyday manifestation to, on the other hand, their claiming that for Socrates 'what *is*' is *objectively real*. This gives us good reason to be suspicious of imposing an objective ontology. Next, we focus our attention on the fact that Socratic philosophizing begins always with his interlocutors' *doxa*, which is traditionally translated as 'opinion' but which, as chapter

2 indicates, should be understood first and foremost as 'appearance.' Once developed, this insight opens up at least the possibility that Socratic philosophizing might be concerned with *phenomenal being*, rather than objective reality, something that would require a radical reassessment of Socrates' method and its aim or end.

Part 2 then moves through three steps, each of which constitutes a chapter. Chapter 3 investigates the nature of the *alētheia* or 'truth' to which Socrates' elenctic philosophizing is explicitly devoted, and suggests that this *alētheia* is *deinos* or, as it is interpreted there, essentially 'excessive.' Chapter 4 presents the argument that Socrates does not himself have as an ideal any *technē* or 'craft-knowledge' of virtue, but rather seeks only to expose himself and his interlocutors to the being of virtue as unknown. This exposure, however, is by no means merely a self-conscious ignorance; it establishes rather a true and properly human relation to the phenomenal being of virtue. That truthful and proper relation to the being of virtue is to be painfully concerned for it and distressed by its distance, its ungraspability. Indeed, as chapter 5 then shows, this is very precisely that *pathos* or 'suffering' of 'what virtue *is*' with which all the early dialogues end—*aporia* or 'waylessness, frustration' is itself the truthful and proper experience of virtue as it is.

Chapter 6, which by itself constitutes part 3 of the book, offers a detailed interpretation of Socrates' discussion of *andreia* or 'courage' in the *Laches* as a whole. We focus our attention on the *Laches* at this point, not merely because it seems a paradigmatic early Platonic work, but also because this dialogue thematizes that precise facet of human virtue or excellence which becomes evident when confronting what is fearful, distressing, and threatens pain. Implicit here is the claim that, even if this is not its predominantly apparent aspect in all instances (e.g., in those where piety, temperance, wisdom, or justice are more manifest), every occurrence of human virtue for Socrates must be an occurrence of extreme courage for it entails holding out before the painful excess of the being of virtue.

PART I
SOCRATIC PHENOMENOLOGY

1

Setting Aside the Subject-Object Framework in Reading Plato

> Die »wahre Welt«, wie immer auch man sie bisher concipirt hat,
> —sie war immer die scheinbare Welt noch einmal.*
> —Friedrich Nietzsche, *Nachlass*,
> November 1887–March 1888, 11 [50]

ARISTOTELIAN ASSESSMENTS OF PLATO'S SOCRATES

A fundamental tension presents itself to us if we read carefully Aristotle's remarks on Socratic philosophy. This tension should indicate to us that the Socratic philosophical project is worlds away from the modern one with which we are familiar. Indeed, if we linger for a moment within this tension, Socrates must appear to us by Aristotle's lights as a quite perplexing figure.

Before beginning, it is important to note that, for Aristotle, who never experienced Socratic conversation firsthand, Plato's early dialogues seem to present a fair portrait of the historical Socrates.[1] At the very least, nothing Aristotle says concerning the historical Socrates is inconsistent with the character drawn by Plato in his early works. Thus, because Aristotle's image of the historical Socrates seems so thoroughly informed by the persona of Socrates in these works, his assessments of the former can be used in good conscience to illuminate our subject here, which is strictly speaking the latter.

The first of the two relevant remarks comes down to us only secondhand. It is found in Plutarch's responses to the Epicurean Colotes, specifically to

---

*The "true world," however one has conceived of it until now—it has always been the apparent world once again.

the latter's attacks on Socrates and various other philosophers for the purported impossibility of living according to their teachings. We read there,

> Of the inscriptions at Delphi, "Know Thyself" seemed most divine, for it even provided Socrates with the source (ἀρχὴν) of his *aporia* and his searching (τῆς ἀπορίας καὶ ζητήσεως), as Aristotle states in his Platonic writings. (*Adv. Col.* 1118c)[2]

According to the young Aristotle, the simple Delphic imperative to know oneself is the ultimate impetus for the constant searching and questioning of Socrates, which is all that the early dialogues depict. And this imperative, therefore, is the ultimate origin of the *aporia* beyond which Socrates' philosophical activity in the early dialogues never reaches. Apparently, in Aristotle's judgment, that activity should be considered an attempt by Socrates, *originally and primarily*, to come to know himself and to aid his interlocutors in coming to know themselves.

Surely Plato scholars and casual readers of the early dialogues alike would endorse such a claim on some level. However, the possible significance of this description has been largely missed even in the massive wealth of secondary literature that addresses itself to the subject. Either interpreters rest content with understanding Socrates' activity as directed toward self-knowledge in some vague and commonsensical manner, or if they offer any explanation of this, they manipulate the concept 'self-knowledge' to the point of unrecognizability. As one commentator remarks,

> Among the nominees we find, e.g., innately correct beliefs, a self-consistent set of beliefs, the so-called Socratic precepts, virtue itself, and even knowledge of knowledge. Yet with a few exceptions, one candidate is conspicuously absent from the ballots: self-knowledge in the context of the Socratic elenchus is rarely taken to be knowledge of the self.[3]

That is to say, scholars have been largely uninterested in pursuing the most direct path—whatever the "knowledge" aimed at or effected by Socratic conversation, it is in some sense *reflexive*, i.e., it is above all *of one's self*, one's own character, tendencies, or perhaps one's very own thoughts and beliefs, and their unclear or unremarked contents and implications.

Indeed, many interpreters have been able to ignore this implication partly insofar as they equate the Socratic goal of 'self-knowledge,' simply and without remainder, with what is reported in the second of our Aristotelian assessments.[4] In the *Metaphysics*, Aristotle summarizes the Socratic contribution to the search for wisdom as follows:

> Socrates made his central occupation (πραγματομένου) the ethical virtues (τὰς ἠθικὰς ἀρετὰς) and first sought to define (ὁρίζεσθαι) these according to the whole (καθόλου). . . . It is well-spoken to say that he sought the 'what it is' (ἐζήτει τὸ τί ἐστιν). (*Met.* XIII.1078b17–23)[5]

It is the first part of this passage that has been glossed as addressing the issue of Socratic self-knowledge. Rather than seeking all-embracing explanations of natural phenomena, in the words of Cicero, Socrates "first called philosophy down from the sky, placed it in the cities and brought it into the homes, and compelled it to consider life and morals (*de vita et moribus*), and what is good and bad" (*Tusc.* 5.4.10). That is, he turned his philosophical attention *away from the natural world* and *toward human beings*. Broadly speaking, this has been taken as an adequate and perfectly manifest description of the Socratic aim of self-knowledge—we search for knowledge of ourselves with Socrates insofar as we seek definitions of the ethical universals that concern how we should live our lives.

However, the other defining feature of Socratic questioning mentioned here must be considered as well—Socrates asks the 'What is "x"?' question. Indeed, Richard Robinson in his seminal work on Plato's early dialectic follows Aristotle here, identifying this as *the Socratic question*. Examples include 'What is piety?' in the *Euthyphro*, 'What is temperance?' in the *Charmides*, 'What is courage?' in the *Laches*, 'What is friendship?' in the *Lysis*, 'What is fineness or beauty?' in the *Hippias Major*, 'What is virtue?' in the *Meno*, and 'What is justice?' in the first book of the *Republic*, which may well be an independent aporetic dialogue predating the composition of the rest of the *Republic*.[6] Of course, Robinson rightly points out that Socrates' questions in some dialogues also take the alternate form of 'Is "x" "y"?', as is the case in the *Crito*, *Ion*, *Lysis*, and *Protagoras*, for instance. At other times, the 'What is "x"?' form explicitly gives way to this one (*Chrm.* 165b–e, 169c–d, *Grg.* 466a–527e, *Men.* 86c–100b). Nonetheless, as Robinson also notes, Socrates explicitly and repeatedly *prioritizes* the question 'What is "x"?' over all other questions, especially those seeking any particular predication (*Hp. Ma.* 287b–e, *La.* 189e–190a, *Men.* 71, 86d–e, *R.* I.354c, and *Prt.* 360e). Thus, although it "owes its prominence in the earlier dialogues not to spatial predominance but to the emphasis Socrates puts upon it,"⁷ '*What is "x"?*' *is nevertheless the central and characteristic form of Socratic inquiry*, which is precisely what Aristotle highlights in the passage above as a Socratic contribution to the search for the *sophia* or 'wisdom' that is *protē philosophia* or 'first philosophy.'

Any reading of the early dialogues certainly bears this out, for Socrates insistently and with a certain precision demands of his interlocutors that they give an account not just of human virtue (and the various virtues that we shall see as its context-specific appearances), but of 'what human virtue *is*.' What precisely does he have in mind here? To be sure, Socrates never in the early works thematizes Being itself. He does not, for instance, dig beneath the (as yet undifferentiated) special sciences to ask the Aristotelian metaphysical question concerning "being *qua* being (τὸ ὄν ᾗ ὄν)" (*Met.* 1003a21). Neither does he chase after the sufficient reason for the existence of contingent beings as such, asking with Leibniz why there are beings at all, and not rather nothing. And, although he sometimes uses terms that are familiar from Plato's middle dialogues in order to refer to the object of his inquiry, such as *ousia, eidos, idea*, and *paradeigma*, his object here seems not yet the more fully articulated Platonic Idea of the middle period, as that is usually understood.⁸ Thus, we must surely proceed with caution and not simply read back into the early works any or all of the characteristics traditionally associated with the Ideas, as immaterial, intelligible, changeless, eternal, self-same, perfect, paradigmatic, essential causes that are in some way *separated* from the material, sensible, changing, temporal, self-othering, imperfect appearances thereof, which populate the world of our everyday experience. At the very least, we can say that, when Socrates directs his interlocutors' gaze toward his target, 'what virtue *is*,' and away from how virtue initially and immediately appears to them, he does distinguish the being of virtue and gives some indication of how he understands it.⁹

We might say provisionally that the Socratic question 'What is virtue?' seems to gesture toward what belongs in some sense to all virtuous individuals, is the cause in some sense of their being virtuous, and is that according to which these individuals are called or recognized as 'virtuous.'¹⁰ It is unnecessary for us to determine at this point whether Socrates takes the subject matter of his questioning to be separated from and transcendent with respect to material, sensible, particular virtuous things, or whether he takes it to be immanent to them. Rather, we need only say that, given his insistent posing of and emphasis on this question, a *prima facie* central aim of Socratic philosophizing, whether we see this as successful or unsuccessful in

Plato's portraits, seems to be bringing the participants in the discussion into a proper and truthful relation to what we can refer to as 'what virtue *is*' or the being of human virtue.

With this, however, a distinct tension presents itself between the two Aristotelian assessments cited earlier. According to the first, Socrates' discussions aim at some kind of *reflexive knowledge of oneself*, while according to the second, they seek *knowledge of the being of human virtue*.[11] In order to bring the unarticulated but no less pervasive modern bias to light, this tension could be put in the following terms. The Socratic project as described in the first assessment seems directed toward and confined within the horizon of the inquiring subject him- or herself,[12] while in the second, it is directed toward 'what *is*,' or toward what exists as objectively real over against the subject. This would then map onto the Socratic paradox discussed earlier in the introduction. The negative or destructive moment would be in effect a kind of self-knowledge, the subject's recognition that his or her opinions are groundless and disconnected from the objective reality of human virtue, while the positive moment, the sought-after salvific knowledge, would be a certain grasp of this reality.

Given any such bias, the question must arise, at what precisely is the inquiring Socratic gaze directed? In Socratic conversation, does one come to a knowledge of *oneself* or a knowledge of 'what *is*,' as something *other than oneself*? What is especially illuminating here is the fact that the Socratic project seems to us to suffer because of this tension, and yet both Plato and Aristotle are (troublingly) untroubled by it.

The tension made manifest through our consideration of these Aristotelian remarks, when rendered in subject-object terms, should make us suspicious of any interpretation that explicitly or implicitly imposes these categories and consequently settles on two mutually exclusive Socratic projects—a skeptical project whereby the subject would come to know only itself and its own oblivious ignorance or an epistemologically positive project whereby the subject would ultimately establish a secure connection to the objective reality of virtue. In contrast, we might ask how *both* the Aristotelian assessments might be true and essential, even if each in a radically modified sense, and this is precisely what the following chapters attempt to show. The Socratic elenchus does indeed accomplish a radical form of self-knowledge, but this is nothing other than a proper and truthful relation to the being of virtue.

It is generally agreed that this 'proper and truthful relation' for Socrates would be a 'knowledge,' an *epistēmē* or a *technē*, of virtue,[13] the necessary and perhaps sufficient condition of which would be the ability to give Socrates the propositional definition he clearly demands in his characteristic philosophical activity and then to defend that definition from elenctic refutation. I argue later that this is not the case. Rather, Socrates' elenchus, focused as it is on the being of virtue, has the following two aims, one more immediate and the other more remote.[14] First, he sets out directly to interrogate his interlocutors' opinions about virtue, exposing their self-contradictions and their false presumption of just such an *epistēmē* or *technē*-like grasp of virtue thereby. Second, Socrates intends with his refutations alone to bring about a non-epistemic, but nonetheless true and properly human way of relating to 'what virtue *is*' as it is.[15] For this reason, although Socrates demands of his interlocutors a definition of virtue, I resist saying that Socrates' philosophical activity has as its own *aim* something like 'moral knowledge.'

Indeed, the properly wise and true relation established by the elenchus will prove to be the condition of *aporia* itself, with which (in one fashion or another) all of the early dialogues end. This proves to be a quite radical suggestion, to be sure, but we must not presume that in the abundant secondary literature on Plato this suggestion has already been taken up, analyzed, and rejected in favor of more orthodox interpretive approaches. Rather, as we shall see, a nearly universal ontological presupposition has made it impossible even to consider the peculiar truth and wisdom of Socratic *aporia*.

CONSTRUCTION OR DESTRUCTION IN THE EARLY DIALOGUES

The scholarly debate concerning the philosophical project of Plato's early Socrates has been ordered for the most part along a spectrum between two poles, the 'constructivist' and the 'non-constructivist' interpretations of the elenchus.[16] Despite its ostensibly negative results, the constructivist sees the elenchus as *indirectly* producing and justifying some kind of understanding, usually true belief or non-expert knowledge, with regard to virtue. That is, these interpreters, like the later Vlastos, argue that the elenchus establishes the truth, or at least the great likelihood, of the beliefs opposed to those found problematic and explicitly refuted in elenctic discussion. Some claim that an individual elenctic discussion can accomplish this,[17] while others claim this only occurs through many repetitions of the elenchus.[18] Against both of these, non-constructivists see the elenchus as capable only of revealing an interlocutor's ignorance of virtue, as evident in their failure to produce an unassailable propositional definition.[19]

There are, however, very good reasons to hesitate before either of these interpretive options. First, Socrates' many and emphatic admissions of ignorance about virtue throughout the dialogues would seem to speak directly against the constructivist's thesis.[20] Indeed, he often says not only that he lacks perfect wisdom or certain knowledge, but specifically that he does not know the answers to the very questions he is asking. Consider how Socrates clarifies his philosophical project to Critias after the latter presses him to endorse or reject his attempted definition of the virtue in question, *sōphrosunē* or 'sound-mindedness, temperance.' Asking for time to consider how best to address himself to Critias's proposal, Socrates responds,

> But Critias, you are speaking to me as though I were claiming to know the things about which I am asking (εἰδέναι περὶ ὧν ἐρωτῶ) and as though I could agree with you if I wished. But this is not the case. Instead, I investigate with you what is put forth as an answer always on account of my own not knowing (διὰ τὸ μὴ αὐτὸς εἰδέναι). (*Chrm.* 165b–c)

And a bit later on, when Critias becomes defensive and accuses Socrates of seeking not truth, but mere victory in the argument, Socrates protests,

> Oh come Critias, even if I refute you utterly (μάλιστα σὲ ἐλέγχω), how can you believe that the reason I do so is anything other than that very same reason for which I investigate what I myself say—fearing that I might escape my own notice, thinking that I know something although not knowing it (φοβούμενος μή ποτε λάθω οἰόμενος μέν τι εἰδέναι, εἰδὼς δὲ μή). (*Chrm.* 166c–d)

The first passage resonates perfectly with Aristotle's general assessment—"Socrates questioned but did not answer, for he did not assert that he knew (ὡμολόγει γὰρ οὐκ εἰδέναι)" (*SE* 183b6–8). Socrates refuses to either endorse or reject Critias's suggestion *not* for pedagogical or dialectical reasons, but because he lacks the knowledge necessary to do so. Furthermore, Socrates emphasizes at the end of the first passage and clarifies in the second that his entire philosophical activity, his searching and questioning of opinions, arises only *dia* or 'through, on account of' his own acknowledged non-knowing. His philosophizing then serves not to relieve him of this condition, but to maintain him in (even while it introduces others to) a particular kind of self-knowledge—it does not allow him to *lanthanein* or 'escape his own notice' as being non-knowing with respect to virtue.

Taking Socrates (and Aristotle) at his word here is clearly difficult for the constructivist. According to this, his lifelong investigation of virtue has not produced what he would be willing to call 'knowledge' and thus it follows that the elenchus itself does not arrive at a true knowledge of human virtue, neither with every elenchus nor even through many repetitions.

Against this, however, the constructivist sometimes responds that such passages indicate only two distinct levels or modes of 'knowledge.' Socrates distinguishes between real wisdom, which no one he has ever met possesses, and a lesser, weaker, or more limited understanding of virtue and its related notions, which he does claim to possess and that his elenctic philosophizing produces. However, Plato repeatedly *emphasizes* Socrates' self-conscious non-knowing of human virtue as his most salient and apparently praiseworthy characteristic, rather than his possession of some strong or weak knowledge, and the universally aporetic results of the early dialogues serve only to amplify this emphasis for us as we attempt to determine the ultimate aim of Socratic philosophical discussion.[21] What seems to make Socrates who he is, an exemplary human being for Plato, is not what he knows, but what he knows he does not know.

Moreover, if Plato's Socrates were to "know" some set of "generally applicable moral truths,"[22] and thus to possess that very knowledge he pretends to seek along with his interlocutors, whatever his reasons for refusing to share this knowledge, be they pedagogical or substantive, we can at the very least say that the epistemic grasp he enjoys would be the ultimate goal of Socratic philosophy and its ultimate good. The elenctic and aporetic discussion we see repeated in the early dialogues again and again, and which is indeed all that Plato ever presents us with, would then be *a merely propaedeutic step* on the way toward the possession of this resultant understanding and its capacity to direct our actions correctly. And yet, Socrates contradicts this in perhaps the most oft-cited passage in all the early dialogues. In the *Apology*, after his conviction and in a situation where the motivations traditionally cited for his irony would presumably not be in effect, we find him claiming that

> The greatest good for a human being (μέγιστον ἀγαθὸν ὂν ἀνθρώπῳ) happens to be giving accounts of virtue (περὶ ἀρετῆς τοὺς λόγους ποιεῖσθαι) every day, along with the other things about which you hear me discussing and examining myself and others (διαλογομένου καὶ ἐμαυτὸν καὶ ἄλλους ἐξετάζοντος) for the life without examination is not worth living for a human being. (*Ap.* 38a)

As an obviously climactic moment of the *Apology*, this must be read as a considered, careful, and precise statement of Plato's Socrates' philosophical mission. Given this, we note that Socrates does not say that knowledge or wisdom of any kind concerning virtue is the greatest good for a human being. Rather, this status is reserved for precisely that *daily, repeated, always frustrated, and thus endless discussion of virtue* that we find portrayed throughout Plato's early works. As Francisco Gonzalez comments on this passage, "It is easy not to hear what is extraordinary in this assertion: Socrates is claiming, not that elenctic examination in search of virtue *promises* to produce a great good for us, but rather that *it is itself our greatest good*."²³ Indeed, it would seem that the constant, elenctic, *aporia*-producing and sustaining questioning of Socratic philosophizing, and thus even a certain self-conscious way of *not possessing knowledge or wisdom of 'what virtue is,'* is what is supremely good for human beings. This passage seems to bring about a "collapse of the distinctions between knowledge and product, pursuit and possession,"²⁴ such that any interpretation that finds the great benefit of the elenchus in some knowledge or wisdom *beyond* that activity must be rejected in favor of an interpretation that finds this benefit *within the elenchus itself*. Thus, it speaks directly against the possibility of any human being ultimately *possessing* some real extra-elenctic product, some knowledge or wisdom about the issues addressed by Socratic questioning. Moreover, the passage would certainly contradict the assertion of a secret, never revealed, ironically dissimulated Socratic *possession* of knowledge or wisdom. The constructivist's interpretation seems at the very least dubious for these reasons.

And this very same statement from the *Apology* generates a fundamental objection to the non-constructivist's position as well. Socratic philosophy is presented by these interpreters as purely destructive, as merely exposing the ignorance of common opinion about virtue, but providing no alternative to common opinion. This skeptical vacuum would produce a bit of discomfort surely, but it would seem to leave the interlocutors free to slip inevitably back into their initial, unreflective views on virtue in living out their lives and making ethical decisions. If Socratic philosophy achieves no alternative (much less *true*) relation to 'what virtue is' and only exposes the oblivious ignorance of everyday opinion, how can Socrates claim that his mode of philosophizing is nothing short of "the greatest good for human beings"? What, then, would be so supremely beneficial about this purely destructive Socratic elenchus? The non-constructivist seems to have no satisfying response to this question.

In the following chapters, we will concern ourselves with the Socratic elenchus and the relation between its destructive project and truth. For now, we can simply acknowledge that it has proven extremely difficult for the scholars in this debate to cope with what is essentially a refinement of the aforementioned "paradox of Socrates." That is, they have been unable to reconcile the elenchus's explicit and consistent failure with the great benefit that these failed discussions are proclaimed to have for human beings.[25]

Although this interpretive dilemma has been widely acknowledged, the most direct way of resolving it has simply been put out of play due to a certain presupposition about the implicit ontology of the early dialogues. That is, scholars have been unable even to entertain the possibility that the aporia, which Socrates' elenctic being-focused questioning obviously maintains and with which it always ends, is itself understood to be not just the properly human condition, but an epistemologically legitimate and even true relation to 'what virtue is.' If this were somehow the case, we could understand quite unproblematically Socrates' claim that his utterly destructive elenchus itself accomplishes the greatest good for human beings, for it would accomplish what is for him and his interlocutors indisputably necessary for any human being to live well—a true and proper relation to 'what virtue is' as it is. Despite its elegance, this solution has not presented itself for consideration in orthodox interpretations of the early dialogues due to the unquestioned presupposition that for Socrates the mode of being of 'what virtue is' must be objective reality and that the relation to virtue he would seek must be therefore some kind of objective knowledge. If this presupposition is set aside, however, I believe the truth and supreme benefit of Socrates' elenctic and aporetic mode of discussion can become intelligible, making sense of what we initially suffer as 'the Socratic paradox.'

FROM EXCESSIVE BEING TO OBJECTIVE REALITY AND BACK

We must note at the outset that this long-standing and all-determining presupposition of Socrates' objective ontology remains almost entirely unstated. Such silence, however, does not testify against the claim that such a presupposition exists. It indicates, rather, that the position is so deeply ingrained in the dominant, which is to say analytic or Anglo-American, interpretative approaches that it seems not to require thematization, much less justification.[26] This makes it quite difficult to confront directly as a bias. The presupposition tends to surface, however, with the vocabulary employed in the following contexts: 1) In discussing the anti-relativism of Plato's Socrates; 2) in distinguishing Socrates' search for definitions from twentieth-century nominalism; and 3) in excavating an implicit and ordinary or everyday attitude about reality in Plato's thought. Let us examine each of these in turn.

ARTICULATING PLATO'S ANTI-RELATIVISM

We begin with an early work of twentieth-century English scholarship, one that set many of the terms of later discussion even in being vigorously opposed by most later interpreters. In his 1903 *Unity of Plato's Thought*, Paul Shorey puts forward a non-developmental account of Plato's works. In so doing, he argues that the being-focused Socratic search for definition in the early dialogues already indicates "the definite and positive assertion that the substantive essences, or rather the objective correlates, of general notions constitute the ultimate ontological units of reality to which psychological and logical analysis refer us as the only escape from a Heraclitean or Protagorean philosophy of pure relativity."[27] Shorey here exhibits quite clearly a fundamental tendency of twentieth-century Plato scholarship. He emphasizes that Socrates' philosophizing is already directed at the being of virtue, just as I have previously. However, in order then to oppose this position to sophistic relativism, Shorey makes the unwarranted presupposition that Being here must amount to *objective reality*, and consequently that the true, certain, and philosophically required mode of grasping or, better, relating properly to this reality is *objective knowledge*.

Later, and in the same vein, J. L. Ackrill states directly that, for Socrates, "if questions such as 'what is justice?' . . . can be answered . . . justice is a real, objective characteristic."[28] T. H. Irwin writes that, in the early works, "Socrates commits himself to the existence of real kinds and genuine objective similarities that justify our classifying things as we do."[29] And from Terry Penner we hear that "Socrates urges against relativism the objectivity of the *sciences*, and suggests that the knowledge that is virtue is just one more objective science."[30] It is of no consequence to the present argument whether the interpreters in question find the separate, immaterial, intelligible Ideas of Plato's middle period already at work in the early dialogues (as Shorey certainly does), or whether they insist that, although there are Ideas at stake in the early dialogues, these are immanent to particular material things, or whether they reject there any technical role whatsoever for *eidos* and *idea*. What I wish to indicate is simply that, because of his overt anti-relativism, it is concluded that Socrates' 'What is virtue?' question asks after something that has the status of objective reality, be it material or immaterial. David Roochnik offers a perfect summary of this position in his primer to ancient philosophy, writing, "Unlike Protagoras or Gorgias, for whom there was no Truth about questions of justice or goodness, Plato argued time and again that objective knowledge, and not merely opinion, was both possible as well as necessary in living the good life."[31]

Distinguishing Socrates' Search for Definitions from Twentieth-Century Nominalism

The very same vocabulary arises in attempts to stave off a prevalent tendency among contemporary interpreters. That is, because Socrates exhibits a consistent and consuming interest in the definition of ethical terms, his philosophical project is easily, but mistakenly, viewed as commensurate with the "nominalism" of twentieth-century philosophers who practice linguistic or conceptual analysis. In the wake of positivism's violently anti-metaphysical project, these analytic thinkers emphatically and proudly turned their backs on 'Being' as an illusory place-holder responsible for nothing but a myriad of pseudo-problems in the history of philosophical inquiry. They asked *instead* after what we mean by or how we use given universal terms.[32] Many readers of Plato have, as a result, felt compelled to observe that Socrates' search for definitions is something altogether different from this post-positivist movement. In the trajectory traced by the following passages, however, there is an important slippage from the language of 'realism' to the language of 'objective reality' in attempts to combat this perceived interpretive temptation.

In his chapter on Socratic definition, Richard Robinson writes,

> Socrates is also assuming some sort of realism as opposed to nominalism. . . . He is assuming that this form or essence or one in the many is not a word in the mouth, nor a concept in the head, but something existing in the particular Xes independently of man.[33]

Note that Robinson leaves somewhat indeterminate here the status of whatever it is that Socrates searches for in his quest for a definition of 'what virtue is.' He insists only that Socrates' question aims at something ontologically independent of language or thought. Arguing from "the explanations which Socrates gives of his question,"[34] Robinson states a bit further on that they indicate "some sort of realist assumption about the ontological status of this 'essence'"[35] as the aim of the Socratic 'What is "x"?' question. I wish only to note here that, for Robinson, Socratic realism amounts to a target not located ontologically within human language usage or thought. It must be *beyond* these, in some way, and *independent* of them.

R. E. Allen, in his excellent interpretation of the *Euthyphro*, makes a similar observation. He writes,

> The dialectical procedure of the *Euthyphro* cannot be represented as an attempt to discover what the word 'holy' means, coupled with a further attempt to find out whether it applies to anything. For . . . existential import is taken for granted, not demonstrated, in the early dialogues: Socrates and Euthyphro assume there are holy things, and ask what their nature is; and this assumption of existence is made in every early dialogue in which that 'What is it?' question is initially answered by appeal to examples—which is to say in every dialogue in which it is asked.[36]

Allen too wants to distinguish his Socrates from a twentieth-century philosopher of language, and he does so by pointing out the brazen "assumption of existence" made in his conversations. The "existential import" of the term *hosion* or 'holy' is taken for granted by Socrates, in that it is understood to refer manifestly to something in the world, beyond or in excess of the contents of human language or thought.

As far as they go, the claims of Robinson and Allen in these passages are indisputably correct. As they make clear, there can be no doubt that Socrates is some kind of realist and no kind of nominalist, in that he presumes to be asking after 'what virtue *is*' rather than merely what the term means or what we conceive it to be, and he certainly does not reduce the former to the latter. However, a significant transformation occurs if this claim, namely, that 'what virtue is' for Socrates *is something more than* or *exceeds* the contents of human thought and language, slips into the claim that it must therefore be an *objective* reality to which *objective* knowledge would be the proper and truthful relation.

A. E. Taylor provides a particularly illuminating example of this very slippage in his discussion of the *Meno*. In the passage in question, Socrates is insisting on searching with Meno for 'what virtue *is*,' a notion filled out in the discussion as the one *eidos* that all virtuous things must share (*Men.* 72c). As Taylor writes, for Socrates this entails that

> [T]here is no third alternative between realism and nominalism. A universal, unambiguously employed, signifies something or it does not. If it signifies anything, that something is not an arbitrary fiction of the mind; if it signifies nothing, there is the end of all science. Science stands or falls with "objective" reference.[37]

According to Taylor, like Penner, Socrates' search for a proper relation to the being of virtue must be a search for something like a "science" of the objective referent of the term 'virtue.' For the only alternative to this that he can imagine would be simple "nominalism," according to which the term would be understood as referring only to other words or mental contents. These would amount to arbitrary "fiction[s] of the mind" for Taylor's Socrates, precisely because any connection to a world outside the subject would be left unsecured. Thus, because Plato's Socrates seeks knowledge of 'what virtue is' as something *beyond* or *exceeding* human thought or language, it is presumed by Taylor (representatively) that Socrates must operate with an objective ontology and that he must be searching for scientific or objective knowledge as the proper way of relating to or grasping this object.

Excavating the Everyday Understanding of Being in Plato

To conclude this brief and pointed survey, let us turn to a passage once again from Vlastos. He is here introducing a distinction between having an ontology, or an implicit, all-governing understanding of Being, and being an ontologist, or one who is reflective about one's ontological principles and can articulate them more or less systematically. Vlastos is arguing here that Socrates can have the former without being the latter. In so doing, however, Vlastos also makes admirably clear the manner in which the presupposition of, in particular, an objective ontology is *read back into* the early dialogues:

> Can one have an ontology without being an ontologist? Why not? The belief in the existence of a physical world independent of our own mind, stocked with material objects retaining substantial identity and qualitative continuity over long or short stretches of time, is a solid piece of ontology, as entrenched in the mind of the average Athenian then as in that of the average New Yorker now.[38]

Now, I agree with Vlastos that there is an ontological framework implicit in the everyday attitude and I would say that Plato's Socrates might adhere in his investigations to some guiding notion of what it means 'to be' without thematizing Being as such. However, I would call into question the assumption that what we find at work in the early Plato's Socratic discussions is the very same *objective* ontology that is so familiar to us.[39] I would even say that Vlastos is likely right in claiming that, for the everyday attitude of the fourth-century Greek, 'what *is*' might well have been understood as in some sense *exceeding* one's most immediate opinions or perceptions and as not in any way constituted by these. And in any case, this is surely true for Plato's Socrates, as his obvious and consistent anti-Protagoreanism or anti-relativism indicates.[40] However, as represented by the passages assembled here from a few seminal interpreters of Plato, the unsupported interpretive bias of the dominant approaches to the early dialogues becomes evident when what we might call this acknowledged *excessiveness of 'what is'* is identified without comment, much less justification, with the claim that 'what is' is *objectively real.*

Consequences of Presupposing an Understanding of Being as Objective

Having merely indicated the pervasiveness of this vocabulary of objectivity, we have yet to make clear precisely what it entails, i.e., what its logical consequences are. Let us begin by saying quite trivially that, for one who holds an objective ontology, 'what is' has the way of being of an object. Our first inclination here might be to understand an 'object' as a material thing, but that would be an unwarranted restriction of the meaning, as the 'objective idealism' sometimes associated with the middle Platonic works indicates. What is essential to being an object seems to be, in the language of the passages already cited, 1) "retaining substantial identity and qualitative continuity over long or short stretches of time," but also, 2) being "independent of our own mind," or "not an arbitrary fiction of the mind," or existing "independently of man." One cannot speak of something as an object in the ordinary sense, as what exists in the mode seemingly indicated by the common vocabulary of 'objective reality,' unless the thing in question has some persisting presence as what it is and is located in the world outside of and not constituted by the subject who thinks or perceives it. If either of these things is not in place, we are speaking no longer of something with objective reality.[41] This is precisely what most interpreters presume to identify as the aim of Socratic being-focused questioning, whether they state their interpretive bias explicitly or not.

There are two fundamental consequences that follow from this presupposition. First, a concomitant notion of truth will be organized according to what is now, in some sense, a subject-object relation. In order to arrive at truth, one will likely be understood as having to produce a proposition, 'S is p,' that accurately represents or corresponds to the present object and its properties or circumstance, in our case the being of virtue. Of course, for Socrates, this would also be an essential, propositional definition, but that is unimportant in this context. Given objective reality as the aim of Socratic inquiry, the truth he explicitly claims always to aim at will have to be a proposition that represents the independently present object. Second, the status of the initial appearances of the object, i.e., the first, unreflective, pre-philosophical opinions Socrates' interlocutors have about virtue, will also be affected by the introduction of a modern subject-object relation. That is, the 'independence' of the object from our initial human reception of it will almost certainly be taken to entail *a separation of being from appearing*.

In one recent, far-reaching study of philosophy in the modern period, the author describes precisely what is entailed by the Cartesian and then quintessentially modern commitment to a reality that is objective. He writes,

> Everything you think or say stands to be assessed in terms of what is *not* you. The measure of thought is *reality*, and reality is neither created by thought nor controlled by it. Reality is *objective*: its being is distinct from its seeming: what it is does not depend on what we *think* it to be. Our thought is aimed at reality, and when it hits the target, then and only then can we speak of truth.[42]

Now, a portion of this description of the epistemological project of modern philosophy might be applied legitimately to the early Plato's Socrates. To be sure, he wishes to measure what his interlocutors think or say about virtue against 'what virtue *is*.' And for him, whatever its status, this is not constituted by individual or communal beliefs about it. That is, whatever the being of virtue is, it is more than and not 'created by' human thought about it. Without a doubt.

However, the next step in this description, which is of course perfectly accurate with regard to philosophical thought in the modern period, simply does not apply to Socrates' understanding of 'what virtue is.' We read here that, with regard to the objectively real, "its being is distinct from its seeming." That is, objective reality *per se* may or may not be accurately revealed in its initial mode of appearing to us in the everyday, pre-philosophical attitude. It is precisely this *separation* of being from seeming or appearing that necessitated what Descartes calls a "general overthrow of opinions (*generali*

... *opinionum eversioni*)"⁴³ in order to clear away these dubiously ungrounded mental contents and then identify a firm and immovable point, a self-evident, undeniable truth (or truths), from which all knowledge might be rigorously deduced after the model of geometry, thereby warranting the name *scientia*.⁴⁴ With Descartes one sees that the separation of being and seeming quite simply entails that all pre-reflective opinions or initial appearances be suspected of being radically deceptive. Thought must confront the terrifying prospect that all unexamined opinions may be, not just cloudy or partial appearances of 'what is,' but utterly disconnected phantasms, merely subjective illusions communicating nothing about reality. In the traditional approaches to Plato's early works, this separation of being from seeming is, in addition to the demand for propositional truth, carried along with the vocabulary of 'objectivity' and improperly imposed upon the Socratic philosophical project.

The imposition of this particular aspect of the modern conception of objective reality is sometimes quite apparent. For instance, it is right on the surface of Benjamin Jowett's oft-cited remark that Plato is subject to certain insoluble logical problems in the later dialogues because he "separates the phenomenal from the real."⁴⁵ It is also present in some commentators' accounts of the status of *doxa* or 'opinion, belief' for Socrates. We find it for instance in Taylor's book on the historical Socrates, where he again opposes the misplaced nominalism he sees in the tendency to speak of the objects of Socratic inquiry as "'universals,' 'concepts,' or 'class-notions'."⁴⁶ He writes,

> If we would avoid all such misunderstanding, it is best to say simply that the Form is that—whatever it may be—which we mean to denote whenever we use a significant 'common name,' as the subject of a strictly and absolutely true proposition, the object about which such a proposition makes a true assertion. . . . The soul, as we saw, has one single fundamental activity, that of *knowing* realities as they really are. . . . Where the mind is not face to face with a Form, we have only *opinion* or *belief*, a *belief* which may, of course, in many cases be quite sufficient for the needs of everyday life, but we have not *knowledge*; the element of '*necessary* connection' is missing.⁴⁷

Evident here is the assumption of precisely that disconnect between being and seeming identified earlier, as well as the effect it has on the way the interpreter understands both the Socratic search for knowledge and the Socratic critique of everyday *doxa*. Taylor presumes that arriving at knowledge entails securing a "necessary connection" between oneself and 'what virtue is,' while *doxa* clearly suffers from a lack of precisely this connection. Thus, for Socrates' interlocutors, who complacently rely on the mere *doxa* of human virtue, "moral life is at the mercy of sentimental half-thinking,"[48] and thus in danger of a complete disconnect from 'what virtue truly is.' Absolutely crucial is this: the desire for a "necessary connection" to objective reality, the epistemological dream proper to modern post-Cartesian philosophy, is here being imposed upon the Socratic project.

And with this we arrive at the purpose of this admittedly strategic review of scholarship. Having traced these two consequences, we are now able to see precisely how the presupposition of an objective ontology in the early dialogues is responsible for the incapacity in the dominant interpretative approaches even to entertain the most elegant resolution of the Socratic paradox. It becomes impossible for these interpreters to take Socrates at his word and see his ostensibly destructive, elenctic discussion of virtue as itself accomplishing the greatest good for human beings, so long as they see Socrates as confronted with the being of virtue understood as an objective reality.

That is, under the influence of this ontological bias, any such supreme benefit within the destructive elenchus itself is ruled out by the fact that, as Paul Woodruff summarizes, the elenchus "presupposed nothing but the beliefs of Socrates' victims, and . . . it ended nowhere but in the victim's feeling that he did not know."[49] We must try to hear the force of this "nothing but" and "nowhere but." With the assumption of an objective ontology, Socratic elenctic questioning must be seen as beginning with nothing but unsubstantiated and radically suspect beliefs and as therefore arriving nowhere but the victim's internal subjective space, revealed in the harsh light of pure self-conscious ignorance. There can be no truth and, thus, no supreme benefit in the *aporia* of the Socratic elenchus itself, for its negative result entails that Socrates and his interlocutors remain trapped on the subjective side of a subject-object gap, dealing only with opinions and succeeding only in marking the absence of that necessary connection to the objective reality of 'what virtue *is*.'

Richard Robinson makes the following highly illuminating remark regarding a certain tension between how Plato's Socrates seems to understand what occurs in the dialogues and how we tend to read them. He writes,

> Plato's dialectic is often of such a nature that to our minds it ought to be separated from philosophy. To us he often seems to be discussing neither physical nor metaphysical reality, but only the human

logical apparatus of conceptions and terms. But still, in a manner very strange and unnatural to us, he regards himself as talking not logic but ontology.[50]

Although he is ultimately unable to extricate himself from the anachronism outlined previously, Robinson does register the strong resistance in Plato's early works to just this presupposition of objective ontology. He notes, at those moments where Plato's dialogues seem *to us* to be concerned merely with concepts and meanings, with thought and its elements, *for Plato* the topic of conversation seems to be 'what *is*.' The radical gap between appearing and being, between the subjective and the objective, seems "in a manner very strange and unnatural to us" not to exist for Plato.

I suggest that, having confronted this tension and this resistance, we simply refuse to impose the presupposition of objective ontology in approaching Plato's works. Nothing more. I do not presume to have *proven* it false or groundless, a mere imposition of modern ontology on ancient thought. I certainly do not claim to have overturned the results of the brilliant and highly esteemed scholars I have cited here, from whose work I myself have benefited immensely. I hope only to have exposed a general, implicit, indeed utterly undiscussed, interpretive bias in a range of orthodox and seminal approaches to the dialogues and to have indicated how this bias is responsible for the impossibility of exploring a very straightforward, even if for us ultimately quite challengingly strange, approach to the central paradox of the Socratic philosophical project. Let us, simply, put aside this particular presupposition and set about reading the dialogues.

If we do so, I believe we will find evidence there of a radically different ontology at work in Socrates' being-focused elenctic questioning. That is, the being of virtue, understood as otherwise than objective (indeed, as neither objective nor subjective), will prove to be in a properly human way 'grasped,' or much better, related to *truly*, precisely in the condition of *aporia* with which all these early discussions of human virtue end and in the painful *meletē* or 'concern' for that Socrates explicitly aims to provoke. This will no doubt seem bizarre, and we might well ask what kind of radical alternative ontology could account for this. Perhaps, for Socrates, the aim of philosophizing is not a proper relation to *objective reality* at all, but to what we might call *phenomenal being*, where the 'being of virtue' would be understood as that which has always already appeared to us and established a connection to us in our immediate or unreflective experience of our world. It is what already concerns us, calling forth our striving and our thinking, even if this concern needs amplification and our thinking needs refinement through the Socratic elenchus.[51] That is to say, perhaps Socrates seeks the being of virtue as nothing other than what has already presented itself to us, albeit in a self-concealing manner, in what the Greeks would call *doxa*, the beginning point of all Socratic philosophical questioning.

2

On *Doxa* as the Appearing of 'What *Is*'

> Let be be finale of seem.
> —Wallace Stevens,
> "The Emperor of Ice-Cream"

The etymology of the Greek term *doxa* seems to announce a very different relation to 'what is' than does that of 'opinion,' its most common English translation in philosophical contexts.[1] Now, arguing from etymology is rightly viewed with suspicion for a number of reasons. On the one hand, what usually remains unclear is the extent to which any given etymological residue still participates at any particular moment in how ordinary language users understand the term in question, much less in how a particular author understands it in a particular text. On the other hand, such arguments traffic in connections between one element of a given language and the next, often moving among culturally specific worldviews and spanning centuries of historical development, but what they aim to uncover thereby is the worldly reality to which these elements ultimately refer. It is this last step that is often less than clear in arguments from etymology and I will not make such an argument here. Nonetheless, taking these risks into account, we can use a given term's etymology to open up a discussion of the term in specific texts and even to point the way for interpretation, which will then still have the burden of grounding its results in the reading of those texts.

DOXA VERSUS OPINION

We might begin by acknowledging that the usual English translation for *doxa*, 'opinion,' has something intrinsically qualified about it in its usage.

'Opinion' almost always seems to mean 'mere opinion' (unless modified as 'expert' or 'authoritative' or the like), and as such it seems inherently suspect in its connection to what is really the case. When I explicitly state my opinion of something or someone, I am claiming *only* to have an opinion, and I thereby also admit that my judgment may well be missing its mark.

And there is good etymological reason for this essential qualification. Our word 'opinion' derives from the Latin *opinio*, which itself is the noun formed from the verb *opinari*, meaning 'to suppose, imagine, conjecture, deem, believe, think.'[2] All of these common translations can emphasize precisely this same lack of certainty. And if we dig deeper, we can understand why. The root of this verb, its simplest significant element, is *AP-* or *OP-*, for which the lexicon's table of roots gives first simply 'to lay hold,' and second derivatively 'to lay hold for work, work, help, beget; mentally lay hold, suppose.' What is named at the root of *opinari* will seem to us then to be, employing subject/object categories, an action originating on the side of the subject, which then constitutes or seeks to constitute a connection to its object. The subject has an opinion insofar as she or he reaches out toward the object hoping to lay hold of it, grasp it. However, this particular mode of 'laying hold' can always misfire. We sometimes reach out toward an object and lay hold of it only partially, or we lay hold of something else entirely or of nothing at all, which constitutes the occurrence of a false opinion. Indeed, this freedom to err in the laying hold of the world by 'opinion' is manifest in the fact that the very same root, *AP-* or *OP-*, also gives us the verb *optare*, meaning 'to choose, select, prefer.'[3] We might say that the root meaning in our term 'opinion' seems to name the relation of human thought and world *from the side of the subject* or *in an action originating with the subject*. This exposes it from the start to the possibility of an utter disconnect between the opining subject and the world that subject seeks to grasp.

Contrast this with the Greek *doxa* and what its etymology tells us. *Doxa* is a noun derived from the verb *dokein*, for which the Greek lexicon gives two equally common and interestingly opposed meanings.[4] *Dokein*, in the active voice, means 'to expect, think, suppose, imagine; to have an opinion, opine.' However, the verb can also mean, still in the active voice, 'to seem, appear: to appear to be something.'[5] Thus, *dokein* has a unique double valence—Either the subject or the object in the epistemological relation can serve as the grammatical subject of this verb in the active voice. In the relation of the world to human experience or thought, *dokein* names *both* the subject's action toward the object ('I think, suppose, imagine that "x"') *and no less* the object's self-presentation to the subject ('"x" seems, appears to me').[6] Even more crucial, the latter meaning seems to be the more original of the two, for we find that the verb *dokein* is linked to the deponent verb *dechesthai*, as its iterative form, indicating repetition. *Dechesthai* means with respect to things, 'to take, accept, receive,' and with respect to people, 'to welcome.'

At its origin, therefore, the Greek word *doxa* seems to have a directionality opposite to that of its common translation, 'opinion.' For *doxa* names the relation of human thought and world *from the side of the object* or *as an event originating with the object*. Whereas 'opinion,' with its etymological residue of 'laying hold' of something, seems to emphasize a separation to be overcome or bridged, *doxa*, with its residue of 'receiving,' seems to emphasize a connection that has already been established when *doxa* occurs. If I have a *doxa* about virtue, then, this is not an always potentially misfiring attempt to reach out and lay hold of 'what virtue is.' Rather, it is in the first instance an appearance of 'what virtue is' that I have received from the outside, from the world. Indeed, we must recognize here the absence of precisely that radical separation which holds apart our modern binaries, 'inside-outside' and 'subject-object,' for what is 'on the inside,' opinion, is originally understood as always already connected to and revealing of, to some extent, what is 'on the outside,' and it is named accordingly.

PHAINESTHAI AND DOXA

To take just one example from the early dialogues, in the *Charmides* this original meaning of *doxa*, as something like 'received appearance,' seems to be explicitly in play. Socrates narrates here the beginning of his interrogation of Charmides and of the latter's reputed possession of *sōphrosunē* or 'temperance, self-control.'

> Well then, I said, do you think that, since you know how to speak Greek, you could also say this, just as it appears to you (εἴποις δήπου αὐτὸ ὅτι σοι φαίνεται)?
> Probably, he said.
> Then in order that we may divine whether it is in you or not, I said, tell us what you say temperance is according to your *doxa* (τί φῂς εἶναι σωφροσύνην κατὰ τὴν σὴν δόξαν). (*Chrm.* 159a)

Let us attend to Socrates' vocabulary here. We find him beginning a discussion in his characteristic way, asking Charmides for his earnest opinion about 'what temperance *is*.' Notice the parallelism between the two phrases, "how it appears (φαίνεται) to you" and "what temperance is according to your *doxa.*" It seems that one's *doxa* about temperance is nothing other than how temperance initially and ordinarily appears to one. That is, in this passage, *doxa* and 'how "x" appears' are explicitly interchangeable names for the starting point of philosophical questioning.

This parallel serves to reinforce and further clarify the tendency in the meaning of *doxa* that we found indicated by its etymology. The verb translated in the first phrase as 'appear' is *phainesthai*, the passive form of *phainein*, which is itself related to *phaos/phōs* or 'light.' The lexicon tells us that *phainein* means first 'to bring to light,' and then 'to make to appear; to show, make clear or known,' and in its passive form, *phainesthai*, 'to come to light, be seen, appear, be clear or manifest; to appear to be.'[7] The present passive participle of this verb, *phainomenon*, from which we have our English term 'phenomenon,' means literally an 'appearing thing,' a 'thing coming to light or becoming manifest.'

In its undeniable etymological relation to light, I suggest, *phainesthai* points originally toward a specific notion of appearance or phenomenality. Namely, appearing is understood as the *movement* whereby something emerges out of darkness into the light, which is to say, approaches the observer out of a distance and presents itself. This emphasis on an emergence and a movement *toward* the observer seems originally to rule out any reduction to *mere appearance*. Appearance is not first understood as a purely subjective event, something taking place *within* the subject seeking a connection to the world, but rather as a *connection* of some kind that is already accomplished between the world and the observer *through this approaching movement*.

Thus, a *phainomenon* or 'appearance,' as always an appearance *of something to someone*, entails a connectedness between the observer and what presents itself to the observer via the movement of appearing. Moreover, this movement can occur and a connection between the observer and what is presenting itself can thereby be established, *even if the appearance does not wholly and completely reveal or manifest what appears there*. 'What is' can present itself to us even by way of obscure, oblique, indirect, partial, multiple, or self-contradictory appearances. Indeed, the limit case here is the appearance of that which definitively withholds itself, for it is even imaginable that something might present itself to us precisely by not appearing and this too, then, can be a (admittedly paradoxical) mode of appearance. In any case, we might say, playing on this sense of movement that belongs to appearing itself, 'what is' can appear to us and establish a connection even *over an obscuring distance*.

However, there is a strange logic at the heart of appearing, a complex play of sameness and difference.[8] On the one hand, the appearance is *of* what appears. It is, in a certain sense, the same as (because included in) that which appears. The appearance is a feature, an aspect, or an extension of the appearing thing. On the other hand, it is an appearance *rather than* what appears, and thus different from it. That is, the appearance is something that can be distinguished from what appears and then considered separately. And it is precisely this play of sameness and difference that allows for a degradation of the original notion of appearance. Appearance can be and often is reduced to *mere appearance*, to apparition. Just as English does here, Greek can articulate such a degradation to mere appearance by shifting to a different term of similar etymology, from *doxa* to *dokēma* or *dokēsis*, and from *phainomenon* to *phantasma* or even *phantasia*, all the latter of which might be rendered as 'apparition, phantom, vision, or fancy.' However, it must be noted that this is clearly a secondary and derivative sense of appearing. The original meaning of appearance indicated by *dokein* and *phainesthai* is, as we saw above, a movement toward the observer out of darkness and into the light that establishes a connection between what appears and the observer. My claim here is simply that, in the undeniable form that Socrates' philosophical project takes in the early dialogues, the examination of (nothing but) his interlocutors' earnest, everyday *doxai* about virtue, these are approached as *real appearances*, rather than potentially *mere appearances*, of 'what virtue *is*.'

Given this understanding of the *doxa* with which all Socratic questioning begins, we are no longer at a loss to determine how a purely destructive elenchus can establish a connection to the being of virtue, and thereby arrive at a kind of truth and then be a supreme benefit to human beings. That connection has already been established by *doxa* itself. The Socrates of the early dialogues is then a strange, peculiarly ancient Greek kind of *phenomenologist*, one who approaches the earnest opinions of his interlocutors about virtue and attempts to clarify what exceeds those opinions even in already presenting itself by way of them. As suggested above, then, Socratic philosophy would not be aimed at objective being, but rather at *phenomenal being—at 'what virtue is' understood as that which has always already presented itself in the everyday appearances of virtue*. Socrates wants nothing more than what we already in some sense "have."

We may wonder precisely what kind of proto-phenomenologist is Socrates then? Is he Hegelian, Husserlian, Heideggerian? The answer is, as it should be, none of the above.

The historicist ontology of G. W. F. Hegel and Martin Heidegger are surely not shared by Socrates. That is, Being is not for Socrates historically contingent, or that over against which human thought is always situated as it unfolds through a complex historical development in different, epoch-specific forms. It seems likely that, whatever the being of virtue is, Socrates would presume that it is the same for all time, in all places, for all people, even if its appearances are always irremediably context-specific. Nonetheless, the Socratic philosophy of the early dialogues does bear some similarity to the phenomenological aspects of the thought of both Hegel and Heidegger. Hegel's *Phenomenology of Spirit* surely presents the subject and object at each stage in the development of *Geist* as always already connected, although for Hegel unlike for Socrates these are *mutually* constituting, and it is precisely this necessary connection that is recognized and *aufgehoben* or 'sublated' at each following stage in the development of *Geist*. And we could mention Heidegger's consistent approach to Being as more than the objective reality scrutinized by modern science and seized upon by the modern technological gaze, his attention to the Greek conception of truth as *alētheia* or an 'unconcealment' that is indeed presumed by and subtends the *adaequatio intellectus et rei* of the correspondence notion of truth, and his insistence on the 'true' (in this more original sense of 'unconcealing') character of pre-epistemic relations to 'what is,' in particular *Grundstimmungen* or 'fundamental moods, attunements.' Here there seems a deep resonance with what we will identify as the implicit Socratic understanding of 'what virtue is' as non-objective and essentially questionworthy, his evaluation of *aporia* as the truthful experience of virtue, and his attempt to provoke *meletē* or 'care, concern' for the being of virtue as a true and proper human relation to it. Despite these points of similarity, it would surely not serve our purposes to impose either of these thoughtful responses to the modern philosophical problematic onto the crucially ante-modern thought of Plato's early Socrates.

Furthermore, Socrates' questioning of appearances is not to be understood on the model of Husserlian phenomenology, under any of its various manifestations throughout Edmund Husserl's career. Most importantly, Socrates would in no way understand himself to be engaging in a study of the object-constituting structures of consciousness, with its echo of a Kantian transcendental subject. There is very little comparison then between Socratic proto-phenomenology and the radicalized descriptive psychology of the *Logical Investigations*. And there is no more with regard to the *epochē*- or 'reduction'-based study of appearing in *Ideas I*, despite the surface similarity resulting from Husserl's description of his phenomenology as a 'science *of essences.*' The crucial difference here is that Husserl employs the *epochē* to bracket or put out of play the thetic or positing tendency of the natural attitude, which treats the contents of what appears to it as real and external to consciousness. Clearly, the 'existential import' that we found earlier, as characterizing Socrates' being-focused questioning with respect to its object indicates that he engages in no such reduction.

There is one fundamental aspect of all phenomenological thinking, however, that resonates deeply with Socrates' study of *doxai*. All phenomenological thinking begins with the thematization of and focus on the relationship referred to as the 'intentionality' of consciousness, a medieval term retrieved and developed by Franz Brentano and Husserl. That is, phenomenology begins with the recognition that all conscious acts are *of something*.[9] To think is to think something, to fear is to fear something, to remember is to remember something. Against the naturalism of modern science and philosophy, phenomenology proposes to circumvent the epistemological problems brought on by the Cartesian separation of the subject from objective reality by studying instead the relation of consciousness to *this* intentional object, an inviolable connection even when the object in question appears obscurely, obliquely, contradictorily, or as withdrawn, concealed. Every human comportment *has* its intentional object in some sense and thus *has* already that which we are as philosophers called to think or reflect upon, whereas any connection to objective reality is always initially in question and in need of being secured.[10]

Alternatively, if the term 'intentionality' seems inextricable from the autonomous, self-sufficient modern subject usually conceived as responsible for this 'intending,' the same fundamental connectedness between human experience and that which is thought, feared, remembered, etc. has been refocused by Jean-Luc Marion, working out of Husserl and Heidegger, with his emphasis on the phenomenon as the site of *etant donné* or 'being given.' That is, we cannot comport ourselves toward or in respect to this or that thing without its having been presented (or having presented itself) to us in some fashion. Marion writes, "dans son fonds, tout phénomène surgit comme un don, donc que toute phénoménalité advient comme une donation. La possibilité prochaine de la phénoménologie (et donc son essence) consiste dans son auto-compréhension à partir de la logique du don."[11]* Although

---

*At its foundation, every phenomenon surges forth as a gift, and therefore all phenomenality occurs as givenness. The next possibility for phenomenology, and thus its essence, is that of understanding itself according to the logic of the gift.

the implications of each are different, in one crucial respect these two fundamental phenomenological vocabularies of 'intentionality' and 'givenness' can be seen as two sides of the same coin; for phenomenological thinking, all human experience must in a certain sense *have* that which it intends or that which one experiences must *be given* in the experience.

Both entail an inviolable connection between human experience or thought and what appears to us thereby, and in this we have a certain echo of precisely what we uncovered in the discussion of *doxa*. Of course, as an ancient Greek untroubled by the skeptical problems brought on by Cartesian hyperbolic doubt, Socrates' intentional or given object did not need to be contrasted with the objective reality upon which modern philosophy and science set their sights. His is not a retrieval of a relation to Being, but an original, even an organic, *ontological phenomenology*. For Socrates, *doxa*, as related to *dekhesthai*, entails necessarily some sense of 'reception or received appearance,' and thus any *doxa* about virtue can be understood, not as a merely subjective and potentially disconnected 'opinion' of virtue, but always as a receiving of the appearing of 'what virtue *is*.'

In his remarkable series of private lectures now published as *Plato and Europe*, in a chapter entitled "What Is the Phenomenon?," Husserl's student Jan Patocka observes that "mere opinion about things is in a certain way their inadequate and not-independent *givenness*."[12] That is, when opinion is returned to this original sense of *doxa*, it always already 'has' what appears in it or what appears in it 'is given,' and it is precisely the clarification thereof with respect to human virtue that is the aim of the Socratic philosophical project. For this reason, Socratic philosophizing need not engineer a Cartesian *tabula rasa* through ridding us of our *doxai*; it can begin instead *in medias res*, which is to say, from things' initial appearing in *doxa*, and attempt to bring to light nothing but what appears there, i.e., the being of virtue as what is 'intended by' or 'given to' the ordinary, everyday attitude. As evidently a kind of *doxologist*, Socrates comes to stand before us as a peculiarly ancient Greek *proto-phenomenologist*.

Indeed, taking this as our starting point and then simply reading the dialogues closely, excavating that which traditional translations often leave buried, we will encounter a ubiquitous and emphatic focus on *phenomenality* in Plato's texts. We will be following Socrates' own language when we speak of the central binary that organizes his philosophical project as 'Being and appearance,' rather than as 'universal and particular.' The latter pair dominates most orthodox studies of these works, which find Socrates struggling to turn his interlocutors away from particular virtuous things toward what the universal term 'virtue' names and then striving to produce valid arguments about this, which would secure correct and certain conclusions about that objectively real referent. As we shall see, this common vocabulary is not so much wrong so as it is secondary and therefore obscuring of the site in which Plato's Socrates undertakes his philosophical project. We will speak throughout, not with these scholars in logical terms, but with Plato's Socrates in phenomenological terms, emphasizing as he does that he begins thinking and questioning alongside his interlocutors at the site of virtue's appearing in *doxa* and that his aim is to bring to light 'what virtue *is*,' as it is.

PART II

VIRTUE'S ONTOLOGICAL EXCESS AND DISTANCE

3

The Excessive Truth of Socratic Discourse

> Socrates had no need of going elsewhere.... He remained at home, investigating contentiously together with others in conversations—not in order to win over their opinion for himself, but in order to experience the searching out of truth.
> —Diogenes Laertius, *Lives of Eminent Philosophers*

> What if truth were monstrous?
> —John Sallis, *Double Truth*

We turn now to take up directly the Socratic philosophical project as it is portrayed throughout the early dialogues of Plato. Here in the three chapters that comprise part 2, we are interested in the notion of Being that is at work in Socrates' posing of his fundamental question, 'What *is* human virtue?' We will approach this via a consideration of the proper comportment toward the being of virtue that Socrates seems to believe his philosophizing is successful in bringing about.

In the preceding chapters, we found good reason to set aside the dominant presupposition of an *objective ontology* in Plato's early works. Namely, it obstructs an otherwise compelling avenue for resolving the Socratic paradox, i.e., for finding in the ostensibly frustrated Socratic search for a definition of human virtue a nonetheless positive and truthful relation to 'what virtue *is*' and thereby accounting for the supreme benefit Socrates seems to claim in both word and deed for his peculiar philosophical activity. Furthermore, we wish to keep in mind the trace indications of something like *phenomenal being* that we identified in our discussion of the etymology of the term *doxa*. If in the coming chapters we can remain open to an alternative (and for us perhaps quite foreign) understanding of Being, we may see the Socratic paradox with which we began resolve itself through the transformation of our own perspective.

THE INDEFENSIBILITY OF PHILOSOPHY IN PLATO'S *APOLOGY OF SOCRATES*

> Welchem Selbstdenker hat jemals dieses sein "Wissen" genügt, für welchen hat in seinem philosophierenden Leben "Philosophie" aufgehört ein Rätsel zu sein?*
> —Edmund Husserl, "Bestreitung der wissenschaftlichen Philosophie"

In Plato's *Apology*, Socrates undertakes the defense of *an essentially indefensible philosophical project*. This is what generates the great tension of the work and establishes the parameters of his defense. Socrates' philosophizing, which has generated widespread animosity and has in the end led to his being brought up on charges of impiety and corruption of the youth of Athens, is presented in the *Apology* as nothing other than a "testing out (*exetasis*)" of the presumed wisdom and virtue of his fellow human beings (*Ap.* 22a).[1] He summarizes, "Even now I go around searching and examining both citizens and strangers who seem to me wise. And if they then do not appear so to me, I come to the god's assistance and demonstrate that they are not wise" (*Ap.* 23a). This is clearly nothing but the method referred to as the *elenchus* or 'refutation,' whereby, as we have already discussed, Socrates secures an attempted definition of an ethical term from his interlocutor, then solicits a few other opinions, the consequences of which he proceeds to reveal as contradicting his interlocutor's own initial definition. It ends, thus, in the purest demonstration of non-knowledge with regard to human virtue or excellence (*aretē*), on behalf of both Socrates and his interlocutor. This, Socrates states here quite directly, is the central mode of his philosophizing—endless questioning, relentless searching after virtue, without ever arriving at knowledge. It should be noted from the outset that, as such, this project admits of no real philosophical justification.

Indeed, its unjustifiability is the great and substantive "difficulty" that Socrates faces in his defense, on which he explicitly remarks numerous times (*Ap.* 19a, 35e–36b, 37a–b, 37e–38b) and which he implicitly acknowledges throughout by the, as we shall see, unorthodox approach he must take to defend himself. His philosophizing is *per definitionem* unjustifiable for the

---

*For what self-sufficient thinker has this 'knowing' of his ever been enough? For whom, in his philosophizing life, has the term 'philosophy' ever ceased to be a riddle?

simple reason that, in order to justify it, one would have to argue that this activity or way of life is virtuous or excellent, or at the very least, not unvirtuous, vicious, or bad. However, any such argument would require the very knowledge of virtue that Socrates steadfastly and explicitly declares that he lacks (as does everyone else he has ever met). Neither, of course, does Socrates simply admit his guilt, conceding that his activities are impious and corrupting, for neither does he believe this to be the case.

Rather, although Socrates' *apologia* does attempt to 'speak away' (*apo-* + *legein*) the charges he faces, it does so in a complex and indirect fashion. Not attempting to *prove* the benefit or righteousness of his philosophical activity, Socrates must instead seek to bring his judges to question their own grasp of virtue. In recognizing their lack of ethical knowledge, the judges might then come to experience the same distress, the same necessitation that Socrates himself suffers and that motivates his own philosophical questioning and searching. This does not constitute a proper justification of Socratic philosophizing; it is not an argument of any kind in its favor. Instead, it amounts to sharing with his judges the questionworthiness of 'what virtue is,' such that they would feel their own distress and a compulsion to embark on precisely that investigation which Socrates is here tasked to defend. We might say that Socrates hopes to speak away the charges he faces not by the power of proof, but by the *power of the question*.[2]

Given the impossibility of defending himself positively and directly, we seem required to reject a fundamental assumption commonly made by interpreters of Socrates' defense. In his fine monograph on the *Apology*, C. D. C. Reeve states representatively, "Socrates is not examining the jurors, after all. His aim, as we have seen, is to prove his innocence, not to awaken in the jurors a sense of their own ignorance."[3] We are arguing, precisely to the contrary, that Socrates *must* attempt to accomplish with his jurors what his elenctic manner of discussion aims to accomplish with individuals, albeit *mutatis mutandis*.[4] Possessed of the very same self-satisfaction with their own ethical opinions that Socrates encounters among all of his interlocutors, his jurors will initially perceive the Socratic philosophical project as, at best, idle talk worthy of immediate dismissal or, at worst, dangerous talk worthy of immediate condemnation. Socrates' task here is simply to *disrupt this presumed immediacy*, to raise the serious question of his philosophizing among his jurors for the first time or to open them up to this question by breaking them out of the everyday attitude that endorses immediate dismissal or condemnation. That is, Socrates *must* engage in something like *elenctic rhetoric*.[5]

Socrates' *Muthos*

> Dem Sehnenden war
> Der Wink genug, und Winke sind
> Von Alters her die Sprache der Götter.*
> —Friedrich Hölderlin, "Rousseau"

The centerpiece of Socrates' defense is a *muthos* that can be understood to bring about the same effect as an elenctic *logos*. This is, of course, the story Socrates tells of Chaerophon's consulting the oracle at Delphi, of the oracle's declaring Socrates wisest of human beings, and of Socrates' philosophical activity as a response to and ultimately a service on behalf of the god, Apollo (*Ap.* 20c–23b).[6] Before beginning to recount these events, Socrates declares,

> Not mine is the *logos* I will tell (οὐ γὰρ ἐμὸν ἐρῶ τὸν λόγον ὃν ἂν λέγω), but I will refer you to a source worthy of consideration (ἀξιόχρεων). For I will call the god at Delphi as my witness as to whether this wisdom of mine is in fact wisdom and of what sort it is (εἰ δή τις ἐστιν σοφία καὶ οἵα). (*Ap.* 20e)

That is, the god himself will effectively testify to the fact that the condition achieved by Socrates' questioning conversations, the acknowledgment that neither Socrates nor his interlocutors possess a knowledge of virtue, is itself wisdom, indeed properly "human wisdom (ἀνθρωπίνη σοφία)" (*Ap.* 20d).

What is the status of such an appeal to the divine, to one of the traditional Olympian gods? It seems clear that Socrates is at least setting out from within the familiar confines of Greek religion. Importantly, Socrates' discourse takes on thereby the fundamental form of a *muthos*, which is to say, a 'story' or a 'narrative,' but more deeply a discourse that incorporates, rather than overcoming, mediation or distance with respect to its own subject matter, divinity. For the Greeks, *muthos* is the mode of discourse suited to bringing the divine to light *as such*, which is to say, as essentially and originally what exceeds human understanding and power.[7] And *muthos* does so precisely insofar as it does *not* claim to reveal its subject matter completely or definitively, instead allowing and acknowledging a degree of indeterminacy and occlusion as proper to its presentation. In hearing a *muthos* about the gods, no Greek would ever presume to have a thoroughgoing, clear, and

---

*For the longing one / the hint was enough, and hints have been / for ages the language of the gods.

definitive understanding of divine being. This is powerfully indicated by the simple fact that the Greeks were long able to support multiple, mutually exclusive explanations and histories in their *muthoi*.[8] *Muthos* would seem then not an authoritative revelation, but a professedly partial, imperfect, mediated, and changing glimpse, a glimpse that would require of anyone who receives it properly active interpretation, questioning, and even imaginative appropriation.[9]

Hesiod, that great compiler and poetic systematizer of myths, marks precisely this in his description of the inspired condition from which he will recite the origins of the gods. In his *Theogony*, he calls upon the Muses, daughters of Mnēmosunē and Zeus, to direct his mythological account. However, even the securing of a divine source does not ensure for his inspired poetic discourse a complete and definitive revelation, for his authoritative witnesses announce from the outset their deeply ambivalent nature. They declare, "We know how to say many false things that seem true" (*Theog.* 27).[10] This ultimate indeterminacy at the authoritative source of Hesiod's account is not overcome, at any point. Rather, it seems essential to Hesiod's still mythical discourse insofar as "it is intrinsic to the mythical . . . that the object is placed outside, is distanced in order to be drawn back again."[11] Or, as Luc Brisson puts it in his book, *Plato the Myth Maker*, myth is essentially "about a 'beyond' which must be located in a distant past or a space which is different from the one in which the narrator and his public reside."[12] That is, the proper subject matter of myths is what is outside, distant from, or beyond with respect to the comfortable, familiar, and presumably known region in which we live out our everyday lives, and this distance and inaccessibility remains intact even in the mythical account of its subject matter. Myth does indeed bring its subject matter to light, but only *along with its being beyond or distant* and thus without presuming to reveal it completely or definitively. And yet, this partial or essentially indeterminate account must be taken seriously, for its subject matter and the origin of the appearing that myth facilitates, the divine, is as Socrates states, *axiochreōs* or 'worthy of consideration' (*Ap.* 20e).[13]

Indeed, the insurmountable distance and mediation between the divine and the human, which is properly acknowledged by mythical discourse, is marked as well by the oracular mode of communication through which the gods speak to human beings only at a great remove.[14] As Marcel Detienne observes in *Les maîtres de vérité dans la grèce archaïque*,

> Le monde divin est fondamentalement ambigu. . . . Les dieux connaisant la "Vérité," mais ils savent aussi tromper, par leurs apparences,

par leurs paroles. Leurs apparences sont toujours énigmatiques, elles cachent autant qu'elles découvrent.¹⁵*

Crucial here is the fact that a certain ambiguity, an enigmatic and hidden character or even perhaps a deceptiveness, belongs to oracular communication *per se*. As Detienne indicates, borrowing the words of Aeschylus's *Agamemnon*, oracular speech, "like a young bride, only reveals itself through veils" (*Ag.* 1178–1179). And of course, Socrates' *muthos* grounds itself in divine wisdom only by way of just such oracular communication, the Delphic pronouncement.¹⁶ Socrates indicates that he himself understands this and responds by acknowledging, not presuming to overcome, its essential ambiguity and hiddenness. For when he receives word that the god has declared no human being wiser than he, his response is: "Whatever does the god mean to say? What is he riddling (αἰνίττεται)?" (*Ap.* 21b).¹⁷ He then sets to questioning and interpreting the meaning of the god's perplexing pronouncement.

In two well-known episodes, Herodotus testifies to the commonly acknowledged obscurity of divine communication, which would thus encourage, rather than prohibit, interpretation and questioning as a proper response. When the Athenians were advised by the oracle that they should rely on a "wooden wall" in order to fend off the Persian invasion, they did not simple-mindedly commission the services of an army of carpenters. Rather, they set about investigating and questioning the murky counsel of the god and ultimately wagered that he was referring to the navy's wooden ships (*Hist.* 7.141–142). And Herodotus also tells the story of the great Lydian king Croesus, who had petitioned the oracle's guidance, asking whether or not he would defeat the Persians in battle. When the oracle answered that, if he attacked the Persians, he would bring down a mighty empire, Croesus assumed that the empire to fall was Cyrus's rather than his own. This did not come to pass. Herodotus writes, "As he misinterpreted what was said and made no second inquiry, he must admit the fault to have been his own" (*Hist.* 1.91–92).

In sum, it seems that Socrates' reception of the oracle's assessment as an occasion for questioning and investigation exhibits a quite standard understanding of oracular speech, that very understanding articulated by Heraclitus—"The lord whose oracle is in Delphi neither speaks out nor conceals,

---

*The divine world is fundamentally ambiguous. . . . The gods know the "truth," but they also know how to deceive, by way of their modes of appearance, by way of their speech. Their modes of appearance are always enigmatic, they conceal even as they reveal.

but gives a sign (οὔτε λέγει οὔτε κρύπτει ἀλλὰ σημαίνει)" (DK 22 B 93). Socrates' defense gathers itself around a *muthos* grounded in an oracular sign, and therefore in an obscure and mediated indication from a perhaps irremediably distant and inaccessible divine source. It seems clear then that the wisdom and even virtue mythically attributed to Socrates here are not intended to be received by the jurors as definitively, simply, and conclusively proven.[18] Rather, by way of the divine pronouncement, Socrates' wisdom and the philosophizing that sustains it should themselves become *axiochrea*, worthy of consideration and investigation.

SOCRATES' *LOGOS*

And yet, in the passage just cited, Socrates explicitly refers to the account of his own wisdom, not as a *muthos*, but as a *logos*—"Not mine is the *logos* I will tell" (*Ap.* 20e). We must recognize, however, that in so doing, he seems to be evoking a passage from Euripides' *Melanippe*. Although this work has been retained only in secondhand accounts and fragments, Eryximachus claims to be quoting directly from this play when he says in Plato's *Symposium*, "Not mine is the *muthos* (οὐ γὰρ ἐμὸς ὁ μῦθος)" (*Symp.* 177a). It seems likely that Plato has Socrates referencing the same apparently well-known line here in the *Apology*, but substituting the term *logos* for the expected term *muthos*.

What then is the significance of this substitution? Are we to understand Socrates here as offering a *logos*, which in its opposition to *muthos* would seem to be a reasoned, thus definitive and compelling, revelation of its subject matter? Or is he perhaps offering a peculiar kind of *logos*, one that operates within the parameters and limits established by *muthos*? That is, not overcoming the essential mediation and distance that characterize the relation between mythical discourse and its subject matter, but assembling reasons and using argument for the purpose of revealing its subject matter with *precisely that same indeterminacy and questionworthiness*. Socratic philosophy could lay claim to inheriting the mediation and distance of the traditional Greek religious worldview, even if in a radicalized form, despite the stark contrast between Socrates' attitude and the pseudo-pious self-satisfaction of his accusers. We should perhaps try to hear Socrates' substitution as holding together the expected term *muthos* and the stated term *logos* in their tension, but invoking them both.[19]

At least this would seem consistent with Socrates' extremely unorthodox defense, for he seeks to share with the jurors precisely that initial need to question which the god's pronouncement granted him and he does so by giving the jurors reason to doubt their own presumed certainty about what wisdom and virtue are and about who possesses these.[20] To be sure, this is not only the condition that the oracle provoked in Socrates himself; it is the very same condition he strove to pass along to others through elenctic *logoi*. He shared it with the representatives of the three classes of purportedly wise individuals (politicians, poets, and craftsmen), those whom he first approached systematically in trying to interpret the oracle, and then with anyone who would agree to speak with him, "citizen or stranger" (*Ap.* 23b), in service to the god's will as his project had led him to understand it.

Socrates indicates the open and questioning attitude that the story is intended to provoke when he states his ultimate interpretation of the oracle. He says,

> It can be hazarded (κινδυνεύει) that the god is in reality wise and with this oracle he is saying that human wisdom is worth little or nothing. And he seems (φαίνεται) to say, "This man, Socrates . . . ," using my name and making me a paradigm, as if to say, "That one among you, human beings, is most wise, who like Socrates knows that he is worth nothing with respect to wisdom. (*Ap.* 23a–b)

Note the ways in which Socrates' tempers the conclusiveness of his interpretation here. The god's assessment is not perfectly manifest even after it has been subjected to an entire lifetime of testing and scrutiny by Socrates. Its meaning remains an open question, something even now to be 'hazarded' or 'risked' (*kinduneuein*). And this term appears not only here at the end the oracle story, but also at its outset, the two occurrences thereof effectively bookending Socrates' *muthos/logos*; there Socrates says of his peculiar brand of human wisdom, given Apollo's oracular endorsement, "I hazard (κινδυνεύω) that I am wise in possessing this" (*Ap.* 20d). Moreover, even after he has arrived at this understanding of the oracle's meaning through his extensive investigations into the wisdom of his fellow citizens, Socrates is still explicitly working with what *phainesthai*, 'seems' or 'appears' to be the case, not immediately with what clearly and definitively *is* so.

The central *muthos* of the defense functioning as an elenctic *logos*, the jurors should come to feel the need to engage in precisely the same questioning that constitutes Socrates' own philosophical project. That is, they would, were he successful, come to experience the activity of Socratic philosophizing not as having been proven virtuous or wise, but simply as *necessitated of them*, suspending their condemnation or dismissal. And indeed, as we shall ultimately come to see, this result, the painful experience of this necessitation or distress, is for Socrates nothing other than the *truth* with respect to 'what human virtue *is*.'

Given the radical and unorthodox mode of his defense, the presentation of Socratic philosophizing in Plato's *Apology* can be read as doubled. On the one hand, Socrates *describes* his lifelong philosophical elenctic activity for his jurors. On the other hand, in his defense he *performs* that very same philosophical project, breaking the jurors out of their everyday attitude and drawing them into the questioning of 'what virtue is.' As we proceed, we will do well to take into account both of these aspects and their reciprocally illuminating relation in reading the *Apology*.

THE *PROOIMION* TO SOCRATES' *APOLOGIA*

Socrates begins his defense with a *prooimion*, or a short 'way or path' (*oimos*) 'before' or 'toward' (*pro-*) what is to follow. Whatever requires a *prooimion* is not immediately accessible from where we are. It lies a bit removed and can be reached only by way of a preliminary transposition, a relocation of the audience. Of course, such introductions were rhetorically standard and Socrates' employment thereof is on some level unremarkable. However we dare not imagine that for him it is serving its standard, *merely* rhetorical function. Rather, his employment of a *prooimion* should be understood as considered and as *substantively* necessary, which would entail that Socratic philosophizing, the subject matter of the oration that will follow, is not immediately accessible to the jurors from within their everyday, pre-philosophical attitude.

The Rhetorical Discourse of Socrates' Accusers

> Having read a defense speech written for him by Lysias, the philosopher Socrates remarked, "A fine speech, Lysias, but not fitting for me." For it was clearly more rhetorical than philosophical.
> —Diogenes Laertius, *Lives of Eminent Philosophers*

In effecting this transposition, in bringing his listeners into a condition from within which they might be able to receive his self-presentation, Socrates opposes the peculiar way of discourse to be pursued in his defense speech to that way of discourse just employed by his accusers.[21] It is often enough remarked that, whereas the accusers have just spoken as rhetoricians, Socrates will speak in his defense as a philosopher. But what might this distinction mean for Socrates here? What is peculiar about his philosophical way of discourse? Indeed, this is precisely what is at issue in his defense and we must allow the text to determine our understanding of this distinction.

As to the discourse of his rhetorically gifted accusers, Socrates opens by discussing the *pathos*, usually translated as the 'emotion' or 'feeling,' that their manner of speaking has aroused in him: "How you, men of Athens, have been affected (πεπόνθατε) by my accusers, I don't know. I myself, at any rate, was almost made by them to forget myself (ἐπελαθόμην), so persuasively did they speak. And yet, almost nothing they said was true (ἀληθές)" (*Ap.* 17a).[22]

Self-forgetting seems to be a very real danger of rhetorical persuasion. Important is the fact that, in observing rhetoric's power to bring about the opposite, Socrates effectively thematizes *self-knowledge*. If the rhetorical discourse of his accusers can bring about the forgetting of oneself, then it seems that the opposed philosophical discourse might arouse self-recollection. But in what sense? Precisely how might his listeners be intended to recollect *themselves* upon hearing Socrates' way of discourse?[23]

Socrates uses a form of the verb *paschein* here, which in the active voice has a passive meaning: 'to suffer, undergo, be affected by' something. This verb generates from its aorist stem the noun '*pathos*.' If upon hearing this we immediately reduce the phenomenon Socrates is describing to the register of feeling or emotion, with their common associations for us, we will be denying what is explicitly spoken by the Greek term. We tend to think of an emotion or a feeling as a merely subjective occurrence, an *internal event*, which may or may not arise from or reflect in any accurate way reality, the *outside world*. By contrast, the term *pathos*, insofar as it derives from *paschein*, is explicitly an 'undergoing' or a 'suffering' *of something*, the grammar of the term insisting on the 'intentionality' of the experience or the 'givenness' of what is undergone or suffered. Indeed, it might best be rendered as 'affect,' so long as we hear this as entailing a 'being affected by' that which is 'outside' us, by our world. Thus, one's *pathē* or 'affects' cannot be understood as mere emotions or feelings, for they are essentially named as a mode of being in contact with whatever provokes them and imposes them upon us. Just as we found previously with *doxa*, *pathos* itself seems to establish a legitimate and necessary connectedness between us and what is intended by or given in the *pathos*, such that the breeching of the boundary between the internal and external has always already occurred in this experience. *Pathos* announces itself, therefore, as a certain way in which we receive the world's self-presentation.²⁴

For now, we should simply remark that, although Socrates is clearly critical of the *pathos* generated by rhetoric insofar as it entails a self-forgetting and allows the rhetorician to persuade his or her audience despite saying nothing true, this does not entail that he opposes the generation of *pathos* altogether in discourse. There may well be another necessary and philosophical *pathos* that his own discourse generates in its audience, one which entails self-recollection and a proper or even *truthful* relation to what provokes it.

Socrates then indicates that the thoroughly untruthful rhetoric of his accusers brings about self-forgetting through the use of "beautified arguments (κεκαλλιεπημένους γε λόγους), embellished (κεκοσμημένους) with words and phrases" (*Ap.* 17b–c). The verb *kalliepēsthai* means literally 'to make *kalos* with *epea*' or 'beautiful with words.' But what precisely does this imply here? The *Hipparchus*, although not authored by Plato, can nonetheless provide us with an insight into how this word was generally used. In the course of the dialogue's treatment of greed, the character Socrates playfully tosses off the rhyming jingle *kai hōra kai chōra*, which we might render as 'both season and soil.' He then remarks in passing that this is "one of the clever phrases with which the legal experts beautify (καλλιεποῦνται) their speeches" (*Hipparch.* 225c.). It seems that the verb *kalliepēsthai* is used to refer to the beautification of one's speech in a manner that is, like Socrates' jingle, *purely ornamental* or *non-substantive*. It is to add effects or elements to speech, such as rhymes or rhythms, in a manner that does not serve what seems then to be the essential function of *logos* or 'discourse,' that of a gathering together (*legein*) of the subject matter in such a way that allows it to come to light and present itself. This does not entail that rhythm and ornament are *always* antagonistic to truth, but only that they can be so in the hands of rhetoricians expert in law-court speech-making.

Returning to the *Apology*, Socrates identifies his accusers as speakers of precisely this variety, remarkably at home in the law-court, unlike himself (*Ap.* 17a–18a). And the purely ornamental character of this beautification is then amplified by the participle *kekosmēmenos*. The verb here, *kosmein*, does derive from the noun *kosmos*, meaning 'order, form,' and then of course 'world, universe.' This might seem to imply that the activity named by this verb would have a more substantive function—one could impose a *kosmos* upon one's speech according to the *kosmos* of its subject matter, for instance. However, because order for the Greeks always entails beauty, the verb *kosmein* comes to mean primarily, 'to make beautiful by embellishing or adorning something.'[25] This is the sense still detectable in our word 'cosmetic.'

Given the kind of embellishment these words denote, no *logos* that takes its form completely from that which it aims to bring to light could be described as *kekalliepēmenos* or *kekosmēmenos*, even if the form of such a thoroughly substantive discourse were pleasing or even if its luminous clarity could itself be seen to exhibit a certain beautiful order. Any act of beautification, in the sense Socrates is assigning to his accusers' rhetoric here, imposes elements and structure *not in the service of bringing the subject matter to light*. Such seemingly harmless ornamentation in speech has deep and serious implications for Socrates, as will become clearer when we turn to his characterization of how he will proceed in his own speech.

Socrates' Way of Discourse in His Defense

Socrates next describes his own way of discourse, drawing a precise and essential opposition to rhetorical discourse as characterized earlier. He says that he will proceed in his defense "without purpose, speaking with whatever words occur [to him] (εἰκῇ λεγόμενα τοῖς ἐπιτυχοῦσιν ὀνόμασιν)" (*Ap.* 17c).[26] Both of these characterizations come into focus when opposed to the rhetorician's way of speaking.

As to the first, in promising to speak *eikē(i)*, Socrates is not declaring that he will proceed 'randomly,' as the term is sometimes rendered, but rather that he will speak of his subject matter, in this case, himself *qua* philosopher, without allowing any *external* or *additional aim*, such as the persuasion of his jury members, to determine the path his discourse will take. This refusal to allow his discourse to be determined by the requirements of persuasion should not be taken to mean that Socrates is uninterested in acquittal. Rather, he will energetically seek acquittal but he will do so strictly by gathering his philosophical activity together in speech in order to bring it to light for his jurors.[27] Precisely insofar as it lacks any *external* or *imposed* aim or purpose, Socrates' way of discourse will thus differ from the rhetorician's.

Turning to the second characteristic, Socrates promises to use whatever words 'present themselves to him' or 'occur to him.' The term he uses is the verb *tunchanein*, here with the prefix *epi-*, meaning then 'to hit, meet with, light or fall upon.' Related to *tuchē*, this verb refers to an unplanned or uncontrolled occurrence to which one must submit. Socrates will not plan out or order *beforehand* the words and expressions he will use. Instead, avoiding the meticulously pre-planned mode of the rhetorician ordered in the service of external and prior aims or motivations, Socrates will allow the words to come to him, he will submit to them and let them arise according to what must come to appearance.[28] As the rest of the speech shows, however, his speech is no less ordered and careful for this. It is by no means pell-mell or confused due to this promised lack of planning. From where then do the word choices and structure come, if they do not come from any prior determinations? The answer—Socrates allows his speech to come to him and to derive its order, not from his own aims or purposes, his desires or intentions, but *exclusively from the subject matter of his discourse in its coming to appearance*.

Illuminated by the forceful and direct opposition Socrates constructs, it seems that the additional, non-substantial elements in rhetorical speech imply necessarily that in this mode *logos* or 'language' pursues an *additional* aim or purpose, i.e., an aim outside of or beyond what is essential to the *logos* itself. The rhetorician, as one who beautifies and ornaments his or her language in non-substantive ways, does not seek to bring the subject matter to light, but instead allows what is spoken of to remain hidden, while nonetheless seeking to persuade his or her audience *concerning that very subject matter*. This way of speaking of something while allowing what is spoken of to remain obscure and hidden is essential to rhetoric insofar as it places speech first and foremost in the service of the additional aim of persuasion. However, unlike mythical discourse, which *explicitly* allows its subject matters a certain indeterminacy and opacity in its way of bringing them to appearance, rhetorical discourse allows its subject matter to remain hidden while *hiding this very hiddenness* in order to persuade its audience. In this lies the very essence of rhetoric for Plato's Socrates.

From this essential critique, we begin already to see what kind of peculiar self-forgetting belongs to the *pathos* generated by standard rhetorical discourse, and by contrast what kind of self-recollection and *pathos* might arise with Socratic discourse. In order to persuade, the rhetorician must present his or her subject matter to the listener along with the claim that 'the way things are' has been completely or sufficiently captured and illuminated by the speaker. When the listener has been affected by rhetorical persuasion, therefore, the *pathos* aroused is always in part an *epistemological satisfaction*, or a certain confidence that things have been powerfully and thoroughly brought to light. When rhetoric is successful, it may well produce other *pathē*, from rage to compassion, but there is always, no matter the subject or purpose, an accompanying confidence that the position arrived at by way of the rhetorical display enjoys the exhaustive or at least satisfactory illumination of its subject matter. And yet, as indicated earlier, the manner of presentation that is essential to rhetoric, its superfluous beautification and ornamentation, dictates for Socrates that, although 'the way things are' is spoken of and supposed to be brought to light, it remains *necessarily* obscured or hidden in order to serve the additional aim or purpose of the rhetorician's discourse. The rhetorician arouses therefore a necessarily *false* confidence in his or her listeners regarding their own clear and immediate grasp of the subject matter being displayed. This *pathos* of confidence in one's grasp of 'what is' would then seem to be the mark of *self-forgetting*, according to Socrates.

This implies, in a very preliminary way, that the self to which Socratic discourse might wish to return its listeners is one *not* situated in a position of such direct proximity with regard to 'what is.' Furthermore, if we find that Socrates wishes to provoke a *pathos* in his discourse, it will perhaps involve suffering the lack of a direct and clear grasp, submitting to the pain and distress of distance.

Socratic Truth as *Deinos*

The *prooimion*'s dramatic opening opposition, between the Socratic and rhetorical ways of discourse, points us to the precise manner in which Socrates will be, as his accusers had warned the jury members, "terrific at speaking (δεινὸς λέγειν)" (*Ap.* 17b). For Socrates does admit that he will be a *deinos* speaker, not at all in being a gifted rhetorician, but rather only if this is understood as "one who speaks true things (τὸν τἀληθῆ λέγοντα)" (*Ap.* 18a).[29] In this deceptively simple claim, an ambivalence within the term *deinos* should trouble our reading, an ambivalence we find addressed explicitly in Plato's *Protagoras*. There, Socrates remarks,

> . . . Prodicus often admonishes me concerning the word *deinos*, whenever I praise you or someone else saying, "Protagoras is a wise and terrific man (Πρωταγόρας σοφὸς καὶ δεινός ἐστιν ἀνήρ)." He asks me then if I am not ashamed to be calling good things terrific (τἀγαθὰ δεινὰ καλῶν). For, the terrific (τὸ . . . δεινόν) is bad. No one ever speaks at any rate of 'terrific wealth,' 'terrific peace,' or 'terrific health,' but of 'terrific disease,' 'terrific war,' or 'terrific poverty,' the terrific here being bad (ὡς τοῦ δεινοῦ κακοῦ ὄντος). (*Prt.* 341a–b)

Prodicus, that lover of precise and prescriptive verbal distinctions, attempts to delineate the two apparently opposed meanings of this term and reject one of them. That which is *deinos* can indeed be 'marvelously strong, powerful' and then 'clever, skillful,' and in these senses positive. However, the decisive term even in these positively tending meanings is 'marvelous,' which points toward its negative valence. For strength is '*kratos*' and clever skillfulness is '*technē*,' but only when these are 'awesome,' and thus in part 'overwhelming' and even 'terrifying' in their manifestation, are they properly *deinos*. We should note that, in this its fundamental meaning, the adjective does not seem to refer to an objective property possessed by whatever subject it modifies so much as it refers to the experiential content of one who comes into contact with this thing. As Socrates himself defines them etymologically in the *Laches*, *deina* are those things that *parechein* or 'bring along with, hold alongside, or thus inspire' *deos* or 'fear' (*La.* 198b). Thus, the adjective *deinos* seems to refer to that which it modifies only by way of the *affective* impact, the *pathos* of one who is exposed to that thing—the *deinos* is first and foremost awe-*inspiring*, wonder-*provoking*, or terror-*inducing*.

In his remarkable translation of Sophocles' *Antigone*, Friedrich Hölderlin brings to light in an especially powerful way this dynamic experience. In the first stasimon of the play, Sophocles' "Ode to Human Being," Hölderlin translates the famous opening line *polla ta deina* as "Ungeheuer ist viel" (*Ant.* 349).[30] *Ungeheuer* is usually rendered into English as 'monster' or 'monstrous,' but we are able to unpack its meaning further. The term indicates a disruption of the familiar, a radically strange appearance, for it derives from the Old High German *hiuri*, meaning 'friendly, dear, familiar,' negated here with the *Un-* prefix. In this, Hölderlin's translation actually helps us to identify the core phenomenon named by the original Greek *deinos*, i.e., a dramatic exceeding of the limits of the familiar, the ordinary, the everyday.[31] That which is *deinos* presents itself by shockingly destabilizing the structures of intelligibility according to which our experience of our world is usually unreflectively being ordered. To suffer what is *deinos* is to be set out before that which presents itself within the breakdown of one's comfortable and secure understanding of one's environment. The experience is therefore in its essence an *exposure to excess*, not in a quantitative sense, but simply as that which resists being delimited and made intelligible, not merely frustrating our specific expectation, but calling radically into question what we presumed to be the limits of 'what is,' even of the possible. This can be positive or negative in valence, ultimately benefiting or harming us, but it is *per se* disruptive and, thus, troubling. In the end, *deinos* seems to refer not properly to the object in question at all, but to the movement that is this disruption, this breakdown and exceeding of our experiential categories, and it does so by way of the *pathos* that attends exposure to such a disruption.

Thus, in his ironically self-deprecating comment, there is a profound indication of what Socratic discourse aims to accomplish. That is, we might not limit our reading of Socrates' comment to the one obvious direction (if *deinos*, then only in telling the truth), but instead, troubled by the ambivalence of the term *deinos*, we might pause and realize that it can be read in the opposite direction as well (if telling the truth, then only as *deinos*). If we take *deinos* to mean 'clever, skillful,' then Socrates' discourse will only be so if this means telling the truth and not perpetrating the beautified and ornamented obscuration he associates with his accusers' rhetoric. However, if we hear in *deinos* something more ominous, something more original and unsettling, then we might understand from this that *the truth Socrates promises will be excessive, overwhelming, and disruptive, perhaps even generating thereby a certain truthful* pathos *or suffering*.

Despite being one of the most striking aspects of Socrates' defense, his intensely declared commitment to truth is often not subjected to interpretation, being instead understood in the most pedestrian of ways. Socrates declares that, whereas his accusers have said almost nothing true, he will tell "the whole truth (πᾶσαν τὴν ἀλήθειαν)" (*Ap.* 17b). And this pledge of truthfulness is repeated no less than eight times throughout his defense (*Ap.* 18a, 24b, 28d, 31c, 32b, 33c, 34b, 38b). It is not the pledge of truth nor even its repetition that are remarkable in the context of a law-court defense, however. Defendants would have been expected to promise just this. What *is* remarkable is the *generality* of the commitment to truth Socrates here declares. As Thomas Meyer puts it in his detailed study of Socrates' defense in the context of Attic rhetoric, "Diese Formulierung hat etwas Ungewöhnliches. Wird in der Gerichtsrede die 'volle Wahrheit' angekündigt, dann nur mit Bezug auf eine konkrete Aussage, nicht im allgemeinen und in so feierlicher Weise wie hier."[32]* Meyer sees in this *ungewöhnlich* or 'out of the ordinary' generality an emphatic commitment to maintaining a certain attitude toward whatever subject matter presents itself to be discussed. Meyer tells us that, in the rhetorical discourse of the standard law-court speech (echoing precisely what we saw earlier), the speaker "macht sich zum Herrn über die Sache,"

---

*This formulation has something uncommon [about it]. If in forensic speech the "full truth" is mentioned, then this is only in connection to some concrete statement, not in general and not so solemnly as here [in the *Apology*].

utilizing the *Sache* or 'subject matter' for his or her external aims. Socrates, by contrast, is claiming in the *prooimion* to do just the opposite, claiming to attempt "die Sache selbst zur Geltung kommen zu lassen und sie in ihrer Eigengesetzlichkeit zu zeigen."³³* Thus, Meyer concludes that in Socrates' way of discourse, the truth to which Socrates commits himself requires that "Der Sprecher ist hier nicht der Herr über die Sache, nur ihr Interpret."³⁴†

What kind of truth, then, does this quasi-hermeneutic Socratic attitude aim to accomplish? It is clear that Socrates sees himself as devoted to truth insofar as he assumes an attitude toward his subject matter in which he does not impose his will upon it as a rhetorician but instead aims to allow it to come to light in his discourse. But what precisely does this involve? According to the presumptive and almost self-evident meaning of 'truth' for us moderns, Socrates would be pledging that his defense speech will manufacture nothing but a correct correspondence between its own discursive representation and the objectively present reality that it describes (in this case, the objectively real character of Socratic philosophizing). Is this not all that Socrates' emphatic pledge to tell the truth amounts to?

The very term that Socrates uses, the Greek word translated here as 'truth,' *alētheia*, indicates at least the possibility of another, more original significance. Heidegger, over the course of his career, drew attention to the radical implications of this Greek term, to which Socrates would seem to commit himself in dramatic fashion. *Alētheia* can be understood as an abstract noun formed of the *alpha privativum* joined to the root *lēth*-, which relates it to such terms as *lēthē*, 'forgetting,' *lathrē*, 'secretly,' and *lanthanein*, 'to escape the notice of, remain hidden.' And indeed, an understanding of the word *alētheia* explicitly according to these constituent parts has been identified in the usage of Greek writers from Homer to Plutarch.³⁵

Pindar, for example, is surely playing on this meaning when, in opening his tenth Olympian Ode he calls on *alētheia* as a remedy against forgetting. He writes,

> Recall (ἀνάγνωτε) for me the Olympian victor, son of Archestratos, where it is written in my mind, for owing him a sweet song I have forgotten it (ἐπιλέλαθ'). O Muse, you and Zeus's daughter, Truth

---

*[In court rhetoric, the speaker] makes him/herself master over the subject matter . . . [while Socrates is claiming here] to allow the subject matter itself to become valid and to display it in its autonomy.

†The speaker here is not master over the subject matter, only its interpreter.

(ἀλάθεια), with guiding hand protect me from the rebuke of harming a guest-friend with falsehoods (ψευδέων). (*Ol.* X.1–6)

Truth as *alatheia* is here undeniably opposed, not simply to the *pseudos* as 'false,' but to *lelathēnai* or to 'having forgotten.' And this sense is undeniably present in the definition offered in the *Etymologicum Magnum*, an anonymous twelfth-century Byzantine lexicon compiled from earlier sources. The author writes simply, "*Alēthes* is that which does not fall away by means of *lēthē* (ἀληθὲς τὸ μὴ λήθῃ ὑποπίπτον).''³⁶ Indeed, in his aforementioned study, Detienne maps with extraordinary detail and breadth of scope the structural relations and specifically the various related binary oppositions within which the term *alētheia* functions in ancient Greek thought from the archaic to the classical periods. On this basis, Detienne presents the *alētheia-lēthē* couplet as a simple fact. He writes, "La triple opposition de Mémoire et d'Oubli, d'Eloge et de Blâme, de Lumière et de Nuit, dessine très précisément la configuration qui donne à *Alétheia* sa signification. *Alétheia* est une puissance que Pindare . . . invoque aux côtés de la Muse, quand il 'se souvient'."³⁷* Detienne, although partly critical of Heidegger's etymological speculations, nonetheless finds in his meticulous study that *alētheia* was clearly understood in opposition not only to the *pseudos* or 'lie, falsehood,' but also to *mōmos* or 'blame,' *sigē* or 'silence,' and *nyx* or 'night,' but also very definitely to *lēthē* or 'forgetting, concealment.' Detienne writes, "En terme formels, *Alétheia* s'oppose à *Léthé* comme elle s'oppose à *Mômos*. Elle est du côté de la Lumière: *Alétheia* donne brillance et éclat, 'elle donne du luster à toutes choses'."³⁸†

To be sure, Heidegger might at some points seem to be grounding an account of the decadence of Western thought in the etymology of this term, locating a fundamental transformation from truth as *alētheia* to truth as representational *orthotēs* or 'correctness' in the thought of Plato, specifically in the *Republic*'s Allegory of the Cave.³⁹ This account, along with some of Heidegger's broader claims about the philosophical import of *alētheia*, may well be greeted with a certain suspicion. However, even his most vocal critic on this issue, Paul Friedländer, cannot deny that the Greeks from Homer on

---

*The triple opposition of Memory and Forgetting, of Praise and Blame, of Light and Night, delineates very precisely the configuration that gives to *Alétheia* its signification. *Alétheia* is a power that Pindar . . . invokes alongside the Muse when he "remembers."

†In formal terms, *Alétheia* is opposed to *Léthé* as it is opposed to *Mômos*. It is on the side of light: *Alétheia* gives brilliance and clarity, "it gives luster to all things."

saw in *alēthēs* an opposition to *lath-*, *lēth-*, and *lanth-*.⁴⁰ That is, regardless of the term's actual etymological origin and broader significance, the Greeks *could and did understand alētheia* and its variants as the compound of a root having to do with concealment, hiddenness, or forgetting preceded by the negating *alpha* prefix.

We should ask, then, of what significance is the fact that, when the Greeks intended something we might like to call 'truth,' the word they used would have been *heard* as 'un-concealment, un-hiddenness, or un-forgottenness'? This question has been more or less completely ignored by orthodox analytic scholars of ancient philosophy, while continental readers often employ the Heideggerian translation, *Unverborgenheit* or 'unconcealedness,' without consideration or explanation of its most fundamental implications. Taking up this question, we might make the initial and quite banal observation that, under this conception of truth, whatever is rendered truthfully in discourse or thought would necessarily be that which is previously and initially concealed, hidden, or forgotten. It must have previously escaped our notice (*lanthanein*). But that which is concealed, that which escapes our notice, and that which we forget all have one thing in common—they belong *per definitionem* to our experience of the world prior to being unconcealed, noticed, or recalled. Consider the following.

First, whatever is for instance visually concealed or hidden from us must stand nonetheless *within our field of vision* as concealed or hidden. I cannot say that the Parthenon is concealed or hidden from me visually at this moment, for it is thousands of miles away. Indeed, even if I were standing in the ancient Agora looking northwest, i.e., in the opposite direction of the Acropolis, I could not understand it properly as hidden or concealed from view. Rather, only if the Parthenon is standing before me, *situated within my purview*, but obscured by something, say by another closer building or by fog, only then can I speak of it in this way. *Concealment or hiddenness is altogether different from and indeed eliminates the possibility of both nonexistence and absence.* And likewise, second, I can only recollect or be reminded of that which I have already experienced in some fashion. Anything that I can describe as retrieved from *lēthē* or 'forgetting' is something that I have previously known or perceived. *Un-forgetting or recollecting is altogether different from the overcoming of complete ignorance or obliviousness.*⁴¹

To take Greek 'truth' seriously as *alētheia*, therefore, is to recognize an *always prior self-presentation or appearance* of that which is then rendered 'truthfully' by being brought to light in discourse or thought. To accomplish this truth in thinking or speaking is to draw something out of its condition of hiddenness, concealment, or forgottenness, but this would not entail *establishing* a relation to an objective reality, which by definition may or may not be presenting itself to us in our initial experience, as we saw earlier in chapter 1. Rather, what is entailed by *alētheia* is a bringing to light of that which is *always already appearing to us*, even though in admittedly obscure or even unnoticed ways, which require of us an uncovering or retrieval via interpretation, refinement, or clarification. We arrive at the truth, then, not by reaching out and laying hold of that which was absent from our initial experience or of that about which we were potentially ignorant or oblivious, but rather by drawing out that which was necessarily already in some sense there in our experience *but concealed* or by recovering that which we have already experienced or perceived but then *forgotten*.

We must at this point recall that, along with the *presupposition* of an objective ontology in Plato's early dialogues, we have set aside the presupposition of a subject-object structured relation between human thought and its world. Thus, we can no longer simply presume that Socrates operates with the familiar modern conception of truth as correspondence between subjective representation and objectively present reality. Indeed, the alternative and for us radically strange conception of truth as 'unconcealment' or 'unforgottenness' resonates compellingly with our consideration of *doxa* in chapter 2. There we found an indication that Socrates' philosophizing, as an interrogation of *doxa*, proceeds through the clarification and bringing to light of that which always already appears in our initial and pre-philosophical opinions about virtue. Insofar as it aims to generate a proper relation to 'what virtue *is*' by means of this interrogation, Socrates would seem to direct his questioning toward something we called *phenomenal being*, rather than the objective reality that as such may or may not be appearing in our everyday, untested opinions. Given this, it would seem that the *alētheia* to which Socrates dramatically devotes himself does indeed want to be understood as 'unconcealment,' a bringing to light of that which can be shown to initially present itself to us in *doxa* as concealed, or in an obscure, partial, multiple, or somehow inadequate way.

How should we now understand Socrates' pledge that his discourse will accomplish the "whole truth" (*Ap.* 17b)? What is entailed by the fact that Socrates pledges a general attitude toward his subject matter that will bring about 'truth' as unconcealment? At the very least, we can note that Socrates could accomplish the truth of his subject matter in discourse by means *other than* propositions or statements re-presenting the present attributes of an objectively real thing. That is, if for example his subject matter were *essentially questionworthy*, leaving aside for a moment what precise ontological condition this would entail, telling the truth would involve Socrates effecting the unconcealment of his previously concealed subject matter *as such*, which is to say, *as concealed, hidden, and, thus, questionworthy*. And the proper and true form of discourse for unconcealing the essentially concealed or questionworthy would be the question itself, not the propositional definition.

What is crucial for our present discussion is that this consideration of the term *alētheia* allows us to see precisely how the truth Socrates pledges in his *apologia* not only can be, but also must be *deinos*, or fundamentally excessive, overwhelming, disruptive. For this is the only form of truth that is suited to the defense of his indefensible philosophical activity. Rather than showing his jurors that his philosophical activity truly is virtuous and worthy of pursuit, which is an impossibility, Socrates aims to disrupt their comfortable, entrenched, presumed understanding of virtue and thereby expose them to what exceeds that understanding. Recognizing the concealment that characterizes virtue's initial appearances to them, its way of concealing its own concealment, virtue becomes in this moment troubling, terrifically or distressingly unconcealed as questionworthy. This does not amount to replacing their old opinions with Socrates' own concerning virtue nor does it mean "proving" the virtuous character of Socratic philosophizing. It rather calls forth nothing but the jurors' own questioning and searching, their own engagement in just that project for which Socrates has been put on trial.[42]

Socrates' Way of Discourse in His Philosophical Activity

Up to this point, we have been focused on the opposition Socrates articulates in the *prooimion* between his own way of discourse in his defense and that of his accusers. However, because Socrates' defense proceeds not *ad captandum vulgus*, but *ad mutandum vulgus*, it must *perform* and not only describe the elenctic *logos* he employs in his philosophical activity. Insofar as this is the case, Socrates' characterization of his defense speech is also fundamentally a characterization of his philosophical activity itself. And Socrates states as much directly, when he asks of his jurors,

> [I]f you hear me making my defense in the same *logoi* (διὰ τῶν αὐτῶν λόγων) with which I have been accustomed to speak both in the *agora* near the bankers' tables, where many of you have heard me, and elsewhere, do not be surprised or cause a disturbance. (*Ap*. 17c)

Of course, Socrates intends here at one level simply that he will be using common language, not the pseudo-elevated and puffed up verbiage of the former speakers. And he is also likely noting that he intends to engage in a specific example of his standard elenctic questioning with one of his accusers, Meletus (*Ap.* 24c–28b).[43] However, a deeper level of meaning is not thereby excluded, and it is indeed necessitated by the unorthodox approach Socrates must take in his defense of an indefensible philosophical project. That is, Socrates is announcing that his *logoi*, his 'accounts, discourses, or arguments,' will be precisely those that he employs as a philosopher in his conversations with his fellow citizens, not in their form, but in their function. Indeed, his way of discourse in his philosophizing and in his defense speech are the same.

If this is so, then everything we have learned so far applies not only to his defense, but to his philosophical project itself as carried out in his perpetually frustrated, elenctic conversations. That is, in these conversations Socrates proceeds by avoiding extraneous and obscuring embellishment, thus without the additional aims this would entail, and by allowing his discourse to be determined by nothing but the subject matter that presents itself to him to be questioned and interpreted. And Socrates commits himself to this approach in order to accomplish *alētheia*, the bringing of his subject matter out of its initial concealment or hiddenness in *doxa*.

As we have seen, the truth or unconcealment of human virtue that his elenctic philosophizing accomplishes need not entail stripping the being of virtue completely of its concealment via a propositional definition and grasping it by means of a *technē* or *epistēmē*. Indeed, it might involve instead bringing virtue to light *as concealed*, as essentially and necessarily exceeding or withdrawing from our human grasp. Indeed, this would seem to be the case insofar as the *alētheia* that Socratic philosophical conversation provokes will be *deinos* and will involve then the movement or dynamic by which our everyday understanding of our world is disrupted and exceeded. And this would be a truth we experience via *pathos*, a condition of being exposed to and affected by this excess. In contrast to the essential *pathos* of rhetoric, this philosophical *pathos* would also entail a certain self-recollection, as we speculated previously, a recollection of one's distressing position over against the now unconcealed concealment of 'what virtue *is*.' We will return to the question of what kind of self inhabits this site and what kind of 'knowledge' of oneself this *pathos* would provide. For now, we are interested in what relationship or comportment to the being of virtue Socratic philosophizing succeeds in bringing about.

We must now go on to determine whether the Socratic, elenctic investigation of 'what virtue is' does in fact accomplish this radical form of *alētheia*, this excessive truth or truthful excess, and its *pathos*. Indeed, this is precisely what we will find as we move from the philosophical activity Socrates describes and instantiates in his defense to that which is portrayed throughout the rest of the early dialogues.

4

The Sheltering of *Technē* versus the Exposure of Human Wisdom

> What is known I strip away,
> I launch all men and women forward with me
>   into the Unknown.
>   —Walt Whitman, "Song of Myself"

We focused our attention last chapter on Socrates' emphatic commitment to a *deinos* or excessive form of *alētheia* or 'truth, unconcealment,' not only in his defense speech, but more importantly in his philosophizing itself. Plato's early Socrates is indeed one who can say with conviction, "Nothing pleases me, unless it happens to be true (εἰ μὴ τυγχάνει ἀληθὲς ὄν)" (*Euthphr.* 14e), but the truth he is speaking of should not be understood too quickly.

A relevant passage presents itself in the *Gorgias*, at a moment when Socrates is attempting to convince his interlocutor to carry on with their elenctic discussion to its end and not leave it unfinished. Which is to say, this is a moment when Socrates is urging his interlocutor to continue despite the difficulty in order to fulfill the promise of Socratic philosophical conversation. That promise is truth.

Socrates says,

> I think it is necessary (χρῆναι) that all of us are contentiously disposed toward knowing what is true (φιλονίκως ἔχειν πρὸς τὸ εἰδέναι τὸ ἀληθὲς τί ἐστιν) concerning those things about which we speak (περὶ ὧν λέγομεν), and what is false (τὶ ψεῦδος). For it is a good common to all (κοινὸν γὰρ ἀγαθὸν ἅπασι) that this come to be apparent (φανερὸν γενέσθαι). (*Grg.* 505e–506a)

First, Socrates begins from the necessity (*chreos*) that human beings seek *alētheia* and that they do so *philonikōs*, 'contentiously, with a love of victory.' With this term, Socrates is appropriating for his own philosophical purposes a trait elsewhere associated with *eristic*, that "fighting with words (ἐν τοῖς λόγοις μάχεσθαι)" (*Euthd.* 272b, see also *Prt.* 360e) which sophists or rhetoricians would practice and teach. Unlike such verbal combat, however, which would disregard truth and seek only victory in debate (or perhaps also the glory, power, and wealth that might accompany victory),[1] Socrates identifies a fundamentally human *philonikia* that aims at *alētheia*.

For Socrates, it seems, no matter their situation, in their basic task of making themselves at home in their world and in carrying out their various projects, all human beings hold dear (*philein*) the winning out (*nikē*) of the true (*alēthes*) and the false (*pseudos*), concerning that which they gather together and thereby bring to light in discourse (*legein*). Of course, we do dissimulate and misdirect when it suits our purposes, but even when we do so it seems that we wish to and even usually presume to have distinguished the true from the false for ourselves.

Insofar as doing so constitutes a *nikē*, however, a 'victory' for which we must struggle against some basic resistance, it would seem that in the way our world presents itself to us first and for the most part the true and the false are indiscriminately mixed. In our everyday attitude, we do not properly mark or observe the distinction between the two. Note however that, and this is crucial, Socrates explains this fundamentally human victory as the marking of the true and the false, or letting what is unconcealed and what is concealed shine or become apparent (*phaneron*), bringing these to light (*phōs*) as such. He does not propose the elimination of all concealment, but instead aims at a certain comportment toward unconcealment through which it would emerge in its distinction from, but also then in its proper relation to, concealment. Socrates puts forth and secures his interlocutors' implicit agreement that letting *this* come to light, i.e., letting the true and the false in their distinction and relation present themselves to us, is a good (*agathon*) common to all human beings.

Indeed, in the *Charmides'* search for a definition of *sōphrosunē* or 'sound-mindedness,' Socrates employs very similar language when he states the purpose of his philosophical activity. Responding to Critias, who has become defensive after his first attempts at definition have been refuted, Socrates pledges that his centrally elenctic activity is not motivated by an eristic desire merely to win an argument or to humiliate his interlocutor. He continues,

> [T]his then is what I say that I am doing now—examining the *logos* most of all for my sake, but also perhaps for the sake of my friends. Or do you not think it something that is, I dare say (σχεδόν), a good common (κοινὸν . . . ἀγαθὸν) to all human beings that each of the things that are (ἕκαστον τῶν ὄντων) come to be apparent (γίγνεσθαι καταφανὲς) as it is (ὅπῃ ἔχει)? (*Chrm.* 166d)

Here, that common good toward which every human being is disposed *philonikōs* is described as a letting 'what is' become *kataphanes*, 'very apparent' or 'manifest,' 'as it is' or, more literally, 'how it holds itself.' We must oppose this to the way that 'what is' presents itself when it appears as it is not or as it does not hold itself. This should then inform our understanding of the true and the false in our passage from the *Gorgias*. Truth or unconcealment is the coming to appearance of 'what is' in the way it holds itself, while the false is the coming to appearance of 'what is' as it does not hold itself. As Socrates indicates in the *Gorgias*, this aim toward which all human beings are disposed whether they acknowledge it or not, would generally be understood as entailing some kind of *eidenai* or 'knowing' relation to 'what is.' We might be tempted to see here a prefiguring of the claim with which Aristotle boldly opens his *Metaphysics* (*Met.* I.980a22)—Socrates enters the project of elenctic discourse with a notion of the human being as essentially striving to arrive at *eidenai* or a 'knowing' relation to 'what *is*.'[2]

However, consider what Socrates says in both the *Charmides* and in the *Gorgias* concerning the condition to which his philosophical activity has brought him, a condition he then shares with others through that same activity. After Critias has pressed him to endorse immediately the suggested (and even seemingly thoroughly 'Socratic') identification of *sōphrosunē* with 'self-knowledge,' Socrates says,

> But Critias, you are speaking to me as though I were claiming to know the things about which I am asking (εἰδέναι περὶ ὧν ἐρωτῶ) and as though I could agree with you if I wished. But this is not the case. Instead, I investigate with you what is put forth as an answer always on account of my own not knowing (διὰ τὸ μὴ αὐτὸς εἰδέναι). (*Chrm.* 165b–c)

And a bit later on, when Critias becomes defensive and accuses Socrates of seeking not truth, but mere victory in the argument, Socrates protests,

> Oh come Critias, even if I refute you utterly (μάλιστα σὲ ἐλέγχω), how can you believe that the reason I do so is anything other than that very same reason for which I investigate what I myself say—fearing that I might escape my own notice, thinking that I know something although not knowing it (φοβούμενος μή ποτε λάθω οἰόμενος μέν τι εἰδέναι, εἰδὼς δὲ μή). (*Chrm.* 166c–d)³

Socrates' philosophical activity seems to have had, up to this point, only one benefit—the particular self-knowledge entailed by not escaping one's own notice as non-knowing with respect to the being of virtue.⁴ That is, one comes to *know oneself* with Socrates, not by coming to know what one is or the species to which one belongs, not by introspectively cataloging the contents of one's consciousness, and not by taking a critical turn and analyzing the possibility conditions for one's conscious experience or knowledge of the world—in fact, not in *any* epistemologically positive sense at all. Rather, one comes to know oneself exclusively *as not knowing 'what virtue is.'*

Returning now to the *Gorgias*, Plato's Socrates states very directly here as well that he himself does not possess any knowledge with regard to what he is always addressing in his own discourse—human virtue or excellence.

> I will go through the *logos* then, as it appears to me to hold (μοι δοκῇ ἔχειν). But if I appear (δοκῶ) to agree with myself as to 'the things that are' (τὰ ὄντα), but not with you, then it is necessary to make a move and refute me (βάνεσθαι καὶ ἐλεγχειν). For I at least am not saying what I say knowingly (οὐδὲ . . . ἔγωγε εἰδὼς λέγω ἃ λέγω), but rather I am searching in common with you (ζητῶ κοινῇ μεθ' ὑμῶν), such that when what is being said by a discussant appears to me (φαίνεται), I am the first to go along with (συγχωρήσομαι).⁵ (*Grg.* 506a)

Here we have a typical statement of Socrates' peculiar form of self-knowledge, sometimes referred to as, 'Socratic ignorance.'⁶ Socrates claims straightforwardly not to speak *eidōs* or 'knowingly' with respect to that which he addresses in his philosophical questioning.

In *The Concept of Irony: With Continual Reference to Socrates*, Søren Kierkegaard brings to light just what this kind of Socratic self-knowledge or Socratic self-conscious ignorance entails. Or more precisely, he makes very distinct the utter poverty of this form of self-knowledge, so long as we insist (as Kierkegaard does) on imposing the modern subject-object model onto Socrates' philosophical project. He writes,

Now it is certainly true that the phrase γνῶθι σαυτόν can designate subjectivity in its fullness, inwardness in its utterly infinite wealth, but for Socrates this self-knowledge was not so copious; it actually contained nothing more than the separating, the singling out, of what later became the object of knowledge. The phrase "know yourself" means: separate yourself from the other . . . Socrates again has a completely negative result. This principle, "know yourself," is entirely congruous with [Socratic] ignorance.[7]

One of Kierkegaard's rare virtues as an (ultimately Hegelian) interpreter of Socrates is that he does not leave obscure or unarticulated the modern paradigm he is imposing. His analysis makes perfectly clear that, once one presumes to find in Plato an earlier unresolved stage in the development of the modern subject-object relation, Socrates' self-knowledge or self-conscious ignorance must appear necessarily as "a completely negative result." That is, Socrates identifies no "wealth" or "fullness" in the "inward" contents of subjectivity, nor does he succeed in establishing a certain connection to what is external and objectively real. Rather, by Kierkegaard's modern lights, Socrates endeavors *only* to "separate" the object of knowledge from his interlocutors in their unsecured subjective experience by means of his questioning and the self-knowledge that comes about by that process is Socratic ignorance understood as self-conscious subjective isolation.

Let us take a moment to remark the pervasive language of appearing (*dokein, phaneron, kataphanes, phainesthai, alēthes*) and being (*ta onta, ti estin, echein*) throughout these passages, which, if we simply refuse to mask it with comfortingly familiar translations, should call to mind the radical difference between Socrates' project and the typical modern philosophical project. Socrates is not speaking of epistemological certainty and truth as correspondence to an objective reality, nor of the failure to arrive at such certainty or such correct correspondence. Instead, he is speaking rather loudly of unconcealment and of bringing to light that which appears to us as it *is*. This, he declares, is not just his own aim, but that of his interlocutors themselves, *qua* humans. As for the 'knowing' relation we would usually associate with this aim, Socrates reports that even after extensive searching and the perpetual practice of the elenctic philosophizing he favors, he has arrived at no such knowledge.[8]

And this returns us to the Socratic paradox with which we began in the introduction. Socratic philosophizing aims at the truth with respect to 'what human virtue or excellence *is*,' something Socrates and his interlocutors agree would be a good for human beings, and yet he steadfastly denies to both himself and his interlocutors the sought-after *knowledge* with which that truth would usually be identified. Despite this, we recall Socrates' statement in the *Apology* that this very elenctic activity is the supreme good for human beings.

> The greatest good for a human being (μέγιστον ἀγαθὸν ὂν ἀνθρώπῳ) happens to be giving accounts of virtue (περὶ ἀρετῆς τοὺς λόγους ποιεῖσθαι) every day, along with the other things about which you hear me discussing and examining myself and others (διαλογομένου καὶ ἐμαυτὸν καὶ ἄλλους ἐξετάζοντος) for the unexamined life is not worth living for a human being. (*Ap.* 38a)

Thus, we are led to suspect that, even if it does not arrive at a knowing relation, Socratic elenctic conversation *itself* nevertheless succeeds in bringing about the aforementioned "common good (κοινὸν ... ἀγαθὸν)" (*Grg.* 506a, *Chrm.* 166d), i.e., the truth concerning the being of virtue or the allowing of 'what virtue *is*' to become apparent *as it is*, rather than as it is not. Only thus would it be, in and of itself, the greatest good for human beings to engage in Socratic philosophizing perpetually or "every day."

One obstacle to this interpretation, however, is the pervasive scholarly opinion that finds Socrates himself declaring the ideal and truthful human relation to the being of virtue to be a *technē*, a 'craft-knowledge, art, or skill' of virtue, even if he also admits that this ideal is never or rarely achieved by human beings. If the interpretation presented in these chapters is correct, we must argue against this common reading,[9] one that extends back in a certain respect all the way to Aristotle (*EN* 1116b5–7, 1144b18–22, *EE* 1216b3–11, and *MM* 1182a15–24, 1190b28–32). We must show that, for the Socrates presented in Plato's texts, the proper and true relation to virtue is *not even ideally* a *technē*-like grasp of 'what virtue *is*.'

In this chapter, Socratic philosophizing will prove to find its aim, its benefit, and its truth in 'human wisdom,' which is nothing other than that self-knowledge of acknowledging one's non-knowing with respect to virtue. This is to be understood even in direct *opposition* to a *technē*-like, knowing grasp of the being of virtue, but this opposition does not entail (as our modern subject-object framework would require) that Socratic 'human wisdom' amounts to the merely skeptical result that is self-conscious ignorance, understood as subjective isolation or disconnectedness from what is objectively real. In order to support this claim, it will be necessary to analyze here the precise character of the *technē* to which Socrates places his human wisdom in illuminating opposition. Next chapter, we will then turn to the 'suffering' or *pathos* that is concomitant with human wisdom and the *melesthai* or 'being concerned by' 'what virtue *is*' in its withdrawal from our grasp, which itself constitutes the positive moment of Socratic elenchus, as a true and legitimate relation to the being of virtue. For now, we are interested in its negative moment, and we begin again with the *Apology*, where Socrates identifies the sophists as the ones who articulate and even presume to possess a *technē*-like understanding of virtue, after which he differentiates himself from these sophists in precisely this respect.

SOCRATES VERSUS THE SOPHISTS

Recall that Socrates' task in the *Apology* is that of bringing himself *qua* philosopher to light before his jurors by way of elenctic rhetoric. He hopes to make his philosophical questioning of everyday *doxa* appear worthy at least of consideration by undermining his jurors' own presumed understanding of 'what virtue *is*,' allowing this to appear for the first time as questionworthy to them.

In doing precisely this, he finds himself required to distinguish his philosophical activity from those other pursuits with which it has long been confused, a confusion that has aroused *misplaced* suspicion and animosity. Socratic philosophy is, as we have seen, indefensible. Indeed, it is essentially suspicious and, because of its disruptive character, even essentially dangerous, but not for the same reasons as natural philosophy and sophistry. Socrates thus takes care to distinguish his philosophical project from both of those endeavors. He hopes thereby to address what he sees as the older, long-standing, unofficial charges against him, which he articulates explicitly along the lines of Aristophanes' satirical portrait in the *Clouds* (*Ap.* 18c, 19b–c)[10]— Socrates is seen by the many as one who "studies things in the heavens and below the earth, makes the weaker argument the stronger, and teaches these things to others" (*Ap.* 19b).

Distinguishing himself from the first group, those whom Aristotle will refer to as "students of nature" or *phusiologoi* (*Met.* I.986b14, I.990a3, *De An.* 426a20), Socrates simply states that the subject matter of his constant questioning conversations is not the same subject matter with which they are concerned. As a student of human virtue exclusively, not of *phusis* or 'nature' in general, Socrates does not engage in the potentially iconoclastic questioning of the traditional notion of divinity or its radical redefinition, which went hand in hand with pre-Socratic speculation about all-governing and eternal *archai* or 'first causes, sources, or principles' of everything that is (*Ap.* 26d–e, see also *Phd.* 96a–100e, *Phdr.* 229b–230a).[11] In order to demonstrate that he is no student of nature, Socrates need only ask at his trial whether anyone in the audience has ever actually heard him discussing natural phenomena and putting forth cosmological theories, as would be proper to this field of inquiry. In response, the crowd remains perfectly silent (*Ap.* 19c–d).

Contrarily, in order to distinguish himself from the sophists Socrates cannot point to a simple difference in subject matter, for there is none. The sophists speak and teach primarily concerning the very same single topic about which Socrates converses—human virtue or excellence. Plato's Socrates indicates at numerous points that this is what he takes to be the sophists' central activity (*La.* 182c, *Hp. Ma.* 283c, *Prt.* 319a, *Grg.* 519c–d). The older Aristophanic charge, that Socrates and the sophists practice and teach the art of dissembling argumentation, stands in for the broader implicit charge that they claim to teach what is required to live well or excellently as a human being.[12] And Socrates' task of defending himself on this count is thereby complicated.

Socrates must then point to a demonstrable difference between *the divergent modes* in which he and the sophists address themselves to their shared subject matter—he, unlike the sophists, has never undertaken "to teach (παιδεύειν) human beings and charge a fee for it" (*Ap.* 19d). He repeats these claims numerous times in his defense, insisting that he has never been anyone's teacher (*Ap.* 20c, 33a, 33b) and that he has never received money for his conversation, often offering his poverty as proof (*Ap.* 31b–c, 33a, also see 23b). What might seem a relatively insubstantial distinction is in fact quite crucial, for entailed here is the claim that, whatever Socratic conversation accomplishes, it is not *paideia* in any conventional sense. In order to claim to teach someone in the familiar way and then charge a fee for it in good conscience, one would have to presume to possess some determinate and even quantifiably valuable skill or teachable form of knowledge, something that might be successfully and justifiably exchanged for payment. Socrates denies ever having engaged in *paideia* in this sense, importantly implying that whatever benefit his philosophical activity might offer, it is not through the possession and transmission of something exchangeable or quantifiable.

Socrates then ironically praises any such ability as "a fine thing" (*Ap.* 19e). Gorgias, Prodicus, Hippias, and the like surely seem to have some such knowledge, which allows them to travel to any city and persuade the young people to leave the company of their fellow citizens and elders, paying to learn instead from these sophists (*Ap.* 19e–20a). Here we have some indication of why the sophists generated such suspicion and animosity—in taking over the role of educators of virtue, they usurped the position that the citizens of any given *polis* would have presumed for themselves.[13] For now, it is simply important to note that Socrates' praise of the sophists is an example of his *complex irony*.[14] That is, Socrates endorses *neither* the sophistic claim to be able to teach virtue, *nor* the simple-minded and thoughtless condemnation of the sophists who make such a claim (see *Men.* 90e–92e, *Euthd.* 303c–d, *Prt.* 316c–d). His comment should be read neither as a straightforward positive statement, 'Sophistic *paideia* is a fine thing,' nor as its opposite, the negation, 'It is not a fine thing.' Instead, Socratic complex irony is intended to put both of these in play, requiring of his audience that they neither simply reject nor affirm sophistic *paideia* in its suspicious departure from and implicit critique of traditional, communal, and familial educational practice. Rather, it would seem that, responding properly to such irony would involve the jury's coming to experience this as an important and undecided question.

Spelling out in a bit more detail precisely what it is that the sophists claim to possess, Socrates reports a conversation he had with the well-known Callias, who (Socrates makes a point of remarking) has spent far more money on sophists than anyone (*Ap.* 20a).[15] Socrates asks him,

> Callias, if your two sons were colts or calves, we could find and engage an expert (ἐπιστάτην) for them, one who would make them fine and good with respect to their appropriate virtue (τὴν προσήκουσαν ἀρετήν). One among the horse breeders or farmers, perhaps. Now, since they are humans, do you have in mind some expert for them? Is there some expert in this sort of virtue, the human and political kind (τῆς ἀνθρωπίνης τε καὶ πολιτικῆς)? (*Ap.* 20a–b)

Socrates here identifies the single focus of his own investigations, which he shares with the sophists—*human and political virtue or excellence*. He asks Callias whether there is some *epistatēs*, someone with 'expert' knowledge, whom Callias might employ to instill in his sons the excellence appropriate to human beings, which every human would seem to seek and every father would seem to desire for his sons. This expert knowledge of virtue would make such a teacher, like a horse breeder or a farmer, the possessor of a *technē*, an 'art, skill, or craft-knowledge.' What Socrates puts in the form of a question, Callias puts in the form of an emphatic assertion—"By all means (Πάνυ γε) . . . his name is Euenus, of Paros, and he charges five minas" (*Ap.* 20b).

Responding, Socrates significantly returns the sophistic possession of a teachable *technē* to the hypothetical and then deepens the irony of his presentation. "I thought Euenus happy, if he truly does possess this *technē*, and teaches it for so little" (*Ap.* 20b). In fact, five minas was no mean sum for anyone, and especially not for Socrates. Indeed, when Socrates later names the largest monetary penalty he could possible pay, he suggests one mina (*Ap.* 38b), which is the equivalent of one hundred drachma, one drachma being the sum paid in fifth-century Athens to a laborer for a whole day's work. Thus, just one of Euenus's seminars would have cost as much as a day-laborer's wages for nearly a year and a half.

Moreover, the entire presentation of sophistic education is colored by the introduction of the figure of Callias as their spokesman. Socrates seems to ask, who is more a product of the sophistic *paideia* than Callias, who has spent so extravagantly on it? And yet, Callias was a figure legendary for licentious behavior, shady business dealings, political machinations, and poor household management. Deborah Nails sums him up as "a grotesque, if fascinating, figure in Socrates' and Plato's immediate environment, a man controlled by his passions, notably lust and greed, whose reputation was earned while he lived, not contrived by later gossips of the Hellenistic period."[16] And Aristophanes parodies him for just such a lack of self-restraint and for having a lusty, uncontrolled temperament in both the *Birds* and the *Frogs* (*Brd.* 283–286, *Fr.* 428–430). This is significant, insofar as effective satire, such as that of Aristophanes, does not generate its comically critical portrait out of thin air, but rather functions by exaggerating and making ridiculous what is already commonly believed about an individual or event.[17]

From this passage then we should take the following: Socrates clearly emphasizes that it is the sophists who claim to possess and to be able to teach a *technē* of human and political virtue. And no less clear is the fact that Socrates places their claim in a thoroughly questionable light. In direct opposition to the sophists, Socrates concludes this discussion by frankly admitting that he does not have any such teachable *technē* (*Ap.* 20c).

Socrates then introduces an imaginary objector, who observes that, even if it is the case that he differs from the sophists on such a fundamental level, to have wound up on trial and facing exile or execution he must nevertheless have been engaged in "something other than what the many do (ἀλλοῖον ἤ οἱ πολλοί)" (*Ap.* 20c). Indeed, in order to attract such suspicion and even antipathy, he must have been engaged in something "quite beyond the common (περιττότερον)" (*Ap.* 20c). This term is a comparative form of the adjective *perittos*, derived from the preposition *peri*, meaning in this case, 'exceeding or beyond.' We should hear this remark as resonating with the *deinos* or 'excessive' character of the truth Socratic philosophizing generates. And Socrates accepts this assessment without qualification, setting out then to show the jury specifically how he differs from the many and in precisely what way his activity, although it does not lay claim to the sophisticated *technē* of those paid teachers, is nonetheless something quite excessive.

Socratic inquiry has been characterized here as that which breaks through and exceeds the boundaries or the limits of a given site, the site of human life as lived within the confines of the everyday attitude. But how does it do so, precisely?

> Perhaps I will seem to some of you to be joking, but know well that everything I will say to you is true. For I have indeed come to have this reputation, men of Athens, by nothing other than a kind of wisdom. What kind of wisdom? Human wisdom (ἀνθρωπίνη σοφία), perhaps. For I hazard (κινδυνεύω) that I really am wise in this way, while those of whom I was just speaking are perhaps wise with some wisdom greater than what accords with the human (μείζω τινὰ ἢ κατ' ἄνθρωπον σοφίαν σοφοὶ) or else I can't say what [it is]. For I, at any rate, do not know this and whoever says that I do is lying and slandering me. (*Ap.* 20d)

It is nothing other than Socrates' peculiar *human wisdom*, arrived at and maintained by way of his elenctic philosophical activity, that is quite excessive and that differentiates him from the many.[18] Indeed, Socrates exposes the everyday attitude to that which always already exceeds it, but which escapes the many's notice as such. And Socrates does so not by gaining access to this excess or by coming to know or grasp it in a definition; rather, his philosophical project serves to mark what is abidingly beyond our human understanding.

We must attend closely to the language Socrates uses, in order to be clear about the crucial oppositions at work in this passage. The sophists' *technē* of virtue is described as not merely marking an excess of the site inhabited by the everyday attitude, not merely breaking or disrupting the boundary. Instead, it posits something that is *meizōn* (comparative of *megas*) or 'greater' than this, and then presumes access to that superior region. This is vital. Socrates distinguishes his own wisdom from both the everyday attitude of the many and the *technē* of virtue presumed by the sophists—*his own human wisdom is marked as "quite beyond" the former, but without presuming to accomplish the transcendence of the latter to what is "greater."*[19]

Most importantly, Socrates does not in this passage merely confess his own *personal* failure to possess such a *technē* of virtue. Rather, he states clearly that while his own wisdom seems to him *properly human*, the wisdom the sophists presume to possess seems *improper to human beings as such*. This amounts to a violent rejection of the *technē*-model and, taking it seriously, we should be very suspicious of any interpretation that finds Socrates advocating a *technē*-model of virtue, even as an unattainable regulative ideal for his questioning.[20]

Indeed, Socrates' language in this passage is surely intended to paint the sophistic presumption of possessing and teaching a *technē* of human virtue as hubris. Note that this passage is followed immediately by Apollo's oracular testimony, in which the god seems to confirm that Socrates' mode of knowing only that he does not know *is itself* wisdom for human beings (*Ap.* 20e). That is, Socrates proceeds to 'ground' (by way of a *muthos*) the propriety of this wisdom for human beings in the pronouncement of the god whose oracle at Delphi bore the central inscription "Know thyself (Γνῶθι σαυτόν)," which was to be understood specifically in the context of such other inscriptions as "Nothing in excess (Μηδὲν ἄγαν)," "Fulfill the limit (Ἐπιτελεῖ πέρας)," "Bow down to the divine (Προσκύνει τὸ θεῖον)," and finally "Curtail hubris (Ὕβριν μείσει)."[21] As with his appeal to Apollo in general, Socrates' gesture toward the hubris of sophistic *paideia* need not entail that he begins from an unquestioned belief in the tenets of traditional Greek religion. Socrates after all does not *assert* sophistic *paideia* to be hubristic, but ironically praises it in such a way that this question should arise according to the jury members' own presuppositions.

Plato's *Euthydemus* also raises the question of whether the claim to possess any such sophistic wisdom or *technē*-like grasp of virtue might be improper to human beings as such and, thus, hubristic. There, when the two eristic debaters, Euthydemus and Dionysodorus, claim that their new occupation is itself virtue and that they believe they can teach it better and faster than anyone (*Euthd.* 273d), Socrates responds, "By Zeus! What a thing to say! Wherever did you find this godsend (ἕρμαιον)? . . . If you now truly have this knowledge (ἐπιστήμην), then be propitious (ἵλεω εἶτον)—You see, I at least am truly and artlessly (ἀτεχνῶς) addressing you as gods (ὥσπερ θεώ)" (*Euthd.* 273e).[22] Although all in good fun, this passage surely draws a sharp contrast between the teachable *technē* (or *epistēmē* in this instance)[23] of virtue, claimed by these two sophists, and Socrates' own *technē*-less condition. He indicates that, if they truly possess it, this knowledge would be a *hermaion* or a 'gift of Hermes,' that god whose primary charge it is to facilitate communication between gods and mortals.[24] Indeed, Socrates' request that these two be *hilaos* or 'graceful, propitious' recalls the language of supplication or prayer, and he then states directly that the possession of such knowledge, again *if* in fact they do possess it, would be enough to qualify these two as gods.[25]

In the *Gorgias*, Socrates remarks ironically that he is "wonder-struck (θαυμάζων)" by the *dunamis* rhetoric claims for itself as a *technē* that would allow its practitioners to advise the city on important political and ethical issues.[26] Socrates then clarifies that "the greatness of its scope appears at least to me to be something *daimonic* (δαιομνία γάρ τις ἔμοιγε καταφαίνεται τὸ μέγεθος οὕτω σοποῦνται)" (*Grg.* 456a). Here too, Socrates marks the sophistic claim to possess a *technē* of human and political virtue as something explicitly wondrous and greater than the human, with the implication that any human who claims to possess it would be guilty of hubris.

Hubris is a familiar concept in Greek religious ethics, but we should take time to recognize a fundamental aspect of the phenomenon it names. Pindar gives us some insight when, in the thirteenth *Olympian Ode*, he writes of "Hubris, the bold-speaking mother of *Koros* (Ὕβριν, Κόρου ματέρα θρασύμυθον)" (*Ol.* XIII.10). Translators of the ode almost invariably render the term *koros* as 'excess,' thereby supporting the general tendency to identify hubris simply with 'wanton violence' or 'lawlessness,' and these are no doubt aspects of what is named in Greek by the word *hubris*. We are at risk of misunderstanding, however, if we do not attend to the more original meaning of *koros*, which is 'one's fill, satiety,' and then, 'surfeit.' Furthermore, we must consider that, in Pindar's poetizing of hubris, he reverses the proverbial causal ordering, evident in Solon's aphorism, "*Koros* begets (τίκτει) hubris, when much prosperity comes to humans of imperfect mind (νόος ἄρτιος)" (*Solon* 6.3–4, see also Hesiod's *Theog.* 153). The reversibility of these terms points to a single, double-edged phenomenon.

What is hubristic for human beings is fundamentally a feeling of *sufficiency*, of satisfaction, an attitude that would then support the violent, aggressive, or lawless acts of self-assertion that the term *hubris* often names. Consequently, any sense that one possesses enough of or what is required of power and understanding, so as to be able to act and assert oneself with complete confidence and even aggressiveness, would be to presume to overcome the very inadequacy that would seem to define the human condition.

To avoid hubris is indeed to recognize proper limits, often simply the laws of one's city, religious practices, or even informal social codes, but the deeper implication is that to be human is to *suffer* needfulness, to live with not having enough of wisdom or power, and hubris is the overlooking of or failing to suffer one's *essential insufficiency*.

The "human wisdom" to which Socrates is willing to lay claim would be excessive and disruptive with regard to the everyday attitude, and other than what characterizes the many, but it would also differ from the presumptuous and hubristic, teachable *technē* of the sophists. It would seem to require operating *within*, not overcoming, the essential limitations of the human condition associated in religious ethics with hubris, which is to say, Socratic wisdom would involve the suffering of an unmastered excess, of something with respect to which we find ourselves necessarily wanting.[27]

And indeed, this non-hubristic wisdom proves to be accomplished simply by Socrates' not thinking that he knows when in fact he does not know (*Ap.* 21d). Human wisdom is nothing other than acknowledging and not overlooking one's non-knowing, or recognizing that one is "worth nothing in truth with respect to wisdom (οὐδενὸς ἄξιος ἐστι τῇ ἀληθείᾳ πρὸς σοφίαν)" (*Ap.* 23b). And Socrates tells us directly that his entire philosophical project consists in the generation of just this acknowledgment.

> Thus, even now I go around, in accordance with the god, seeking out and examining anyone who I think might be wise, among both fellow citizens and strangers. And as soon as I do, if he does not appear to me to be so (μοι μὴ δοκῇ), in service to the god, I display that he is not wise. (*Ap.* 23b)

This and this alone Socrates declares to be his entire *ascholia*, his 'business, occupation,' and we are compelled to acknowledge its undeniably destructive or negative aspect.

Before we delve deeper into what precisely is entailed by the emphatically negative or destructive character of Socratic philosophizing, it is important to note that the only 'knowledge' Socrates is concerned to deny, both to himself and to human beings as such, is the *technē* of virtue. He often claims to have perfectly adequate knowledge of "many inconsequential things" (*Euthd.* 293b), such as "quickness (ταχυτής)" in the *Laches* (*La.* 192a–b) or "shape (σχῆμα)" in the *Meno* (*Men.* 76a) or "what all large things are large by" in the *Hippias Major* (*Hp. Ma.* 294a–c), and he clearly sees the practitioners of other crafts as possessing sufficient knowledge with respect to their specific subject matter (*Ap.* 21d–e). Socrates only denies himself and us the *technē*-like knowledge of anything "fine and good (καλὸν κἀγαθὸν)" (*Ap.* 21d), or of "the greatest things (τὰ μέγιστα)" (*Ap.* 22d)—and these are simply whatever has to do with what living well, excellently, or virtuously as a human being *is*, which would be the best, the most important, indeed the most necessary knowledge for a human being to have.

All of the groups that Socrates reports having systematically examined and refuted take themselves for wise in that they presume to have *this* knowledge of human excellence or virtue. The politicians presume to be able to make decisions about life in their *polis* (*Ap.* 21b–e), the poets presume to be able to educate human beings on the most fundamental issues of human life (*Ap.* 22a–c), and the craftsmen, their legitimate confidence in their craft extending beyond its proper domain, presume they know how to live well as human beings because they know how to do their work (*Ap.* 22d–e). Socrates is only interested in the question of virtue, i.e., in the question of living one's life well, and with respect to this neither he nor anyone he has ever examined seems to have what he would call a *technē*-like knowledge.

We will move on next chapter to investigate the positive aspect of the condition that is the acknowledged non-knowing of virtue or human wisdom, in order to determine how the being of virtue should be understood, if its truth is *deinos* or 'excessive,' such that Socratic philosophizing can accomplish its supreme benefit for human beings in nothing other than bringing them to *aporia*. In order to do so, however, we must first determine what precisely characterizes the *technē* of virtue to which Socrates dramatically opposes his own human wisdom.

FROM SHELTER TO EXPOSURE

The Greek term *technē* seems to derive from an Indo-European root, *tekÞ-*, which Julius Pokorny speculates had a quite specific meaning: "flechten, das Holzwerk des geflochtenen Hauses zusammenfügen."[29]* This 'weaving' together of a covering or cloak or this 'joining together' of a shelter would seem to provide the original phenomenal context of the term *technē*. And this etymological origin is still reflected in a family of derived Greek terms, such as *teichos*, 'wall, city-wall, fortification, or castle,' and the verb *stegein*, 'to cover

---

*. . . to weave, to join together the intertwining woodwork of a house.

closely, shelter, protect.' Latin attests to the existence of this root as well with terms such as the verb *tegere*, meaning 'to cover, shelter, protect, cloak,' and the noun *tectum*, meaning 'roof, shelter, dwelling.'

The term *technē* appears then to point back to the act of making a shelter, of fending off the elements, of bringing together a secured and protected dwelling place. Of course, it is then broadened to encompass any craft, skill, or art, but the sense of establishing and securing a dwelling place for oneself in the world is maintained. Crafts are, after all, those activities through which we act upon our environment, ordering it for our use or pleasure and thereby providing a site for the project of living out our lives.[29]

From very early on, however, *technē* was not limited to the physical act of making or doing, but encompassed as well the understanding of our world that directs these ordering actions. In his work on the relationship between *technē* and *aretē*, Jorge Kube traces the development of the former term from Homer to Plato. He shows that *technē* had long indicated primarily an understanding of the world, rather than primarily a productive or practical activity.[30] He cites a moment from the *Odyssey* as an early and indicative text. When Demokodos, the famed singer of the Phaiakians, tells the tale of how Hephaistos trapped Ares as he lay with Hephaistos's wife, Aphrodite, it is the victory of the crippled Hephaistos's *technē* over Ares' physical swiftness and strength that produces boisterous and approving laughter among the gods (*Od.* 8.327 and 332). Kube finds in this passage an indication that "*Technē* löst durch diese Antithese allmählich ihre Verbindung mit handwerklichen Disziplinen und bezeichnet die sich im fachmännischen Können manifestierende intellektuelle Fähigkeit überhaupt."[31]* One sees here already an emphasis on the knowledge or understanding that enables one to take action and secure one's situation, sheltering oneself by explaining and, thus, mastering in thought the previously uncontrollable and unintelligible aspects of one's world.

The *Technē-Tuchē* Antithesis

These etymological observations concerning the original and core meaning of *technē* find strong support in Martha Nussbaum's articulation of the "*technē-tuchē* antithesis," which she presents as central to Greek ethical thought from

---

*Through this antithesis, *technē* gradually loses its connection with various kinds of crafts and comes to mean the intellectual capability that manifests itself in expert proficiency.

fifth-century tragedy through Plato and Aristotle. In *The Fragility of Goodness*, she focuses on the way in which the menacing role of *tuchē* or 'chance' was addressed in the *eudaimonistic* ethics of Greek thinkers and poets, which is to say, in their understanding of how one should live one's life in order to accomplish *eudaimonia* or 'true happiness, flourishing.' She moves from the tragic view of *tuchē* as a destructive but unconquerable force in human affairs, through what she sees as the transcendent and rationalist aspirations of Plato's "anti-tragic theatre" in his middle-period, to the anti-intellectualist return to an immanent view of human ethical judgment with Aristotle. In tracing this development, Nussbaum writes, we should understand *technē* primarily in light of the contrast "between living at the mercy of *tuchē* and living a life made safer or more controlled by (some) *technē*. . . . *Technē*, then, is a deliberate application of human intelligence to some part of the world, yielding some control over *tuchē*."[32] Her language emphasizes an exposure to *tuchē* over against the security and shelter provided by the ordering and controlling power of *technē*.

Tuchē, however, situated in this antithesis, should not be taken for simply a breakdown in causal connections or 'chance,' as it is usually translated and then understood. More deeply, Nussbaum suggests, "Its basic meaning is 'what just happens'; it is the element in human existence that humans do not control."[33] There is here an important insight into the world that *technē* overpowers, eliminates. For *tuchē*, as Nussbaum indicates, names a certain experience of our world, whereby events arise before us from out of a region that exceeds the familiar or comfortable domain of the seemingly manifest. Occurrences present themselves without explanation or anticipation, thereby marking a boundary between an illuminated here and an inscrutable there, enforcing a sense that our understanding of and therefore power over the world in which we find ourselves is radically finite or limited. The question for Nussbaum's Greeks is first, can we eradicate *tuchē* in this sense from human ethical life altogether or not, and then, if we could eradicate it, would it cost us our very humanity to do so.[34]

What Nussbaum's revealing discussion of this antithesis brings to the fore is the original sense of sheltering and securing that we noted before, initially against the elements, but now more broadly against *that which exceeds our understanding and power*. Indeed, *technē* seems to be the intellectual capacity for sheltering ourselves or for providing ourselves with a dwelling place secured against *the excessive*, whether we refer to this by way of what emerges from it (*tuchē*) or by way of our suffering experience of it when it wells up, presents itself, and affects us directly (*to deinon*).[35]

The Socratic Understanding of *Technē* in Light of *Metaphysics* Alpha

This understanding of *technē* as sheltering and securing human life against the excessive is quite precisely attested, both by Socrates' own conception of *technē* in the early dialogues and by the fifth- and fourth-century Greek understanding of *technē* in general.[36] We will look to Aristotle's study of what constitutes a *technē* in the *Metaphysics* as an indicator of the latter.[37] Despite the decades that surely separate the composition of Plato's early dialogues from these Aristotelian lectures, using Aristotle in this way is justified because of the basic philosophical method he employs. That is, his fundamentally (in the Aristotelian sense) *dialectical* approach demands that he begin his consideration of any given subject matter, in this case *sophia* or 'wisdom,' with a thoroughgoing review of *endoxa*, or with "the appearances [of the subject matter] to all or to most or to the wise (τὰ δοκοῦντα πᾶσιν ἢ τοῖς πλείστοις ἢ τοῖς σοφοῖς)" (*Top.* 100b22–23).[38] Aristotle thus strives first to record those serious, thoughtful, and common ways in which his subject matter appears and has appeared to people, thereby grounding his discussion. The crucial moment for us in *Metaphysics* Alpha's examination of *endoxa* is Aristotle's observation of the greater *sophia* that we generally grant to those who seem to possess a *technē* over those who operate according to what seems mere *empeiria* or 'experience' (*Met.* I.980b22–982a3). Here in Aristotle's more or less systematic discussion, we are able to locate a viable and thoughtful reflection of the general contemporary conception of *technē*.

The salient characteristics of *technē* identified by Aristotle are the following: 1) *Technē* promises shelter and security against the excessive, through the eradication of any pertinent region beyond our understanding's grasp, 2) *Technē* is an explanatory, thus teachable, understanding of our world, and 3) *Technē* entails an immediate grasp of 'what "x" *is*' or the being of its subject matter.[39]

In *Metaphysics* Alpha, *technē* is primarily approached, consistent with our general considerations earlier, not as a physical activity, but as an intellectual capacity or a way of understanding our world. Indeed, *technē* is by no means superior, and is even sometimes inferior, to *empeiria* when it comes to "doing or acting (πράττειν)" (*Met.* I.981a13–15). The superiority that belongs to those comporting themselves by *technē*, or the greater *sophia* that is attributed to them, is not due to greater efficacy in action, but rather to the following: "Those who have experience (ἔμπειροι) know the 'that,' but not the 'why,' whereas the others [those with *technē*] know the 'why' and the cause (τὴν αἰτίαν)" (*Met.* I.981a28–30).

So long as one operates on the basis of *empeiria*, even if one has put away a great stock of related experiences in one's memory and can on this basis intervene effectively in certain situations to bring about desired ends, one nevertheless continues to receive events as (to use Nussbaum's phrase) "what just happens." That is, as at least in part arising from *tuchē* and, thus, as *excessive*, emerging inexplicably from beyond what is manifest or apparent. A healer may know from trial and error that a given herb is beneficial for a patient with a certain set of symptoms and he or she may even be able to group together past and present instances of that condition as the same. This entails, however, no understanding of why the condition has arisen, nor how the herb will bring about health. These eventualities, both the sickness and the health, are experienced as coming forth from the world's unfathomable depths and presenting themselves.

Only with the shift to *technē* is that region of unfathomability eradicated, illuminating the entirety of the event. Only through a technical understanding of the 'why' and the *aitiai* or the 'causes, explanations' of the sickness and the health does one rid one's world of this threatening and abyssal depth. Events within the purview of one's *technē* become demystified, explainable, and even anticipatable. No longer responding to unpredictable occurrences, one can plan and take action to fend off danger and error. *Technē* as a way of understanding one's world therefore provides shelter and security by eliminating its menacingly ungraspable excess, laying everything out as manifest on a flattened plane of causal relations, thereby establishing one's judgments, when *technē* is properly employed, as unimpeachable and certain with respect to that which *technē* knows.

And a craftsperson can on this basis *explain* his or her sheltering knowledge to another and thereby *teach*, rather than merely exemplifying what to do in a given specific circumstance in response to a given eventuality. He or she can give a *logos* or an 'account' of what has caused the event and therefore explain what one must do in response to this in any circumstance whatever in order to bring about the desired result (*Met.* I.981a13–15, also I.981b7–9).[40]

At another point in what we refer to as the *Metaphysics*, Aristotle expands this notion of *technē*, emphasizing the role of one of his four causes, the *causa formalis*, in the understanding or seeing possessed by the expert craftsperson. He writes,

What comes to be from craft is that of which the *eidos* is in the soul [of the craftsperson] (ἀπὸ τέχνης δὲ γίγνεται ὅσων τὸ εἶδος ἐν τῇ ψυχῇ)—and with *eidos* I mean the 'what it was to be' of each thing and the primary being (εἶδος δὲ λέγω τὸ τί ἦν εἶναι ἑκάστου καὶ τὴν πρώτην οὐσίαν). (*Met.* VII.1032a32-b2)

Aristotle offers the *technai* of medicine and house-building as examples (*Met.* VII.1032b11–14). Practitioners can be said to have such *technai* only insofar as in performing their various actions they hold the idea (*eidos*) or the being (*ousia*) of health or house in mind, which Aristotle defines as the *to ti ēn einai* or literally the 'what it was to be' the health or the house that will come into existence through the work of *technē*, but conceived *aneu hulēs* or before it is instantiated in its material component (say, flesh or building stones) (*Met.* VII.1032b13–14). There can be misfires in the actual work of any given craftsperson, of course, even when the *technē* is pursued properly, for the entire performance of a *technē* requires not only the unerring intellectual perception of the *eidos* or *ousia* (*APo.* 71b9–72a14), but also the always imperfect assessment of the material particulars on which and the specific material conditions in which the technical action is taken.[41] However, what is crucial here is that, insofar as one is working with a *technē*, the 'what it *is*' or the being of one's subject matter is immediately held or grasped—one has the being of the thing *in one's soul*, Aristotle insists. This is vital for our considerations. *Technē* entails for Aristotle *the direct intellectual grasp of 'what 'x' is.'*

In sum, we see that *technē* appears here as sheltering or securing against excess, explanatory, and immediately proximal and grasping with respect to the being of its subject matter. All three of these aspects are consistent with Socrates' own discussions of *technē* in the early dialogues.

Before we proceed, however, we should note that in Greek usage through Plato and even up to Aristotle's more or less precise differentiations, *technē* is used interchangeably with a number of other terms.[42] Indeed, we have seen this already in the passage cited earlier from the *Euthydemus* (*Euthd.* 273e), where Socrates speaks of the divine and teachable eristic skill of the two pancratists as an *epistēmē*. We might add to this two particularly clear examples from the *Protagoras* and the *Laches*. In the former, describing virtue in its contextually determined manifestation (i.e., the art of measuring pleasure in order to make ethical judgments), Socrates shifts back and forth indiscriminately between *technē* and *epistēmē*, and ultimately refers to "whatever craft (τέχνη) and knowledge (ἐπιστήμη) this is" (*Prt.* 357b), making no distinction at all between the two terms. And when, having converted into a formula something he has apparently heard from Socrates' previously, the sophisticated general Nicias responds to the question of 'what courage is' by identifying courage with *sophia* (*La.* 194c–d), Socrates turns around and asks him precisely what the nature of this *epistēmē* (*La.* 194e) might be and this is then later on explicitly discussed as one possible *technē* among others, such as medicine and farming (*La.* 195b–c). Thus, given the general and the specifically Platonic tendency to treat these terms as equivalent, and given also that Plato's Socrates does not have nor does he believe he needs to have a consistent technical vocabulary (*Chrm.* 163d, also *Prt.* 358a, *Ion* 532e), we will not be disturbed if we find Socrates speaking sometimes of a *technē* and sometimes of an *epistēmē* or *sophia* of virtue, nor even if we encounter other nouns (*gnōmē, gnōsis, mathēsis,* and *phronēsis*) and other verbs (*epistasthai, eidenai, sunienai,* and *gignōskein*), often apparently used to refer to the very same condition of the soul. We will simply have to determine from the context whether the condition of the soul in play in a given passage is that to which we are referring here as *technē*.[43]

In the *Euthydemus*, where *sophia* has been identified with excellence in such *technai* as flute-playing, steersmanship, generalship, medicine, and carpentry (*Euthd.* 279d), Socrates marshals Clinias's commonsense notion thereof in order to argue that "*sophia* being present, the one in whom it is present has no need of good fortune (σοφίας παρούσης, ᾧ ἂν παρῇ, μηδὲν προσδεῖσθαι εὐτυχίας)" (*Euthd.* 280b, see also Polus at *Grg.* 448c).[44] Wisdom in the context-specific sense of expertise in a *technē* explicitly represents a mastering understanding and control, whereby one overcomes exposure to *tuchē*. This passage indicates quite clearly the way in which *technē* would shelter us, securing us against the abyssal depth and threatening excess that sometimes seems to well up in our experience of our world.

This shelter from *tuchē* is also indicated by another point with which Socrates finds his interlocutors in complete agreement—someone operating with a *technē* (or *epistēmē* or *sophia*) with regard to his or her subject matter should be treated as an authority, since his or her judgments on that subject will be free from error (*Chrm.* 171d–172a, *La.* 184e–184b, *Cri.* 479c–d, *Grg.* 490b–c, *R.* I.340d–341a). That is, the understanding that is a *technē* would be sufficient to more or less ensure good judgment within its field of expertise, and this trustworthiness points to the ability to secure human endeavors against and eradicate the threat of *tuchē*, the unknown or the unanticipated.

Moving to the second and third characteristics of *technē*, in the *Gorgias* Socrates' fundamental critique of rhetoric foreshadows precisely a distinction we saw Aristotle making earlier in the *Metaphysics*. There, Socrates makes the straightforward argument that rhetoric fails to qualify as a *technē* (although it claims to be such) and is instead a mere *empeiria* (*Grg.* 462b–c). Indeed, it is a shameful form of "flattery (κολακεία)" (*Grg.* 463b), grounded in nothing other than the rhetorician's past experience of the many's initial and thoughtless preferences. Socrates then focuses on its non-explanatory character in arguing against its status as a *technē*. He states,

> I say that it is not a *technē*, but an *empeiria*, because it has no account (λόγον) at all of the things it brings forth (προσφέρει) nor that by which it brings them forth, no account of whatever these are with respect to their nature (τὴν φύσιν), with the result that it is not able to state the cause of each thing (τὴν αἰτίαν ἑκάστου). But I do not call a thing that is without an account (ἄλογον πρᾶγμα) a *technē*. (*Grg.* 465a)

It seems that for Socrates, a *technē*-like knowledge would allow its possessor to *logon didonai* or 'give an account.' Specifically, to give an account of the *phusis* or the 'nature' of its subject matter, which would then allow the possessor of the *technē* to provide the *aitiai* or 'explanations, causes' of each thing that is relevant to this subject matter. It is clear then that, as with Aristotle, a *technē* is explanatory, i.e., one who possesses it knows not only what is the case but why this must be so, making it, therefore, teachable.[45]

And, as we would also expect from our look at Aristotle, we have ample evidence that the *phusis* someone with a *technē* would know is just that to which Socrates usually refers in a questioning mode as 'what "x" is.' In the *Laches* for instance, before embarking on the project of educating the sons of Melesias and Lysimachus in virtue, i.e., before presuming to exercise an explicitly teachable understanding of virtue, Socrates asks, "To begin, is this not necessary? To know 'whatever virtue is' (τὸ εἰδέναι ὅτι ποτ' ἔστιν ἀρετή)?" (*La.* 190b).

Indeed, in this light, Socrates' characteristic question in the early dialogues, 'What is "x"?,' itself becomes significant. Given that Socrates' philosophical method seems to involve, centrally, asking for an account or a definition of the being of virtue, an explainable grasp of 'what virtue is' (sometimes by way of what are for him its context-specific appearances such as courage, temperance, justice, wisdom, and piety), this central and persistent question can be and often is understood as a demand that his interlocutor exhibit an explainable *technē*-like grasp of the being of virtue.

Consider Socrates' remarks at the end of the *Protagoras*. As Socrates insists on drawing to its close the elenctic discussion of the great sophist's initial claim to teach virtue, an ornery Protagoras accuses Socrates of shamelessly *philonikein* or 'loving victory.' Socrates in effect assures him that this is so only insofar as he is guilty of the love of winning out the truth, or precisely that which we discussed at the beginning of this chapter. He says,

> But I am asking after all these things for no other reason than wanting to search out how things hold concerning virtue and whatever it itself is (τί ποτ' ἐστὶν αὐτό, ἡ ἀρετή). For I know that, if this were to become clear (τούτου φανεροῦ γενομένου), that about which you and I have each stretched out a long discourse would become manifest (κατάδηλον γένοιτο)—me saying that virtue is not teachable and you saying that it is teachable. (*Prt.* 360e–361a)

If their discussion had been able to make 'what "x" *is*' become *phaneron* or 'apparent,' bringing this to light, Socrates knows that the specific property of x, namely, its teachability or unteachability, would become *katadēlon*, 'manifest,' thoroughly *dēlos* or 'clear, visible, evident.'

The sense here, which we miss if we think in terms of certainty and logical validity, is that by grasping the being of x in a *logos* they would overcome the indeterminacy and obscurity with which it currently appears. 'What "x" *is*' would appear directly and immediately (become *phaneron*), which is to say that it, in its movement into appearing (*phainesthai*), would cease to be received from out of the distance beyond one's grasp or by way of intervening and obfuscating mediations. Instead, by having such a *technē*-like knowledge of our subject matter, in this case 'what virtue is,' all things fine and good, all the "most important things" (*Ap.* 22d), would become manifest, and one would make unimpeachable decisions regarding virtue or excellence. As with Aristotle, possessing the *technē* or *epistēmē* of virtue that Socratic questioning clearly requires of one, insofar as one could contain or master 'what virtue is' in an account or definition, would entail *a clear and immediate grasp of and direct proximity to the being of virtue*. Indeed, although scholarly discussions of the early dialogues often distinguish many different aspects of Socrates' understanding of *technē* (infallibility, accuracy, authority, and the ability to give a definition and defend it in the course of an elenchus), these all derive, for Socrates, from the direct and proximal grasp of 'what *is*' that *technē* would as such seem to enjoy and from the clarity of appearance that this ensures.

When Socratic philosophizing is viewed in light of Aristotle's treatment of *technē*, Socrates' demand that his interlocutors know and explain to him 'what virtue is' presents itself quite distinctly as a demand that they possess a *technē*-like understanding of virtue. For Socrates, then, if anyone *were* to possess the *technē* of virtue that his questioning demands and that the sophists presume, that individual would have an understanding of the world providing shelter and security against excess or *tuchē*, an explanatory and thus teachable form of knowledge, and an immediate or direct grasp of the being of virtue. It is in opposition to precisely this conception of *technē* that Socrates places his notion of human wisdom.

The Non-Knowing of Virtue as Socrates' Aim

We should note at this point that Aristotle himself surely does not take Socrates to be *rejecting* the *technē*-model of human virtue, but quite the opposite. In the *Magna Moralia*, we find a straightforward statement of the general Aristotelian assessment—Socrates "made the virtues *epistēmai*" (*MM* 1182a16).[46] And Aristotle states elsewhere that for Socratic ethics, "the aim is to know virtue (τέλος τὸ γινώσκειν τὴν ἀρετήν), and to investigate 'what justice is' (τί ἐστιν ἡ δικαιοσύνη), 'what courage is,' and each of the other parts" (*EE* 1216b2–6). That is, Aristotle observes Socrates in the early dialogues posing his central 'What *is* virtue?' question (again, often focused on its various context-specific appearances—courage, temperance, fineness, etc.) and demanding that his interlocutors teach him and give an account of their *technē* or *epistēmē*-like understanding thereof.

In addition, Aristotle surely noted the frequent overt comparisons between virtue and various *technai* throughout the early dialogues. Indeed, a whole host of craftspeople are on parade here alongside the virtuous human being as *comparanda*, from doctors, generals, steersmen, measure-takers, and grammar teachers, to athletic trainers, flute-players, farmers, cobblers, cleaners, and cooks (*Ap.* 20a–b, *Euthphr.* 11e–14c, *La.* 198d–199a, *Chrm.* 164a–166d, 174b–175a, *Euthd.* 274e–275a, 288d–292e, *Alc. I* 103a–109c, 111a, *Prt.* 355e–357, *Grg.* 464b–466a, 490b–491b, *R.* I.341c–342e).

From all of this, Aristotle seems to conclude that the *telos* or 'aim' of Socrates' philosophizing is a *technē* or an *epistēmē* of virtue, or that such an understanding of virtue is the *ideal* pursued by Socrates, even if he himself never arrives at it (on this, see *SE* 183b6–8). Indeed, it is just this apparent "intellectualist" aspiration that Aristotle perceives in Socratic and Platonic ethics, i.e., the paradoxical equation 'virtue is knowledge,' against which Aristotle often argues and which he proposes to correct with his conception of virtue as a well-habituated and phronetically reasoning *hexis* or 'disposition' (*EN* 1105b20–1107a26).[47]

However, we are compelled to disagree with Aristotle's interpretation of the ultimate *telos* of Socratic philosophizing as we find it in the text of Plato's early dialogues, while admitting that the complex project portrayed in these works can surely point the reader in that direction. As we have seen, Aristotle is certainly correct in observing that Socrates asks of his interlocutors that they give him an account of 'what "x" is' with regard to virtue and that they teach and explain the 'why' or 'cause' for each related thing. For Aristotle, and for Socrates as we have seen, this is indeed a *demand* that his interlocutors exercise a *technē* of virtue.

Nevertheless, Socrates need not for this reason be seen as *advocating* the technical model of virtue, even as an ideal. Rather, although the Socratic philosophical project does on the surface require a *technē*-like grasp of the being virtue, it should be seen to *aim at* and even *accomplish* an altogether different relation. In the *Apology*, when Socrates introduces the *technē*-model of human virtue, in addition to denying that he himself possesses any such knowledge, he associates this *technē* with the sophists and characterizes it as out of accord with essential human insufficiency, i.e., as *hubristic*. Furthermore, he presents his own lifelong philosophical project there as *purely* elenctic, as simply refuting his interlocutors in their false pretense to knowledge with respect to human virtue. This activity aims at and results in the only wisdom he is willing to claim for himself and others, the properly human wisdom that is *nothing other than* the acknowledging of *not* having a *technē*-like grasp of virtue.[48] Nonetheless, as we have seen, Socrates declares that *this* activity, the elenctic discussion of virtue and the human wisdom it brings about and sustains, is itself the greatest good for human beings.

Given this, we must be very reluctant to accept any interpretation that sees Socrates either as arriving at a *technē* of virtue or even as arriving at a modified and more modest form of knowledge, which would establish *technē* nevertheless as the regulative (if ultimately unattainable) ideal toward which Socratic philosophizing strives.[49] Any such interpretation insists on locating the supreme benefit and aim of Socratic philosophizing precisely where Socrates resists placing it—an epistemologically positive result that is external to or comes in some sense after the acknowledging of one's non-knowing. By contrast, it seems necessary to take very seriously Socrates' simple identification of the benefit of his philosophizing and human wisdom, the acknowledging of one's non-knowing with respect to virtue that is brought about and maintained by the elenchus.

At one point in his fine study, *Socratic Wisdom*, Hugh Benson addresses himself to a potentially problematic fact, often identified by scholars as evidence for the modest but nevertheless epistemologically positive result just mentioned. Namely, the fact that Socrates throughout the early dialogues seems to make occasional, inadvertent claims to know things about virtue, despite his frequent and emphatic assertions of his own humanly wise non-knowing. Focusing on the *Apology*, Benson writes,

> . . . I have found it difficult to understand why some scholars . . . distinguish between two kinds of knowledge, one weak and the other strong, and claim that here in the *Apology* in claiming human wisdom Socrates is claiming weak knowledge of various moral truths, while in disowning divine wisdom Socrates is disavowing strong knowledge of moral truths. . . . Nothing in this passage from the *Apology* suggests that Socrates' human wisdom resides in knowledge of any kind, except perhaps knowledge of his ignorance. Socrates is not wiser than his contemporaries because he has more weak knowledge and no more nor less strong knowledge than they do. He is wiser than they are because he recognizes that he fails to have knowledge of any sort when he does not. Socrates' human wisdom, at least as far as the Delphic oracle story is concerned, consists simply in this recognition.[50]

Benson goes on to conclude that his assessment here of Socrates' claims in the *Apology* is consistent with all of the early dialogues. Socrates identifies as his superior wisdom the acknowledged non-knowing of 'what virtue is,' and this constitutes the sole benefit and promise of the philosophical activity he is forced to defend in the *Apology*. The superior wisdom Socrates possesses, and which he shares with others by way of his elenctic questioning, is clearly *not* some other weaker form of knowledge on its way toward or approximating a *technē*.

Indeed, this is the major contribution of Benson's interpretation of Socratic method, for he argues compellingly against the pervasive current tendency to look for some unstated and epistemologically positive product of Socrates' philosophizing in which its real benefit would reside. Benson's book is focused on the epistemological aspect of the early dialogues, trying to determine what concept of knowledge is at stake in Socrates' questioning.

However, the Socratic conception of knowledge that Benson meticulously articulates, as with our discussion of *technē* earlier, appears in the dialogues *only in being completely and thoroughly disavowed by Socrates*. This leaves Benson with "a genuinely skeptical Socrates,"[51] insofar as the supreme benefit and aim of Socratic philosophizing, human wisdom, "does not amount to an assertion of [even] unclear, fallible, or nonexpert knowledge of anything."[52]

Although there is plenty of reason to agree with Benson's observation that Socrates does not locate the benefit and aim of his elenctic project in the acquisition of knowledge about virtue, of either a strong *technē*-like variety or a more modest weak variety, we should not find that this leaves us with Socratic skepticism with respect to virtue. The consequence Benson draws here is only necessitated by the anachronistic presupposition of an epistemological subject-object relation and its attendant objective ontology.[53] This becomes clear if we investigate his interpretation of the knowledge Socrates disavows and shows others to lack, which Benson defines as a "power or capacity (*dunamis*) to make judgments resulting in an interrelated coherent system of true cognitive states involving a particular object or subject matter."[54]

Although clearly integrating elements of a coherence theory of truth, Benson's definition of the "knowledge" Socrates disavows operates wholly within the framework of the correspondence theory. The systematic complex of cognitive states entailed by knowledge of x, gathered around and founded upon a definitional account of 'what "x" is,' would be true according to Benson's model insofar as they accurately re-present a complex of objectively present conditions. It is only thereby that "a knowledge-*dunamis* grasps its *object* in a particularly strong or complete way."[55] The possession of such an accurately representational and more or less systematic set of cognitions about the objectively real conditions of virtue would power unerring judgments pertaining to virtuous behavior. Note that in our discussion, we have characterized the knowledge or *technē* that Socrates disavows *not* in terms of the correct and certain re-presentation of a present objectively real object, *but rather* in terms of the complete illumination of and proximity with respect to that which first appears in *doxa*. This distinction makes all the difference.

Given Benson's presupposition of an objective ontology and of the correspondence notion of truth proper to it, insofar as the elenchus results in a pure revelation of non-knowing with respect to virtue, he is bound to discover in this a gap between Socrates' interlocutors' own internally contradictory complex of beliefs or *doxai* about virtue and the objectively real properties of 'what virtue is.' *If* this were Socrates' conception of the being of virtue, i.e., *if* the being of virtue were an objective reality from which we could be wholly disconnected and to which we would have to establish and secure a relationship through accurate and justified re-presentation in thought and discourse, *then* the elenchus would indeed result in a skeptical condition, an unveiling of the participants' ignorance, or of the merely subjective and isolated, disconnected character of their opinions about virtue.

However, if we simply resist presupposing this subject-object framework as has been suggested, the real and legitimate relation that is constituted by just this epistemological failure might present itself. That is, the negation or destruction of the interlocutors' everyday opinions would *not* amount to these individuals' even potential disconnection from the being of virtue. Rather, these *doxai* would be revealed as obscure, partial, oblique, and multiple appearances of 'what virtue is,' as inadequate and not qualifying as 'knowledge,' but as always nevertheless legitimate appearances of the being of virtue. Thus, the result of a destruction of our *doxai* is not skeptical, not a potential solipsism or subjective isolation. Instead, as a *disruption* of *doxa*, Socratic elenchus amounts to a disruption of one legitimate relation to or appearing of 'what is' that results in another legitimate relation to or appearing of 'what is.' The latter is a relation that Socrates has come to wager is true and humanly wise, even if still questioning and at a distance, and he therefore attempts to bring this about and maintain it with his philosophical conversations.

Finally, it is important to note that the *emphasis* on the condition of acknowledged non-knowing as the principal result and apparently sole benefit of Socratic philosophizing is by no means limited to the *Apology*. Rather, it remains consistent throughout the early dialogues. Indeed, Socrates' most consistent and most emphatic description of himself is surely that he is non-knowing with respect to human virtue and its various aspects (*Euthphr.* 5a, 11b–e, 14b–c, *Chrm.* 165b, 175c–176b, *La.* 199e–200e, *R.* I.337d–e, 354b–c, *Hp. Ma.* 286c–e, 304d–e, *Hp. Mi.* 372b, *Ly.* 223b, *Prt.* 361c, *Grg.* 509a, *Men.* 71a, 72b, 80d).[56] Throughout these discussions, Socrates is contrasted with his interlocutors explicitly and repeatedly insofar as he maintains himself in a condition of non-knowing, whereas they presume to know.

Simply put, if we are able to do so, we should locate the supreme benefit of his philosophizing where Socrates himself expressly places it—the human wisdom that he emphasizes, both in the *Apology* and consistently throughout the early dialogues, in describing his elenctically sustained condition. We hope to be in a position to better understand this through having clarified the conception of *technē* to which Socrates dramatically opposes the result of his elenctic activity. That is, the condition that Socratic elenctic questioning brings about, which constitutes its truth and its supreme benefit, would seem to be: 1) An exposure to excess (as opposed to the sheltering and securing of *technē*), 2) An ultimately non-explanatory and non-teachable experience of the unfathomable depths of our appearing world (as opposed to *technē*'s flattened and all-manifesting plane of causal relations, which explains everything relevant and allows for straightforward *paideia*), and 3) A questioning and distant relation, but a relation nonetheless, to the being of virtue (as opposed to the immediate and mastering grasp and direct proximity of *technē*).

We have arrived at this by taking seriously Socrates' opposition to the sophistic *technē*-model of virtue and his constant emphasis on the ostensibly negative or destructive aspect of the elenchus, i.e., its generation of human wisdom. Next chapter we will focus on Socrates' positive articulation of this very condition in terms of *meletē* or 'concern' and *lupē* or 'pain.'

Socrates and the *Technē*-Model of Virtue

Before we turn to an elucidation of the positive aspect of this anti-technical, which is to say, exposed, non-explanatory, and distant, but true and humanly wise comportment toward the being of virtue, we must briefly explain why Socrates, as we have seen, demands of his interlocutors a *technē*-like grasp of 'what virtue is,' such that Aristotle and others have misinterpreted the ultimate *telos* of his philosophizing. Indeed, why does he often seem to introduce the *technē*-model of virtue, securing his interlocutors' agreement that virtue can and should be conceived as such, if in fact he is fundamentally opposed to this analogy? The answer to this question emerges with the recognition that Socrates does not take himself to be "introducing" the *technē*-model at all. Rather, he is simply drawing his interlocutors into an explicit statement of the sheltering, explanatory, and immediate grasp of 'what virtue is' *that all of them already presume to possess*.

In the early dialogues, we can group the individuals whom Socrates encounters into two general categories—the sophisticated and the unsophisticated. On the one hand, we often find Socrates in conversation with those who presume to have elevated themselves above the everyday attitude of the many through education—sophists or rhetoricians, their committed pupils, rhapsodes, and religious experts. On the other hand, we also witness Socrates relishing every opportunity to engage in conversation with the youth of Athens, with unformed young men about to embark on their public lives as citizens of the *polis* and even, in the case of the *Lysis*, *paides* or 'adolescents.'[57] Despite the importance that this distinction might have for considerations of the pedagogical mode and mood of the questioning Socrates employs with different interlocutors, what is far more important is the presumption of an understanding or knowledge of virtue that these groups share. Both the sophisticated and the unsophisticated alike presume to have a satisfactory understanding of virtue.

The sophists, experts, and rhapsodes lay open claim to such an understanding, even if they do not always or initially articulate their claim in precisely this way. Their presumption to advise the city on ethical and political matters or to teach individuals concerning how to live well as human beings *would entail* for Socrates a *technē*-like grasp of virtue. Protagoras admits to as much directly (*Prt.* 318a–319a), while Gorgias does so only with a bit of prompting (*Grg.* 461b, also 460a). As we have seen, Euthydemus and Dionysodorus presume to have arrived at an *epistēmē* of virtue (*Euthd.* 273d–274a), and even Ion the simple-minded rhapsode is led to realize that, given how he understands his own mastery of Homeric poetry and given the significance he perceives in that mastery, he presumes knowledge of various important *technai* (*Ion*, esp. 530b–c). Hippias the polymath claims just such a grasp of virtue inadvertently, insofar as he claims to know 'what the fine is' (*Hp. Ma.* 286d–e, 296d), as does Critias in the *Charmides*, when he is shown to assume an understanding of the good itself (*Chrm.* 174b–e). Finally, in declaring it to be definitively the "advantage of the stronger" (*R.* I.338c), Thrasymachus claims to "know (εἰδέναι)" (*R.* I.337d, 338a) precisely 'what the just is,' as well as what wisdom and virtue are (*R.* I.348d–349a). To be sure, this is why he finds Socrates' plodding and frustrated discussion with Cephalus and Polemarchus so intolerable (*R.* I.336a–d). In short, Socrates' sophisticated interlocutors are all explicitly confident in their understanding of virtue, such that their judgments about related matters will be authoritative and they presume to be able to explain and teach this understanding to others.

However, Socrates' unsophisticated interlocutors are possessed as well of a false confidence in their grasp of 'what virtue is.' Indeed, Socrates perceives such an assumption as necessary to any decision we make in leading our lives according to our everyday attitude. Although he is a sophisticated interlocutor and the dilemma he faces is extreme, Socrates' assessment of Euthyphro's decision-making applies to all the decisions we make, from the most significant to the most pedestrian. Socrates says at the end of their opening discussion,

> For if you did not know clearly (σαφῶς) the pious and the impious, you would never have ventured to prosecute your father for murder on behalf of a servant. . . . Now I know well that you think you know clearly (σαφῶς . . . εἰδέναι) the pious and the not pious. (*Euthphr.* 15d–e)

For Socrates, every time we presume in our everyday mode to be able to decide on this over that, every time we choose something as good or we pursue our own happiness or well-being, we operate under the assumption of "knowing clearly" 'what virtue *is*.' Indeed, it is in this context of decision-making that we see precisely the interchangeability of the various vocabularies Socrates employs. Always following its context-specific appearance in the conversation in which he is currently involved, which is to say, always speaking "without [external] purpose, speaking with whatever words occur [to him] (εἰκῇ λεγόμενα τοῖς ἐπιτυχοῦσιν ὀνόμασιν)" (*Ap.* 17c), Socrates sometimes speaks of this ultimate aim in light of which all of our decisions are made not as 'what virtue is,' but as *to agathon* or 'the good' or as *eudaimonia* or 'true happiness, flourishing' (even extraordinarily as *hēdonē* or 'pleasure,' *Prt.* 355e–356e). That is, Socrates most often wants his interlocutors to acknowledge that "it is by *aretē* that we are good" (*Men.* 87d–e) and by which "we live well (*eu zēn*) and happily (*eudaimōn*)" (*Chrm.* 176a, also *Grg.* 470e, *Cri.* 48b), but he can also ask them to affirm that "The good is the end (τέλος) of all actions and it is necessary that everything we do is for the sake of that" (*Grg.* 499e, also *Chrm.* 173a–174d), as well as that "We all desire to be happy (εὐδαίμονες . . . εἶναι)" (*Euthd.* 282a). Whether he refers to this as *aretē*, *agathon*, or *eudaimonia* (or even as *hēdonē* in its contextually radicalized sense), Socrates sees that every comfortable decision we make in our everyday mode presumes an immediate and unproblematic grasp of this ultimate end. Socrates alone, extraordinary in maintaining himself in a questioning attitude, would seem to make his decisions and take action otherwise in relation to 'what virtue is.' In any case, even his unsophisticated interlocutors, insofar as they embody the everyday human attitude, are to be understood as presuming a satisfactory understanding not just of this or that state of affairs or specific issue, but of the being of virtue itself. It is the task of Socratic elenchus to undermine just this false confidence.

This confidence is most dramatically highlighted in the early dialogues by the fact that even Socrates' unsophisticated interlocutors again and again perceive his basic question, 'What is human virtue?,' as bizarrely facile.[58] Although already having been a student of Gorgias, Meno is first and foremost presented as a young man in search of an education in virtue, a project Socrates undertakes to help him with. When in the course of this, Socrates admits that he knows neither whether virtue is teachable nor even "whatever virtue altogether is (ὅτι ποτ' ἐστὶ τὸ παράπαν ἀρετὴ)" (*Men.* 71a), Meno's response is disbelief. He asks, "But, Socrates, do you truly not know 'what virtue is' (ἀληθῶς οὐδ' ὅτι ἀρετή ἐστιν οἶσθα) and should we report this about you to those back home?" (*Men.* 71b). Little does Meno suspect that this comportment itself already realizes in a sense the entire *telos* of Socratic philosophizing—*alēthōs* or 'truly' not knowing what virtue is. That is to say, Socrates aims to bring about among his interlocutors the acknowledgment of not possessing a *technē*-like knowledge, which *itself* exposes them in a truthful mode to the excessive being of virtue.

In any case, the admission clearly scandalizes Meno, implying that he operates under the general expectation that everyone shares in an understanding at least of what human virtue is. One might object that Meno's expectation here is peculiar to Socrates, i.e., that it is surprising only that a reputedly wise man does not know 'what virtue is.' However, a little later on, Meno responds to Socrates' request for an account of the being of virtue by stating confidently, "But it is no difficult thing (οὐ χαλεπόν) to say, Socrates" (*Men.* 71e). That is, unlike the intricacies of some specialized *technē*, which would be a difficult thing for everyone except a few experts to explain, giving an account of 'what virtue is' should not be at all difficult for anyone.[59]

In their discussion of courage as one of "the parts of virtue (τῶν τῆς ἀρετῆς μερῶν)" (*La.* 190d), the older but still humble and unsophisticated general, Laches,[60] voices precisely the same everyday presumption when he is asked by Socrates to state "whatever courage is (ἀνδρεία τί ποτ' ἐστίν)." He responds confidently that it is "not a difficult thing (οὐ χαλεπὸν) to say" (*La.* 190e).[61]

And when Socrates begins their discussion by asking the youthful Menexenus and Lysis whether they are friends, they respond in unison, "Absolutely (πάνυ γε)" (*Ly.* 207c). With this, Plato has the two boys express complete confidence in their understanding of *philia*, that aspect of human *eudaimonia* that will be the topic of the entire subsequent discussion. Socrates, of course, goes on to show them in the course of this conversation that their confidence is altogether unjustified.

We see that Socrates' unsophisticated interlocutors as well, simply in living out their everyday lives, presume what for him would amount to a *technē*-like knowledge of virtue. Again, this is so even if they would not necessarily refer to their relation to virtue as a *technē* and even if they are sometimes hesitant to state their views openly. As one interpreter puts it, among Socrates' interlocutors, "the pretension to knowledge is varied in form although ubiquitous in nature: everyone needs to be freed of it, whether they profess it or simply live according to it."[62] Indeed, insofar as sophistry and rhetoric are obligated to cater to, please, and flatter the many (*Grg.* 462a–465e, also see *R.* VI.492a–493a), Socrates sees the sophisticated practitioners of these as trafficking in nothing other than refined reflections and secondary articulations of the everyday attitude's *doxai* about virtue, which is to say, of the everyday attitude's presumed immediate and, thus, *technē*-like grasp of the being of virtue.

In sum, there is another explanation for Socrates' apparent invocations of the *technē*-model of human virtue, one that is consistent with his characterization of this very model as sophistic and hubristic. Socrates employs the *technē*-model simply in attempting to bring to the surface, articulate, and make precise *what is already presumed by both his sophisticated and unsophisticated interlocutors*.[63] He thereby encourages them to claim a form of knowledge that they themselves will recognize, according to the general conception of *technē*, as explanatory and thus teachable. Having done so, he is then able to perform his elenchus toward its apparently desired result. For when the interlocutor has proven unable to give an account of virtue (or to explain and teach it), this should occasion the recognition that one does not have precisely that *technē*-like grasp of virtue which one had previously presumed. In short, one can come to know that one does not know.

We should say, therefore, that Socrates' elenctic questioning is not employed in pursuit of an ultimate *technē*-like understanding of virtue; rather, the *technē*-model of virtue is employed in the service of the elenchus, in order to bring about the acknowledgment of non-knowing that is its whole and proper aim.

5

The Truthful Elenctic *Pathos* of Painful Concern

> There are four natures, those of plants, of beasts, of humans, and of God—the latter two, which are rational, have the same nature, but they are distinguished in that the one is immortal while the other is mortal. Regarding these, then, the good of the one, God, is fulfilled by his nature, but the good of the other, the human, is fulfilled by concern (*cura*).
> —Seneca, *Epistle 124*[1]

> Apprends à penser avec douleur.*
> —Maurice Blanchot, *L'écriture du désastre*

In the closing lines of the *Apology*, standing now in the shadow of his impending execution, Socrates makes a striking request of his jurors as to their treatment of his sons after his death. He does not ask, as we might expect, that his sons be shown mercy, that they be spared retribution for their father's perceived misconduct. Instead, quite to the contrary, he encourages those who see him as guilty of impiety and corruption to pursue vengeance and to do so relentlessly. He asks only that they avenge themselves on his sons in a particular way—"By paining (λυποῦντες) them in the same way I have pained (ἐλύπουν) you" (*Ap.* 41e).

If we submit to the concentrated intensity of this moment, of this last public request, Socrates makes evident here that his philosophizing achieves its benefit by bringing *lupē*, 'pain, grief, distress,' for it is just this that he asks for on behalf of his loved ones. Our task is to determine the precise character of what must then be this requisite suffering, this *pathos* that belongs essentially to the Socratic philosophical project.

---

*Learn to think with suffering.

ELENCTIC PAIN AND BEING CONCERNED BY VIRTUE

> Each of us holds on to the *doxa* we already have of
> Ourselves, until we suffer (παθεῖν).
>   —Solon, *Prayer to the Muses* (13.33–35)

Surely Socrates' public refutations often produce embarrassment, even humiliation, for those whom he subjects to questioning. However, so long as this remains superficial and has only to do with the one's image or reputation, it remains far removed from the substance of what Socrates must want for his sons. In calling at this moment for them to be pained, Socrates the father must be asking for what will bring them nothing short of "the greatest good (μέγιστον ἀγαθὸν)" (*Ap.* 38a), which is of course precisely what he believes elenctic philosophical discussion accomplishes. And it does so, as we have seen, only and entirely by bringing its participants to acknowledge their own non-knowing of 'what virtue is.' Given what Socrates says here, however, it is clear that this "human wisdom," which is the sole aim of Socratic philosophizing, cannot be understood on a merely epistemological register. Rather, the condition of acknowledged non-knowing with respect to virtue *is itself this pain, this distress Socrates calls for*, and this pain is nothing other than suffering the being of virtue *as not known* or *questionworthy*. This is the deeper and all-destabilizing sting of the gadfly (*Ap.* 30e). As strange as it may seem to us, it is in the pain of the elenchus's negative or destructive moment, and nowhere else, that its positive moment resides. That is, as we shall see, it is with this pain that the *epistemological failure* of Socratic elenchus itself constitutes, in a sense, a *pathological success*.

In order to determine precisely how this is so, we must attend to the vocabulary of *meletē* or 'concern' that Socrates employs in further directing his jurors' vengeful pursuits. This peculiar vocabulary deepens and explains the elenctic *pathos* of pain and distress in its truthful positivity. He continues,

> And if they should appear to you to be concerned toward (ἐπιμελεῖσθαι) possessions or anything else more than virtue, and if they believe themselves to be something, being nothing (ἐὰν δοκῶσί τι εἶναι μηδὲν ὄντες), reproach (ὀνειδίζετε) them just as I have you, for their not being concerned toward (ἐπιμελοῦνται) those things that necessitate [concern] (ὧν δεῖ) and for their thinking themselves worthy (ἄξιοι), being worthy of nothing (οὐδενὸς). (*Ap.* 41e–42a)

This passage is surely to be understood in stark contrast with Socrates' earlier mention of Callias's plans for the education of his own two sons (*Ap.* 20a–c). Whereas Callias, as we saw last chapter, wants his sons to acquire the sophistic *technē* of "human and political virtue" (*Ap.* 20b), and with it success, wealth, and power, Socrates hopes that his sons will be pained, specifically such that they will *epimeleisthai* or 'be concerned toward' virtue.[2]

Why should they be pained and concerned most of all toward virtue? The "answer" to this question is communicated here in Socrates' use of an impersonal verbal expression, *dei*. In all of the ways it appears to us (a variety indicated by the related topics that Socrates investigates, e.g., 'what piety, temperance, courage, etc. are,' 'what friendship is,' 'what fineness is,' 'what the good is,' etc.), the being of virtue is simply that toward which 'it is necessary' to be concerned. *Dei* is a form of the verb *dein*, which the Greek lexicon presents as two distinct verbs, *dein* (A) meaning 'to bind, tie, fetter,' and *dein* (B) meaning 'to lack, miss, stand in need of.' The lexicon then traces the impersonal idiom *dei* specifically back to *dein* (A), although the translation offered for it, 'it is needful, one must,' points obviously to *dein* (B) as well.[3] These lexical fine points are in fact all important. For reflected in them is a fundamental ambivalence in the original phenomenon to which the common expression *dei* points, an original phenomenon that precedes this expression's association with divine, moral, social, or natural laws, all of which impose themselves on human beings and compel certain actions or conduct. What we find named by this expression is a condition whereby one experiences oneself as bound or fettered, compelled to comport oneself in a certain manner, but this compulsion is strangely but explicitly *not* generated by the positive application of force. Rather, the compulsion arises from a withdrawal or a non-presence that leaves one needful and concerned toward that which presents itself *as* withdrawn, hidden, distant, and *precisely thereby* compels one. Having been made needful or made to suffer this non-possession, one would most properly live, think, and act in a wondering, questioning, searching mode, attending to this compelling non-presence in so doing. Indeed, Socrates' use of *dei* here clearly brings this original phenomenal context to the fore, insofar as the proper effect of the compulsion or necessitation that he invokes is not this or that specific enforced action, but *epimeleisthai*, or 'being concerned toward' what compels or necessitates, i.e., the being of virtue.

For Socrates, in all aspects of its appearance to us, 'what virtue is' should affect us in this way—it should distress us and necessitate our concerned comportment toward it. Just as we saw with respect to the "great difficulty"

(*Ap.* 19a) of his own defense, Socrates here in his closing request is not and cannot be asking the Athenians to convince his sons by means of positive arguments on behalf of the virtue or excellence of their father's mode of philosophizing, i.e., of leading an examined life. Rather, Socrates asks only that his fellow citizens impose pain on his sons, that pain of being properly concerned toward 'what virtue is,' which is just what he claims to have done throughout his life. For anyone who earnestly suffers it, this would compel or necessitate one, *of its own original power*, to lead a life of Socratic philosophizing.[4] Indeed, *lupē*, *meletē*, and *dei*, or 'pain,' 'concern,' and 'it is needful,' are here all markers for the very same condition, the same *pathos*. It is precisely this *pathos* that Socrates aims to provoke in his philosophizing and that he asks his jurors to provoke in his sons.

Furthermore, should his sons be concerned more toward wealth or honor or anything else, they should 'be reproached, upbraided, disgraced' (*oneidizesthai*).[5] We might note that not being properly concerned toward virtue is equated here with thinking oneself to be something, although one is in fact *mēden*, 'nothing,' and also with thinking oneself *axios* or 'worthy,' although being worthy of *ouden* or 'nothing.' These are rich (and somewhat shockingly nihilistic) indications of the kind of *self-knowledge* entailed by the *pathos* of Socratic philosophizing. For now it should be clear that, if his sons were to think too highly of themselves, they would do so only by failing to suffer the properly painful concern Socrates wants for them.

There is no indication in Socrates' dying wish for his sons that this condition would or should be overcome. Indeed, there is every indication that this properly painful concern, this suffering of one's needfulness and worthlessness, would itself amount to arriving at a certain paradoxical kind of adequacy or worthiness. For Socrates, it seems, just as acknowledged non-knowing is human wisdom, suffering pain and needfulness in some way might be *eudaimonia* or 'true happiness, flourishing' for human beings. Pained in any case, and shamed if they do not suffer this pain—that is what Socrates wants for the ones he loves and all that he wants for them.

MELETĒ IN THE *APOLOGY* AND *APORIA*
THROUGHOUT THE EARLY DIALOGUES

Many other passages in the *Apology* attest as well to the significance and centrality of this notion of painful concern for Socratic philosophizing. Indeed, Socrates declares his aim again and again to be nothing but provoking *meletē* with respect to virtue. And yet, despite the remarkable repetition and emphatic character of such statements, this theme has been largely neglected in the secondary literature, surely because taken for a merely emotional, subjective, or preliminary aspect of the epistemic condition at which Socratic questioning is understood to be primarily directed. Let us consider just a few of these passages.

After the guilty verdict is handed down and he is called to propose a fitting counter-penalty, Socrates retrospectively describes his own philosophical activity in the following way:

> I went to each person doing what I say is the greatest good deed (τὴν μεγίστην εὐεργεσίαν)—going here and there, endeavoring to persuade each of you not first to be concerned toward (ἐπιμελεῖσθαι) any of your things before you are concerned toward yourself (ἑαυτοῦ ἐπιμεληθείη) and how you might be as good and wise as possible. Not for the things of the city, but for the city itself (αὐτῆς τῆς πόλεως), and to be concerned toward (ἐπιμελεῖσθαι) other things in the same manner (κατὰ τὸν αὐτὸν τρόπον). What then do I deserve to suffer for being this sort of person? Something good, men of Athens, if it is necessary to judge in truth according to what is deserved. (*Ap.* 36c–d)

Socrates uses the verb *epimeleisthai* three times in this passage. We will return presently to the etymology of this term, its relation to *meletē*, and the significance of *meletē* as what we are referring to as 'painful concern.' For now, we wish only to note that Socrates states in unmistakable terms, first, that his philosophical activity accomplishes nothing short of "the greatest good deed" for his fellow human beings and, second, that this good deed is nothing other than, or beyond, the provocation of *epimeleisthai*, a condition of 'being concerned toward.'

Earlier on in his speech, the sum total of what Socrates wishes to bring to light in his exemplary elenchus of Meletus is the poverty of the latter's *meletē*.[6] He says at the outset,

> Meletus is guilty of feigning seriousness (σπουδῇ), frivolously dragging people down into a dispute, pretending to take seriously and to trouble himself with (σπουδάζειν καὶ κήδεσθαι) matters that have never concerned (ἐμέλησεν) him. I will try to display (ἐπιδεῖξαι) to you that this is how it is. (*Ap.* 24c)

Clearly, Meletus is one who busies himself with virtue, with piety in particular. His participation in prosecuting Socrates is proof of just this. However, such meddling and precipitous zealotry is precisely not what Socrates is after. Socratic philosophizing contrarily aims at that to which Meletus pretends, but that which he has never actually suffered—being concerned, being profoundly, destabilizingly 'troubled, distressed' (*kēdesthai*) by virtue. That is, one's suffering virtue as a *kēdos*, a 'trouble, anxiety, grief.' To be serious (*spoudaios*) about virtue is to suffer in this way, and this is what Meletus surely has never done, however much he presumes to speak in the name of virtue and piety.

Socrates then engages in a typical elenchus to bring Meletus's blameworthy pretension to light. He asks Meletus whether he considers it of the greatest importance that the young be made as good as possible, to which Meletus responds in the affirmative. Socrates then demands, "Tell these men, who it is that makes them better. For it is clear that you know, or at least it concerns you (δῆλον γὰρ ὅτι οἶσθα, μέλον γέ σοι)" (*Ap*. 24d). Meletus's crowd-pleasing response, "these jurymen here" (*Ap*. 24e), is then revealed as inadequate through a very quick *reductio ad absurdum*—all of the other Athenians improve the youth of Athens, while Socrates alone corrupts them, and this despite the fact that in all other areas of human endeavor, it is only a select few who are thought capable of providing real benefit (*Ap*. 24e–25b). As with every elenchus, the interlocutor proves to hold inconsistent opinions pertinent to virtue and, thereby, not to have mastered virtue in the manner he presumed. Socrates finally remarks,

> You are not to be believed, Meletus, not even (it seems to me) by yourself. For this man seems to me, men of Athens, to be wholly hubristic and unrestrained (ὑβριστὴς καὶ ἀκόλαστος), and he brought this indictment against me artlessly (ἀτεχνῶς), out of some *hubris*, lack of restraint, and youthful rashness (ὕβρει τινὶ καὶ ἀκολασίᾳ καὶ νεότητι). (*Ap*. 26e–27a)

It is not Meletus's inability to answer Socrates' questions that is condemnable, but rather his *hubris*. Recall that, in chapter 3, we found *hubris* to name an overlooking of or a failure to suffer one's fundamental human insufficiency. And just now, we found the painful concern that Socratic elenctic questioning should provoke to be the avoidance of *hubris*, thus understood, and a suffering of one's needfulness, one's non-knowing. Socrates is appropriating here the traditional religious notion of *hubris*, identifying it with the failure to presume a painfully concerned attitude toward the being of virtue. For Socrates, this condition would be simply antithetical to the self-righteousness that Meletus's indictment exhibits.[7] In sum, what shows Meletus's lack of knowledge (his acting *atechnōs* or 'artlessly')[8] with respect to virtue is his refutation in the elenchus, but what shows his shameful failure to be concerned by virtue is his presumptuously self-satisfied, *hubristic* prosecution of Socrates.[9]

Lastly, at the moment in his defense when Socrates proclaims that he will not cease his philosophical activity even upon threat of execution, he promises as long as he lives to go on approaching others and asking:

> Are you not ashamed (αἰσχύνῃ) of being concerned (ἐπιμελούμενος) for as many possessions and as much repute and honor as possible, while you are neither concerned toward (ἐπιμελῇ) nor think about (φροντίζεις) wisdom or truth or how it is best for your soul to be? And if one of you should dispute this and say that he is concerned (ἐπιμελεῖσθαι), I shall not let him go, but shall question him, examine and elenctically test (ἐλέγξω) him, and if he should seem to me not to have achieved virtue, but says that he has, I shall reproach (ὀνειδιῶ) him for treating the things worth much as the least important and the most trivial things as the most. (*Ap.* 29d–30a)

Once again, and multiple times in this passage, Socrates employs terms related to *meletē*, indicating that he aims in his philosophical activity to bring about the condition of painful concern. And once again, what is *aischros* or 'shameful' and what deserves *oneidizein* or 'upbraiding' in Socrates' eyes is the failure to suffer just this pain or the presumption of having a perfectly sufficient and immediate grasp of virtue.[10] In addition to these, there are numerous other passages in the *Apology* that explicitly frame this painful *meletē* or 'concern' as the condition Socratic philosophizing aims to provoke in its participants (*Ap.* 30a–b, 31b, 32d, 40e).

In the other early works of Plato, the terminology of *meletē*, central to the *Apology*, gives way largely to that of *aporia* and forms of its related verb, *aporein*. For *aporia* the lexicon offers 'difficulty, being at a loss, being wanting, embarrassment, perplexity, distress,' a field of meanings that resonates already with the constellation of *meletē*, *lupē*, and *dei*, analyzed previously. Indeed, it is with reference to this term that the early dialogues are categorized generally as *aporetic*. Much more important is the fact that Socrates himself uses this language with remarkable frequency in those passages where he is describing precisely that condition which his philosophizing brings about and centrally aims to bring about (*Chrm.* 167b, 169c–d, *La.* 194b–c, 196b, 200e, 304c, *Ly.* 216c, 223b, *Hp. Ma.* 286c–d, 297d, 298c, *Euthd.* 293b, *Grg.* 462b, *Men.* 80a–d, 84a–c).

Consider the following two remarks. Socrates sums up his philosophical endeavor in the *Protagoras*, saying, "In discussing with you, I want nothing other than to look thoroughly at those things about which I am myself every time in *aporia* (ἃ αὐτὸς ἀπορῶ ἑκάστοτε, ταῦτα διασκέψασθαι)" (*Prt.* 348c). Here Socrates states that the subject matter of his philosophizing is that which provokes *aporia*, perplexity, distress. Were it not for that pesky adverb, *hekastote* or 'each time, every time,' one might wish to maintain (in the face of the preceding evidence) that this passage indicates only an *initial* and *preliminary* condition of *aporia*, which would be properly or at least ideally overcome through positive philosophical argumentation, presumably by arriving at some understanding of what was only provisionally experienced as questionworthy. Instead, Socrates indicates here that this aporetic condition is not overcome even in the long run, but recurs (for him as well) each time and with every elenctic conversation. And this is then only amplified at the end of the *Hippias Major*, where Socrates describes the condition in which he sustains himself through a life of elenctic philosophical investigation in the following way: "I wander around and am in *aporia* always (πλανῶμαι μὲν καὶ ἀπορῶ ἀεί)" (*Hp. Ma.* 304b–c). We might even look to the *Meno*, which is sometimes held up as a dialogue that initiates Plato's move toward a less exclusively elenctic, thus less destructive, philosophical project. There Socrates responds to Meno's comparing him to a stingray or torpedo fish in the following way. He says,

> I am similar to a torpedo fish, however, only if the fish is itself numb and then makes others numb. But if it is not so, then I am not similar. For it is not the case that I myself am well on my way (εὐπορῶν) when I make others suffer *aporia* (ἀπορεῖν). Rather, I am myself most of all in *aporia* (ἀπορῶν) and only thus do I make others suffer *aporia* (ἀπορεῖν). (*Men.* 80c–d)[11]

That is, *aporia* seems to be a condition not merely preliminary to making philosophical progress for Socrates. It is not merely a necessary cleansing that would then be surpassed by epistemological gains. Rather, it is here described as the abiding end-result and, as we have argued with reference to *meletē*, in a sense the aim of the central elenctic activity of Socratic philosophizing.

And we should note here that there is very good reason for the terminology of *meletē* to be central to the *Apology*, while *aporia* becomes predominant in the other dialogues. In his defense, Socrates emphasizes the active response to virtue's becoming distressing and painful, the way of life that maintains a condition of being concerned toward virtue, which Socrates himself has exemplified, to which he calls his interlocutors, and which he is tasked in the *Apology* to defend. In the other early dialogues, as depictions of Socratic conversation *in vivo*, his interlocutors (and he along with them) experience the disruption, the shattering of their previous, confidently held opinions. In describing this experience, it is the pain and distress, rather than the concerned response, that is brought to the fore, and Socrates thus speaks of *aporia*. This change in vocabulary reflecting then merely a change in emphasis, *meletē* and *aporia* should be viewed as two sides of the same coin.

A PHENOMENOLOGICAL CONSIDERATION OF *MELETĒ/APORIA*

> The want of an object, and, still more, the search for an object, imply in a certain sense the knowledge of that object.
> —F. H. Bradley, *Essays on Truth and Reality*

Meletē derives from the verb *melein*, which in the active voice means 'to be an object of care, thought, or anxiety.' In the most basic usage of this verb, the one who cares will be in the dative case, which is usually understood as a dative of reference, but which should be refined to what we might call a *dative of appearance*. Unless one is being intentionally paradoxical or clever, one cannot say that something is a concern to a given individual, if it does not appear to him or her, or if he or she in no way experiences it as such.[12] *Meletē*, thus, names a condition in which something is a concern *with reference to me*, but more precisely in which something *appears or presents itself to me* and *thereby affects me* in a concerning way. Originally, it is only in the passive voice that the concerned individual becomes the grammatical subject of this verb—*melomai* means 'I am concerned' by something and the deponent *epimelōmai* means, strictly speaking, 'I am concerned toward' something and then 'I care for, attend to' something.

From a modern perspective, we might very well tend to understand *meletē* as naming the interior condition of a psychologized subject, i.e., as a caring about something that as such may or may not involve the accurate mental re-presentation of the objectively real and externally present thing about which one presumes to care. Indeed, by this light, its relation to reality affects the status of one's caring *qua* care not in the least. I can care legitimately or successfully about leprechauns although they do not in fact exist, precisely because for us 'caring' denotes only that my internal state exhibits the specific associated characteristics (e.g., linking the intentional object to my own happiness, being willing to make sacrifices for its benefit, etc.). According to its modern conception, caring has not been secured in its relation to, and therefore does not entail a necessary correspondence with, the real character of its object.

By contrast, just as we have found to be the case with *doxa* and with *pathos*, the Greek complex of *meletē* and *melein*-based verbs announces from the outset and entails a *relatedness* to what we would initially think of as an 'exterior,' i.e., to the world or to 'what is.' For, to have *meletē* is understood as *being affected by something*, being touched by or in contact with what provokes concern. In this case, however, the grammar of our English term 'concern' (in contrast to the grammar of other terms such as 'care,' 'love,' or 'desire') retains this essential relatedness, even if it is almost impossible to hear it over the ubiquitous humming of our subject-object bias. We say, 'It concerns me' or 'I am concerned by it,' and only secondarily, 'I concern myself with it.' This latter signification, which the Greek has as well in the middle voice and deponent forms, indicates the act of directing one's concerted attention toward something and it is substantively, not merely morphologically, secondary. That is, *epimeleisthai*, sometimes translated as 'attending to, studying' or 'having charge of, overseeing,' can occur only once one has been concerned by that toward which one then directs attention and effort.[13] To return to the *Apology* for a moment, although it is clear that Socrates encourages a life of this secondary *epimeleisthai* as well, 'attending to or studying' virtue in the sense of questioning it, the fact that the condition provoked by his elenchus is *essentially* painful and distressing indicates that his aim is more fundamentally to bring about the suffering of that primary *pathos*, that *meletē* or 'being concerned by virtue,' within which it would be possible for one to attend to and study just that which one experiences as distressingly unknown or unmastered.

Thus, *meletē* indicates a human condition radically unlike that usually associated with the modern subject and its internal space of representation and decision, the contents of which would then need to be secured in their connection to an externally present objective reality. For one who is related to one's world or to 'what is' by *meletē*, the 'inside' is nothing other than the site for the appearing of and being affected by what is 'outside,' such that any radical severance or gap in the concerned relation is excluded from the outset.[14] The Greek thereby indicates that even prior to any philosophical verification or reflection, the condition of 'being concerned' is itself understood as *always already legitimately and necessarily connected to* that which appears to us in a concerning way, even if this concerned relation is pre-epistemic or not *technē*-like. That is, even if, and perhaps truthfully only when, the appearance through which we are concerned remains questionworthy and, thus, distressing.

Insofar as they constitute a concerted attending to that which first concerns us, any questioning, investigation, defining, or giving of a *logos* or an 'account' would operate within a relation established by *meletē*, by 'being concerned.' In these secondary modes, we would direct ourselves toward a world to which we are always already connected by our concern. This is vital, for we can conclude that 'what *is*,' as that which we would come to know or understand, is definitively *not* conceived here as an objective reality. *Qua* objective, any such reality, as we saw earlier in chapter 1, may or may not be connected to its initial, unsecured appearing to us in our pre-reflective comportment. For the Greeks, rather than an objective reality, what we would aim to know in striving for a *technē* is what we already 'have' in a certain sense, as the intentional object or as that which is given within its already appearing to us, presenting itself, and affecting us in a concerning way. What Socrates seems to uncover is that painful aspect of the being of virtue that his interlocutors might have glimpsed in the initial condition of being concerned.

Finally, the originally passive suffering that is at the very heart of *meletē* would seem to indicate that, no matter how valid or persuasive, no *logos* can ever *generate* the condition of being concerned in its most fundamental sense. Our concerns can be made more poignant or more pressing or less so through discourse or argumentation, and what concerns us might be clarified and refined through investigation or analysis. However, we cannot properly speaking *create* or *compel meletē*, either in ourselves or in others.[15] It is simply not in our power to do so, for *meletē* in its original sense is not the *act* of a subject at all, but, as its grammar insists, an undergoing, a *pathos* triggered through the affective contact with that which places us in a relation of concern.

And *aporia* is just another name for the very same condition. The word *aporia* is an abstract noun constructed from the *alpha privativum* and the noun *poros*. This term, *poros*, first named specifically a 'means of passing a river' or a 'ford,' recalling the experience in earlier times of bodies of water as the menacing and all but impassable limits of one's world. More broadly *poros* comes to name any 'way through or over an impasse' and figuratively then a 'means of achieving, discovering, or providing' something.

In its deepest reserves, this term bears a fundamental relation to *peras*, 'end, limit, boundary.' That is, *poros* has been determined to derive from the related verbs *peirein* or *perē(i)n*, which mean, respectively, 'to pierce, run through' and 'to pass through, over, or across, traverse; transgress.' The links between these verbs and *peras*[16] are manifest in their form, but in their meaning these links are very peculiar indeed. Think of how strange it is that these verbs, *peirein* and *perē(i)n*, share an etymological origin with the verb *perainein*, 'to bring to an end, finish,' and then 'to limit, impose a limit' and, in the passive voice, 'to be limited, finite.' That is, these verbs all bear a clear relation to *peras* insofar as they have something to do with 'end, limit, boundary,' but in manifestly contrasting modes.

On the one hand, with *perainein*, one refers to a *peras* as an impassable obstacle, a confinement, conducting oneself thus within that limitation or imposing it as such on something or someone else. On the other hand, with *peirein* and *perē(i)n*, the etymology of these terms indicates no less an experience of the *peras* or of just such an impassable obstruction, an impossibility of moving beyond, and the compelling confinement of the limit—but one experiences the *peras* here *precisely in pushing through or beyond it*. According to the etymological origin they share with *perainein* then and in a sense simply bizarre for us, the verbs *peirein* and *perē(i)n* would also be heard as something like, 'to limit,' but in the mode of touching and experiencing the limit, playing or being at the limit, precisely in passing through or over it. The Greek reports here that, in a breeching of the limit that lives up to its name, there must also be a *limiting*. All this is hidden away in the recesses of the term *poros*, and we draw it out here only to prepare for the equally strange relation to the limit that is the lack of a *poros*, or what Socrates calls *aporia*.

For *aporia* is *precisely not* the failure to constitute a connection to that which lies beyond the *peras*, beyond the limit. This can be put in very concrete terms. If one were to learn that there is an impassable obstacle along the path from the *agora* in the center of Athens to the port of Piraeus, but one had no idea where or what the Piraeus was and no intention or desire to go there, this situation could not be referred to as *aporia*, even if we might technically be able to identify here some form of 'waylessness.' One experiences *aporia* only if one encounters the obstacle when one is already *toward* the Piraeus, if one is already on the way there and 'knows' it in some qualified sense as his or her desired destination. What is indicated, then, by the phenomenon named by *aporia* is an always prior relatedness and even a *pre-understanding* or *foreknowledge* of that which we experience aporetically. Just as the breeching of the limit that is a *poros* is always also a suffering of that limit as such, the suffering of the limit that is *aporia* is always already, in a certain sense, a breeching thereof.

It should be clear that, as long as we view the *aporia* at which Socrates' philosophical questioning aims along subject-object lines, we will be incapable of understanding it. It will remain a mere epistemological failure, with perhaps an accompanying psychologically or emotionally painful component. But where the modern sees a threatening chasm, a severance between the subject and its object, the ancient Greek fears only *distance*, a painful remove between us and that which appears to us, a withdrawal of 'what is' behind its initial and immediately accessible appearances. Virtue has always already *dokein* or *phainesthai* to us and by means of this movement of 'appearing' it has traversed the distance that both binds us to what appears, to 'what virtue *is*,' and holds us from it. In our everyday mode, it is precisely the distance in this relation that remains hidden; the questionworthiness that results from the concealment of 'what virtue is' behind its appearances is what goes unnoticed or is forgotten. Indeed, the *aporia* that results from Socratic questioning is simply the yawning into view of this distressing distance between us and 'what virtue is,' that distance which the movement of appearing has been covering and covering over.[17]

SERENITY IN THE INTERPRETATIONS OF NEHAMAS, VLASTOS, AND THE STOICS

In insisting on the centrality of pain and distress for Socratic philosophizing, the interpretation being developed in these chapters finds itself in tension with the orthodox view on yet another point. The orthodox view sees Plato's Socrates as serene. We find a very focused articulation of this common attitude in Alexander Nehamas's fine book, *The Art of Living*. Here Nehamas identifies a tension between Plato's Socrates' admitted non-knowing of virtue and the undeniable and consistent performance of virtue in his conduct, on which Plato seems to insist throughout the early dialogues. He writes,

> However we ultimately specify the precise sense of Socrates' disavowals of ethical knowledge or his views regarding the nature of *aretē* and its role in the good life, we will leave the main question I

want to raise unanswered. We may attribute to Socrates fallible beliefs about *aretē*, or the uncertain assurance that consistent dialectic victory affords, or any other cognitive state weaker than knowledge in the strictest sense of the term. We may construe the strict knowledge he desires in any manner we want—as deductive knowledge, as technical or expert knowledge, or even as the knowledge only the gods possess. But the fact remains that in Plato's eyes Socrates, though he lacked that knowledge, always acted in a virtuous manner. No one was ever more consistently virtuous, no one managed to act as well as he did, without exception, over the course of his whole life. Without exception: but also without explanation. For being reliably good is one of the central results of possessing the strict knowledge that Socrates considered necessary for *aretē* and that he was convinced he lacked. That is the real paradox of Socrates.[18]

We have wrestled in previous chapters with a number of articulations of the Socratic paradox, and to these Nehamas adds his own here.[19] He observes that, no matter how we address the central interpretive problem of the early dialogues (i.e., what kind of relation to the being of virtue Socratic philosophizing succeeds in bringing about), the paradox as he presents it here persists. It makes no difference whether one argues, as we have, that Socrates is centrally and significantly non-knowing with respect to virtue, that he has true beliefs but not knowledge, or that he has a certain modest kind of "knowledge," even if not the full-fledged *technē* or *epistēmē* of virtue he so often and so explicitly admits to lacking. Regardless, according to Nehamas, we must acknowledge that Plato presents us with a Socrates who *both* does not possess the knowledge required for unfailingly virtuous conduct *and* nonetheless never fails to conduct himself virtuously.

Indeed, Vlastos had already gestured to this perplexing aspect of Plato's characterization of Socrates. In "Socrates' Disavowal of Knowledge," Vlastos first introduces what is commonly taken for a central Socratic doctrine or tenet—virtue is knowledge and vice is ignorance. Given this, Vlastos then notes the following apparent inconsistency in Plato's portrait of Socrates: "[I]f he has no knowledge, his life is a disaster, he has missed out on virtue and, therewith, happiness. How is it then that he is so *serenely* confident that he has achieved both?"[20] Citing this very passage from Vlastos, Nehamas himself thematizes and endorses the *serenity* attributed here to Plato's Socrates. That is, Nehamas and Vlastos both find it extremely puzzling that Plato presents a character who is adamantly and significantly non-knowing with respect to virtue, but who they take nonetheless for extraordinarily serene, composed, and secure in the righteousness of his own conduct. Nehamas speaks specifically of "Socrates' confidence that he possesses *aretē* and happiness" and ultimately claims that "Socrates' paradox is that he is aware that he lacks what he believes the art of living requires [according to Nehamas, a *technē*-like mastering knowledge of virtue] but is still its best practitioner."[21]

To understand the significance of their position, it will help to note that their emphasis on Socratic *serenity* and *confidence* effectively returns Vlastos and Nehamas to a Stoic interpretation of Socrates. For the Socrates of the Stoics was a sage exemplary for his *tranquilitas* or 'imperturbedness,' and precisely therefore a model of virtue and self-discipline.[22] He was someone who unfailingly imposed *logos* on his soul, bringing himself into harmony with the cosmic *logos* and, thereby, living well and securing for himself *eudaimonia* and *ataraxia*, 'flourishing' and 'freedom from disturbance.' Consider what Cicero sees as Socrates' defining characteristic: "It is a splendid thing to maintain equability (*aequabilitas*) throughout one's life as a whole (*in omni vita*) and to keep always the same mien and the same expression on one's brow (*idem semper vultus eademque frons*); this, we know from history, was the case with Socrates" (*De Off.* 1.26.90).[23]

When Plato puts forward Socrates as exceptionally and unfailingly virtuous (and when Plato's Socrates himself exhibits contentment with the life that he has lived, *Ap.* 37b, *Grg.* 522d, and even see *Phd.* 117b–c), Vlastos, Nehamas, and the Stoics all presume that Socrates' consistently excellent character could only arise from a *technē*-like grasp of 'what virtue *is*' or from the employment of one's *logos* or 'reason' imposed unfailingly upon one's actions. Unlike the Stoics, however, Vlastos and Nehamas attempt to take Socrates' explicitly admitted lack of adequate knowledge of virtue seriously, and are thus perplexed by what they find. Indeed, Nehamas even believes that, until he introduces what are often seen as the psychological and metaphysical innovations of the middle period, Plato himself remains perplexed by his creation, the fictional character of Socrates in the dialogues. Socrates is in Plato's own assessment, "a divine accident, a surd, an inexplicable phenomenon, a lucky stroke who, ironically concealing himself from his interlocutors, remains opaque to his own author as well."[24]

This chapter presents an interpretation that is able to accommodate the elements that Vlastos and Nehamas find so paradoxical in Plato's portrait—Socrates' acknowledged non-knowing of virtue and what is emphatically presented as his consistently exemplary conduct. Although it is necessary to resist their identification of a (suspiciously Stoic) Socratic serenity or self-certainty, as well as their assertion that Socrates leads a life confident and settled in its *possession* of virtue and happiness, it is nonetheless necessary to acknowledge a certain sameness and consistency that Plato seems to emphasize in his portraits of Socrates. Already in the early dialogues Plato's Socrates is being portrayed as "of all those we have known, the best and otherwise the most practically wise and the most just (τῶν τότε ὧν ἐπειράθημεν ἀρίστου καὶ ἄλλως φρονιμωτάτου καὶ δικαιοτάτου)" (*Phd.* 118a). However, as we shall see, the wisdom and virtue that Plato's early Socrates consistently embodies are emphatically human, which is to say coincident with his *aporia*, with its painful concern for and distressing distance from 'what virtue is.' Socrates' truthful and properly human relation to virtue could not be more antithetical to serenity and self-certainty.

To be sure, Socrates could be relatively confident in his avoidance of that "most blameworthy want of knowledge (ἀμαθία ... ἐπονείδιστος), that of thinking one knows things one does not know (οἴεσθαι εἰδέναι ἃ οὐκ οἶδεν)" (*Ap.* 29b, and see also *Alc. I.* 117e–118a). But this would amount to a strange form of serenity indeed and not the one supposedly identified by Vlastos and Nehamas. This Socratic serenity would be purchased only at the expense of constantly questioning one's ever-emerging situation-specific opinions about virtue and thereby maintaining a painful and distressed awareness of one's own not knowing what one needs to know. It is, if anything, something like a *meta-serenity*, which would reside only within and on the basis of constant self-disturbance, self-interrogation, distress, and pain.[25]

Kierkegaard acknowledges something like this meta-serenity when he writes of Socrates' elenctic self-knowledge, "The reason Socrates could be satisfied in this ignorance was that he had no deeper speculative craving. Instead of speculatively setting this negativity to rest, he set it far more to rest in the eternal unrest in which he repeated the same process with each single individual."[26] That is, Socrates is content with what Kierkegaard sees as the purely negative or destructive character in the elenchus, but this is something altogether different from the kind of quietude and self-satisfaction or "rest" that would accompany the positive result of successfully speculative knowledge about objective reality. Rather than such serenity, Kierkegaard suggests that Socrates achieves a certain kind of "rest" only by giving himself over completely to the "eternal unrest" of perpetually repeated elenctic questioning. Along with Kierkegaard (although *sans* the subject-object relation he imposes), we must oppose the serenity that Nehamas and Vlastos find in the early dialogues (and that they find so paradoxical). Instead, we will focus our attention on that troubled comfort of Socrates' relentlessly self-disruptive and *aporetic* relation to 'what virtue is.'

MELETĒ/APORIA AS ITSELF THE *ALĒTHEIA* OF 'WHAT VIRTUE IS'

Let us recall that our challenge from the outset has been to find our way between, or, better, beneath the two poles of interpretation in the orthodox scholarly approaches to the early dialogues. We have sought to avoid conceiving of the elenchus as either on the one hand, purely negative or destructive, a project producing only the skeptical result of self-conscious ignorance, or on the other hand, epistemically positive, a project for arriving at a *technē*-like understanding of virtue or even at some weaker form of understanding that would still have *technē* as its ideal.

We are now in a position to see the pain, concern, needfulness, or *aporia* themselves as constituting the elenchus's positive moment. Of course, we are only able to perceive it as such after having from the start set aside the pervasive scholarly presupposition of a subject-object ordered relation between human experience and its world, a move that has then found compelling support throughout our interpretations of the dialogues as well as in the etymology and grammar of Greek terms such as *doxa, pathos, alētheia, meletē, aporia*, and others. The condition toward which all Socratic questioning in the early dialogues leads is indeed more than merely a defeatist skepticism, but it is also more than a preliminary step on the path toward an epistemologically positive result. Rather, the *meletē* or *aporia* that the elenchus provokes and sustains simply *is* the *deinos* unconcealment of the being of virtue that we found suggested in the *Apology*.[27]

Indeed, this condition should appear to us now in a very precise and point-by-point opposition to the sophistic *technē* model we found Socrates rejecting in chapter 4. Rather than providing *shelter*, Socrates' questioning brings about *exposure to excess*. Not arriving at an explainable and thereby teachable understanding of virtue, Socrates brings about a *pathos* of 'what virtue is,' a suffering of it as questionworthy that can only flare up in the moment of a crisis in which one's own previously confident opinions are disrupted and exposed as inadequate. And not arriving at a directly proximal grasping or epistemic possession of the being of virtue, Socrates instead brings his interlocutors to experience the *distressing distance* thereof.

There are two consequences of this interpretation of Socrates' philosophical project, with respect to two central issues—that of Being and that of the everyday attitude. We must take very seriously what is entailed by the fact that *aporia* has been identified as itself the unconcealment of the being of virtue, in the precise sense of overcoming the concealment of concealment that characterizes the *doxa* of the everyday attitude. If virtue is indeed *truthfully* experienced in the mode of human wisdom and the painful concern it entails, in our exposure to its exceeding our grasp and withholding itself as distant, then 'what virtue is' must be *per se* excessive and distant.

Upon hearing this claim, it might be objected that these are relational or perspectival categories, terms that indicate how an object stands relative to our individual position or perhaps at most relative to the position of human perception and cognition in general. Something can be excessive *with respect to* attempts to contain it, to delimit, grasp, and thereby master it. Something can appear distant or faraway only *from us*, from our present location. To declare the being of virtue distant and excessive *as such* seems like an obvious category mistake.

However, we must remind ourselves that, having in chapter 1 set aside in the presupposition of objective ontology in reading the dialogues, we have come to see Socratic questioning as directed at *phenomenal being*. Socrates seeks 'what virtue is' as nothing other than that which has already presented itself to us by way of the movement of appearing, or via the initial appearances to us that constitute our *doxai*. What Socrates' elenctic interrogation of *doxai* brings to light is that the being of virtue is concealed in its initial appearance. What is concealed in its initial everyday mode is the being of virtue in its concealment, its being questionworthy, or distant and excessive. If *this* concealment is what comes to light in the truthful or unconcealing experience of virtue that the elenchus provides, then the very mode of being of 'what virtue is' must itself be understood as distance and excessiveness. That is, it is not due to personal failing or even due to human finitude that we prove unable to arrive at an adequate definition of virtue and the *technē*-like proximal grasp such a definition would entail. Rather, the failure arises from the being of virtue itself, and the proper, wise, and truthful experience thereof is nothing other than the pain of being concerned for it and the posing and holding open of the question 'What is virtue?' This is the most radical and, for us moderns, the strangest aspect of our interpretation of Socratic philosophizing in these chapters. Implicit in Socrates' philosophical project and the truth at which it arrives is the *ontological excess and distance of virtue*.

Second, this concerned relation to the being of virtue must *already* characterize the everyday attitude itself, even if in a deficient mode. For, as our phenomenological considerations have indicated, the condition of *meletē* or 'being concerned' cannot be *generated* either in oneself or in others by argument or by persuasive discourse. Indeed, Socratic questioning must be conceived as neither engineering nor even as redirecting concern, technically speaking. Even as we acknowledge the hortatory and protreptic aspects of his project, we must see Socrates as encouraging his interlocutors neither to engineer (and so much less so, to *decide* to engineer) a concern for the being of virtue that they previously lacked nor even to shift a pre-existing concern from another object to this one. Rather, the various worries and pursuits, the various decisions and actions of the everyday attitude all indicate for Socrates that the many *have already been concerned by* 'what virtue *is*,' even if they are so in an oblique or untruthful way. Socrates must be seen to bring this concerned condition to light, intensifying it, making it painfully palpable and undeniably distressing.

Indeed, in the last passage we read from the *Apology*, Socrates indicates that the *meletē* he aims to provoke is not at all generated by the *elenchus* but stands rather as its precondition. Recall that Socrates there describes himself as asking others if they are not ashamed of their lack of concern for virtue. He then states clearly: "if one of you should dispute this and say that he is concerned (ἐπιμελεῖσθαι), I shall not let him go, but shall question him, examine and elenctically test (ἐλέγχω) him" (*Ap.* 29e). That is, the concern for the being of virtue *must precede* Socratic questioning and elenchus; Socrates merely aims to change its modality, from concealed to unconcealed as such.

We will see these two fundamental consequences more clearly, and in their necessary interrelation, if we trace this shift in the mode of 'being concerned' for the being of virtue as it unfolds in an exemplary elenctic conversation. That is, if we attend to Socrates' method in a specific dialogue, carefully considering how he undertakes the disruption of his interlocutors' comfortable everyday opinions. This is precisely what we undertake in the next chapter with respect to the *Laches*.

DISTANCE AND EXCESS VERSUS TRANSCENDENCE OR IMMANENCE

> Aber indes ich hinauf in die dämmernde Ferne mich sehne . . .*
> —Friedrich Hölderlin, "An den Äther"

If interpreters discuss to any extent the ontological status of that after which Socrates' 'What is "x"?' question asks, they tend to take their bearings from

---

*But in that I stretch myself out into the fading distance . . .

the "theory of Ideas" in Plato's middle dialogues, as it is traditionally understood, and often from Aristotle's critique thereof. As is well known, Aristotle differentiates Plato from the historical Socrates in part by claiming that the former introduced a *chōrismos* or a 'separation' between Ideas and their material instantiations.[28] He writes of Socrates in the *Metaphysics*,

> He is rightly said to have examined the question "What is 'x'?" . . . But Socrates made neither the things according to the whole nor their definitions separate (τὰ καθόλου οὐ χωριστὰ ἐποίει οὐδὲ τοὺς ὁρισμούς). The others [Plato and the other "friends of the Ideas"], however, separated them, and called beings of this sort 'ideas' (οἱ δ' ἐχώρισαν, καὶ τὰ τοιαῦτα τῶν ὄντων ἰδέας προσηγόρευσαν). (*Met.* 1078b23–32)

"Socratic" is, thus, the interest in 'what is' and in arriving at definitions that are *katholou*, the orthodox rendering of which is 'general, universal.' Properly "Platonic" thinking emerges when these *definienda* are understood as *chōrista*, usually translated as 'separate, existing separately, or abstract,' and perhaps also only once these come to be referred to with the technical terms *idea* and *eidos*. What this separation entails for Aristotle is a matter of some scholarly disagreement,[29] but when the ontology of the early dialogues is taken up at all it is usually framed by this Aristotelian critique.

Some interpreters argue that the Socrates of the early dialogues is a fully "Socratic" and not yet "Platonic" thinker. Although Socrates does speak of *idea* and *eidos* in some of the earlier works, these occurrences can be understood largely according to the general pre-technical usage of the terms. There is, by these readers' estimation, no developed "theory of Ideas" whatsoever, either concerning their ontological status or their methodological role in Socrates' discussions. Other scholars would agree that the early dialogues present a 'Socratic' Socrates, but this second group argues for a different, "Socratic theory of Ideas." Here the *definienda* of Socrates' discussions in the early dialogues are not yet the *chōrista* entities of Plato; they are already Ideas, but understood to be *immanent* in the material particulars that take their form.[30] Still a third group argues that the Socrates of the early dialogues is already a proponent of the fully developed "Platonic" theory of *transcendental* Ideas, understood as separate, changeless, perfect, intelligible paradigms, which are ontologically prior to their instantiations.[31] These interpreters argue not only from the use early on of the terms *idea* and *eidos*, but also from Socrates' occasional mention of terms that will become central in the middle period, such as *ousia* and *paradeigma*, as well as various explanatory phrases used throughout the dialogues to describe 'what "x" is.'[32]

Once having entered into this scholarly dispute, the task of determining the ontological status of *idea* and *eidos* in the early dialogues does indeed present itself. More specifically, however, one feels compelled to ask whether these are *immanent* or *transcendent*, deciding the issue of a Socratic ontology then in one of these two directions. And yet, before posing just this question, it should be noted that the terms *idea* and *eidos* are only used with any emphasis or frequency in the *Euthyphro* and the *Meno*. Thus, the investigation of any such earlier "theory of Ideas" seems from the outset a somewhat questionable undertaking.[33] The simple preponderance of other expressions throughout the early dialogues in itself indicates that *idea* and *eidos* are merely two elements in the broad and varied descriptive vocabulary employed by Plato's Socrates in approaching 'what virtue *is*.' Scholarship has become focused on *idea* and *eidos* here only because these terms have been understood to play a more central role later on in the middle period.[34] The surer path, however, seems the one that approaches from the more general problem of the status of the being of virtue, the central concern of all Socratic discussion. Only after that question has been posed and discussed would we then consider asking what descriptive function the terms *idea* and *eidos* might serve. Thus, let us ask accordingly after the status of that to which these terms, among others, point.[35]

Rather than employing the language of immanence or transcendence, we have argued that the being of virtue at which Socrates always ultimately directs his questioning is *excessive* and *distant*. We came to the specific vocabulary of excess through our discussion of the *deinos* truth to which Socrates commits himself (*Ap.*17b–18a) and the essential description of his "human wisdom" as being *perittoteros* or 'quite in excess of or beyond' what the many do, without presuming to ascend to what is *meizōn* or 'greater' than human, to which the sophistic *technē* of virtue lays claim (*Ap.* 20c–e). The vocabulary of distressing distance we found in a careful consideration of the *aporia* with which every Socratic conversation ends. Once viewed not as a condition of being disconnected or severed from that by which one is concerned, the *meletē* of *aporia* can be seen rather as a pre-understanding of that which does present itself and establish a connection in *doxa*, but which is recognized then as frustratingly inaccessible, withheld, or withdrawn behind its multiple initial appearances.

Does this amount to replacing traditionally accepted and time-worn terms with foreign and vague metaphors? Distance and excess are, indeed, metaphors or images, but that alone is no objection. So ultimately are such terms as 'immanence' and 'transcendence.' With their prefixes *in-* and *trans-*, these terms employ a latent *spatial* imagery to describe the *definiendum* at which Socrates aims. Their metaphorical character, therefore, makes 'distance' and 'excess' no more obscuring than these traditional terms, and their foreignness should in fact be seen as a virtue, for it is as such that these terms become conspicuous and requiring of careful attention. Giving them such attention, we see that the vocabulary of excess and distance, in addition to arising from the Platonic text itself, allows us to describe with precision that to which we relate in *aporia* or in the condition provoked by Socratic questioning, which resists categorization as either transcendent or immanent. Indeed, our terms resonate with what Drew Hyland has referred to as the paradoxical "finite transcendence"[36] of this condition. That is, what exceeds or withholds itself behind its initial and proximal appearances is hereby experienced as such from within the limits of the site of that appearing; we abide within *doxa* while pointing beyond it and to its limits.

The distance here under consideration is specifically a *distressing distance*, a *far-away-ness*. It is a distance that *must* be traversed, which stands between *here*, where we are, and *there*, where the being of virtue is, as that which concerns us and necessitates (*dei*) our nearing it and coming to know it. And the excess to which one is exposed by the elenchus is that which one glimpses only in the crisis, in the disturbing breakdown of one's own presumed grasp, when that which one believed one had constrained, controlled, and possessed slips through one's fingers and escapes. Thus, the spatially metaphorical character of transcendence and immanence is of a significantly different sort than that of distance and excess. Immanence and transcendence are *objectively spatial*. They imply two distinct regions in objective reality, one located above and definitively outside of the other. Unlike the objective spatiality inherent in these metaphors then, distance and excess are intended to characterize the *phenomenal being* of virtue, and thus are understood as *relatively spatial* or, to employ a term coined by Edward S. Casey, *placial*.[37] That is, the space or place that our terminology entails is not conceived as existing independently of one's experience of it, but is instead essentially ordered around us and characterizes the world only in its appearing to us. Indeed, the *placiality* of distance and excess belongs essentially to the site opened up by *meletē*, by our being originally *concerned* by the being of virtue, compelled to be toward it in its withdrawal. In truthfully suffering the distressing distance and excess of 'what virtue *is*,' the site or the place in which we find ourselves is experienced for the first time as sprawling, stretching outward toward a receding horizon.

What we have arrived at, then, is the conclusion that Socrates practices a peculiarly Greek form of *radicalized ontological phenomenology*. Working backward through this tripartite designation, his philosophical project is *phenomenological* in that it engages in the questioning of initial appearances, of which our everyday *doxai* are the articulated report. And this qualifies as an *ontological* phenomenology insofar as what is to be drawn out of those initial appearances is not understood as the essence, idea, or concept of a consciousness, transcendental or otherwise. Rather, what emerges into truth through the questioning of *doxa* with Socrates is 'what virtue *is*' or the being of virtue (i.e., the *phenomenal being* of virtue). Finally, this ontological project should be considered a *radicalized* phenomenology in the precise sense that the study of appearances is pushed to its very limit. Socratic phenomenological thinking does not merely clarify appearances but it undertakes even to let the inapparent or the non-appearing appear *as such*. That is, when the Socratic phenomenological approach to virtue is "successful" it marks the limit of virtue's appearing to us, disturbing our *doxai* and pointing thereby beyond them to what is present in *doxa* only in exceeding it, or to what comes to appear as withholding itself even in its utterly truthful appearance to us.

What remains is to trace precisely this transition as it occurs over the course of an entire Socratic conversation. For this we turn specifically to the *Laches* and we do so for two reasons. First, this dialogue presents a paradigmatic example of Socratic philosophizing, which is to say, a clear and straightforward transformation of the everyday attitude into *aporia*, a movement from *doxa* to the *deinos* unconcealment of virtue's essential concealment. Second, given the interpretation being set forth here, it is fitting that we take up specifically Socrates' examination of *andreia* or 'courage.' This is so, not because this virtue is more important for Socrates than others (such as wisdom, temperance, justice, or piety). Not at all. Rather, we take up Socrates' discussion of courage in the *Laches* now because it is there preliminarily defined as the proper comportment toward *ta deina* or 'excessive and fearful things,' and it is precisely the *deinos* or 'excessive' aspect of Socratic truth that I have been arguing has been overlooked in previous scholarship on the early dialogues.

PART III

SOCRATIC VIRTUE IN THE FACE OF EXCESSIVE TRUTH

6

The Courage of Virtue and the Distant Horizon of the Whole in the *Laches*

> Abtun
> will ich die Wünsche, jeden andern Anschluß,
> mein Herz gewöhnen an sein Fernstes. Besser
> es lebt im Schrecken seiner Sterne, als
> zum Schein beschützt, von einer Näh beschwichtigt.*
> —Rainer Maria Rilke, "Unwissend vor dem Himmel meines Lebens"

"You have seen the man fighting in armor" (*La.* 178a). So begins Plato's *Laches*. We find ourselves in attendance at a demonstration of individual armed combat, precisely that in which most able-bodied citizens of Athens would be expected to engage as hoplites fighting for their city. The man in question, a certain Stesilaus, promises for a fee to teach those put in his charge to fight expertly in this capacity. Two concerned fathers, Lysimachus and Melesias, have asked two accomplished generals, Nicias and Laches, to accompany them to the event, hoping for advice as to whether they should enlist their sons in this training as a part of their education. Someone eventually notices Socrates milling around nearby, presumably having come to take in the spectacle as well.

The dialogue consists of five sections. It begins with a prologue in which the *dramatis personae* are introduced and the differences between their basic dispositions become initially evident (*La.* 178a–184c). Socrates then enters the discussion and sets about bringing his interlocutors to refine the question they themselves have been asking (*La.* 184c–190b). Once the question

---

*I want / to do away with desires, with every other attachment, / to accustom my heart to its ownmost distance. Better / it should live in fear of its stars, than / sheltered by appearance, soothed by nearness.

to be posed has been articulated as 'What *is* courage?' Socrates then undertakes an elenchus with each of the two generals, first Laches (*La.* 190b–104b) and then Nicias (*La.* 194b–199e). The generals and Socrates having together proven unable to arrive at an adequate definition of courage, the dialogue ends with an *aporetic* epilogue or an indication of how they are all to go forward given the condition in which they now find themselves (*La.* 200a–201c).[1]

The dramatic tension that orders the dialogue from the outset is between the *epideixis* or 'demonstration, display' just given by Stesilaus (*La.* 179e, 183b, 183d, 185e, 186a, 186b) and the altogether different kind of *epideixis* given by Socrates in his elenctic conversation with the two generals. This opposition is explicitly resolved in the final moments, when all involved, comparatively evaluating their experiences of these two displays, declare their intention to entrust the education of their sons and themselves to Socrates rather than Stesilaus (*La.* 200c–201c).[2]

An *epideixis*, from the verb *epideiknunai*, is most literally a 'pointing' with one's *daktulos* or 'finger' *epi* or 'toward' something. Precisely thereby, it can be a 'showing forth' of that to which one points and then even a 'proof' of what is shown. In the simple act of pointing, the Greek notices, what is right there before us can come to show itself; it can emerge from its prior hiddenness and be disclosed as it is. Stesilaus wishes in his demonstration to point to himself, such that his perhaps previously unremarked possession of an impressive and teachable skill will come into view, thereby persuading others to learn from him and, more importantly, to pay him for the favor. Socrates wishes to point as well toward that which is always there in our everyday world, that which looms unnoticed before us, but that to which he will have us attend is not at all himself or something in his possession. Indeed, it is the very unpossessability or excess of 'what virtue *is*' that Socrates will *epideiknunai* or 'point out' and allow to show forth and he will do so in the only manner proper to it, i.e., through the elenchus. We might hear then at the close of Socrates' demonstration an altered echo of the opening line of the dialogue: "You have seen the man fighting to strip himself and his companions of their armor altogether, exposing himself and them to what is truly *deinos* or 'terrific'—the being of virtue."

FINITE TRANSCENDENCE AND SOCRATIC "BEING WITH"

Over the past few decades, it has become a much more common practice in scholarship on the dialogues to take into account the dramatic frame in which Plato always situates philosophical thinking.[3] That is, interpreters more and more frequently thematize the fact that Plato decided not to write treatises (as he could well have done), a textual form that at least tends toward impersonal, ahistorical, and non-context-specific truth claims. Plato decided rather, along with some of his contemporaries, to write dialogues.[4]

To respect this fact interpretively entails recognizing that, as Hyland puts it, "the single most distinguishing feature of the Platonic dialogue compared to other formats of philosophic writing is that the dialogue always begins in a specific place, a specific situation, within which the limitations as well as the possibilities of each dialogue arise."[5] In *Finitude and Transcendence in the Platonic Dialogues*, Hyland argues that his employment of the dialogue form tells us something profound about Plato's view of philosophizing itself. Namely, dialogues *qua* dialogues do not only point the reader to the content of what is discussed in them and provide arguments and justifications for various positions, they also manifest for the reader the simple fact that philosophical thinking always occurs within a specific situation, undertaken by a specific person in response to specific conditions. Thus, "the situation itself within which the dialogue occurs—the place, the occasion, the temporal exigency—all have the effect of presenting the interlocutor with an initial limitation, an occasion of finitude, that he or she must confront."[6] According to Hyland, the dialogue form should itself bring to the fore an always initial confrontation with finitude or limitation, i.e., with the specific set of conditions and factors that both delimit philosophical thinking and provide the conditions for the appearances with which it inevitably begins. Philosophical thought always begins as *situated*, as specifically contextually delimited.

Hyland then sets out the three basic responses to this situatedness. These are "domination, submission, or an acknowledgment of the finitude that transforms it into possibility."[7] One might strive to overcome the limitation of one's initial perspective and ascend to a non-contextual or absolute vantage point. Contrarily, one might accept the biases of one's pre-reflective position and resign oneself to the merely relative value of all human judgments. Or finally, one might find one's way between these two paths, directing oneself toward a world that is accessible by way of its initial context-specific appearances, even while recognizing that these never allow for a completed or definitive grasp of that world. It is this third, more complex and more tenuous mode that Plato's dialogues present and advocate via the ideal of Socrates, according to Hyland.

To be sure, the early Plato consistently presents the first two modes, domination and submission, as unsatisfactory. The unending project of Socratic philosophizing calls into question the sufficiency of our pre-reflective everyday opinions (non-submission) even as it indicates the impossibility of our ever extricating ourselves completely from the ways in which things initially appear by gaining a perfect, authoritative, or *technē*-like grasp of 'what virtue is' (non-domination). Following along with Plato's Socrates, one comes to recognize that although the initial appearances of virtue are not 'what virtue *is,*' this remains irremediably in excess even of the critical or enlightened perspective one has gained. Hyland employs a deliberately paradoxical formulation to capture this condition provoked by Socratic questioning: *finite transcendence*. Rendered in our terms, Socratic philosophizing begins by inhabiting the site of one's everyday attitude and marks the excess or distance of 'what virtue is' without presuming to secure a *technē*-like mastery thereof.

We might here at the outset simply note that Socrates' own descriptions of his philosophizing tend to emphasize quite clearly, repeatedly, and dramatically his manner of immersing himself in the situation of everyday life alongside his interlocutors. Surely, as we have seen, he insists that he himself shares in his interlocutors' *aporia* at the discussion's end (*Chrm.* 175e–176a, *La.* 200e, *Ly.* 223a, *Hp. Ma.* 304c, *Prt.* 361a–b, *Men.* 80c). But he also often emphasizes in conversation that he is "with you (μετὰ σοῦ)" (e.g., *Chrm.* 165b–c, *Hp. Ma.* 372a–e, 376 b–c, *Prt.* 361d, *R.* I.337e, and *Men.* 80d). In the *Critias*, he declares, "I myself, Crito, am eager to examine together with you (ἐπισκέψασθαι . . . κοινῇ μετὰ σοῦ) whether this appears to me otherwise in my present circumstance, or whether it remains the same, whether we should abandon [the former argument] or be persuaded by it" (*Cri.* 46d). And in the *Gorgias*, Socrates deepens this a bit, describing his mode of being with his interlocutors in the following terms: "I myself do not say the things I say with knowledge (εἰδὼς), but rather I search together with you (ζητῶ κοινῇ μεθ' ὑμῶν), with the result that if a disputant appears to me to be saying something, I will be the first to go along with him (ἐγὼ πρῶτος συγχωρήσομαι)" (*Grg.* 506a, see also *Men.* 86c).

Socrates' mode of philosophizing requires that he inhabit his interlocutors' everyday situation with them, *koinē(i)* or 'in common,' and that he *sunchōrein* or 'go along with' them in that attitude, seeing the world from that point of view. Indeed, this is throughout the dialogues referred to as *sunousia* by Socrates, literally a 'being together,' but often translated as 'intercourse' or 'congress' in the hopes of catching the Greek term's sometimes sexual connotation (esp. *Thg.* 129e–130e, where Socrates sums up his philosophical activity, referring to it multiple times as *sunousia*, but also *Thg.* 122c, *Prt.* 335c, *La.* 201c).[8] However, even in being with his interlocutors in this intensified fashion, in having immersed himself there with them, Socrates sets about transforming the very site they inhabit together. Or better, he does not transform it, properly speaking, but brings to light an aspect of that everyday site that, though always already there, remains unnoticed as it is.

SOPHISTICATION AND THE EVERYDAY ATTITUDE IN THE INTRODUCTION OF THE TWO GENERALS

In the first section of the dialogue, before Socrates begins his elenctic questioning, we become acquainted with the two generals, Laches and Nicias. They are presented initially in their contrasting assessments of the value of receiving training in what is referred to variously as Stesilaus's *mathēma* or 'that which is learned' (*La.* 182c, 182e, 184b), his *epistēmē* (*La.* 182c, 184c), or his *technē* (*La.* 186c, also 185a). Nicias initially sees learning the *technē* of fighting in armor as bringing with it bodily fitness, advantage in combat, a desire for further study, and most importantly greater confidence in battle (*La.* 182c). He thus recommends the boys' undertake this study. Contrarily, Laches advises against buying what Stesilaus is selling. Surely all learning is good in some insignificant sense, but time and energy being finite, one must choose among many possible courses of instruction. If Stesilaus is successful in teaching anything at all, of which Laches is very skeptical, whatever he teaches is not courage, but something of no importance (*La.* 184b). The deeper contrast between the generals' basic attitudes, which becomes evident over the course of the dialogue, is already implied in their opening estimations of Stesilaus.

Laches is a man of action. For him, both the world and we ourselves are revealed truly in *prattein*, in 'doing, acting,' not in *logoi* or 'speeches, discussions, arguments.' When Laches declares that he has seen the man Stesilaus in actual combat performing quite ridiculously, he claims to have seen him "in truth, truly demonstrating against his will (ἐν τῇ ἀληθείᾳ ὡς ἀληθῶς ἐπιδεικνύμενον οὐχ ἑκόντα)" (*La.* 183d).[9] Notice the emphatic repetition of *alētheia* and *alēthōs* here, whereby Plato makes unmistakable Laches' absolute faith in what presents itself in action, and so in ordinary pre-reflective experience. Later, Laches admits that he might well seem to some a *misologos*, a 'hater of discourse,' for he judges a human being's words wholly and completely with reference to his or her *erga* or 'deeds' (*La.* 188c–189a). *Logos* for him is at best secondary, an epiphenomenon, which should take its measure from whatever appears to be true in pre-reflective experience. With respect to any operation by which *logos* might presume to clarify, call into question, or correct this always initial mode of relating to the world—operations such as analysis, definition, explanation, argumentation, or even elenctic questioning—Laches is extremely suspicious. And wholly anathema from his perspective is the possibility that the *logos* might even be required to arrive at a truth not available in the ordinary unquestioned first appearances of things.

By contrast, Nicias is presented as a lover of *logoi*, in the specific sense of sophistic speeches and arguments, learned distinctions and formulations. Indeed, later on he will state straightforwardly that he believes that any expert's knowing (*eidenai*) amounts to nothing other than the ability to say (*eipein*) of his subject what sort of thing it is (*hoion*) (*La.* 195c); one's skill comes to light principally in *logos*, not *praxis*. His responses to Socrates' questioning will prove to be definitions and differentiations he has merely received from others, manifestly not insights gained from his own experience. In the elenchus to come, Nicias first regurgitates what he believes to be a Socratic doctrine (that courage is simply a kind of wisdom), a supposition which Socrates significantly and without hesitation leads into difficulties. Nicias responds then by adding to it a fine verbal distinction that, as Socrates recognizes immediately, he has received from the sophist Prodicus by way of a certain Damon (*La.* 197c–d). Laches' polar opposite, Nicias thinks in a way that remains utterly abstracted from his pre-reflective experience of the world, trafficking instead in empty verbal or conceptual formulas.

According to the types we identified in chapter 4, Laches is an unsophisticated interlocutor, content with the apparent self-evidence of what presents itself in everyday experience, and Nicias is a sophisticated interlocutor, believing in the truth and power of the teachable and exchangeable refinements thereof. The condition at which Socrates' elenchus aims and even arrives is presented here in the *Laches* as, in a certain sense, between these two and, in another sense, in radical opposition to both. That is, just as we found in the *Apology* in chapter 3, the human wisdom that is accomplished in the moment of *aporia* is *perittoteros* or 'quite excessive or beyond' with respect to the everyday attitude, while it simultaneously declines the transcendence of and abstraction from this attitude to what is presumed to be *meizōn* or 'greater,' a *hubris* he diagnoses in the sophists' presumptive possession of a *technē*-like grasp of virtue (*Ap.* 20c–21a). However, Socrates' position is no mere compromise between those of Laches and Nicias, for he aims to provoke an exposure to what exceeds and subtends both the everyday attitude and the presumed sophistic *technē* of virtue, the withdrawn ground that appears in the *doxai* of both, but is remarked by neither.

In fact, it would be accurate to say that the basic attitudes of Laches and Nicias are strictly speaking not distinguished from one another at the most fundamental level, since the latter is in Socrates' eyes utterly parasitic on the former. That is, given that Nicias's faith in technical abstractions is explicitly sophistic, it should be understood as merely mirroring in more articulate and refined forms one or more of the familiar opinions of precisely that everyday attitude in which Laches remains immersed. Plato's Socrates consistently paints sophistry as beholden to the everyday attitude insofar as its wares, its techniques and its verbal formulas, are for sale and must therefore operate according to the many's vague but already established notions and reflect their values. In the *Gorgias*, Socrates disparages the core of sophistic *paideia*, rhetoric, as a mere *empeiria* or a 'knack based on experience' for flattering or gratifying the many (*Grg.* 462a–465e). The sophistic rhetorician must tell people, in clever and polished ways, some aspect of what they want to hear and already presume to know.

If we look beyond the early dialogues, Plato's Socrates in the *Republic* has not altered his assessment in the least. Rejecting the widespread tendency to lay the corruption of the youth at the feet of a small group of paid educators, Socrates argues instead that it is the many who are centrally responsible for their city's decay. They are themselves already, as he says, the "greatest sophists of all" (*R.* VI.492a). He then goes on to explain the relation between these two groups, declaring that

> Each of those paid private teachers, whom the people call sophists and consider to be their rivals in *technē* (ἀντιτέχνους), teaches nothing other than the convictions of the many (τὰ τῶν πολλῶν δόγματα), those things they express (δοξάζουσιν) when they gather together. Indeed, this is what the sophists call 'wisdom.' (*R.* VI.493a)

Socrates sees sophistry as presuming to transcend the everyday attitude, but as never even being concerned by what exceeds that attitude's *doxai* and therefore remaining inextricably bound to and wholly immersed within it.

Socrates' project is therefore to be understood as a 'demonstration' of that which exceeds the everyday attitude, and sophistry as well, by association. Again, what is vital to understanding Socrates' elenchus as a form of *epideixis* is the fact that this excess must always already be there in the world of the everyday attitude, as already appearing to that attitude in a certain way, concerning it even and constituting thereby its character. Indeed, the being of virtue is that which is already calling forth the actions and decisions of the many, already giving form to their opinions and tenuous notions. And Socrates' method of 'pointing out' this excess is simply the posing of the question, 'What *is* virtue?' combined then with the elenchus as the holding open of that question. Indeed, in a sense, the Socratic elenchus accomplishes nothing other than making more emphatic that which presents itself faintly in the opening question his interlocutors are always so confident they can answer. With this, Socrates accomplishes his demonstration of virtue *as questionworthy*, which is to say, as painfully concerning and distressingly distant.

THE UNITY OF THE QUESTION 'WHAT *IS* VIRTUE?'

When Socrates is present, any question can be the pebble that breaks the surface of the pond, shock waves reverberating outward in ever more encompassing questions. These latter questions are always already there as the context of the initial question, and the broadest in scope and most important of these is always, for Socrates, 'What is virtue?' For this question asks simply how to live well and therefore extends its reach to the entire world in which human life and *praxis* take place.

The *Laches* begins with the very concrete and practical question of whether Lysimachus and Melesias should have their sons train with Stesilaus. After the two generals give conflicting counsel, Socrates enters the discussion, declining an offer simply to cast the deciding vote in the matter. He indicates that what is to be decided here presents itself in such a way that "it necessitates (δεῖ)" making a choice "by knowledge (ἐπιστήμη)," rather than merely "by majority (πλήθει)" (*La.* 184e). Contrary to much scholarly opinion, this statement and others like it are not indications of Plato's moral intellectualism, i.e., of his Socrates' *own* conviction that being virtuous requires some kind of knowledge of 'what virtue is' (often brought as evidence are *Euthphr.* 4d–5d, *Hp. Ma.* 304d–e, *Ion* 531a–532c, *Men.* 71a–b).[10] Rather, Plato presents Socrates only as *asking* his interlocutors whether there are not some instances where they would find themselves persuaded less by the majority and more by someone of proven expertise. Melesias agrees that there are, and all others present are complicit in his agreement. Socrates is thus bringing his interlocutors to the realization that the issue with which they are faced presents itself *to them*, here and now, as requiring knowledge in order to make trustworthy judgments (whether that of the sophists to whom Nicias turns or of the men of action in whom Laches places his trust).

With this, the initial question opens up into another question. Socrates asks, in presuming to give knowledgeable counsel as to whether the young men should be enrolled in this form of study, would one not also presume to be "expert in caring for the soul (τεχνικὸς περὶ ψυχῆς θεραπείαν)" (*La.* 185e), which is to say, expert in how a human being will be made better with respect to his or her soul? All agree. Socrates suggests, therefore, that they first undertake a discussion of whether any of them are in fact such experts in this particular *technē*. He asks then, should this not be decided in the same way that one would evaluate any claim to possess a *technē*? Would one not ask if the claimant had studied with someone of recognized expertise in the area? As one must expect him to do, given his skepticism about sophistic instruction, Laches objects at this point, saying, "But what's this Socrates? Have you not noticed that some come to be more expert (τεχνικωτέρους) without teachers than with them?" (*La.* 185e). Socrates takes his point, and asks if nevertheless one would only trust these autodidacts if they had "some well-executed product of their *technē* to demonstrate (ἐπιδεῖξαι) to you, and not just one but many" (*La.* 185e–186a), to which Laches assents. They set out then once again, asking whether any of them can prove their possession of this *technē* by pointing either to the acknowledged expert from whom he learned it or to the pupils whom he has improved by way of it (*La.* 186b–d).

Socrates declares that he himself can claim no such *technē*, having neither discovered it for himself nor learned it from anyone (*La.* 186e). Let us attend carefully to Socrates' language in what follows. He observes that, in contrast to him,

> [Nicias and Laches] appear indeed to me (δοκοῦσι δή μοι) to be able to educate a human being. For, they would never have shone forth (ἀπεφαίνοντο) so fearlessly (ἀδεῶς) concerning what pursuits are beneficial or harmful for the young, without knowing sufficiently what there is to know (ἐπίστευον ἱκανῶς εἰδέναι) as regards these things. (*La.* 186c–d)

That is, in answering the first question, they have both, by their own measure, presumed a *technē*- or *epistēmē*-like grasp of what here presents itself as 'to be known.' In so doing, they appear or shine forth, they *dokein* or *apophainesthai*, as 'without anxiety or fear (*adeēs*).' This is the first time Socrates introduces the theme of courage here, and it is important to note both that courage explicitly presents itself via the movement of appearing and that it seems initially associated with the sheltered confidence provided by the presumption of a *technē*. One wonders, first, what the relation is between this initial appearance and the being of courage that appears through it and, second, what kind of alternative form of courage might be characterized by the human wisdom to which Socrates has just confessed.

Socrates suggests that the two generals submit to interrogation with respect to the *technē*-like grasp they both must, as has become clear, presume to possess (*La.* 186e). Substantiating the results of our earlier discussion, Socrates neither introduces nor endorses the *technē*-model of virtue—indeed the dialogue as a whole seems structured to undermine confidence in precisely this model. The *technē*-model of virtue is presumed by both Socrates' sophisticated and unsophisticated interlocutors here, a presumption he merely brings them to articulate very distinctly *as such*, i.e., as a *technē*. At this point, both agree to submit to questioning. Nicias gives a jolly endorsement of Socratic elenctic discussion, describing it as a pleasant and quite familiar activity for him (which should make us highly suspicious of the degree to which Nicias has really experienced the truthful pain and distress of Socratic *aporia*).[11] Laches agrees as well to submit to Socratic questioning, but only because he holds Socrates to be a man who knows whereof he speaks, for he has seen Socrates comport himself admirably in action at Delium (*La.* 181a–b).

The second question unfolds at this point into a third. Socrates says that we could proceed as planned, asking what teachers the generals have had or what individuals they have made better, but he has another suggestion: "There is an inquiry (σκέψις) like this one, which will carry [us] into the same [place] (εἰς ταὐτὸν φέρει), but an inquiry which I dare say is more from the *archē* (μᾶλλον ἐξ ἀρχῆς)" (*La.* 189e).

What is crucial here is that the third question and its investigation promises to bring us *eis to auton* or literally 'into the same' as the second, which itself was shown to contain the first. This indicates that the first two questions were already asking after and leading us into an experience of what is encountered as questionworthy in the third. The privilege of the third question is explicitly *not* that it asks after a different object, something more vital or relevant. Rather, leading us "into the same," the third question's privilege lies in its doing so more directly from the *archē* or from the 'beginning, origin, source.' We might ask, the origin of what? The beginning or source of what? The context provides only one answer—the third question proceeds more directly from the origin *of the questioning or inquiry itself*, more directly from that which in its presentation to us affects us and draws us into questioning.

Socrates then sets out upon this other more direct inquiring path. "Aren't these two now (νῦν) asking us for advice on how virtue might be added to the souls of their sons, making them better?" Laches agrees and Socrates goes on, "Then is this necessitated of us in order to begin (ἡμῖν τοῦτο γ' ὑπάρχειν δεῖ), to know whatever virtue is (τὸ εἰδέναι ὅτι ποτ' ἔστιν ἀρετή)?" (*La.* 190b). This is the more direct path from and into the powerfully necessitating *archē* of the original practical question facing us *nun* or 'now.' We feel compelled to ask simply, "What is virtue?" Already in the fathers' desiring or striving toward their sons' proper education, already in their being concerned by what is at stake in their practical decision, that on which the third question focuses directly was acting as the *archē*, the beginning and the source. Through their initial conversation, this *archē* has now come more clearly into view as that which necessitates our knowing it, indeed as what affects us by compelling us to have precisely that directly proximal, *technē*–like grasp of 'what it is,' that which Nicias and Laches *appeared* to have in giving their initial counsel.

We should see here a substantiation of precisely what we found to be required in our phenomenological consideration of *meletē* and *aporia*. That is, the condition of being concerned toward the being of virtue is already present in the everyday attitude, even in its sated and contented presumption of direct proximity and mastery. For Socrates, in every single moment, in every single *nun* or 'now' of everyday life, where decisions must be made, we are already suffering that condition of being concerned, that momentary terror of the undecidable, that *aporia* that his questioning aims to intensify. Even here we are exposed to and concerned by that very same distressingly distant being of virtue that is the ultimate *archē* of Socratic questioning, an *archē* that originates it, governs it, and necessitates it, but precisely in its withdrawal, its concealment.

Socrates then restates the question, with an addition. He asks, "For if we do not somehow know virtue by the whole, whatever it happens to be (εἰ γάρ που μηδ' ἀρετὴν εἰδεῖμεν τὸ παράπαν ὅτι ποτε τυγχάνει ὄν), in what way can we become advisors as to how it might best be acquired?" (*La.* 190b–c). Notice Socrates' not insignificant employment of the particle *pou* or 'somehow,' which at least opens the possibility that the kind of "knowing" that would be proper to "whatever virtue happens to be" might not be the presumed proximal and comfortable *technē*-like grasp that we might initially believe is necessitated of us.

Furthermore, already here Socrates is indicating how he will bring this initial appearance of 'what virtue is' into its proper self-presentation as it is, into its truth. He does so with the simple adverbial accusative *to parapan*, which is the phrase *para pan* or most literally 'to the side of the all or whole' or 'by the all or whole,' now become a single term and made substantive with the definite article. This phrase is usually translated as 'altogether' or 'absolutely.' Consider Rosamond Kent Sprague's representative translation of Socrates' question: "If we are not absolutely certain of what it is, how are we going to advise anyone?" However, such a translation perpetrates an egregious anachronism. The force of *pan* having been eliminated, what we hear in this translation is a Socrates invoking 'absolute certainty,' that paradigm of truth proper to the modern or Cartesian subject who presumes to enjoy indubitable because immediate contact with his or her own internal contents and then seeks to secure an equally indubitable access to external objective reality. Socrates is not, however, speaking of certainty at all, but loudly of relating to the being of virtue in some sense 'by or toward the all, the whole.' The significance of this will become clearer when we observe precisely what Socrates accomplishes with his elenchus, specifically with respect to the horizon within which virtue is appearing to his interlocutors.

Socrates then suggests that they focus their discussion on an "easier" target, replacing the third with a fourth and final question. He says,

> Let us investigate not concerning the whole of virtue directly (περὶ ὅλης εὐθέως)—perhaps a greater task (πλέον)—but first let us see concerning some part thereof (μέρους τινὸς πέρι) whether we are sufficiently disposed with respect to knowing (ἱκανῶς ἔχομεν πρὸς τὸ εἰδέναι). For us, it is likely (τὸ εἰκός), the inquiry will be easier (ῥᾴων). (*La.* 190c–d)

Having placed his interlocutors before the question, 'What is virtue?' Socrates suggests that they not investigate this "perhaps greater question" *eutheōs* or 'straightforwardly, directly,' but that they instead focus on a *meros* or a 'part, portion' of this whole, an investigation that is "likely" easier. We should notice that this does not rule out the possibility that what follows will itself be a non-straightforward or indirect consideration of the being of virtue.

In the secondary literature on the early dialogues, Socrates is often presented as holding a conviction opposed to the one he states here. That is, many scholars argue that the 'unity of virtue' is a Socratic principle, doctrine, or belief. With this it is intended that for Socrates all of the various virtues, such as courage, piety, temperance, and justice, refer to the same condition of the soul (and also that he believes this condition to be, in a fundamental sense, a form of wisdom or knowledge).[12] As we have observed, what characterizes the figure of Socrates in Plato's early dialogues most emphatically and consistently is his "human wisdom (ἀνθρωπίνη σοφία)" (*Ap.* 20d), or that he acknowledges his own non-knowing of virtue. Indeed, it is not his knowledge or his correct convictions, but his non-knowing of virtue that seems to account for, however paradoxically, the superior and even heroic status of this man as presented in Plato's works, which in sum constitute the greatest tribute ever paid by a student to his or her teacher. Given this, we would do well to try to explain Socrates' relation to this unity of virtue not as Socrates' presuming to know something, but in terms that are consistent with his going about "*always* in *aporia*" (*Hp. Ma.* 304b–c).

In order to do so we need only attend to the fact that what we find here, and in every such case where a Socratic "doctrine" might be suspected, is not Socrates stating his own opinion, belief, or understanding, but *inhabiting the site of appearing with his interlocutors*. This is the vital function of what has been referred to as the Socratic "say what you believe" requirement (*Cri.* 49c–d, *R.* I.346a, *Prt.* 331c, *Grg.* 500b),[13] as well as of his constant requests for consent from his interlocutors. That is, Socrates requires his interlocutors to state earnestly the way the subject matter of the questioning appears to them and he will brook no hypothetical answers to his questions. Furthermore, along the way Socrates secures the interlocutors' agreement that the subject matter appears each time to require the next step in the argument. In addition to ensuring that the interlocutor himself will be refuted rather than an abstract definition, and consequently that the interlocutor will most likely suffer some actual distress and pain at the refutation, these tactics also effectively situate Socrates and maintain him *at the site of the interlocutors' everyday attitude*, such that the elenchus has only *their opinions* or the way the issue appears *to them* with which to work. It then develops and articulates those initial appearances, pointing to unnoticed consequences or aspects, but it *never presumes to transcend them*. In the passage just cited, Socrates is saying there are *merē* or 'parts, portions' of the whole of virtue, and the task of coming to know the whole is 'greater,' while coming to know the part is 'easier' . . . does it not *seem* or *appear* to be so here and now *to you*, my partner in this investigation? Laches agrees that it does seem so to him. As we shall see, it is precisely this relation between 'what virtue is' and its 'parts'—meaning *both* the particular virtues *and* the particular virtuous individuals and actions that present themselves as virtuous in various ways—that will become problematic in the elenctic discussion that follows, thereby provoking *aporia*.

Having situated the purportedly easier within the purportedly harder question, Socrates thereby allows the being of virtue to loom menacingly in the background throughout the ensuing conversation. The form in which virtue appears first in the present context of evaluating the merits of hoplite training is courage, and Socrates therefore suggests they ask after "what courage is (τί ἐστιν ἀνδρεία)" (*La.* 190e). In the elenctic refutation of Laches, the being of courage will be shown to withdraw behind the various particular occurrences or appearances of courage. But courage itself will then in discussion with Nicias be shown to be an occurrence or an appearance of 'what virtue is,' which then itself withdraws even further into the distance behind the individual virtues. The interlocutors will thus come to realize that this "greater" and "less easy" question, which they set aside at the outset, necessitates a proper answer and makes them needful even in their relation to its "parts," to courage and to various particular virtuous or courageous individuals and actions.

BEING MANY EVERYDAY

In the working open of the question that organizes the second section of the *Laches*, we have seen Socrates placing his interlocutors first before the great and difficult question, 'What *is* virtue?' and then before the "easier" question, "What is courage?" And we have traced the manner in which Socrates has unfolded these questions out of his interlocutors' original practical question. We might say that Socrates uncovers not so much what claims or positions are entailed by their beliefs, but what questions are entailed by their questions, or what questions precede and provide the context within which they face practical decisions.

Indeed, these may be questions the interlocutors have struggled with or they may be questions that have barely or never arisen as such in the decisions the interlocutors have made. Euthyphro stands before the practical question of whether to prosecute his father for murder (*Euthphr.* 3e–5a), while Meno explicitly wonders whether virtue is teachable (*Men.* 70a). Perhaps less distinctly, but no less significantly in Socrates' eyes, Hippias stood before a question in deciding that a given discourse is fine or beautiful (*Hp. Ma.* 286a–e), Charmides in deciding how to respond to the praise he routinely receives (*Chrm.* 158c–d), Lysis and Menexenus in deciding to consider themselves friends (*Ly.* 211d–212a), and Crito in deciding for and planning the escape of Socrates (*Cri.* 44b–46a). Protagoras faces a particularly fraught question in deciding to pursue the life of a sophistic educator (*Prt.* 316c–317c), as does the young Hippocrates when he decides to enlist as the former's student (*Prt.* 310b–311a). And in devoting themselves to the "arts" of the rhapsode and rhetorician respectively, so did Ion (*Ion* 530b–c) and then Gorgias, Polus, and Callicles (*Grg.* 447b–d) all face some virtue-related decisions. In all of these cases, when in discussion with them, Socrates sees himself as articulating the all-encompassing question that his interlocutors themselves already face, although they do so in the deficient mode of presuming to possess a perfectly satisfactory answer. That is, he sees the everyday attitude (and its sophistic reflection), even in its most pedestrian considerations and decisions, as already *concerned by the being of virtue itself,* but in the mode of presuming to enjoy a sheltering *technē*-like proximity to and grasp thereof.

Once we have properly focused our attention on the relations between these questions, we can then understand Socrates in his elenchus not as introducing a *new* question, nor as engineering a *new* concern among his interlocutors. This rids us of the scholarly problem of whether Socrates identifies a quasi-metaphysical object over above or at least as analytically distinct from the particular material things with which the everyday attitude busies itself. Socrates understands himself to be introducing nothing new, but merely bringing to light the being of virtue that is always already concerning or presenting itself as questionworthy in the usually fleeting moments of pause and unremarked spaces of openness that occur in practical decision-making.[14] Even in his struggles to identify and distinguish 'what virtue is' from particular virtuous things, Socrates proceeds by asking for assent at every step and therefore relies upon his interlocutors' already existing, even if vague and inarticulate, concern for the *being* of virtue. Socrates' elenchus brings his interlocutors to see that they are already concerned by the being of virtue in their most ordinary pursuits *and* that in the everyday attitude that characterizes these pursuits the being of virtue is not appearing to them 'as it is.' That is, the *technē*-like, proximal grasp they presume to enjoy in the everyday attitude in fact conceals the being of virtue. We might ask at this point, if the being of virtue is itself always already concerning us and appearing to us in the everyday attitude, why does it do so here 'as it is not'?

Aristotle on Socrates and Definition *Katholou*

There is a clue in one of the essential Aristotelian assessments of Socratic philosophizing cited in chapter 1. We found there Aristotle summing up Socrates' contribution to *sophia* and *protē philosophia* in the following way: "Socrates made his central occupation (πραγματομένου) the ethical virtues (τὰς ἠθικὰς ἀρετὰς) and first sought to define (ὁρίζεσθαι) these according to the whole (καθόλου). . . . It is well-spoken to say that he sought the 'what it is' (ἐζήτει τὸ τί ἐστιν)" (*Met.* XIII.1078b17–23).

Socratic discussion is characterized here by its interest in human virtue, rather than for the natural or cosmological phenomena that drew the attention of his predecessors. Nevertheless, Aristotle highlights that Socrates demands from his interlocutors a *horismos*, one of Aristotle's common terms for 'definition' (e.g., *APo* 91a1, *Top.* 139a26, *Met.* 1031a1), which would account for virtue *katholou*, an adverbial phrase often translated in such a context as 'generally, universally.'

As we have seen, the explicit demand for a definition of virtue that Aristotle rightly observes need not lead us to presume Socrates' own endorsement of the propriety of securing the *technē*-like grasp this would entail. Rather, it should be seen as a response to the being of virtue's appearing to us in everyday contexts as necessitating or requiring our knowing relation to it. Socrates operates within his interlocutor's presumption to have already met that requirement or having already satisfied that concern. Aristotle's description here is instructive, nonetheless, insofar as he rightly identifies the central mode of Socratic elenchus, i.e., Socrates places his interlocutors and himself before the question 'What is virtue?' by asking for a *horismos katholou* or what is usually understood as a 'universal definition.'

Horizein is a verb most often translated as 'to define' and it occurs in this sense in the early dialogues (e.g., *La.* 194c, *Euthphr.* 9c–d, *Chrm.* 163d, 171a, 173a, *Grg.* 453a, 475a, 491c, 513d). However, we should keep in mind that the verb derives from the noun *horos*, which is originally a 'boundary' or 'border' (e.g., *Grg.* 470b), but also the 'marker,' 'landmark,' or 'boundary stone' that indicates the perimeter of something or identifies it (e.g., *Hp. Ma.* 283b2, *Ly.* 209c), and then figuratively a 'definition' (e.g., *Grg.* 488d). Thus, *horizein* is first and foremost 'to draw a perceptible boundary around something,' tracing its extent and distinguishing it from its surroundings, marking it out. In so doing, one allows the thing in question to emerge from these surroundings as distinct and thereby present itself, e.g., as a unified plot of land, a single piece of property. Our English 'horizon' stems from this term as well, as the ultimate limit of the visual field, within which specific visible things take their place and present themselves in their relations with one another.

What we wish to note here is the original sense of distinguishing, marking out, specifically in allowing something to present itself. The term thus points back to what, according to the lexicon, is a more original power of *legein* as 'gathering together' and 'laying out' and it points thereby beyond the technical sense of definition as a determining of genus and differentia or as a listing of the necessary and sufficient properties of the object defined.[15] In requiring of his interlocutors a *horismos*, Socrates is most fundamentally asking them to gather together the *definiendum* by 'horizoning' it or by drawing a differentiating boundary around it, thereby bringing it to light. If we hear only our settled and later sense of 'definition' here, we lose the original phenomenon that *horizein* names, the sense of bringing together by marking out and distinguishing, which is fundamentally a bringing something to light or an allowing something to appear more clearly.

What Aristotle describes with great precision, then, is Socrates' elenctic task as we have understood it, i.e., as beginning with his interlocutors' *doxai* and striving to allow what already appears there to present itself 'as it is.' Aristotle emphasizes in this that, for Socrates, the horizon that is required in order to bring the being of virtue to light truthfully is *to holon* or 'the whole,' the entire world in which human *praxis* is taking place and already finds itself, rather than some partial or limited context within that whole. Not accepting the way virtue appears in this or that specific situation as his interlocutors do, Socrates leads them to cast their gaze out toward that horizon which encompasses these various situations and thereby to view virtue for the first time *kata holou* or most literally 'according to the whole.' However, as we have already seen in our consideration of the truth of Socratic *aporia*, within the horizon of this whole that Socrates requires us to consider, the being of virtue appears as in excess of its context-specific appearances. The whole is invoked without the comprehension or circumspection thereof, by way of which 'what virtue is' would be successfully defined and grasped. This releasing of the interlocutor's gaze from its confinement in this or that context of everyday life is precisely what we find in the *Laches*, but also in every instance of the elenchus throughout the early dialogues. Socrates again and again labors to draw his interlocutors out of the confines in which virtue is now appearing to them, an appearing they articulate in the *doxai* that provide the starting point for the elenchus.

To Socrates' question, 'what *is* courage,' Laches answers, exhibiting the untroubled and precipitous confidence of the everyday attitude, "It is not, by god, difficult to say (οὐ χαλεπὸν εἰπεῖν). For if someone is willing to remain at his post to fight the enemy and not flee, it can be well said that he is courageous" (*La.* 190e). Socrates' response is instructive. He says that Laches has not answered *his* question, which concerned the being of courage, but a different question (*La.* 190e), namely, how does courage appear in his particular present context. With his mention of two different questions here, the one Laches has answered and the one that was posed, Socrates references the way in which practical questions are embraced by *his* question. Then Socrates lists a number of other individuals in whom courage also undeniably presents itself, but in quite different ways within different horizons of appearance: soldiers who fight while retreating, sailors who risk the dangers of sea travel, those who stand the trials of sickness and poverty, and even those who bravely hold up under the pressures of desire or pleasure. Laches agrees that all of these individuals appear courageous. Thus, Socrates asks, "try then to say first what courage is, being the same in all of these (ἀνδρείαν πρῶτον τί ὂν ἐν πᾶσι τούτοις ταὐτόν ἐστιν)" (*La.* 191e).

Here we should not understand Socrates to be putting forth an essential property of his own implicit conception of Being; i.e., the being of courage is that which is the same in *all* courageously appearing individuals. Rather, he is simply capitalizing on Laches' own inarticulate sense that, insofar as we can and do name what appears in all of these contexts with the same name, 'courage,' what appears here and is named as such is the same in each case. Socrates asks Laches to no longer view courage within the single context in which he first articulated his definition, but to gather these and view them within the whole in which they must exist together, and then state how virtue *now* appears. This is less a move from the particular to the universal than it is a shift in the context in which courage appears, from a limited horizon to the horizon of the whole.

And it is precisely this that Socrates' questioning accomplishes in all of his elenctic discussions. We might consider just a couple of examples in order to understand more clearly the quintessentially Socratic broadening of horizons.[16]

Meno 71D–73D

In the *Meno*, Plato puts in the mouth of the eponymous character an extremely illuminating, if uncritical, remark about the everyday attitude's confinement in multiple restricted horizons. When Socrates poses his characteristic question with regard to virtue itself, "What would you yourself say virtue is?" (*Men.* 71d), Meno responds that for a man it is efficacy in public and private matters, for a woman it is managing the home and submitting to her husband, for a child it is something else, and something else again for the elderly and for the enslaved. Meno sums up, "And there are very many other virtues (ἄλλαι πάμπολλαι ἀρεταί), with the result that there is no *aporia* involved in speaking of virtue concerning 'what it is' (ὥστε οὐκ ἀπορία εἰπεῖν ἀρετῆς πέρι ὅτι ἐστίν)" (*Men.* 72a). Occurring within a Socratic conversation that will itself lead to *aporia*, Meno's observation is particularly striking. For he emphasizes that it is explicitly *thanks to* its confinement in multiple discrete horizons of appearance that the everyday attitude is never at a loss to say 'what virtue *is*.' It appears in one context as efficacy, in another as managerial competence, in yet another as obedience. In the specific circumstances in which we find ourselves, some course of action usually appears as clearly choiceworthy or good. That is to say, as virtuous or excellent, as what is to be done.

Meno also indicates that, as confined within each one of these contexts, one equates 'what virtue *is*' with its appearance. This is crucial. For it is explicitly not by being *unconcerned* or *untouched* by the being of virtue that the everyday attitude avoids the *aporia* Socratic elenchus provokes. It is rather, precisely as Meno states, by failing to distinguish the being of virtue from its multiple site-specific appearances that the everyday attitude is able to avoid the distress and pain that belong to *aporia*. These appearances are so suffocatingly close and compelling, so mesmerizingly familiar and immediately identifiable as choiceworthy, that one can merely rush about in the pursuit of one proximal apparent virtue after the next. It is in this way, in its complete immersion in specific contexts of appearance, that the everyday attitude remains untroubled by the distance and excess of the being of virtue. Until, that is, Socrates intervenes and disrupts this immersion, bringing his interlocutors to see their lives not only as taking place within these various discrete and cloistered horizons, but also always within that exceeding whole, that distant horizon which encompasses all the others but refuses us a comprehending overview.

Socrates' response is ironic. He says that Meno's answer amounts to "some great good-fortune (πολλῇ τινι εὐτυχίᾳ)," for in seeking *one* virtue Socrates finds himself provided with "a whole swarm (σμῆνος) of them" (*Men.* 71a). This term, *smēnos*, is particularly apt here, for it offers an evocative image of the everyday attitude that Socrates associates with contentedly accepting a multiplicity of context-specific appearances of virtue. On the one hand, the term names a 'swarm' of bees, or what presents itself as a furious throng, buzzing about *en masse* in frenetic activity. On the other hand, it names their compartmentalized dwelling place, their 'hive.'

Socrates then endeavors to drag Meno from the current context in which virtue is appearing to him. He tells Meno to "stop making many out of one (παῦσαι πολλὰ ποιῶν ἐξ τοῦ ἑνός)" (*Men.* 77a), and tries to focus Meno's inquiry on what he has described as "the same virtue of all [human beings] (ἡ αὐτὴ ἀρετὴ πάντων)" (*Men.* 73c). Thus, he asks Meno to answer, "according to the whole, saying of virtue 'what it is' (κατὰ ὅλου εἰπὼν ἀρετῆς πέρι ὅτι ἐστίν)" (*Men.* 77a). Socrates' language of *pan* and *to holon* here indicates precisely what we found emphasized in Aristotle's assessment. Socrates' questioning seeks to release Meno from his bondage before the multiple and initially satisfying context-specific appearances of virtue. When Meno then finally attempts to look beyond these specific contexts and take them all together, when he makes an explicit effort, admittedly feeble, to say how virtue appears in the horizon of this whole, he states the virtue is "to rule over people" (*Men.* 73c). Socrates responds, acknowledging Meno's shift in perspective, "that is indeed what I am seeking" (*Men.* 73d), although he goes on to dispense with it *in the very next sentence*, reminding Meno of a counterexample he himself had introduced, namely, that the virtue of a slave or a child obviously cannot reside in ruling over people.

EUTHYPHRO 5C–7A

Another illuminating passage is found in the *Euthyphro*, where Socrates is depicted in conversation with a self-proclaimed religious expert. Socrates asks,

> Now (νῦν) tell me then, by Zeus, what just now in fact (νυνδὴ) you were maintaining you know so clearly, what sort of thing you would say the godly is, and what the ungodly is, both concerning murder and concerning other things (περὶ τῶν ἄλλων). Or is this, the pious, not the same as itself (αὐτὸ αὑτῷ) in every *praxis* (ἐν πάσῃ πράξει)? And is the impious not on the one hand the opposite of the pious in all cases (παντὸς) and, on the other hand, like to itself and having some one *idea* (μίαν τινὰ ἰδέαν)? (*Euthphr.* 5c–d)

From Euthyphro's prior practical decision to prosecute his father Socrates draws him to pose the question before which he already stands, the question of 'what piety *is*,' for which Euthyphro believes himself to have an adequate answer.

Socrates goes on to demand of Euthyphro that he release his view from any particular context of appearance and take in the whole of human *praxis*, stating then what is the same or like to itself in "all" of the various pious-appearing actions. That is, as Socrates here explains, that same *idea* or that 'look' that all individuals present insofar as they appear to us as pious. We will discuss next section the varied vocabulary Socrates employs to articulate the distinction between being and appearance. For now, we are concerned only with the shift in horizons Socrates is attempting to bring about through his questioning.

Euthyphro's first response fails miserably in its attempt to let virtue appear *katholou*, remaining instead clearly confined to the very specific context in which he now finds himself. He says, "well, I say that the pious is what I am doing now (νῦν), to prosecute the wrongdoers in cases of murder or of temple robbery, or those who fail to do the right thing in other cases of this sort" (*Euthphr.* 5d–e). As Socrates points out (*Euthphr.* 6d), Euthyphro's account of 'what *is* pious' fails because there are many cases where the look of piety presents itself, but which quite obviously fail to be encompassed by his definition. Euthyphro, catching on, revises his answer admirably, declaring "what is dear to the gods is pious, what is not dear to them is impious" (*Euthphr.* 6e–7a). Socrates' response is significant. He says, "Wholly beautiful (παγκάλως) and just as I was asking you to answer, thus have you now (νῦν) answered. Whether also truly (ἀληθῶς), that I do not yet know, but clearly you will teach me that the things you say are true (ἀληθῆ)" (*Euthphr.* 7a). It must be noted that Socrates makes a distinction here between the inadequate answer Euthyphro first gave and this revised answer. The distinction has nothing to do with the second answer's being true, for that has yet to be tested and, indeed, the answer will prove insufficient under scrutiny. And Socrates must be at the very least suspicious of the inadequacy of Euthyphro's response even at the start of the discussion, given the quickness with which he leads Euthyphro into difficulties (*Euthphr.* 7a–8a). Nonetheless, this answer pleases Socrates. It is at least the right *way* of responding; it is responding finally to Socrates' question, not some other question.[17]

Socrates praises Euthyphro's answer simply because the latter has attempted to state what piety is, not in any specific context, or in response to any specific situation. Not only in the case of a son prosecuting his father, but also for the seer, the priest, the one who wishes to make an offering at the temple, etc. This is the move that Socrates praises, for Euthyphro himself has agreed that 'what piety *is*' cannot simply be the context-specific appearance in this or that situation. It is not one way in one context, but another way in another. Whatever truly *is* pious, courageous, or virtuous for a human being, must be one and the same throughout all these specific contexts in human life.

What is of great significance in these passages from the *Meno* and *Euthyphro* is that Socrates can praise even the *attempt* to answer with a view to the whole of all human contexts. He does so, not because the truth of 'what virtue *is*' has been arrived at (*Euthphr.* 7a), nor because he hopes that this will provide a component of or a step toward the ultimate definition of virtue. Rather, he does so because in giving such an answer, his interlocutor has expanded his horizon from any specific context of human life to include that which exceeds it, the enveloping horizon opened by the question, 'What *is* "x"?'

SOCRATES' INTERLOCUTORS AND THE CONFUSION OF APPEARANCE AND BEING

Although scholarship is divided as to the nature and significance of the interlocutors' initial misunderstanding in such passages, John Burnet offers a clear statement of the most basic and most common interpretation thereof. He writes, "In several of Plato's dialogues Socrates is made to criticize the confusion of the universal . . . with some particular of which it is predicated."[18] That is, Socrates' characteristic question, 'What is "x"?' is supposed to be ambiguous in Greek. His interlocutors take him to be asking them to point to one or more x's, particular things that possess the quality or property, 'x-ness.' But Socrates intends to be asking for a definition of the property 'x' itself.[19] In this scenario, Socrates and Plato are to be credited with recognizing this ambiguity and for making a definition of the latter central to both the philosophical and practical understanding of virtue.

Nehamas has argued forcefully against this common view.[20] He is skeptical, in effect, of attributing such obtuseness to Socrates' interlocutors with regard to the use of universals or abstract properties. In his article on the topic, Nehamas interprets the relevant passages, arguing that, although it has seemed so to many interpreters, Socrates' interlocutors are not in fact pointing to a particular thing in their responses to the 'What is "x"?' question. Rather, according to Nehamas, they give general explanations of virtue that are simply not general enough, universals that are not universal enough.[21]

After laying out his textual grounds for questioning the common interpretation, Nehamas points out that the traditional view seems to entail a situation that is somewhat difficult to accept as the condition of Socrates' interlocutors. That is, they seem in these passages to "find nothing problematic in the idea that there is an entity, the *F* or *F*-ness, that the predicate *F* names," which Socrates lays out at the start of the discussion and which they so often affirm without hesitation. However, they simultaneously "always take the question 'What is the *F*, or *F*-ness?' to be concerned only with *F* particulars."[22] Can it be that, for example, Euthyphro affirms that 'the pious' is that which is the same and alike in every such action and that this is the *idea* or 'look' that all pious things present (*Euthphr.* 5c–d), and then three lines later says, "This particular act, my prosecution of my father, is a sufficient answer to your question about the referent of 'the pious'"? If this were the general situation among the contemporaries of Socrates, we would also have to assume that "Socrates, faced with an antecedently understood use of adjectives as general terms and with a domain of particular objects to account for that use, insisted that such terms also have a different, referential use and introduced a new domain of objects in order to account for it."[23] As Nehamas indicates, this sounds implausible and it is simply not in accord with what we find in the dialogues. Socrates does not seem to be generating *ex nihilo* a different use for the term 'virtuous,' which would thereby be seen as referring not to virtuous things, but to some heretofore unknown entity at least analytically distinct from these.

As an alternative, Nehamas suggests that the Greek copula at work in Socrates' 'What *is* "x"?' question might not function as it does in English, i.e., "to indicate that the individual named by the subject-term is a member of the class of those possessing the attribute expressed by the predicate-term."[24] Rather than indicating membership in a class of objects possessing some property, the Greek copula, Nehamas surmises, may have been understood as "To be *a* is to be *F*."[25] In normal Greek, to say that 'A beautiful maiden is wondrous' might have been understood as equivalent to saying '*To be* a beautiful maiden is *to be* wondrous.' In this scenario, Socrates is not introducing a *new* referential use of the adjective. He is not suggesting that 'beautiful' refers not only in general to all the particular things in the class, but also and perhaps more properly to some other thing, the entity 'the Beautiful,' not identical to these, with which nobody seems familiar because Socrates is introducing it for the first time. Rather, Socrates can be understood as simply "showing his contemporaries that given this naming use of predicate-terms, to which they all agree, neither Charmides, nor his beauty, nor being a beautiful youth, nor even physical beauty in general, can be beautiful; that is, what it is to be beautiful."[26]

As far as I understand it, I am in agreement with Nehamas's alternative interpretation of the confusion of Socrates' interlocutors and of the function of the Greek copula. His interpretation rejects that, in the passages in question, there is a confusion regarding the relations of universals, or class names, and the particular members of these classes. Instead, returning now to our terminology (which follows the dialogues' own emphasis on phenomenality, but which Nehamas himself would likely find suspect), this interpretation finds a confusion between 'what "x" is' and its appearances. Socrates' interlocutors identify the various immediate 'x' appearances in limited contexts with 'what "x" *is*.' In order to show them that this identification is false, Socrates relies on their own already implicit preconception of *what it means to be something*. Or even more precisely, he relies on their own implicit distinction between 'what is' and 'what appears to be,' which is already in play in any everyday disagreement concerning the truth of any given issue.[27] Socrates neither replaces nor alters their understanding of this distinction, but rather, by securing their affirmation, holds the interlocutors to their own inarticulate notion of Being and then brings the being of virtue to light as troublingly in excess of and withdrawing behind its initial appearances.

Surely even in the most ordinary situations, when conflicting opinions arise we find ourselves distinguishing between appearances and 'what *is*.' The paradigmatic situation in which this would come to light for the Greeks is the assembly, where the many gather together to discuss the affairs of the city. They accept the counsel given by some, while they reject that of others. Some activities they praise, others they blame, remaining always at the level of the everyday attitude (see *R.* VI.492b–493e). When we decide these disputes not by the threat or use of force, but by means of discourse and argument, this necessarily occurs with reference to the truth. That is, in such disagreements, each party claims that his or her opinion is the truth of the matter or 'the way things *are*,' while the other party's opinion is merely the way the matter appears to him or her. Here, we operate according to a nebulous preconception of appearance and Being, the former as *to the other* and the latter as what we grasp in *our own* assessment.

Indeed, in a certain sense, as G. C. Field observes in *The Philosophy of Plato*, the question of 'What is?' already haunts the everyday, pre-philosophical world.

> [It] is not, as some modern writers have seemed to suggest, a question invented by philosophers for their own amusement. On the contrary, it arises inevitably as soon as we begin to reflect on our most ordinary thought and experience. All our thinking and investigation from the first is an attempt to find out what is real or what is really the case, as opposed to what only appears to be. This

distinction between reality and appearance is, therefore, assumed in our ordinary experience from its earliest stages. . . .[28]

Philosophical thinking simply radicalizes this already troubling question, problematizes this already operative distinction between Being and appearance. Indeed, Socratic thinking is a philosophical approach to ethics, rather than a dogmatic or practical approach, only insofar as it reflects upon the everyday attitude's existing preconceptions of Being and appearance and employs these in the framing of its question, 'What *is* virtue?' Socrates does not produce a theoretical statement on the meaning of Being, but he does make explicit some always prior notion thereof in directing his interlocutors' in their responses to the ethical question that concerns them.

The most compelling evidence for this reading is that Socrates never has to *argue for* the various aspects of 'what "x" is' that he introduces. When he articulates these and then imposes them as requirements for defining the being of 'x,' the interlocutors always affirm them immediately (or as soon as they understand them) as what must be proper to 'what "x" is' insofar as it *is*. They then attempt to answer accordingly. After this, of course, it is by just these agreed upon criteria that their own *doxai* will prove inadequate. The adequate *logos* or *horismos* of 'what "x" *is*' for Socrates would gather together and distinguish, allowing to come to light, what presents itself in *all* things that we call 'x' (*Euthphr.* 5c–d, *La.* 191c–e, *Hp. Ma.* 288c–289d, 300a–b) and in *only* these things (*Chrm.* 160b–d, 161b, *La.* 198a–199e, *Prt.* 328b–333b, *Men.* 74a). It will identify that same one *dunamis* or 'power' (*La.* 192b–c) or *phusis* or 'nature' (*Grg.* 465a) by which they all *are* x or the *idea/eidos* or 'look' that they have by which they all *present* themselves as x and can be recognized as such (*Euthphr.* 5d, *Men.*72c). When Socrates asks his 'What *is* "x"?' question, he is able to direct his interlocutors toward such an aim (even if having usually to clarify that aim), without anyone ever rejecting the assumption that to define 'what x *is*' would be to define just this.

Socrates is not introducing a new use of adjectives and new objects to which this usage refers. Rather, he is drawing out the implicit consequences of an already present pre-understanding of Being, of 'what "x" *is*.' This is not to say that all of Socrates' interlocutors would have or even could have articulated these aspects of their pre-understanding. Certainly not. We need only recognize that what Socrates offers to aid his interlocutors in answering his 'What is "x"?' question are not innovations, but rather elucidations of already present unreflective presuppositions about what it means to *be* something.

It seems then that, to a certain extent following Nehamas, what has been seen as a "confusion of particulars and universals" is better explained with reference to the relation of being and appearance, and to the everyday attitude's entrapment by the latter as already discussed. That is, in his discussions with them, Socrates' interlocutors show that they have been unable to suffer the questionworthy status of 'what virtue is,' unable to acknowledge the distance that stretches between the immediate appearances of virtue in the various contexts in which one always initially finds oneself and this. They have been able to avoid the questionworthy being of virtue by remaining entrenched within these limited contexts and by accepting the immediate appearances of virtue there as 'what virtue is.' They have not asked about what gathers together all the various appearances of virtue in all the various contexts of human life and what makes them all virtuous insofar as they are such. In his refutation of their appearance-based opinions, Socrates utilizes their own implicit pre-understanding of what it means to be something in order to bring his interlocutors to see the ontological inadequacy of the various appearances of virtue they have accepted as truth.

APORIA AND THE TRUTH OF APPEARANCES

Über dem Nirgendssein spannt sich das Überall!*
—Rainer Maria Rilke, "Taube, die draußen blieb"

Returning now to the final two sections of the *Laches*, we find Socrates beginning again by offering an example of the kind of definition he is looking for. As is always the case in such moments, that which Socrates is able to define unproblematically (and that over against which he and his interlocutors need suffer no *aporia*) is of minimal significance for human life, whereas the term Socrates then asks his interlocutor to define in like fashion inevitably belongs to "the most important things" (*Ap.* 22d), which is to say, those things central to our human pursuit of virtue, excellence, or living well. Socrates selects for himself *tachos* or 'swiftness, speed.' Although it appears differently in running, playing the lyre, speaking, learning, and the like, nonetheless if one were asked to shift one's perspective to include all of these cases together and define it, one would not hesitate to say it was the "power of accomplishing much in little time" (*La.* 192b).

---

*Over 'being-nowhere,' the 'everywhere' stretches itself!

Catching on and thinking back to Socrates' varied list of courageously appearing individuals, Laches declares, "It appears now then to me (Δοκεῖ τοίνυν μοι) to be some endurance of the soul, if indeed it is necessary to speak about all these concerning courage by nature (εἰ τό γε διὰ πάντων [περὶ ἀνδρείας] πεφυκὸς δεῖ εἰπεῖν)" (*La.* 192b–c). We see here that Plato has Laches speaking of how courage is *nun* or 'now' *dokein* or 'appearing' to him, i.e., after at least trying to cast his view beyond the specific individual horizons of the everyday attitude toward the horizon of the whole. He still questions whether it is necessitated (*dei*) of them to do so, however. Socrates answers emphatically, "But it is indeed necessary (ἀλλὰ μὴν δεῖ), if we wish to answer the question posed to us" (*La.* 192b). That is, given our pre-understanding of what it means to be, the question, 'what *is* courage' demands of us that we not tolerate the atomized multiplicity of the everyday attitude, where each of the various and conflicting appearances is taken in its specific context *to be* courage. By the minimal requirements of our own vague notion of Being, whatever *is* courageous cannot be both one thing and its opposite, e.g., standing ground and retreating. Therefore, in coming to confront the question 'What *is* courage?' that had already been encompassing our initial practical question, we find ourselves directed toward what *necessitates* our defining it *katholou* or 'according to the whole,' in order to determine what is the same, rather than different, in the various appearances of courage.

We should note the language Socrates uses in describing the position from which he responds to Laches' definition and from which he launches his elenchus thereof. He says, "Now then, this is what appears to me at least—it is not so that all endurance, I think, appears to you as courage (τοῦτο τοίνυν ἔμοιγε· οὔτι πᾶσά γε, ὡς ἐγῷμαι, καρτερία ἀνδρεία σοι φαίνεται)" (*La.* 192c). Socrates indicates here a division in the 'self' he sees as the recipient of the appearances of virtue. Immediately after Laches says *dokei toinun moi* or 'it appears now then to me' that courage is endurance of the soul, Socrates can say that (still *toinun* or 'now then' and thus sharing this 'now' with Laches) he suspects that this is not simply the case. Notice that Socrates does not say that Laches is failing to consider certain examples, nor that Laches is incognizant of the logical consequences of his claim. He says, rather, that, having cast their eyes out toward the encompassing horizon of the whole, something *is now appearing* to Laches, although the latter has not been able to articulate it in his definition. As the *aporia* toward which Socrates' elenchus is headed will show, what is already appearing even to Laches is the *excess and distance* of 'what courage is,' and ultimately even 'what virtue is.' Indeed, this is always already appearing to him, affecting him and concerning him, even in his everyday attitude, but it is hidden or concealed *as it is* through his identification of immediate appearance with Being. Through elenctic questioning, Laches comes to stand before this already-at-work complex appearing and the indication thereof is that 'what courage is' becomes inescapably painful, distressing.

The *aporia* hidden in Laches' experience comes quickly to light under scrutiny (*La.* 192c–194b). Laches has said that courage is the soul's endurance under pressing or threatening circumstances. However, courage is, simply *per definitionem*, virtuous or excellent and, therefore, again *per definitionem*, a fine thing. But some forms of endurance are not at all fine, for foolish endurance would seem to be disgraceful while wise endurance would seem praiseworthy. Agreeing to this, Laches refines his definition of courage to 'wise endurance of the soul.' However, when we attentively compare how wise or knowing endurance appears to us with how an endurance that lacks this reassuring or sheltering wisdom appears to us, the latter shines forth as the more courageous of these two comportments. Indeed, Socrates asks us to imagine a businessman going forward risking capital in an investment, a doctor persisting in the imposition of an unpleasant remedy on a patient, and a soldier holding out in battle. To the extent that these individuals appear to do this out of perfectly confident calculations or to the extent that they *know* what the outcome will be and are thus secured against the unforeseen eventualities of *tuchē*, they do not appear courageous to us. When individuals stand before *ta deina* or 'fearful things,' we seem to identify courage less in those individuals who proceed "with *technē*" (*La.* 193c), and more in those who proceed without it. Indeed, sheltered by their *technē*, the individuals who wisely endure seem not to stand exposed to *ta deina* at all. According to Laches' earlier admissions, courage is appearing to him in contradictory ways as both wise and foolish endurance.

After the elenchus, Laches confesses to *aganaktein*, 'feeling a violent irritation or being vexed, grieved' (*La.* 194a–b). Socrates thus suggests that they bring Nicias into the discussion, given what Socrates emphatically refers to as their shared *aporia*. Indeed, he uses terms related to *aporia* three times in a little over four lines to describe the condition at which they have together arrived by way of his philosophical activity (*La.* 194c).

Laches, of the two generals with whom Socrates speaks equally here, is the one after whom the dialogue is named and seemingly the one who succeeds in suffering *aporia*. By contrast, although the elenctic refutation of Nicias is no more or less logically conclusive, it seems to leave him somehow unconcerned. He begins with what he believes to be a Socratic precept: For human beings to be good is simply to be wise and to be bad is simply to be ignorant, from which he suggests that anyone who is courageous, insofar as this is a way of being good, must also be wise (*La.* 194b–c). Specifically, this wisdom would be the *epistēmē* "of fearful and daring things (τῶν δεινῶν καὶ θαρραλέων)" (*La.* 194e–195a). Nicias presents this as a resolution to the previous discussion, somehow remaining oblivious to the fact that his claim is (at least *prima facie*) contradicted by the phenomenological evidence just presented by Socrates and Laches. Namely, those who proceed by a technically calculating wisdom or sheltering knowledge appear not even to stand before *ta deina* at all and seem less courageous than those who proceed without this.

After a short fractious exchange between the two generals, Socrates again begins to direct the questioning. Nicias claims that courage is a knowledge of what is to be feared and what is not, but this surely disallows any brute beast from being courageous, despite the fact that certain beasts are widely considered to be so. Following Prodicus and his practice of making fine semantic distinctions, Nicias wishes to distinguish *andreia* or 'courage' from *aphobia* or 'rashness, fearlessness,' the former being reserved for human beings and even only for those few who comport themselves with *sophia* or *epistēmē* with respect to what is *deinos*. Socrates next takes a moment to remind Nicias of their earlier agreement that courage seemed to them to be "a part of virtue (μέρος ἀρετῆς)" and that "there being other parts, these altogether were called virtue (ὄντων ἄλλων μερῶν, ἃ σύμπαντα ἀρετὴ κέκληται)" (*La.* 197e–198a).

Nicias having once again affirmed this notion of virtue as a clear aggregate of parts, Socrates proceeds by having him agree that things to be feared are future evils and things to be hoped for are future goods. However, any *technē* or *epistēmē* knows what it knows, its proper subject matter, regardless of its temporal placement—in knowing 'what health is,' a doctor's knowledge must claim to range equally over past, present, or future instances of health. But then the same must be true of courage, entailing that in knowing the fearful and the hopeful, its proper object of knowledge must be the good and bad as such, with the result that all good and bad would fall under its authoritative judgment. If this is the case, however, courage thus defined cannot be considered a mere part of virtue, but must rather be the whole of it. For anyone who knows the good and the bad would seem to be not only courageous, but also temperate, just, and pious. Thus, Nicias and Socrates come into difficulty, insofar as what appears to them as one part of virtue also appears to them as "virtue altogether (σύμπασα ἀρετή)" (*La.* 199e). The being of virtue, therefore, placed somewhat ominously in the background at the outset of the conversation in order to investigate courage, surges forth at the end as an open and troubling question.

In the elenchus of Laches, 'what courage is' withdrew behind its conflicting initial appearances in *doxa*. And in the elenchus of Nicias, 'what virtue is' withdrew behind the *merē* or 'parts,' the various context-specific aspects by way of which human excellence initially presents itself to us.[30] We are returned then, by the elenchus, to the beginning and source of the questioning, to its *archē*. Recall that the elenchus began bringing to light our relation to 'what virtue is' as necessitating (*dei*) our knowing it. With Nicias and Laches, we had simply identified the initial appearances of virtue within the various contexts of the everyday attitude as 'what *is*' and it was this that allowed us to presume a direct proximity to and a confident *technē*-like grasp of virtue, thereby quieting the concern or satisfying the need that nonetheless already characterizes our everyday attitude. We fell prey to the power of appearance itself, its power to conceal itself *as appearance*. That is, the movement of appearing simultaneously hides the essential excessiveness of what appears by way of it (Being) and precisely thereby proclaims what it presents us with as 'what *is*.'

In overcoming this initial concealment, the Socratic elenchus accomplishes the *alētheia* or 'unconcealment' of 'what virtue is.' In this lies its great benefit, for by way of it we enter into a truthful relation to the being of virtue. However, this relation is nothing other than the exposure to its excess and it occurs only in the crisis of *doxa*, the disruption of the familiar and trusted categories according to which we have been organizing our experience of the world and making our decisions in *praxis*. In being situated before and even struck by its withdrawal behind appearances, its abiding questionworthiness, we suffer the *deinos* unconcealment of the being of virtue.

We are not, thereby, freed from our immersion in the multiple atomized contexts of everyday life, for we still find ourselves nowhere else but at these sites of virtue's initial appearance. And yet, although nothing has changed, everything that presents itself is now transfigured in our experience of it. For in the *pathos* that the elenchus has provoked, in our being painfully concerned by 'what virtue is,' we remain before its initial appearances but these are received *otherwise*. As we have seen, employing nothing other than our own vague notion of what it means to be something, in posing the question of the being of virtue, we have been brought to experience the various isolated horizons of everyday life within the one all-encompassing, but uncomprehended, horizon of the whole. In doing so, in casting our gaze out toward that distant non-totalizing horizon, even if always from the site already inhabited by the everyday attitude, we are no longer *toward* the many discrete and proximal appearances of virtue. We might say now that, from this same site, we have now come to be *toward* that one virtue that appears in exceeding them and remaining questionworthy within the horizon of the whole.[31]

In the *pathos* brought about by the elenchus, then, these proximal appearances no longer seem so manifest and lucid, becoming instead troublingly crepuscular, emerging from out of the murky distance. This is altogether different from discovering one's ignorance of or obliviousness to virtue, for we are not threatened with the possibility that these initial appearances are purely subjective illusions, fantastical inventions of our subjectivity. Rather, in our being exposed to the *excessive measure* that is the being of virtue, we see our own formerly trustworthy *doxai* as that which 'what *is*' exceeds, but nevertheless as that whereby 'what *is*' first presents itself, even if in multiple, partial, obscure, oblique, contradictory, and ultimately unsatisfactory ways. This is precisely the sense of Socrates' ironic remark to the rhapsode Ion: "I say nothing but true things (τἀληθῆ), in the manner of any common person (ἰδιώτην ἄνθρωπον)" (*Ion* 532d). Socrates does indeed say nothing *more* than *doxa* and he therefore remains adamantly at the site of and does not transcend ordinary human life. However, his peculiar elenctic way of "saying" *doxa*, which brings *doxa* into conflict with itself and marks its limit, accomplishes a truth or an unconcealment quite foreign to the everyday attitude, bringing to light 'what virtue is' in its excessive and distant mode of being.

The immediate everyday appearances of virtue are now for us traces or hints, which when experienced as such spur us on to further questioning, further investigation. Not however with the aim of finally arriving at a *technē*-like knowledge, not as though pursuing some regulative ideal, but simply as the necessitated response to the being of virtue's withdrawal, or as the comportment imposed on us by that which now necessitates (*dei*) our knowing it in a painfully concerning way.

In the *Laches*, both the naïve confidence of the everyday attitude and the reflected confidence of sophistic wisdom have been shown to presume a *technē*-like proximal grasp of the being of virtue, and precisely thereby to falsify how it appears to us. It is Socrates' *aporia*, the dialogue indicates, that is the truthful or unconcealed relation to 'what virtue is.' However, we must resist declaring for this reason that Socrates is presented by Plato as wise, virtuous, or courageous, even if in a radically redefined and challenged, non-*technē*-like sense. Doing so is to fail to suffer what is so troubling about the result of the elenchus, the truthfully questionworthy appearance of virtue itself. In the *Laches*, as in all of the other dialogues, it is not the case that we are encouraged by Plato to emulate Socrates because we see him, even in failing to define virtue, as *exemplifying* it, as knowing *how* to be virtuous even in not knowing *what* virtue is.[32] Instead, as we saw in the *Apology*, even Socrates' philosophizing itself remains in question, indefensible because the terms of its possible defense escape it by its own admission. We are indeed to engage in Socrates' elenctic project, not however in emulation of him, but because we ourselves have come to suffer *our own* necessitation, *our own* pain motivating a questioning comportment. Indeed, Socrates insists on just this in the closing section of the dialogue.

THE SOCRATIC HERE AND NOW

> I stand in a far place.
> —Robert Lowell's rendering of Aeschylus's *Oresteia*

After the elenctic conversations, which is to say, after the alternative demonstration by Socrates, the generals recommend that the fathers place their sons in Socrates' care rather than in Stesilaus's, enlisting the former to help the boys become as good as possible. Socrates agrees to help, for it would be shameful to refuse any such request, but he reminds them that in the foregoing discussion he certainly "did not appear as knowing (ἐφάνην εἰδῶς)" (*La.* 201a). They should in no way single him out as an expert or a teacher of 'what virtue is,' "for indeed, now we have all come likewise to be in *aporia* (νῦν δ' ὁμοίως γὰρ πάντες ἐν ἀπορίᾳ ἐγενόμεθα)" (*La.* 201a).[33] Socrates suggests that they not abandon, therefore, their search for a teacher. We hear him then calling his interlocutors to join with him in the further pursuit of precisely that task in which they have been engaged. Indeed, what he calls for here is precisely the mode of his philosophical endeavor in the *Apology*—questioning those who presume to be wise with respect to virtue.

In consenting to join his interlocutors in the search for a teacher, Socrates is prepared to offer only one directive: "I do not advise that we remain as we are now (νῦν)" (*La.* 201a). This is an intentionally provocative line, for it captures the strangeness of the promise of Socratic philosophizing. At the very end of the *Laches* (*La.* 201a), Socrates twice repeats the very same drumbeat of the 'now' that we have heard throughout the passages previously cited (*La.* 190b, 192b, 192c, *Euthphr.* 5c, 7a). Again and again Socrates asks us to situate ourselves before appearances and say how 'what virtue is' presents itself to us 'now.' The moment that Socrates wants us to experience is a moment torn from its past and its inherited doxastic certainties, as well as torn open toward its future by our acknowledged needfulness, our being painfully concerned by and not in present possession of 'what virtue is.'

However, we must not understand this too quickly. What Socrates articulates here in temporal terms is precisely what we have been discussing here in spatial (or placial) terms. Recall that we found the Platonic dialogue emphasizing the situated character of philosophizing. Socrates places himself emphatically *with* his interlocutors at the site or the 'here' of their everyday opinions. However, his way of inhabiting the site is to expose its inhabitants to what painfully exceeds it. As establishing contact with excess *qua* excess, we found the Socratic elenchus to be aligned with what Hyland calls "finite transcendence."[34] At the end of the *Laches*, Socrates articulates the temporal aspect of this human condition. The 'now' in which Socrates situates his interlocutors is emphatically *not* a 'now' pointing ahead to a future moment when that need will be satisfied, when that painful concern will be quieted. From a life of elenctic discussion, Socrates is ready to *kinduneuein* or 'hazard' that human wisdom might be nothing other than the acknowledged non-knowing of virtue that is *aporia* (*Ap.* 23a–b). That is, as we have seen, he would wager that the *pathos* of painful concern, being distressed by the distance of 'what virtue is,' is the truthful experience of what presents itself already in our *doxai*, the unconcealment thereof 'as it is.' But in this wager we must understand Socrates to be neither asserting that virtue is knowable, striving then to realize this ideal, nor making the equally dogmatic skeptical claim that virtue is unknowable. Rather, this question must remain troublingly open.

Socrates and his interlocutors find themselves in this 'here' and 'now,' this *aporetic present*, and he encourages them to hold out, to endure their shared exposure to the *deinos* truth of the being of virtue and their being encompassed by the distant horizon of an abyssal non-totalizing whole.[35] The necessitation that compels their enduring in that site and in that moment with Socrates is not that of self-assured righteousness. It is instead the necessitating force of the open question. Knowing here and now their non-knowing, possessing here and now their non-possession of virtue, not aiming to overcome this condition, Socrates calls them instead to courageously attend to this condition's own requirements.

Conclusion:
Aporia in the Middle Dialogues

> Platon hat Weisheit und Lehre zu geben. Aber so sehr ist jenes sokratische Grundgesetz noch in ihm gebietend: auch ihm hieße ein Wissen 'Betrug,' das für alle gleich und immer in gleicher Weise gültig wäre. Man philosophiert von einem stets wechselnden Blickpunkt aus, mit einer bald kleineren, bald größeren Weite des Horizonts, in einer immer verschiedenen Höhe und Richtung des Betrachtens. . . . Und das Gute ist zwar weit entfernt von Gnaden seines Gegensatzes zu bestehen. Aber erkennbar und benennbar ist allerdings das Licht nicht ohne das Dunkel.*
>
> —Paul Friedländer, *Platon I*

The foregoing chapters have hopefully cast a transfiguring light on Plato's early Socrates. We began with the suggestion that Socrates' elenctic questioning might be aimed not at objective reality, but at the phenomenal being of virtue. That is, Socrates might be seeking only to clarify that which is always already *dokein* or 'appearing' to us in our most basic, everyday, prereflective *doxai* or 'opinions' about what is virtuous, excellent, or good. Having first simply opened up this possibility, we then found Socrates engaging in that very pursuit, his questioning being aimed above all else at the *alētheia* or 'unconcealment' of 'what virtue is,' but in a very specific sense. For Plato's early Socrates, this truth being *deinos*, 'terrific or excessive,' the proper mode

---

*Plato has wisdom to offer and much to teach. However, the fundamental Socratic law remains so very much in command within him. For him too, any knowledge that would be the same for all and that would be valid always in the same way would be called a 'fraud.' One philosophizes out from a constantly shifting point of view, with at one moment smaller and at another moment broader horizons, with an ever-changing height and direction of contemplation. . . . And the Good will indeed be far removed thanks to its opposites. But the light is after all unknowable and unnamable without the dark.

in which this is accomplished is not (even ideally) the unmediated grasp of a *technē* or *epistēmē*. Rather, the truthful relation to the being of virtue is that condition in which virtue's distressing ontological excess or distance emerges from its prior everyday concealment. Indeed, this truth proved to be nothing other than the pained 'concern' or *meletē* that Socratic elenchus provokes, the common name for which is *aporia* or 'waylessness.' By recognizing the unwarranted presuppositions and impositions arising from our own still persistently late modern perspective, we were able to open ourselves to the strange project of Socratic philosophizing in Plato's early works and its radical ontology.

This approach and the interpretation at which it arrives have found support at every turn, from the explicitly phenomenological aspects of Plato's own vocabulary (which are so often obscured in translation) to the many specific passages and arguments that our approach was able to illuminate compellingly. However, the very strongest endorsement for our approach is surely its satisfying resolution of that central Socratic paradox with which we opened our inquiry and to which we have returned throughout in its various forms and manifestations, that paradox we found still plaguing the traditional or orthodox interpreters of the early works. That is, we have been able to explain how Socrates can consider his elenctic and apparently destructive mode of conversing about virtue to be, in and of itself, nothing short of "the greatest good for a human being (μέγιστον ἀγαθὸν ὂν ἀνθρώπῳ)" (*Ap.* 38a, see also 36c). No longer reduced to self-conscious ignorance or subjective isolation from what virtue objectively is, the *aporia* that Socratic questioning provokes can now be understood as *itself* the truthful and properly human relation to the being of virtue. One lives one's life well as a human being, Socrates wagers, not by knowing or possessing but by suffering 'what virtue is' in its distance and excess.

As this interpretation draws to a close, the question surely arises as to whether Plato breaks in fundamental ways with this Socratic proto-phenomenological project in the works usually understood to belong to his "mature" middle period. Surely most readers and scholars would find relatively improved prospects for human knowledge or wisdom in these works, as well as a more articulated theory of how 'what is' relates to its material and sensible instantiations, and an ethic or politics consisting no longer of pure Socratic questioning but rather (at least, it might seem, ideally) of applying a knowledge of eternal moral laws or principles to one's individual or communal life. In sum, the middle Plato is generally approached as the Plato of the Ideas, which is to say, as having made a fundamental advance at the ontological, epistemological, and ethical/political registers over his own earlier, tentative searching. As Werner Jaeger describes Plato in his magisterial three-volume study, *Paideia*:

> Indem er das Läuterungsfeuer des sokratischen Nichtwissens durchschreitet, fühlt er sich fähig, jenseits desselben zu der Erkenntnis des absoluten Wertes vorzudringen, die Sokrates gesucht hatte, und durch sie der Wissenschaft und dem Leben die verlorene Einheit zurückzugeben. Aus dem sokratischen φιλοσοφεῖν entspringt die platonische "Philosophie."[1]*

No doubt, Jaeger's comment expresses a quite common view. In response, however, we might ask ourselves whether, in the experience of reading the Socratic discussions that still make up the middle-period works and in comparing these to the likely earlier dialogues, do we find the stark contrast to which Jaeger here gestures? As dialogues they are every bit as much portraits of the emphatically situated, thus context-delimited and character-specific acts of *philosophein* or 'philosophizing' that we encounter early on. But do the middle works nevertheless manage to present us with anything like a complete, definitive, and more or less systematic articulation of a Platonic "philosophy"? Of Platonism? Perhaps not.

This is surely not the place to undertake a comprehensive study of Plato's middle dialogues and their relation to those of the early period. What is possible, however, is to consider the middle-period works now in relation to the radical interpretation of the earlier dialogues offered in the preceding chapters. To this end, I suggest that we consider very briefly three moments from the *Cratylus*, *Republic*, and *Phaedrus*, moments in which we might hear distinct echoes of what we found characterizing the early Socratic philosophical project. These three brief studies altogether have a quite modest aspiration. They hope only to suggest that something like the same truthfully *aporetic* relation to 'what *is*' might persist into Plato's middle period, even if Plato's vocabulary and argumentation have changed and developed in significant ways.

---

*As he passes through the cleansing fire of Socratic ignorance, [Plato] feels that he is then able to press beyond this to that very knowledge of absolute value for which Socrates had been searching, and through this to return a lost unity to scientific understanding and life. Out of Socratic *philosophein* sprang forth Platonic "Philosophy."

IDEA/EIDOS AS 'LOOK' AND PHENOMENAL BEING IN THE MIDDLE DIALOGUES

Although we could contest various orthodoxies regarding the middle dialogues and the mature Platonism they purportedly espouse, let us here simply grant that, as Socrates remarks in the *Phaedo*, the Forms or Ideas are indeed "those things that we are always making a fuss about (ἃ θρυλοῦμεν ἀεί)" (*Phd.* 76d).[2] It has often been remarked that Plato devotes relatively little space to defending or clarifying the precise character and function of these entities that have loomed so large in subsequent interpretations, but it is nevertheless undeniable that when Plato's middle-period Socrates undertakes his familiar 'What is "x"?' questioning, he now understands himself to be asking after an Idea, and this in a seemingly more central and articulate sense than when he had previously used the term (e.g., in the *Euthyphro* and *Meno*). Furthermore, understanding the measure by which he and his interlocutors' questioning and thinking must proceed as principally an 'Idea' has significant repercussions for Socrates. And yet, even if we grant this and allow our approach to the middle-period works to play out within the space opened up and organized by what has been referred to (although never by Plato) as a "theory of Ideas," we will still find right here at the center of this orthodox position evidence that Plato's Socrates continues to think *phenomenal being*, rather than objective reality. And within this quasi-phenomenological project, we will then find indications of an abidingly modest or anti-hubristic Socratic assessment of the extent to which we human beings are able to overcome the mediation and distance of our relation to 'what is,' i.e., to the Ideas.

We might begin simply by attending to the etymology of the more or less interchangeable Greek terms *idea* and *eidos*, usually translated as 'Idea' or 'Form,' given that Plato does often employ them.

> [I]t is well known, but cannot be too often repeated, that the word Idea in this connexion is a very misleading transliteration, and in no way a translation, of the Greek word ἰδέα which, with its synonym εἶδος, Plato frequently applies to these supreme realties. The nearest translation is 'form' or 'appearance,' that is, the 'look' of a person of thing.[3]

Although expressing a complaint that the terms *idea* and *eidos* are often misleadingly translated and although calling for a return to the etymological root of these terms, i.e., a return to 'appearance' or 'look' as more original meanings, the author of these remarks is not Heidegger or one of his adherents. Rather, this passage is taken from the opening page of G. M. A. Grube's seminal work, *Plato's Thought*.

While we do well to follow Grube's suggestions as far as they go, our specific worry about translation is quite different from his, as is what we presume to learn from considering the etymological origins of these terms. Indeed, his concern is that the English term 'idea' falsely suggests mental contents, a possession of the mind or perhaps (in a Kantian sense) a structure imposed on experience by human understanding. This would be misleading according to Grube insofar as Plato's 'Ideas' do not exist within the subject. Because he "insisted on the possibility of knowledge and upon the existence of absolute values," Plato felt compelled "to establish the existence of an objective, universally valid reality, and this he found in his Forms or Ideas."[4] It is for this reason that Grube favors the translation 'Form,' insofar as this could indicate a structure or *Gestalt* that exists outside the mind, ordering its material instantiations and allowing them to be recognized as this or that kind of thing.

In avoiding one pitfall with Grube we encounter another. For, although these entities, as Socrates describes them, surely do not exist in any sense within the soul or subject, neither are they mind-independent shapes or objective organizing forces. Instead, they operate *within the movement of phenomenality*, prior to skepticism's introduction of a schism or chasm between subject and object. That is, the terms *eidos* and *idea* derive from the verb *idein*, which functions as the aorist form of the verb *horan*, 'to see.' They mean, therefore, and as the lexicon tells us, first and foremost 'that which is seen,' or even better 'the seeing of something.' Grube indicates as much when suggesting that we take note of 'look' or 'appearance' as original meanings. What he misses, however, is that most originally, as the 'look' or 'appearance' of something, the *eidos* or *idea* is *eo ipso* not something an object possesses independently of its appearing, but rather something that only *is* in being presented *to us*. Some scholars will note, usually following Heidegger,[5] that the terms *idea* and *eidos* derive from the verb 'to see,' and they may even haphazardly toss in 'look' as a translation thereof. This might occasionally lead to a critique of Greek ocularcentrism, but the notion that these terms are heard by Plato and his contemporaries as 'look' rarely leads to any deeper interpretive insight in approaching the dialogues.[6]

Striking should be the fact that, according to Plato's middle-period ontology as it is traditionally understood, what *is* most of all, the *idea/eidos*, belongs emphatically to the movement of coming into appearance, to *phenomenality*. An important consequence of the non-objectivity of the idea/eidos is that initial, everyday, pre-reflective opinions always entail the appearing of 'what is,' i.e., the self-presentation of the *idea/eidos* or 'look.' This is so even if these initial appearances are obscure, partial, oblique, multiple, or contradictory. Insofar as someone *seems* to us beautiful, the look of Beauty is presenting itself there at the site of that individual, insofar as someone *seems* to us just, the look of Justice is presenting itself there, and so on.⁷

Consider that initial moment of Socrates' introduction of the Ideas in the *Republic*. In Book V, Socrates has just made the dramatic claim that the *polis* will have no rest from injustice and suffering unless ruling and philosophizing are somehow made to belong together (*R.* V.473c–e). He is then tasked with distinguishing the true philosophers from the pretenders, which he does by means of two different arguments—an esoteric argument for the initiated or for those experienced in discussion with Socrates (*R.* V.475e–476d) and an exoteric argument for those not included in this circle of intimates (*R.* V.476d–480a). In the first of these, Socrates tells Glaucon that *with him* it should be easy to explain who the "lovers of seeing truth or unconcealment (τοὺς τῆς ἀληθείας . . . φιλοθεάμονας)" (*R.* V.475e) are, although it would perhaps be difficult with someone unpracticed at moving from initial appearances to the Ideas. Note Socrates' emphatic language of appearing or phenomenality throughout this section, a section that serves as the best, clearest, and most direct introduction to the Ideas to be found in the middle-period dialogues.

Socrates first asks Glaucon if the beautiful is the opposite of the ugly, and if these are therefore two, each being one. Glaucon agrees. Having established the principle that the beautiful must be one, rather than many, he continues,

> And the same account holds concerning even the just and the unjust and the good and the bad and all other Ideas (πάντων τῶν εἰδῶν). Each is itself one, but by means of their being together or in common (κοινωνίᾳ) everywhere with actions and bodies and one another, each appears as many appearances (φανταζόμενα πολλὰ φαίνεσθαι ἕκαστον). (*R.* V.476a)

Here, the *truth* that the real philosophers love is not just any sight or sound, not just any experience of something that might be secured, but strictly the emergence of 'what *is*' from what initially appears to us. That is to say, the philosopher loves the unconcealment of the one 'look' of, e.g., the beautiful, that look which must be presenting itself wherever something appears as beautiful according to, as Socrates states here, the *koinōnia* or contextual 'complex' of relations in which it is situated.

The proto-phenomenological project we found at work in the early dialogues would seem by no means suspended with Plato's concerted turn to a vocabulary of *idea/eidos* in the middle dialogues. Indeed, this vocabulary serves if anything to emphasize the fact that 'what *is*' for Plato in the middle period *remains* phenomenal being, rather than objective reality. The middle Socrates continues to ask after, discuss, and bring to light or clarify in dialectic that which is already appearing to us in our initial experience of the world, striving for its unconcealment just as he had in the early works. Our question then, is whether in the middle period there is any indication that the relation to the Ideas that Socratic philosophizing would aim to provoke might be abidingly aporetic? Or is that early model replaced with an epistemologically more positive model, which would entail a replacement as well of the Socratic ontology of excess and distance and the ethics of elenctic questioning? That is, do we find in the middle-period works any sense that the Socratic project of bringing the Ideas to light *as they are* might still involve, not overcoming, but suffering more intensely the distance and excess of 'what *is*'?

ALĒTHEIA AS DIVINE WANDERING

In the *Cratylus*, Socrates presents an etymology of the term *alētheia*. To be sure, the entire series of etymologies that constitute the greater portion of this dialogue are essentially and explicitly comical. Socrates confesses as he rattles them off in a flurry that he feels taken hold of by "inspiration (ἐνθουσιασμός)" (*Cra.* 396d), a force that endows him with wisdom that he himself calls "daimonic" (*Cra.* 396d) and "wild and laughable" (*Cra.* 426b).

These light and playful etymological definitions do perform a vital dramatic function, however. The dialogue opens *in medias res*, Socrates being asked to moderate an already failed discussion between Hermogenes and the eponymous Cratylus as to the nature of the correctness of names. Hermogenes defends a conventionalist position, arguing that names are assigned arbitrarily to what they name by *nomos* or 'custom.' Cratylus holds that names, insofar as they are names at all, must imitate and be naturally like their referents. However, Cratylus refuses to defend or even explain what precisely his naturalism entails.

It is just this anti-dialectical posture of Cratylus that calls forth Socrates' etymologies. Their purpose in the drama seems to be to draw Cratylus out of his silence, luring him into articulating and discussing his position by encouraging him to align himself with Socrates' inspired etymological wisdom. And this is exactly what the etymologies bring about, for Cratylus eventually enters the conversation claiming the position behind the Socratic etymologies as his very own (*Cra.* 428b–c). His doing so, however, triggers Socrates' confession that he remain doubtful about the position he and Cratylus now seem to share. He then leads them both into difficulties about their linguistic naturalism and its Heraclitean ontology. Neither, of course, does Socrates advocate Hermogenes' conventionalism, for the young man's claim that language is separable from the world it names and thus subject completely to human caprice was early on interrogated and rejected. We might just note that the *Cratylus*, thus, arrives at *aporia* in precisely the same manner as the *Laches*, insofar as both of these dialogues find Socrates pitting two opposed views against one another (one of which is easily mistakable for "Socratic"), exposing them both as problematic, and leaving his interlocutors and the reader without a resolution.[8]

Let us now focus in on the playful etymology of *alētheia* that Socrates presents, keeping in mind the suggestion of the *Laws'* Athenian stranger that human life itself might best be understood as a serious or noble kind of *paizein* or 'playing' (*Lg.* 803c).[9] First, we should remind ourselves of how we have treated both mythical discourse and Socratic irony in the early works. These are not merely false or fictional for Plato, not simply expressing the opposite of 'what is.' Rather, in both cases the subject matter is brought to light as it is, even if it is not definitively or exhaustively laid bare and mastered by human understanding. That is, unlike rhetorical and technical discourse, both of which claim to deliver their subject matter completely, encouraging the listener to make a judgment or take action on the basis of a presumed immediacy, myth and Socratic irony contrarily maintain a certain distance between their recipient and what they bring to light. Indeed, their subject matter should become, as we saw in the *Apology*, *axiochreōs* or 'worthy of consideration' (*Ap.* 20e). But precisely thereby, one should not presume to grasp what is brought to light immediately and authoritatively, but instead should experience it as requiring questioning or investigation. Comic discourse (and in particular the comic etymologies of the *Cratylus*) should be understood as bringing its subject matter to light in something like this fashion.

Although just one moment in Socrates' careering catalogue of etymologies, his treatment of the term *alētheia* here calls attention to itself, due to its unmistakable connection to the central theme of the *Cratylus* entire.[10] That is, at this point Hermogenes has asked Socrates to draw this already extensive series of speculative etymological definitions to a close by taking up *alētheia* and *onoma* or 'name,' "that very same thing we are treating in our present discussion" (*Cra.* 421a).[11] The centrality of these etymologies having thus been indicated, Socrates begins by dissolving *onoma* into its component parts, one of which seems to be *masma*, meaning a 'search,' deriving from the verb *maiesthai*, which as a synonym of *zētein* means 'to search, seek after' and, then, 'to desire.' On this basis, Socrates suggests that we can see what *onoma* means most clearly in the term *onomaston* or 'named thing,' for this seems to be a compressed version of "this is a being for which there is a search (τοῦτο εἶναι ὂν οὗ μάσμα ἐστίν)" (*Cra.* 421a–b).

Crucial here is the following. Socrates' playful etymological definition does not place the name and its function first and foremost within a situation where both the name and the named are adequately grasped. Rather, Socrates situates the name emphatically within the context of searching, seeking, desiring, and thus specifically of *not grasping*. Names refer most properly, Socrates' indicates thereby, to that which is not yet possessed, not yet mastered, to that which appears to us *as such* and draws us toward it in our searching and striving.

Socrates then turns to the issue of truth. He says, "'*Alētheia*' seems like the others in the same respect [i.e., in being compacted]. For the divine motion of being (ἡ γὰρ θεία τοῦ ὄντος φορὰ) is called by this locution, by '*alētheia*,' for it is a '*theia alē*' or a 'divine wandering' (ὡς θεία οὖσα ἄλη)" (*Cra.* 421b).In Homer, *alē* is the word the temptress Circe uses to describe Odysseus's hopeless and desperate voyaging at sea. Precisely in so doing, she hopes to dissuade him and his men from leaving the island of Aeaea (*Od.* X.456–465). We hear then already that this is not a mere moving about or being underway, but, just as the lexicon has it, a '*wandering* or *roaming* without home or hope of rest.'[12] If we have granted that the etymologies Plato has Socrates set forth here at such great length and in such detail are not merely ludicrous, not simply fantastical, then we must ask ourselves what we can make of the notion of 'truth' entailed here? If truth as *alētheia* or 'unconcealment' is itself brought somehow to light in this formulation, what are we to understand about it?

Socrates is certainly not declaring that 'what *is*' is subject to the kind of radical flux or constant self-othering that he knows Cratylus (the Heraclitean) will hear in this statement. Indeed, it is just this flux-ontology that, by the dialogue's end, Socrates will deeply problematize and it is on the basis of that problematization that Cratylus's linguistic naturalism will be led into *aporia* (*Cra.* 434b–440e). Is there some other sense, then, in which the *alētheia* or 'unconcealment' of 'what is' *as it is* might be understood as a 'wandering away from home,' a 'perpetually restless or unsettled roaming'? Is there a *theios* or 'divine' sort of wandering that would accomplish the truth of the Idea, the 'look' of what presents itself to us in our experience? Indeed, for it seems that the *maiesthai* just mentioned, the 'searching, seeking, or desiring' to which what is named properly presents itself, might be just this. That is, the striving for or desiring of the Idea, experienced as *in excess of* its initial appearances to us, would *itself* accomplish this 'divine wandering' that would be the *alētheia* or 'unconcealment' of the Ideas as they are. One's discourse and comportment would be truthful, *not* in putting an end to this wandering, but by wandering in the proper way, by pointing always beyond the initial appearances toward the Ideas as that to which we relate properly in the peculiar mode of not-possessing that is striving or desiring. According to this comic etymology, the Ideas would seem to be, as that by which all appearances must be judged and by which our lives must be led, something like *essentially excessive measures*.

THE GOOD BEYOND BEING AND
THE IDEAS AS EXCESSIVE MEASURES

Even taking seriously the suggestive etymology of *alētheia* in the *Cratylus*, one must wonder what might explain the *ontological* distance or excess of the Ideas, according to the Plato of the middle period? That is, one might well grant that for Plato in these works we are *initially* to recognize the Idea as *exceeding* the various, conflicting, context-determined appearances or instantiations thereof and we should thus experience the Idea as withdrawing behind these, as inaccessible and distressingly distant from the perspective of the everyday attitude of the many. However, with proper education and by the employment of *dialektikē* or philosophical 'dialectic,' are we not eventually or at least in principle able to gaze directly upon the Ideas with the "eye of the soul" (*R.* V.533d)? Ascending the divided line, is there no hope of securing immediate intellectual contact with those realities?

In the *Republic*, by Socrates' own express indications, we find ample reason to doubt the possibility of completing that ascent and of seizing hold of the Ideas as they are. Surprisingly, this essential excess or inaccessibility is not, in the *Republic*, owing to the inevitable distractions and limitations associated with embodiment. No, rather than arising due to the starting point of the philosophical or dialectical ascent, the essential limitation emerges in this case from the pinnacle of that ascent and is then distributed over the entire course.

As just mentioned, Book V presents the philosophers who would rule in the best possible human *polis* as first and foremost those who love *alētheia*. As Socrates explains, there are individuals who acknowledge that 'what *is*' exceeds or is not exhausted by what initially appears (*phainesthai, dokein*) to us, and these individuals desire the *alētheia* or 'truth, unconcealment' of 'what *is*,' the Ideas. This unconcealment of the Ideas from their initially self-concealing appearance in *doxa* would seem to produce *epistēmē* or 'knowledge, understanding' (*R.* V.475e-480a). We come to hope that, after a rigorous educational program that refines their rare natural gifts, the wisdom of the *polis* would be firmly in the possession of these philosopher kings and queens. And that wisdom, we likely presume, would amount to the unmediated noetic grasp of the relevant Ideas, presumably everything having to do with human excellence such as Justice, Temperance, Courage, etc.

However, in Book VI, Socrates introduces the following *aporia* at the very summit of this thinking, after making an explicitly offhanded reference to something that is *meizon* or 'greater' than Justice and the other virtues (*R.* VI.504d). This is, of course, "the Idea of the Good (ἡ τοῦ ἀγαθοῦ ἰδέα)," which is "that by which just things and any other things come to be useful and beneficial" (*R.* VI.505a). Indeed, Socrates tells us that the Idea of the Good is

> that for which every soul hunts (διώκει) and that for the sake of which (τούτου ἕνεκα) it does everything it does. Divining (ἀπομαντευομένη) that the Good is something, but being in *aporia* (ἀποροῦσα), it does not sufficiently grasp (λαβεῖν) 'whatever it is (τί ποτ' ἐστὶν)' and is not furnished with the sort of abiding belief it has about other things. But on account of this, the soul fails to hit upon (ἀποτυγχάνει) the benefit even in these other things, if indeed there is any. (*R.* VI.505d–e)

This is a central and extraordinarily rich passage, but we can only take from it here a portion of what it has to offer. First, given the phenomenological approach entailed by the Platonic vocabulary of *idea* and *eidos* in the middle period, the thought that every single soul always acts *tou agathou heneka* or 'for the sake of the Good' requires us to recognize that the 'look' of the Good is presenting itself to every soul at every moment. It is simply not the case that any of us are ever wholly separated from the Good. Insofar as we have desires, make decisions, and take actions, the Good is appearing to us. The question is only to what extent it is appearing to us *as it is*.

Second and even more important for our discussion here, everything else, every desirable thing, but also every virtue and every other Idea, only appears as desirable, which is to say, *as it is*, when viewed in the proper light of the Good. Indeed, as Socrates continues,

> I suspect that if there is a failure to perceive (ἀγνοούμενα) in whatever way just and fine things are good (ὅπη ποτὲ ἀγαθά ἐστιν), they will not have a guardian for themselves who is worth much of anything if he or she fails to perceive that. And I divine that no one will recognize them adequately before [he or she perceives that] (μηδένα αὐτὰ πρότερον γνώσεσθαι ἱκανῶς). (*R.* VI.506a–b)

Absolutely crucial is the fact that one cannot *gignōskein* or 'discern, recognize, know' any of the virtues, i.e., any of the Ideas of Justice, Courage, Sound-Mindedness, etc., unless one knows *in what way they are good*. One knows all of the other Ideas, that is to say, only when one knows them *in their relation to the Idea of the Good*.

Of course, Plato's Socrates himself refuses to say anything directly concerning the Idea of the Good, despite the pleading of his interlocutors, but offers instead a discussion of its likeness, the Sun. He does so simply because he confesses *not to have knowledge* of the Good itself (*R.* VI.506c–d). Let us not forget that Socrates remains the exemplary human being for the middle Plato. He is "of all those we have known, the best and otherwise the most practically wise and the most just (τῶν τότε ὧν ἐπειράθημεν ἀρίστου καὶ ἄλλως φρονιμωτάτου καὶ δικαιοτάτου)" (*Phd.* 118a). And yet, even this model individual, this man who has made this his *pragma* or 'occupation' and spent a lifetime in relentless investigation of it (*R.* VI.505a), even he remains unknowing with respect to the Good. That is, with respect, not just to this or that object of knowledge, but to the very *sine qua non* for knowledge of any Idea. This Socratic shortcoming should be sobering, to say the least.

And in case there were any question, Plato then goes on to make it perfectly evident that Socrates' not knowing the Idea of the Good (and his consequent imperfect knowledge of every other Idea) results neither from Socrates' own personal shortcomings nor even from some endemic human incapacity. Rather, this non-knowing is necessary due to the character, or better, to the topography of the Idea of the Good itself. That is, the Good is the source of the being of all the things that are, which is to say of all the Ideas. As such, the Good "holds itself still over beyond being, in both rank and power (ἔτι ἐπέκεινα τῆς οὐσίας πρεσβείᾳ καὶ δυνάμει ὑπερέχοντος)" (R. VI.509b). Surely Glaucon's response to this statement, which Socrates terms *geloios* or 'ridiculous,' has the ring of (comic) truth to it—Glaucon yelps, "What a daimonic excess (δαιμονίας ὑπερβολῆς)!" (R. VI.509b). At this point, a profound and all-affecting tension is introduced by the status of the Good as the source of all being, which holds itself *epekeina*, from *ep' ekeina* or 'in that region' rather than *epi tode* or 'in this one,' and thus in a beyond or yonder or in excess with respect to *ousia* or 'being.'

The Idea of the Good, as the Sun in the visible realm, is also the principle and the cause of all *alētheia*, which is to say, the source of the medium in which knowledge relates to and brings to unconcealment what most of all *is*, the Ideas. Even given the evident strangeness of this situation, Socrates issues the following imperative to Glaucon concerning his thinking of the Idea of the Good: "It being the cause of knowledge and truth, think of it as knowable (αἰτίαν δ' ἐπιστήμης οὖσαν καὶ ἀληθείας, ὡς γιγνωσκομένης μὲν διανοοῦ)" (R. VI.508a). Given that it is referred to as an 'Idea,' this seems perfectly reasonable.

However, the Idea of the Good is an Idea unlike any other, indeed one that pushes its own status as such to the limit and beyond. We must recall here the distinction Socrates has very recently drawn between *epistēmē* and *doxa*, between 'knowledge' and 'opinion' (R. V.476e–480a). These are two different *dunameis* or 'powers,' each of them being by nature *epi* or 'toward' different things. Socrates then makes the following very direct statement: "Knowledge is in a sense toward being, to discern what is as it holds [itself] (Ἐπιστήμη μέν γέ που ἐπὶ τῷ ὄντι, τὸ ὂν γνῶναι ὡς ἔχει)" (R. V.478a). If the Idea of the Good holds itself over in excess of and beyond being, beyond the being of the Ideas, it is also *ipso facto* unknowable, for according to Socrates knowledge has as its sole and proper object that which *is*. As we have seen, however, the Idea of the Good is not merely one thing that we would like to know among many others, for as Socrates has made clear, one cannot have true knowledge of any of the other Ideas unless one already has knowledge of the Good. The Ideas are essentially paradigms of perfection in what they are (the Idea of Justice being the best or, as it were, the most 'good' with respect to justice, the Idea of Courage being the best or most 'good' with respect to courage, and so on). Just as one truly "knows" a material and sensible manifestation of Justice *only* by knowing the Idea of Justice that is appearing there and ordering that appearance, one knows the Ideas of Justice, Courage, etc., only by knowing the Idea of the Good that appears through them in their respective perfection. This all-important knowledge of the Good is, however, *per definitionem* impossible.

Here then, in the *Republic*, Plato's Socrates indicates the importance of recognizing that 'what *is*' exceeds the initial appearances that present themselves to *doxa* in everyday life, and he calls us as philosophers to desire and search for *alētheia*, the 'unconcealment' of the Ideas that are presenting themselves there. However, due to the proper and insuperable excessiveness of the Idea of the Good and due to its central role in our arriving at knowledge of the Ideas as such, 'what *is*' would seem to withhold itself from our grasp irremediably.

HUMAN MONSTROSITY AND BEING BETWEEN ONE AND MANY

Finally, we turn to a moment at the very outset of the *Phaedrus*. The passage in question occurs in the framing or stage-setting section of the dialogue and has thus received relatively little attention from orthodox interpreters. Although this is certainly a peripheral moment in this work, a dialogue devoted to the relation between *erōs* and *logos*, it is nonetheless a moment where Plato's Socrates addresses his own mode of philosophical activity in the middle period and brings it to light in a certain way.

The dialogue that bears his name opens with Phaedrus leading Socrates out beyond the confines of the city walls. They are seeking a place to relax while Phaedrus reads aloud the new rhetorical work of Lysias. Along the way, Phaedrus asks Socrates if he believes the story to be true, whereby Orithuia is said to have been abducted from a nearby spot by the god of the north wind, Boreas. Socrates' response rewards close attention (*Phdr.* 229c–230a). He states that he could perhaps reject or criticize the story, as do the *sophoi* or 'wise men.' To be sure, if he wished to be "one of those who argue in a sophisticated manner (σοφιζόμενος)," he could declare that the girl simply came too near the edge and was blown over the rocks by the wind.

He does not see fit, however, to spend his time debunking myths. His reason is that anyone addressing him- or herself scientifically to the question of 'what Boreas is' would be compelled according to the inherently exhaustive, indifferent, and impersonal project of science to go on and question the appearance of the Hippocentaurs, and then the Chimerae, "and then a throng of Gorgons and Pegasuses comes flowing in and a plethora of inconceivable others (ἄλλων ἀμηχάνων) and extraordinary things (ἀτοπίαι) of the kind spoken of by fabulists (τερατολογῶν τινῶν φύσεων)." If someone, "disbelieving (ἀπιστῶν)," wishes to approach each and every one of these mythical appearances, furnished "with some crude wisdom (ἀγροίκῳ τινὶ σοφίᾳ)," that individual will have need "of much leisure time (πολλῆς ... σχολῆς)." Socrates is no such individual.

> And the reason for this is the following. I am not yet able to know myself, and adhere to the Delphic inscription. And to me it seems laughable to investigate other things, while remaining unknowing with respect to this. Having allowed myself to dismiss these [other inquiries] and being prevailed upon concerning these by what is customary, I examine, as I was just saying, not these things, but myself—whether I happen to be some beast more complicated and rather more lusty than Typhon, or whether I am a more tame and simple being, partaking by nature of some divine and gentle allotment. (*Phdr.* 229e–230a)

Socrates' statement of disinterest in the iconoclastic study of nature here surely resonates with the oft-discussed autobiographical passage in the *Phaedo*, where he tells his companions of his initial enthusiasm for and then disillusionment with the Pre-Socratic materialistic mode of explaining what presents itself to us in our experience of the world (*Phd.* 96a–100b). It is a veritable commonplace that Socrates turned away from the study of nature and concerned himself rather with the study of ethical and political matters, and in this sense his philosophizing answers to the Delphic imperative and amounts to a search for self-knowledge. However, this passage seems to oppose Socratic philosophizing to Pre-Socratic natural science not only with regard to its subject matter, but much more importantly with regard to its mode of discourse and investigation, its way of engaging in *logos*.

That is, in this passage, Socratic philosophical *logos* is aligned quite forcefully here with *muthos*, with mythical discourse, in opposition to the sophisticated *logos* of science. It is the natural scientist who reduces everything to what is explicable, intelligible, and, thereby, masterable. This amounts to eliminating from the world precisely that which myth seems to acknowledge and harbor essentially in its peculiar mode of addressing its subject matter, i.e., a limit to human understanding. As we have seen, whereas the ideal for scientific or technical discourse is complete revelation or exhaustive explanation, mythical discourse brings its subject matter to light *as* obscure, unintelligible, withheld (in some way or to some extent). As Kierkegaard puts it, in a line already cited, "it is intrinsic to the mythical . . . that the object is placed outside, is distanced in order to be drawn back again."[13] What requires emphasis here is the fact that this excessive or distant moment is drawn back into discourse and articulated mythically only insofar as the subject matter appears as distant, excessive.

It seems quite clear that, although he does not simply reject the validity of natural science and its explanations, Socrates does wish to place it in a questionable light, suggesting that its project of exhaustive illumination might not be unambiguously positive. In addition to the ironic references to natural scientists as *sophoi* or 'wise men' and their thinking as *sophizein* or 'reasoning sophisticatedly,' Socrates calls their wisdom *agroikos* or 'crude, rustic, boorish,' implying that, in its approach, it lacks the refinement and subtlety required to do justice to the world in which we find ourselves.

Of course, these critical observations do not imply that Socrates aligns himself simply with myth. He is not a proponent of religious belief, as we would understand this today. After all, when he is first asked if he believes the story of Orithuia's abduction by Boreas, Socrates states that it would not at all be out of character for him to reject such a story *tout court* (*Phdr.* 229c), presumably because as a philosopher he is "the sort of man who is persuaded by nothing other than the argument (τῷ λόγῳ) that appears best to [him] while reasoning (μοι λογιζομένῳ βέλτιστος φαίνηται)" (*Cri.* 46b). However, Socrates' remarks here at least indicate that there is some affinity between his peculiar anti-hubristic philosophical mode of discourse and that of myth. In his philosophizing, Socrates would seem to retain a quasi-mythological subtlety and refinement in acknowledging, rather than eliminating, distance and excess in bringing his subject matter to light.[14]

Given this affinity, it is all the more significant that Socrates takes pains to emphasize the radically incomprehensible and ungraspable character of mythical subject matter. Not focusing on the many fabled human forms by which the divine presents itself, which would make the gods and demigods seem nearer or more familiar, he speaks exclusively of the extremely *monstrous* manifestations of the divine. He lists off Hippocentaurs, Chimerae, Gorgons, and Pegasuses as the subject matters of myth and he refers to these mythical beasts first as *amēchanoi*, which is formed as a compound of the *alpha privativum* with the noun *mēchanē*, meaning 'instrument, machine, or way.' That is, these are 'impossibilities' or 'radically extraordinary and inconceivable things,' but more tellingly they are *aporiai* or things for which there appears no 'way, means, or instrument' for reaching and grasping them fully.

And he tells us that they are inconceivable not due to a failing of intelligence or attention on the part of the perceiver, but because they are *atopiai*, usually translated as 'eccentricities' or 'extraordinary things,' but more literally meaning, 'out of place things.' These beings appear to us as unintelligible, because they dramatically exceed the comfortable sphere of recognized and calculable entities. They present themselves *as* explicitly *atopos* or 'out of place' with respect to the familiar region of human life.

Socrates also refers to these as the typical stuff of *teratologoi*, which can be translated as 'marvel mongers' or 'fabulists.' Again, this composite term seems calculated to signal the specifically excessive or distant character of what myth properly brings to light. The word *teratologos* is composed by combining the word *logos*, here the general category of 'speech,' with the word *teras*. A *teras* is translated as 'sign, wonder, or portent,' but then also as 'monster,' and it is most essentially something that points beyond itself, or beyond its immediate appearance. The occurrences recounted by myth mongers or fabulists are strictly those that are taken for 'signs' or 'portents' of something beyond their initial appearances, or beyond the human experience of them.

Focusing our attention on the one suggested translation of *teras*, 'monster,' the mythical beasts listed by Socrates seem to be paradigmatically *monstrous*, from the Latin *monstrare*, meaning 'to point out, exhibit, show forth.' Essential to the phenomenon of monstrosity is the appearance of something as especially apparent or attention-grabbing, but precisely because of its unfamiliar, bizarre, or extraordinary, i.e., essentially 'out-of-place' character. But this attention-grabbing appearance should be recognized as due to some excessive or *not fully apparent* aspect of the monster, something about it so radically strange as to be incomprehensible, incommensurable. Monsters *as such* are *terata*, in the precise sense that they are 'signs' pointing beyond themselves. Paradoxically, they appear or present themselves to us especially dramatically because partly withdrawn in unintelligibility and not fully graspable. But then, with the appearance of the monster (following out for a moment the implications of the Latin root of this illuminating translation), what is also 'shown forth or pointed out,' indirectly, is the great unnoticed *distance* in the sphere of human life, the *distance* of what is essentially withdrawn from human understanding and calculation. By emphasizing the *monstrous* aspect of the proper subject of myth, Socrates makes clear that myth is the appropriate manner of letting *monstrosity* appear, insofar as its mode of self-presentation here continues to point beyond itself to its excess, to what remains distant as such.

This must be allowed to illuminate Socrates' declared philosophical project, self-inquiry, given that he presents himself as suspended between the following two possibilities: He seems to be either "some beast more complicated and rather more lusty (πολυπλοκώτερον καὶ μᾶλλον ἐπιτεθυμμένον) than Typhon" or "a tamer and simpler living thing (ἡμερώτερόν τε καὶ ἁπλούστερον ζῷον), partaking by nature in some divine and gentle allotment (θείας τινὸς καὶ ἀτύφου μοίρας φύσει μετέχον)" (*Phdr.* 230a). Note that *both* of the possible accounts Socrates offers of his own nature are *mythical* in character. Socrates appears to himself as stretched between either the more terrible, hundred-headed Titan on the one hand and the tamer, simpler animal with a divine aspect on the other. Whatever way this might be decided, Socrates appears to himself *as monstrous* in any case, leaning either more toward the multiple or the simple.

Recall our discussion earlier of 'being many everyday' in the early dialogues. Most emphatically in the *Meno* and in the *Laches*, we found Socrates confronting his interlocutors always in their everyday attitude, which was distributed among various discrete contexts of appearance. In each of these contexts, 'what virtue or excellence/goodness is' appears in context-delimited ways and draws us desiringly toward itself as we make decisions and take actions. What we do not do, except when Socrates confronts us with the question, is ask 'what virtue *is*?' and acknowledge a distinction between what virtue *is* and how it initially *appears*. As we have seen already, Meno's response to this question is most illustrative, for he answers that for a man virtue is efficacy in public and private matters, for a woman it is managing the home and submitting to her husband, for a child it is something else, and something else again for the elderly and for the enslaved. Summing up, he says, "And there are very many other virtues (ἄλλαι πάμπολλαι ἀρεταί), with the result that there is no *aporia* involved in speaking of virtue concerning 'what it is' (ὥστε οὐκ ἀπορία εἰπεῖν ἀρετῆς πέρι ὅτι ἐστίν) (*Men.* 72a). Socrates then encourages Meno to try to catch a view of "the same virtue of all of these [human beings] (ἡ αὐτὴ ἀρετὴ πάντων)" (*Men.* 73c) and, later, as "according to the whole, concerning virtue, 'what it is' (κατὰ ὅλου . . . ἀρτῆς πέρι ὅτι ἐστίν)" (*Men.* 77a).

Socrates' unmistakably mythical description of himself in the *Phaedrus* thus seems to map quite nicely onto that *aporetic* condition we saw him trying to provoke throughout the early dialogues as the truthful experience of the being of virtue. There, Socrates' 'What *is* "x"?' question always aims to disrupt or breech the multiple discrete everyday contexts in which virtue is initially appearing to us and in which we presume to grasp it with a *technē*-like comfort and immediacy. Drawing us beyond these and toward the all-encompassing horizon of the whole, Socrates' elenctic questioning by no means effects the transcendence of those immersed perspectives, but it does incline its participants toward the single being of virtue that they recognize for the first time as what is presenting itself in those multiple and various appearances even while it remains always in excess of them.

The philosophical project of the early dialogues thus understood does not seem to have been abandoned or superseded, at least note by the Socrates of the *Cratylus*, *Republic*, and *Phaedrus*. Rather, his philosophical project seems to have delivered him over to the very same condition, suspended between the multiple contexts of the everyday attitude and the all-encircling horizon of the whole that opens with the question of what virtue or the good *is*. The strangeness of the early Socrates has become monstrosity. For him truth is a wandering in perpetual exile, but a divine wandering, on that points always past the initial appearances toward the Ideas, and ultimately toward the Good beyond being, beyond knowledge. However, and this is vital, his playful notion of truth, his understanding of the Good's ontological excess, and his own discourse's affinity with myth and antagonism toward demystifying science all seem to indicate that Socratic philosophizing does not aim at overcoming the essentially human monstrosity it acknowledges. Rather, the human life that Socrates seems to model for us here in the middle dialogues is a certain way of being a monster, a way of living in philosophical conversation with others such that one is always toward that which can be properly brought to light only in the moment we suffer its disturbing excess, its distressing distance.

Notes

INTRODUCTION: SOCRATES AND THE
HERMENEUTIC OF ESTRANGEMENT

All translations from Greek and Latin are my own unless otherwise noted.

1. The translators of Hans-Georg Gadamer's *Wahrheit und Methode* introduce the neologism 'traditionary text' in order to render into English the German term Überlieferung. Although often translated simply as 'tradition,' this certainly loses the active sense of the German verbal noun, which names literally a 'delivering over.' For Gadamer specifically, the traditionary text is not a past and finished sum of cultural concepts, values, and historical events, but rather something that is handed over to us and addresses us as though in conversation. Not at all disinterested, we feel ourselves rather tasked to understand it, apply it to ourselves, and respond. It is this aspect of being addressed and made responsive that most characterizes our relation to traditionary texts. Gadamer writes, "Der Interpret, der es mit einer Überlieferung zu tun hat, sucht sich dieselbe zu applizieren" (Gadamer, 1960, 329). For their discussion of the term 'traditionary text,' see J. Weinsheimer and D. G. Marshall (1997, xvi).
2. Vlastos (1991, 2).
3. Vlastos (1957/58, 496–516), emphasis added.
4. Vlastos (1957/58, 502).
5. Vlastos (1957/58, 503). It should perhaps be noted that Vlastos later makes a change to this summary, a change important for understanding the logical function of elenctic argument, but not its end or aim. In his article "The Socratic Elenchus," Vlastos (1983b) rightly observes that, of the thirty-nine elenctic arguments in the early dialogues (according to Robinson's count [1953]), none of them seem to bring about the strong,

self-contradictory result he describes above. It is not the case that the interlocutor's initial claim p itself eventually yields ~p. Instead, the interlocutor states p, and then additionally is led to state q, r, s, etc., these other opinions being used to deduce ~p. In any case, the result is the same—the interlocutor is shown *not to have the knowledge he presumed he possessed*, the implicit premise being that anyone who holds contradictory opinions relevant to virtue does not have what one would call 'knowledge' thereof.

6. In his seminal essay "Socrates' Disavowal of Knowledge," Vlastos (1985, 2–4) definitively eliminates one possible solution to the paradox—irony. He offers a most concise argument against the long-standing suspicion that, in the early dialogues, Socrates' claim not to have the knowledge he seeks is 'ironic' in the simple and uninteresting sense of 'dissembling, deceitful' (as Thrasymachus alone seems to claim at *R.* I.337a). In so doing, Vlastos rejects his own earlier assessment, Vlastos (1971, 7–8), as well as that of Gulley (1968, 69) and Guthrie (1975, 123–124, 131–132). For other denunciations of Socratic irony as a resolution to the paradox, see Irwin (1977, 39–40), Lesher (1987), and Brickhouse and Smith (1994, 32).

7. Vlastos (1983b).

8. In the radicalized philology carried out both in *Die Geburt der Tragödie* and in its extensive unpublished companion volume *Die Philosophie im tragischen Zeitalter der Griechen*, Nietzsche is surely fascinated by the Greeks' foundational role in establishing the concepts and values that are our inheritance and by their consequent capacity to illuminate our present historical moment. However, it must be emphasized that the ultimate benefit of the philological study of Greek thought and culture resides for Nietzsche in its capacity to point *beyond* the horizon of our historical present. As he writes in a collection of notes from 1875 entitled "Wissenschaft und Weisheit im Kampfe," "Das griechische Alterthum als classische Beispielsammlung für die Erklärung unsrer ganzen Cultur und ihrer Entwicklung. Es ist ein Mittel uns zu verstehen, unsre Zeit zu richten und dadurch zu überwinden" (1980, 173, 6[2]). Nietzsche even sees the study of the ancients as pointless and highly suspect if it lacks a certain 'untimeliness': "[D]enn ich wüßte nicht, was die klassische Philologie in unserer Zeit für einen Sinn hätte, wenn nicht den, in ihr unzeitgemäß—das heißt gegen die Zeit und dadurch auf die Zeit und höffentlich zugunsten einer kommenden Zeit—zu wirken" (1874, 241, Vorwort). The task of thinking what I am calling the 'strangeness'

of the figure of Socrates would bring forth his untimeliness in precisely this sense.

9. In establishing the order of composition of Plato's works, there is little trustworthy external evidence, such as Aristotle's remark that the *Laws* was written after the *Republic* (*Pol.* 1264b24–27), as well as some internal evidence: e.g., the cross-references between dialogues that tell us that the *Sophist* was composed before the *Statesman* (*Sph.* 217a, *Plt.* 257a, 258b), but perhaps after the *Parmenides* (*Sph.* 217a), which is perhaps before the *Theaetetus* (*Tht.* 183e); also the *Timaeus* is between the *Republic* (*Ti.* 17b–19b) and *Critias* (*Ti.* 27a). Given this dearth of evidence, in speculating on the dialogues' order of composition we are left either to stylometric analysis (*Sprachstatistik*) or to the more substantive but also more speculative assessments of the probable development of Plato's thought. The former counts the frequency of particles, response phrases, prose rhythms, and other elements such as the Isocratic intolerance of hiatus (following a word ending in a vowel with another word beginning in a vowel). Although there are some discrepancies in the various accounts and a few cusp dialogues end up on one side or the other of a division (specifically, *Men.*, *Euthd.*, *Mx.*, *Prm.*, and *Tht.*), there is a great deal of conformity among stylometric analyses as to which dialogues belong to the early (see main text), middle (*Phaedrus*, *Phaedo*, *Republic* II–X, *Symposium*, *Cratylus*), and late periods (*Parmenides*, *Theaetetus*, *Sophist*, *Politicus*, *Timaeus*, *Critias*, *Laws*). The consistency of these results is remarkable, given that various analysts have employed radically different and independent criteria. Furthermore, again with some exceptions, most substantive, developmental accounts simply reinforce these three divisions and their order. Either of these two means of chronological assessment might be dubious on its own, but their mutually reinforcing character makes the three basic divisions and their order quite compelling in my opinion, while the ordering *within* these divisions remains for us, if more vexing, less important. On the stylometric approaches, see the fine survey and evaluation of previous scholarship in Brandwood (1990) or (1992). For supporting substantive chronological assessments, see Guthrie (1975, 39–56) and Vlastos (1991, 45–80). For some compelling critiques of the traditional chronological ordering, see Howland (1991) and Nails (1992). In response to these critical assessments, I would simply say that, although I do believe these now orthodox divisions to be fundamentally sound and I am relatively comfortable with the claim that the group of dialogues treated here as 'early' are indeed

so, this is not in fact necessary for my interpretation. Ultimately, I offer an interpretation of a Socratic philosophical project portrayed with more or less consistency throughout *these* texts, regardless of their date of composition.

10. We might say that all of the dialogues being treated here are alike *aporetic* insofar as they all problematize how to live well as a human being, or 'what human virtue truly is,' without ever arriving at what they themselves seem to indicate is the sought-after satisfactory definition or form of knowledge. This *aporia* is produced in most cases by the elenctic refutation of an interlocutor's *doxai* about virtue. Vlastos (1983b) notes that three dialogues do not seem to proceed by means of the elenchus, technically defined—the *Lysis*, *Hippias Major*, and *Euthydemus*, and to this list we should obviously add the *Menexenus*, which contains no elenchus at all. The first two are not elenctic by Vlastos's estimation because "Socrates proposes all the theses which are discussed and refutes all the theses which are refuted." This is, however, not a terribly important distinction, given that there are many instances of Socrates suggesting answers to his own questions throughout the thirty-nine examples of standard elenctic argument in the early dialogues (by Robinson's count [1953]). What is vital is that Socrates secures the interlocutor's agreement at each step, i.e., the interlocutor's affirmation that this is how the issue appears to him as well, thereby ensuring that his interlocutors themselves are subjected to the elenchus even when Socrates is the one proposing the definitions or answers. Especially illuminating here is the *Meno*'s elenchus of the servant, where Socrates gives a professedly paradigmatic display of the method and nonetheless suggests many of the answers to which the boy merely assents (*Men.* 82b–84a). Thus, Vlastos's hesitation on this count seems unwarranted. The *Euthydemus* is a special case, insofar as Socrates here confronts eristic, or "fighting with words (ἐν τοῖς λόγοις μάχεσθαι)" (*Euthd.* 272b), in the persons of the pancratists, Euthydemus and Dionysodorus. This practice is very close to the elenctic project of Socrates, which explains his ironic enthusiasm for it, but in its fervor to defeat an opponent eristic lacks the elenchus's *protreptic* aspect, its turning of the interlocutor toward 'what "x" is' and encouraging a questioning, seeking, and concerned attitude. However, as I hope to show in part 2, this *protrepein* or 'turning toward' should not be understood as an addition to the destruction of Socratic elenchus, but rather as an essential aspect thereof, insofar as Socratic elenchus when it is successful provokes a painfully concerned attitude

in its participants. In the *Euthydemus*, Socrates must emphasize the protreptic moment in the face of the indiscriminately and mischievously (non-truth seeking) destructive display of eristic, but the end result is the same as with a standard Socratic elenctic discussion—the interlocutor is left with the recognition that he does not know what he must know (for Socrates, 'what virtue is') and is rendered thereby *needful* of this knowledge. The *Menexenus* is especially strange, as it presents a Socratic funeral oration, which he claims to have learned from Pericles' mistress, Aspasia. It has been suggested that Plato's motivation in writing such a work might have been to show that he too was capable of writing elevated and compelling oratory, thereby making evident that he chose to pursue philosophy not because he was inept at rhetoric, but because he thought it a superior means of attaining human excellence. While this may well be the case, the philosophical significance of the dialogue as a whole remains to be determined. We must consider here the explicitly ironic tone (in Socrates' complex sense of irony) of Socrates' introduction to the topic of rhetoric (*Mx.* 234b–235c), of which he will then go on to give an example. He begins by observing that rhetoricians are those who engage in "colorful embroidering with words (τοῖς ὀνόμασι ποικίλλοντες)," and by means of this they offer their audience members not only the praise the latter truly merit, but also praise they do not. Rhetorically ornamented speech is so powerful, indeed, that it brings its audience to believe even this false praise, now experiencing themselves as transformed, improved. Socrates states that the rhetoricians, thus, "bewitch our souls (γοητεύουσιν ἡμῶν τὰς ψυχάς)," producing a resonating spell from which even he only recovers three or four days later, when, as he says, "I am reminded of myself and perceive that I am on the earth (ἀναμιμνῄσκομαι ἐμσυτοῦ καὶ αἰσθάνομαι οὐ γῆς εἰμι)." As we shall see in chapter 3, this echoes distinctly and fundamentally the critique of rhetoric that we will find in the *Apology*—by means of embellished speech rhetoric is able to present its subject matter even in concealing how things truly *are* with it, generating both false confidence and self-forgetting. That Socrates' opening praise of rhetoric should be received as ironic is indicated explicitly in the *Menexenus* by the eponymous interlocutor's response—"Oh Socrates, you are always making fun of the rhetoricians" (*Mx.* 235c). Thus, given its introduction, Socrates' own rhetorical praise of the Athenians in the *Menexenus* should leave the citizens who hear it in a condition of something like *aporia*, edified and inspired by the historical and contemporary catalogue of their virtues but wondering deeply if they in fact possess what rhetoric has led them to believe they possess. See Benson (1990, 141–144) for a discussion that also presents all the early dialogues as broadly *aporetic*.

11. Thus, although the *Apology* often serves here as a touchstone of sorts, the following interpretation is not limited in its significance to that work alone. Indeed, it must be admitted that the following cannot even claim to offer in its course a thoroughgoing interpretation of that work. Although many passages from the *Apology* are taken up as key passages for understanding Socratic philosophizing and are therefore interpreted in depth and repeatedly, many other important aspects and themes of the *Apology* do not receive extensive treatment here: e.g., Socrates' later responses to the formal charges he faces, his complex religious beliefs, the source of the authority he grants to his nay-saying *daimonion*, and his extraordinary attitude toward death and the afterlife. A full interpretation of the *Apology* would need to address in greater depth these and other issues, and to situate them each in turn with a view to that work as a whole. This is not the task undertaken here.

12. The most compelling and original work focused centrally on this issue has surely been that of Drew Hyland. Any of his studies of Plato not only display but argue for, with great subtlety and clarity, the necessity of taking into account the dramatic context of what is said in the dialogues. However, the chapter entitled "The Place of Philosophy" in *Finitude and Transcendence in the Platonic Dialogues* offers a discussion where this is the central issue. See Hyland (1995, 13–34). See also these major contributions that depart explicitly from the orthodox, exclusively argument-focused approach: Gadamer (1931), Klein (1965), Strauss (1966) and (1983), Sallis (1975), Tigerstedt (1977), Benardete (1984), Gonzalez (1998), and Gordon (1999).

CHAPTER 1. SETTING ASIDE THE SUBJECT-OBJECT
FRAMEWORK IN READING PLATO

1. On this very claim, see Vlastos (1991, 91–98) and also Guthrie (1971b, 35–39).
2. Plato explicitly discusses the Delphic oracle's injunction to "Know Thyself" at various points (*Ap.* 20e–23b, *Chrm.* 164d, *Alc. I* 124a–b, *Prt.* 343b, *Phdr.* 229e, *Phil.* 48c, and *Lg.* XI.923a).
3. Rappe (1995, 2).

4. Gonzalez (1998, 61) is a noteworthy exception to this rule. Making use of Gilbert Ryle's well-known distinction, Gonzalez argues that Socratic "dialectic" in the early dialogues has as its aim (and indeed itself performatively realizes) a 'knowledge how' (to be virtuous), rather than a 'knowledge what' (virtue is). In addition to the fact that this knowledge "cannot be expressed in propositions/definitions," it is a kind of self-knowledge, insofar as "its 'object' is not completely external to the knower." Although none of them have taken the ontological approach I advocate here, other writers who have to some extent *emphasized* a kind of self-knowledge as at least an aspect of the central aim of Socratic philosophizing are Cornford (1933, 302–309), Annas (1985), and Brickhouse and Smith (1994, 17–18, and esp. 85).
5. In the ellipsis between these two statements is a parenthetical remark about Democritus and the Pythagoreans. Cf. *Met.* I.987b2–5, XIII.1086b2–5, and *De Part.* 642a.25–30.
6. See Vlastos (1991, 248–251) for a catalogue of the overwhelming scholarly consensus on this issue.
7. Robinson (1953, 49).
8. Some scholars' views on the issue notwithstanding. See Shorey (1903), Cherniss (1945, 4), Allen (1970, 136), and, although with quite a different approach and aim, Annas (1999). For accounts of an earlier "theory of Ideas" without *chōrismos* or 'separation' between *eidos* and instantiation, see Ross (1951), Dodds (1951, 20–21), and Prior (1985) and (2004).
9. I am inclined to agree with John Burnet that if this issue were not in play in the works of the early Plato, he wouldn't qualify as a philosopher. Burnet (1914, 9) writes, "If we look at Greek philosophy as a whole, we shall see that it is dominated from beginning to end by the problem of reality (τὸ ὄν). In the last resort the question is always, 'What is real?' Thales asked it no less than Plato or Aristotle; and, no matter what the answer given may be, where that question is asked, there we have philosophy."
10. For a discussion of these three aspects of the object of Socrates' 'what is "x"?' question, see Teloh (1981, 2) and Benson (2000, 108–111).
11. In his book on the epistemology implicit in Socratic philosophical activity, Hugh Benson argues that there are eight distinct aims of the Socratic method. He finds these enumerated in the account Socrates himself gives in the *Apology*, but then sees ample evidence for these very same aims in the activity of Socrates as depicted in the other early dialogues as well.

He writes, "These aims are (1) interpreting the statements of others, (2) testing or examining the knowledge of those reputed (by themselves or others) to be wise, (3) showing those who are not wise their ignorance, (4) learning from those who are wise, (5) examining oneself, (6) exhorting others to philosophy, (7) examining the lives of others, and (8) attaining moral knowledge" (Benson 2000, 17). Although all of these various aims will be in play at one point or another in the following chapters, it would seem that our two Aristotelian assessments emphasize aims (5) and (8) explicitly.

12. Eva Brann is delightfully dismissive of just this possibility. She writes that, when Socrates takes up the issue of self-knowledge in the *Charmides*, "he doesn't mean rummaging around in your own 'subjectivity'" (Brann 2004, 77). Of course, I agree completely with Brann. The point of this discussion is simply that, if we make explicit the subject-object structure that is implicitly imposed on the dialogues in orthodox scholarship, *then* the Socratic concern with self-knowledge threatens to reduce itself to such "rummaging" so long as it secures no bridge to external objective realities.

13. Other terms that might be added to this list and that Socrates uses in a non-technical, sometimes interchangeable manner are, among still others, *gnōmē, gnōsis, mathēsis, sophia,* and *phronēsis,* and the verbs *epistasthai, eidenai, sunienai,* and *gignōskein.*

14. Benson (2000, 21–23).

15. I refer here to Socrates' philosophical project as directed toward 'what virtue is,' although this might seem initially to be true in the *Meno* alone and perhaps in the *Apology*, given Socrates' explicit indications throughout that the principle concern of his philosophizing (which he shares with the sophists) is "human and political virtue" (*Ap*. 20b). Other conversations focus on the being of particular virtues (courage, temperance, justice, piety) or of other ethically significant terms (fineness, the good, friendship). I refer to the aim of Socrates' questioning simply as virtue for it will be my contention that Socrates always wants his interlocutors ultimately to experience this as questionworthy, even when the conversation first focuses on a specific virtue or a related ethical theme. We will have occasion to discuss this in detail in chapter 6, but we might remark already that this does not entail the thesis that Socrates himself believes in the "unity of virtue," as is so often claimed. He does not. Rather, he remains, as he constantly says, non-knowing with respect to 'what virtue is.' When he invokes the apparent unity of the virtues this is a

means of opening up the *question* of 'what human virtue is,' not at all an answer or a part of an answer. This is evident in Socrates' common elenctic tactic in the discussion of a single virtue or what will appear to us initially as in some undefined sense a *meros* or 'part' of virtue as a whole—Socrates leads his interlocutors to see that they have inadvertently identified what they themselves believe to be only a 'part' of virtue with another part or with the whole, thereby indicating that they do not know what they thought they knew. In the *Laches* for instance, it becomes clear that Nicias has identified courage with wisdom and then with the whole of virtue (*La.* 194b–199c), both of which Socrates proceeds to problematize rather than endorse. In the *Charmides*, *sōphrosunē* or 'temperance' moves away from a "knowledge of knowledge" and toward some knowledge of the Good (*Chrm.* 173a–176a). And in the first elenchus of Protagoras, the famous sophist is brought to *aporia* when his tidy structure of atomized specific virtues, parts of the whole of virtue, is quickly demolished through Socratic questioning (*Prt.* 329b–333e). In all such cases, it is as though Socrates perceives in his interlocutors a presumption to have answered the question of 'what human virtue is,' which is always just the question of how to live well as a human being, only insofar as they presume that it involves the possession of all or some of the parts, which they see as more easily graspable than the whole (see *Men.* 79b–e, where Socrates scolds Meno for just this tendency). As we shall see, to such a "divide and conquer" approach to virtue, Socrates opposes not "unite and conquer," but "unite and bring to light 'what virtue is' as abyssally questionworthy"—a slogan one labors to imagine as a rallying cry, to be sure. Socrates finds again and again that the *question* of 'what each of the individual virtues are' always opens up to the question of 'what virtue is,' and vice versa. Socrates would seem then to be making only the simple and characteristic observation that we call all these various things by the name *aretē*, which is to say, in them 'what virtue is' appears to us and this is why we name them all by the same genus term. And he might well observe that, whenever we are faced with the question and when we do embark on the project of trying to define them, we tend to always see the comportment they name as entailing some kind of wisdom. However, this is not a presumption to know one important element in the definition of 'what virtue *is*' (e.g., that virtue always involves all virtues, or that it always involves wisdom or knowledge), but merely an aspect of virtue's *appearance* to us, behind which it withdraws. Given this, we refer here to Socrates' philosophical questioning as directed at the being of human virtue or excellence *simpliciter*, although different aspects or different context-specific appearances thereof are in play in different contextualized discussions. For a review of the standard positions and a more traditional approach to Socrates' advocacy of the unity of virtue, see Penner (1971).

16. See Brickhouse and Smith (1984, 186), Gonzalez (1998, 9 and 21), and Benson (2000, 35) for the use of these terms.
17. Vlastos (1983b), (1985), and Penner (1992). Although in a less technical sense, both Goldschmidt (1947, 74–75) and Guthrie (1975, 132) seem to see the overall impact of a Socratic conversation as somehow indicating, if not providing a conclusive argument for, the correct answers to Socrates' questions.
18. Reeve (1989, 37–53) and Brickhouse and Smith (1994, 3–72). See Benson's (2000, 35) observation as well that his proclaimed non-constructivism is nonetheless compatible with this form of, as it were, long-run constructivism.
19. Robinson (1953, 7–32), Ryle (1966, 119–120), Kraut (1984, 249–256), MacKenzie (1988), Stemmer (1992, 142–143), and Benson (2000, 187–188). Shorey (1933, 105) calls the elenctic method of Socrates in the early dialogues "the negative dialectic," and Taylor (1926, 34) writes of an elenctic dialogue that "The result of the whole discussion is negative." See also Vlastos (1956) and (1983a). Something like non-constructivism seems to be entailed by Stokes's reading of Socrates' pure questioning method. See Stokes (1986, 1–35).
20. Brickhouse and Smith offer the following list (1994, 30): *Ap.* 20c, 21d, 23b; *Chrm.* 165b–c. 166c–d; *Euthphr.* 5a–c, 15c–16a; *La.* 186b–c, 186d–e, 200e; *Ly.* 212a, 223b; *Hp. Ma.* 286c–e, 304d–e; *Grg.* 509a; *Men.* 71a, 80d; *R.* I.337e. To this, we might add Aristotle's comment in the *Sophistici Elenchi*, where he is discussing "the essential aim of the dialectical art and of examination" (*SE* 182a35–6). Aristotle writes, "Socrates asked questions and did not answer them, for he confessed that he did not know" (*SE* 183b6–8).
21. See also Grote (1865, 291–292), who already writes disdainfully of this approach: "Interpreters sift with microscopic accuracy the negative dialogues of Plato, in hopes of detecting the ultimate elements of that positive solution which he is supposed to have lodged therein, and which may be put together so as to clear up all the antecedent difficulties."
22. Brickhouse and Smith (1994, 18).
23. Gonzalez (2002a, 180).

24. Ibid.
25. There are two important, relatively recent interpretations of the Socratic project that address this issue centrally and at length: Brickhouse and Smith (1994) and Benson (2000). Both of these works offer subtle, thoughtful, and comprehensive interpretations of the relevant passages in the early dialogues, and I will be referring to and taking guidance from their arguments throughout the following chapters. However, I fundamentally disagree with both. In *Plato's Socrates*, Brickhouse and Smith offer a constructivist interpretation, arguing that Socratic elenchus is sufficient not only to expose the inconsistency of the interlocutors' own beliefs about virtue and, thus, of the lives they lead, but also that through many repetitions it gives one "good reason to think" that there are certain "moral propositions that everyone would be better off having" (1994, 21). The benefit of the elenchus resides ultimately in identifying and encouraging such beliefs, even if these fall short of the definitional and unerring moral wisdom that Socrates demands of himself and his interlocutors. In his *Socratic Wisdom*, Benson offers a non-constructivist account. His principle goal is to articulate the knowledge at which Socratic philosophizing aims, and he concludes that what would count as knowledge or wisdom for Socrates is ultimately "a power or capacity (*dunamis*) to make judgments resulting in an interrelated coherent system of true cognitive states involving a particular object or subject matter" (2000, 220). Benson's argument on the whole is compelling and well supported, and I don't disagree with his basic claim. However, as discussed later in chapter 4, I believe that the form of knowledge Benson has identified is not Socrates' own ideal, but a certain (somewhat anachronistic) formulation of what is implicit in the presumed moral expertise of Socrates' interlocutors. In asking his interlocutors for a technical and thus definitional knowledge of virtue, Socrates is holding them not to his own standard, but to theirs, a standard that, once they have articulated and agreed to it with Socrates, they themselves fail to meet. In any case, since this knowledge is virtually unattainable, Benson sees the supreme benefit of the Socratic elenchus as its exposure of blameworthy ignorance, which he claims merely clears the way for some positive inquiry into human virtue, one that it must be admitted is never portrayed in the early dialogues. For this reason, Benson's Socrates is "a genuinely skeptical philosopher" (2000, 187). As I will show, neither Brickhouse and Smith nor Benson register the real implications of Socrates' claim to have only a properly "human wisdom (ἀνθρωπίνη σοφία)" (*Ap.* 20d),

which is nothing but a knowledge that one does not know, and to bring others to this wisdom, and that "the greatest good for human beings" (*Ap.* 38a) lies in this and this alone. Thus, these works fail to do what the passages demand, which is to find in the very *aporia* that is occasioned and maintained by the elenchus a true, non-cognitive, and properly human relation to the being of virtue.

26. It might be noted that, although they are often criticized in the scholarly literature for what has been referred to as the "willful inaccuracy" and "dazzling mystification" of their unorthodox readings of Plato's Socrates, Hegel and Kierkegaard are at the very least both clear-headed enough to state explicitly the subject-object dualism they presume to find at work in the dialogues. See Hegel (1832–1845, 441–515) and Kierkegaard (1841, 169).
27. Shorey (1903, 27). Shorey also writes later on, "Plato, it must be remembered, does not say what the ideas are, but only that they are in some sense objective and real" (1903, 29). Of course, Plato's Socrates says no such thing anywhere in the dialogues. He couldn't do so, as there is no word or phrase in Greek that translates as 'objective.' As I am arguing, Socrates *is* interested in the *being* of virtue or 'what virtue *is*,' but this does not have the sense of an 'objective reality,' set over against and potentially disconnected from 'subjective mental contents.' Shorey cites the following phrases, untranslated, from the *Parmenides* as evidence: "thought of nothing (νόημα δὲ οὐδενός); . . . being or not being (ὄντος ἢ οὐκ ὄντος); Then won't an idea be that which is thought to be one, always being the same and throughout all (εἶτα οὐκ εἶδος ἔσται τοῦτο τὸ νοούμενον ἓν εἶναι, ἀεὶ ὂν τὸ αὐτὸ ἐπὶ πᾶσιν)" (*Prm.* 132b–c). Note that only terms for 'being' appear in the passage, *on* and *einai*, but nothing that translates as 'objectively real.'
28. Ackrill (1997, 136–37).
29. Irwin (1995b, 149).
30. Penner (1992, 138).
31. Roochnik (2004, 161).
32. Cf. Teloh (1981, 14) and White (1976, xiv and 14–15).
33. Robinson (1953, 57).
34. Robinson (1953, 59).
35. Robinson (1953, 58).
36. Allen (1970, 81–82).
37. Taylor (1926, 133).

38. Vlastos (1991, 58). We should note here, however, the limits of Vlastos's claim to be able to find an "ontology" in the thinking of Plato's early Socrates. Hyland makes the point when he writes the following of his approach to the essentially and emphatically finite thinking he finds Plato always presenting in the dialogues: "[A]nother consequence of the pervasive emphasis in the dialogues on context, on the literally de-fining character of the situation, is that it makes anything like 'systematization' of Plato's thought immensely more problematic than has been recognized by many scholars. Plato never has Socrates, or any other character, speak of his 'moral theory,' nor of his 'theory of forms,' his 'theory of knowledge,' or his 'metaphysics.' Only Platonic scholars speak of such things, and one reason they easily do so is that they ignore the pervasive presence of context, of situational finitude, that informs every specific discussion of ethical issues, of forms, of knowledge, or of Being, in the dialogues" (Hyland, 1995, 7).
39. In his introduction, Robinson (1953, 3) identifies precisely this interpretive pitfall in reading Plato's dialogues. It is the common error he refers to as "*insinuating the future.*"
40. In Nicholas White's *Plato on Knowledge and Reality*, we find some highly representative usage of the vocabulary of objectivity, but only in negative terms to describe what Plato's sophistic opponents deny. For instance, White (1976, 2) writes, "It is a commonplace, though a crucial one, that Plato's philosophical activity was directed toward finding something that could be taken to be certain and reliable knowledge, toward discovering judgments which could be in some manner counted on . . . the sort of view he particularly opposed can be constructed with such terms as 'relativism,' 'skepticism,' 'anti-objectivism,' and the like." And further on, White (1976, 4) mentions "the contemporary tendency to think (at least on occasion) that there is no settling disputes or disagreements and even to think that there are no 'objective' matters of fact which those disputes and disagreements concern." For White, Plato's Socrates, as an anti-'anti-objectivist,' must assume the possibility of objective knowledge of objective reality with regard to virtue.
41. We might still speak of a world outside the subject that has no persisting presence, leaving us with radical Cratylean flux. Or we might speak of something with persisting self-identical presence that exists as some mental content or some subjective element or measure, but not in the world, leaving us with a Berkeleyan idealism or perhaps with Kantian

transcendental idealism. In either case, we do not seem to be speaking about 'objective reality' as it is usually intended.
42. Scruton (1994, 98).
43. Descartes (1641, 19). It should perhaps be noted that, although we mention Descartes as the inaugurator of modern philosophy, we are not using 'objective reality' in the technical sense developed in his Third Meditation. For Descartes, 'objective reality' is what an idea possesses in itself, which seems to correspond to the necessity of its existing—for instance an idea that corresponds to a substance is more objectively real than those that correspond to its accidents or modes, specifically insofar as the latter cannot exist without the former (a distinction that resonates with Aristotle's distinction between *protē* and *deutera ousia* in the *Categories*). Ultimately, Descartes will argue that an idea can only have as much 'objectivity reality' as its cause has 'formal reality,' or reality *simpliciter*, thus making the absolutely necessary existence entailed by God's perfection an argument for God's actual existence. We are using 'objective reality' in the sense that it acquires after Descartes in the project that then dominates all of modern philosophy—mending the radical severance of the subject from its object—and thus more in the sense of Descartes' 'formal reality.'
44. Descartes (1641, 19–22).
45. Jowett (1892, 7). This is mentioned, but not cited, by Shorey (1903, 36). Evoking Kant, Shorey also emphasizes the Platonic Idea as *noumenon* in opposition to *phainomena*, and even introduces comparisons to the *Ding-an-Sich* (27–40).
46. Taylor (1932, 177).
47. Taylor (1932, 178).
48. Taylor (1926, 47).
49. Woodruff (1990, 76). Note that this is Woodruff's description of an interpretive position that is not his own.
50. Robinson (1953, 71).
51. Note that this would not correlate with the "bloß phänomenales Sein" that the Husserl of the *Ideas* attributes to "das Transzendent," and which he opposes to the "absolutes Sein" of "das Immanent." Here the objects posited by the natural attitude in its mode of perception are approached as transcendent (or beyond, external) with respect to consciousness and as only given indirectly via their *phenomena*, while the objects of nonthetic pure consciousness are immanent to consciousness itself and thus given absolutely and immediately. This distinction between modes of

givenness or evidence then determines the ontological distinction. For us, insofar as Socrates poses his 'What is "x"?' question and presumes to approach its referent via its appearances in initial everyday *doxai*, the being of human virtue at which he directs his and his interlocutors' gaze is *phenomenal being*, but not *merely* so. See especially section 44 of Husserl (1913, 80–83).

CHAPTER 2. ON *DOXA* AS THE APPEARING OF 'WHAT *IS*'

1. *Doxa* is also rendered into English as 'expectation, belief, fancy,' 'repute, reputation,' and 'glory.' However, in the translation of Plato's works, 'opinion' is the standard.
2. Lewis (1996, 567).
3. Lewis (1996, 569). Also see the entry for 'opinion' in Partridge (1958, 453–454).
4. Liddell and Scott et al. (1843, 441–442).
5. Liddell and Scott (1891, 177).
6. Otherwise fine translations often tend to wash out the second meaning, rendering phrases such as *dokei moi*, which literally means 'it appears to me,' as 'methinks, I think, or I suppose.' My claim is not that this is utterly wrong or inaccurate. Rather, I wish only to point out that this sense of *dokein* seems to indicate that the word *doxa* may have a very different meaning in the Greek mind than our term 'opinion,' and it seems potentially misleading to hide this difference.
7. Liddell and Scott (1891, 750).
8. Heidegger (1993, §7).
9. Indeed, Heidegger (1992, 597–601) identifies the discovery of intentionality by Franz Brentano and, more profoundly, by Husserl as a *recovery* of a Platonic, or more generally Greek, understanding of *logos*, 'discourse,' as always already pertaining to *to on*, 'being.' He does so clearly in his reading of the passage in the *Sophist*, where the Eleatic Stranger states that "It is necessary that *logos*, whenever it is, is *logos* of something (τινὸς εἶναι λόγον), and it is impossible that it not be of something" (*Sph.* 262e). Heidegger writes, "Die Geschichte der Philosophie, vor allem die der neueren und neuesten Logik, zeigt, daß man diese Einsicht, diese Trivialität, längst wieder vergessen oder nicht mehr Gebrauch von ihr gemacht hat. Man stellt sich die Zusammenhänge so vor: Es gibt Wortlaute, die im Psychischen vorkommen; an diese knüpfen sich auf

dem Wege von Assoziationen sog. Allgemeinvorstellungen; und all dies zusammen spielt sich im Bewußtsein ab. Dann stellt man die Frage, wie diese Assoziationen innerhalb des Bewußtseins objective Geltung haben können für die Dinge draußen. Das ist fast durchgängig noch die Position, auch bei den Besseren. Auch Cassirer z.B. ist grundsätzlich nicht über diese Position hinausgekommen. Man hat also nicht mehr Gebrauch gemacht von dieser Einsicht: λόγος ist λόγος τινός. Sie ist *erst wieder von Husserl entdeckt worden mit seinem Begriff der Inentionalität*" (598).

10. Already in Plato's *Charmides*, there seems to be a clear recognition of something like the intentionality of human experience and the sense that what human thinking is tasked to grasp or clarify is that which pre-epistemic human experience already intends. In this dialogue devoted to the question of *sōphrosunē* or 'sound-mindedness, temperance, self-control,' Critias eventually suggests in response to Socrates' interrogation that the essence of this aspect of human virtue or excellence must be self-knowledge (*Chrm.* 164c–165b). Surprisingly, Socrates and Critias then proceed to show self-knowledge, at least in the mode of an *epistēmē heautou* (*Chrm.* 165c) or *epistēmē heautēs* (*Chrm* 166e), 'knowledge of oneself' or 'knowledge of itself,' as well as any reflexive form of *technē*-like knowing (*Chrm.* 165e, 167a), to be both impossible and worthless. In questioning the possibility of any knowledge that would know itself, Socrates sets out three general classes of relation in which the possibility of their relating to themselves rather than their proper object seems absurd: sense-perception (*Chrm.* 167c–d), other modes of consciousness such as desiring, wishing, fearing, etc. (*Chrm* 167d–168a), and other non-conscious relations such as being greater than, double of, heavier than, etc. (*Chrm.* 168a–d). In the course of making this argument, Socrates seems to presume that, just as something that is greater than something else or the double of something else enjoys a necessary relation to what it is greater than or the double of, so does seeing enjoy a necessary relation to what is seen and fearing enjoys a necessary relation to what is feared. The objects of these conscious acts are entailed by the acts themselves. Knowledge seems to be essentially "some sort of power (δύναμιν) with the result that it is *of something* (ὥστε τινὸς εἶναι)" (*Chrm.* 168a, my emphasis). For a discussion of the *Charmides* where the issue of intentionality is introduced, although as it relates to Hegelian rather than Husserlian phenomenology, see the two articles by Rosen (1973) and (1974). For a discussion from an analytic perspective

of the importance of the vocabulary of *epistēmē heautou* and *epistēmē heautēs* in Socrates' discussion, see Tuckey (1968). In his monograph on the dialogue, Tuckey makes much of the transition from the *epistēmē heautou* or 'knowledge of oneself' to *epistēmē heautēs* or 'knowledge of itself.' Indeed, he views this as "the central problem of interpretation" (1968, 33) in the dialogue. I do not see it as such a crucial point, and I do not think it important whether Socrates introduces the shift or Critias does. What is crucial, as always in Plato's dialogues, is that Critias makes it his own by agreeing to it along the way. This is what is most important for Socrates, i.e., that things honestly appear to Critias in this way, so that in the end Critias himself (and Socrates along with him) must experience the sting of the elenchus, and thereby be exposed to 'what *sōphrosunē* is' *as it is* for the first time. Plato's text moves from *technē* to *epistēmē* freely, and it moves from *gignōskein* to *epistasthai* to *eidenai*, seemingly unconcerned with maintaining rigorous distinctions or a technical vocabulary (*Chrm.* 163d, but also *Prt.* 358a, *Ion* 532e). Thus, given that the language employed in this discussion is so fluid, always trying to capture what is appearing rather than imposing pre-determined and rigid distinctions, the text as a whole seems to point not to this or that formulation, but to the radically Socratic form of self-knowledge with which we are familiar from many other dialogues—awareness of one's own non-knowing.

11. Marion (1991, 72). Marion also writes in *Etant donné: Essai d'une phénoménologie de la donation*, "La donation appartient moins à la phénoménologie, que la phénoménologie ne relève tout entière de la donation. En effet, la donation n'offre pas seulement à la phénoménologie un concept parmi d'autres, ni même l'acte privilégié pour accéder à elle-méme, elle lui ouvre aussi tout le champ de la phénoménalité" (1997, 42).
12. Patocka (2002, 25).

CHAPTER 3. THE EXCESSIVE TRUTH OF SOCRATIC DISCOURSE

1. Even this term, *exetasis*, contains in its etymological recesses a reference to the ultimate aim of Socratic philosophizing—being properly related to 'what *is*.' The term is usually translated as 'searching out' or 'investigation, examination, testing' (*Ap.* 22e), which is no doubt correct. But rather than remaining at a merely epistemological register, as a striving for knowledge or certainty, this term implicitly extends to

the ontological. The noun derives from *ek-hetazein*, the prefix *ek-*, 'out, from,' being joined to a verb that is itself derived from the adjective *eteos*, which seems to be related to *einai*, meaning 'to be.' Thus, in the etymological depths of Socrates' term, we find a hint that his project is a testing out that explicitly aims to make contact with Being, not merely to arrive at correct judgment. The more we can remind ourselves that the terms Socrates uses have different resonances than our own, the less likely we are to impose a modern philosophical sensibility onto the Platonic text. This term and the dynamic to which it points become more central when we note that it is, in Socrates' famous phrase, the *anexetastos bios*, or 'the unexamined life,' that is not even worth living for a human (*Ap.* 38a).

2. Indeed, Plato has his Socrates predict precisely this necessity in the *Gorgias*, when Socrates remarks, "This is the sort of thing that I would suffer if I were brought to court. For I would not be able to speak of any pleasures I have provided [my jurors], ones they would acknowledge as good works and benefits (εὐεργεσίας καὶ ὠφελίας νομίζουσιν), though I envy neither the one who provides such nor the ones to whom they are provided. If someone says that I corrupt the young by bringing them to *aporia* (ἀπορεῖν ποιοῦντα) or that I defame the old by speaking bitter words against them in private and in public, I will not be able to say the truth (τὸ ἀληθές)—that 'I say all these things justly and do this in fact for you, gentlemen of the jury'—nor will I be able to say anything else. Thus, it is likely that I will suffer whatever happens" (*Grg.* 522a–b). It is important to note that Socrates predicts his inability not only to list benefits recognizable to the many, or to his jurors, but also his inability to "say the truth." That is, Socrates will be unable to say the truth, that his activities are in fact just and beneficial, because they are not *simply* so according to the way in which justice and benefit are understood by the many. Socratic questioning will appear "virtuous" and "good," or compelling, only from the immanent perspective of one who recognizes that he or she does not know what virtue and the good are.

3. Reeve (1989, 178). Brickhouse and Smith (1989, 39–47), and much earlier Grote (1865, 157–163), all see Socrates' defense as a straightforward proof of innocence. Only Gonzalez (2002b, 1), to my knowledge, has suggested something along the lines sketched here. He states that "the defense is *ironic* in the true sense of the word: neither literal nor deceptive, but ambivalent." This irony is akin to what I have referred to as Socrates' attempt to raise the question of philosophy.

4. That Socrates undertakes an elenctic defense is also indicated in the fact that he bemoans not having sufficient time for his defense (*Ap.* 24a, 37a–b), which is to say, enough time for extensive and perhaps repeated elenctic argument in order to immerse his jurors completely and solidly within the recognition that, just like Socrates and those others he questions, they do not know 'what human virtue *is*.' As is indicated by the recidivism of some of Socrates' interlocutors, such as Alcibiades, Critias, and Charmides, the position aimed at in Socratic philosophizing is extremely tenuous and cannot be secured—repeated and extensive elenctic conversation is preferable (*Grg.* 513c–d), but still no guarantee. See also the *Crito* on the impossibility of Socrates' defending himself, or persuading his detractors in any conventional sense (*Cri.* 49c–d, 51c). Mitchell Miller interprets these passages in the *Crito* in the following way: "At 51c the Laws put this very strongly: "one must obey the commands of one's city and country, or persuade it as to the nature of justice. . . . By his own account, however, for Socrates in particular to 'persuade [Athens] as to the nature of justice' is an impossibility and, so, not a genuine option" (1996, 130).

5. The Socratic critique of rhetoric in its traditional sense can also be seen as his attempt to ground a radically new kind of rhetoric. Socrates suggests as much in the *Apology* when he states that, if the rhetorical skill required to be "clever at speaking" means "saying true things," then he would agree that he is a "rhetorician" (*Ap.* 17b). We will return to this claim later in this chapter. Cf. *Phdr.* 259e–266d and the *Grg.* 517a, where Socrates explicitly refers to the non-flattering kind of persuasion he contrasts with traditional rhetoric as *alēthē rhētorikē*. Meyer (1962, 119) emphasizes this with respect to our text, writing that "Die *Apologie*, das Werk des Redners Sokrates, ist also auf Züge einer neuen Rhetorik hin zu untersuchen." See also de Romilly (1975, 25).

6. Cf. Hackforth (1933, 88), Brickhouse and Smith (1989, 87–90), McPherran (2002, 114–119) for interpretations that take the oracle story as central to Socrates' defense. Reeve (1989, 21–45, 62–73, 121–124) acknowledges that the story of the oracle is intended as serious, but argues that the grounds for Socrates' faith in his mission are ultimately not religious, but "prudential." West (1979, 118–124) does not deny the centrality of the oracle story, although he interprets it not as an earnest attempt at *apolegein*, but as merely ironic, which for him means no more than playful and boastful. It is, thus, in keeping with the general character of the defense as West sees it. Others who see the story of the

oracle as merely ironic or not serious, but therefore as departing from the otherwise earnest defense, are Burnet (1914, 107), Taylor (1926, 160), Kidd (1967, 482), and Versenyi (1982, 112). However, these arguments against taking the oracle story seriously are grounded in a misunderstanding of the role the divine plays for Socrates. They see this indication of Socratic "religion" as a contradiction to his character as "the sort of man who is persuaded by nothing other than the argument (λόγῳ) that appears best to [him] while reasoning" (*Cri.* 46b). Contrarily, I believe that the role the divine plays for Socrates is wholly consistent with his questioning and his rational elenctic form of argumentation, since the divine for Socrates is not a supreme and self-revealing being issuing unquestionable truths or commandments, but first and foremost an excess that only "saves" one insofar as its oracular utterances disrupt one's complacent faith in appearances by exposing the distance that separates Being from (but also joins Being to) its appearances to us humans.

7. W. K. C. Guthrie observes this excess as the very essence of the Greek experience of the divine. See Guthrie (1975, 10).

8. In "Religion grecque, religions antiques," while discussing how to interpret the evidence of Greek myths, Jean-Pierre Vernant (1979, 12–13) asks, "Un pantheon dispersé, une mythologie faite de pièces et de morceaux, si tel était le polythéisme des Grecs, comment ces homes, dont on célèbre l'exigente rigueur en matière de cohérence intellectuelle, ont-ils pu vivre religieusement dans une sorte de chaos?"

9. Speaking of the early migrations of the Greeks and the mythical mode in which they are recounted, Jacob Burckhardt (1898–1902, I.3) writes, "Denn dieses alles hat zunächst der Mythus dicht in seinen schimmernden Duft eingehüllt, in welchem er so viel Tellurisches und Kosmisches, so viele Religion und Poesie, so viele unbewußte Weltbetrachtung und aufsummiertes Erlebnis mit beherbergt. Die Bilder, welche aus diesem Ganzen aufstiegen, wurden als der fernen Vorzeit Enstprechende festhalten, doch sehr frei und zwanglos. Die stärksten Varianten und Widersprüche, unvermeidlich bei so verschiedenen Ursprung der Dinge, stören die Nation nicht. Dazu kömmt aber eine aushelfende freie Fiktion, namentlich in genealogische Dingen. Frühe wie späte Autoren, auch wenn sie Anspruch auf genaue Erzählung zu machen scheinen, sind und bleiben nicht nur Zöglinge des Mythus und schauen die Dinge mit mythischen Augen, sondern sie fingieren und ergänzen auf eine Art und Weise weiter, welche der ganzen neueren Welt völlig fremd ist."

10. Marcel Detienne traces the development of the notion of truth from

its origins through the archaic and into the classical period in ancient Greece in *Les maîtres de vérité dans la grèce achaïque*. Hesiod, as a poet, is one of these "masters," but the truth to which he can lay claim *qua* poet is, according to Detienne, vastly different from our modern conception of truth and never overcomes but incorporates, mediation and obscurity. Detienne also emphasizes the relationship between the poet's truth and, via the Muses, Memory or *Mnēmosunē*, then drawing a strong connection between *Alētheia* and *Lēthē*, to which we will return later in this chapter. He writes, "Fonctionnaire de la souveraineté ou louangeur de la noblesse guerrière, le poète est toujours un «Maître de Vérité». Sa «Vérité» est une «Vérité» assertorique: nul ne la conteste, nul ne la démontre. «Vérité» fondementalement différente de notre conception traditonelle, *Alétheia* n'est pas l'accord de la proposition et de son objet, pas davantage l'accord d'un jugement avec les autres jugements; elle ne s'oppose pas au «mensonge»; el n'y a pas le «vrai» en face du «faux». La seule opposition significative est celle d'*Alétheia* et de *Léthé*. A ce niveau de pensée, si le poète est véritablement inspiré, si son verbe se fonde sur un don de voyance, sa parole tend à s'identifier avec la «Vérité»" (Detienne, 1967, 27).

11. Kierkegaard (1841, XII.195).
12. Brisson (1998, 7). For a discussion of Socrates and myth in the *Phaedrus* that privileges the vocabulary of 'distance' over the more transcendent-seeming vocabulary of the 'beyond' or 'a space which is different,' see Kirkland (2004).
13. This adjective is a compound of *axios*, 'of like value, worth as much as, worthy of,' and *chreos*, 'want, need; needful matter, business, affair; debt, what is due, duty.' Thus, the god is not introduced so much as 'trustworthy' (Grube), or as an 'unimpeachable authority' (Tredennick), or even as 'a witness who is worthy of credit' (Jowett), but rather as a source that stands us at attention, a source to which we must give its due by attending to it seriously, but which might not speak in a definitively revealing or straightforwardly credible way.
14. In the *Cratylus*, Socrates offers the following comical, but nonetheless revealing, etymology for the name Hermes. Socrates declares here, "Well then, this 'Hermes' seems to be something that concerns the *logos*" (*Cra.* 407e), for the name Hermes derives, Socrates continues, from the phrase *eirein emēsato*, which entails that it was the god Hermes who, depending on the valence of the verb *mēdesthai*, either planned, counseled, plotted, schemed, or contrived the ability to speak for human beings. However,

this gift or this message from the gods, must be considered in the light of the messenger who brings it, Hermes, who Socrates describes as a thief, an *agorastikos* or a 'wheeler-dealer' and as one who is *apatēlos en logois* or 'wily in discourses' (408a). And indeed, as we know from the *Homeric Hymn to Hermes*, this god is the one who already as an infant stole the sacred cattle of Apollo (68–141) and, after being accused of the theft, spoke a false oath to Zeus proclaiming his innocence (368–386). This untrustworthiness or essential ambivalence is then reflected in Socrates' description of Hermes' gift, or the message he brings us, as analogous to the son of Hermes, Pan. That is, our human *logos* is, like Pan, *diphuē* or 'double natured.' Socrates says, "the *logos* signifies (σημαίνει) all things" (408c), but is itself *diplous* or 'double' insofar as it is both *alēthēs* or 'unconcealing' and *pseudēs* or 'obscuring.' The unconcealing aspect of the *logos* is "smooth and divine and dwells with the gods," while what is obscuring is "rough and goatish (τραγικόν)" (408c) and dwells among the many human beings. This is then related to what Socrates calls here the *tragikos bios* or 'tragic life' of the many, which is tragic specifically insofar as the many do not realize the double aspect of the *logos*. They do not experience as such the aspect of the *logos* that would open humans up to the excess of divine wisdom, but instead take the obscuring lower half alone as the sufficient and true whole of language. See my discussion of this etymology and its place in the *Cratylus* in Kirkland (2007b).
15. Detienne (1967, 75).
16. The very mechanics of oracular communication make the mediation and obscurity that characterize it unmistakable. Christiane Sourvinou-Inwood (1996) writes, of the workings of the Delphic oracle, "One possibility is that she [the Pythia] felt that she received partial signs transmitting fragmentary visions—*not* gibberish—and that the *prophētai* interpreted these, shaping them into coherent, if ambiguous, responses; this was not an attempt to hedge their bets, but a result of the ambiguity inherent in the god's signs and the Greek perception that ambiguity is the idiom of prophecy, that there are limits to man's access to knowledge about the future; the god speaks ambiguously, and human fallibility intervenes and may misinterpret the messages." Add to this the apparent fact that the ultimate pronouncements were poetic, delivered in dactylic hexameter (Fontenrose, 1978, 6), and the meaning of divine communication becomes emphatically withdrawn indeed. One note: Fontenrose (1978, 196–232) argues at great length against the aforementioned representation of the oracle's workings, the employment of

the lot-method at Delphi, and also against the essential ambiguity of the oracle's pronouncements. Against Fontenrose on these points, cf. the previous work of Parke and Wormell (1956, 17–45). Fontenrose draws a four-part distinction in order to support his claims, isolating what he calls the "historical responses" (1978, 7), those recorded by a writer contemporary with the pronouncement, from the many other later or more distant accounts, and finds only in the former trustworthy evidence for determining the actual wording of the oracle's responses. After doing so, he concludes that the oracle's wording was not necessarily ambiguous and that this attribution arises only in subsequent legend. Even if his argument were convincing, it does not complicate the point that I am making here, for my point is made equally well if oracular communication *was widely thought of* as essentially ambiguous as it is if its actual wording was ambiguous. My aim is simply to show a general conception of divine communication as non-transparent to mortals, which is indicated in what I am accepting as the mediation of the mantic ritual, but also in the many stories that directly characterize divine communication as profoundly obscure.

17. Cf. the discussion of this verb, *ainittesthai*, and its resonance in Bassett (1928).
18. There seem to have been two methods by which one could consult the Delphic oracle. One was quite expensive, the result of which was a written reply to the petitioner's question. The other was the likely original and relatively inexpensive method of the "two beans." In this, a white and a black bean or stone were placed in a basin atop a ceremonial tripod, from which the Pythia would draw out one or the other, indicating the answer to a yes or no question. See Fontenrose (1978, 219–224), Parke and Wormell (1956, I.18–19), Giebel (2001, 14). Given the notorious poverty of Chaerophon (*Cl.* 103–104) and evidence from the alternative report in Xenophon's *Apology*, Reeve (1989, 29) is surely right to conclude that Chaerophon employed the latter method. However, even given the simplicity of these responses, they remained open to interpretation, as is attested by Socrates' reaction, and suffered therefore from the same irremediable obscurity of divine communication.
19. At *Grg.* 523a, Socrates also thematizes the relationship between the terms *muthos* and *logos*, and there as well he holds them together in tension with one another. Socrates describes for Callicles the afterlife and the respective rewards of the just and unjust ways of life. He says at the outset, "Listen, as they say, to 'an exceedingly fine account (μάλα καλοῦ

λόγου),' which you will consider a tale (μῦθον), but which I consider an account (λόγον). For it is as true (ὡς ἀληθῆ) that I will tell you what I am about to tell you." And in the *Meno*, Socrates introduces the same ambivalence. He refers to his solution to the paradox of learning by way of *anamnēsis* or 'recollection' as a *logos* (*Men.* 86b), but he nevertheless states that it derives from priests and priestesses who "talk about divine matters" (*Men.* 81a) and from poets such as Pindar (*Men.* 81b–c). This peculiar, poetic, and divinized *logos* is also perhaps not entirely true (*Men.* 86b–c), but must be accepted in any case in order to encourage human beings not to abandon questioning and investigation, which will make them "better, more courageous, and less idle" (*Men.* 86b). Sallis (1975, 46–54) advocates something like this tension in his reading of Socrates' appeal to the divine in the *Apology*.

20. Some interpreters have seen in Socrates' interrogation of the oracle's meaning a certain impiety, while others have seen at least a failure to take the divine assessment of his wisdom seriously. For the former, see Burnet (1924, note at 21b), Ryle (1966, 177), West (1979, 106). For the latter, see Hackforth (1933, 94). For a sound rejection of these, see Reeve (1989, 21–28). I am here in agreement with Reeve, as should be clear from the foregoing discussion of oracular communication requiring interpretation and questioning.

21. I believe the brief but powerful opposition of standard rhetoric and Socrates' own way of discourse presented in the *Apology* contains already the more developed Platonic critique of rhetoric. See note 10 in the introduction for a discussion of the *Menexenus*, where Socrates explicitly links rhetoric's employment of ornamented discourse with the power to bring about self-forgetting (*Mx.* 234b–235c). Also, the entire *Gorgias* is devoted to the critique of rhetoric as an *empeiria* or a 'knack' for flattery, which does not strive to bring to light what is truly good (*Grg.* 462b–466a). This critique is then continued and expanded upon even later in the *Phaedrus* (*Phdr.* 259e–272c).

22. Note here that Socrates draws a quite explicit opposition between this verb for forgetting, *epilanthanesthai*, and the adjective *alēthes*, translated here as 'true.' We will return to this vital relation later in the chapter.

23. It might be argued that the opposition of self-forgetting and self-recollection that I have brought to the fore here is peculiar to this circumstance, where Socrates *himself* is the subject of discussion. It could be then concluded that this characterization should not be generalized to the opposition between rhetoric and Socratic philosophizing as such. I

would like to suggest that this is not the case, and that the opposition Socrates introduces here, although initially confined to this particular context, is intended to characterize a fundamental difference between rhetorical and Socratic discourse and, thus, to extend beyond its context. This will be become clear as we read the rest of the *prooimion*.

24. For a related contemporary discussion that wishes to take seriously the cognitive content of emotion, although in a way that does not align precisely with the phenomenological discussion of *pathos* above, see Nussbaum (2003).
25. Cf. Stallbaum's notes on *kekalliepēmenos* and *kekosmēmenos* in Smith's edition of the Greek text of the *Apology* (1863, 103).
26. The significance of this line is often lost in translation. See Grube's (1997b) translation ("from me you will hear . . . things spoken at random and expressed in the first words that come to mind"), which gives the unhappy impression of a Socrates promising to be a reckless babbler. Jowett (1874) ("I shall use the words and arguments which occur to me at the moment") and Tredennick (1954) ("what you will hear will be a straightforward speech in the first words that occur to me") both avoid the first mistake, but at the expense of literalism and by sacrificing the *eikē(i)* altogether. This word *can* mean 'randomly,' but it can also be taken in a privative sense as 'without plan or purpose.' In the *Charmides*, Socrates seems to use it in the former sense when he states that "It is necessary to look at what comes forward in appearing and not go along randomly (τό γε προφαινόμενον ἀναγκαῖον σκοπεῖν καὶ εἰκῇ παιέναι), if someone is the least bit troubled (κήδεται) about himself" (*Chrm.* 173a, see also *Prt.* 326d). Although his usage of *eikē(i)* here is different than what we find in our passage from the *Apology*, note the clear phenomenological vocabulary—Socrates states that it is necessary to establish oneself before the *prophainomenon* or 'what comes forward into appearance before us' and investigate this. In any case, none of the translators of the *Apology* seem to have considered how important the notion of an *external aim* or *purpose* is to the discussion in this context, even given Socrates' criticism of rhetoric discussed earlier.
27. The unorthodox, and ultimately unsuccessful, character of Socrates' defense strategy has led some readers to see Socrates as uninterested in being acquitted for one reason or another. This view was already held by Xenophon, who speculated that it was due to a kind of world-weariness that Socrates engaged in what Xenophon calls "talking big (μεγαληγορία)" (*XAp.* 1), i.e., his deliberately provoking the jurors with his assertions of

the supreme benefit of his philosophizing, not only for him but also for the citizens of Athens (*Ap.* 30a–b, 30e–31b, and esp. 36b–30b). It is also suggested by Epictetus (*Disc.* ii.2.18), and West (1979, 225, 227) seems to agree.

28. Stallbaum (1863, 103) comes close to this in his note on the Greek *tois epituchousin*. He suggests as a paraphrase, "with such words as offer themselves unsought."

29. Socrates makes use of an expression here that we find in Sophocles' *Oedipus Rex*, employed perhaps with something like this very ambivalence. After Tiresias has revealed that Oedipus is the murderer of Laius, Oedipus lashes out, accusing Tiresias and Chreon of plotting against him. It is clear that the *anagnōrisis* is already underway, Oedipus's desperate resistance to the truth itself being a sign of this. When Chreon comes before Oedipus to deny the charge, Oedipus remarks ironically, but already sensing the horrible truth, "You are terrific at speaking (λέγειν σὺ δεινός), but I am bad at learning from you" (*OT* 545–546). Oedipus seems, on the one hand, to be attributing to Chreon a rhetorical skill capable of false persuasion, but, on the other hand, to be indicating that Chreon's words might be pointing to something horrifyingly, unendurably true.

30. A full interpretation of Sophocles' ode would take us too far afield, but it might be noted that the ambivalence Socrates observes in the term *deinos* is precisely what was at stake in Sophocles' portrait of the human here. The extraordinary power and all-embracing mastery of human *technē* is catalogued in the first strophe and antistrophe, where everything from mountains to the sea, from the ox to the bird, has been overpowered by tireless human effort and technological understanding. In this mode, the world presents itself to us as *to be mastered*. However, it can do so only because bounded by a certain unremarked horizon, encircled and constituted by an excess that as such extends beyond our mastering grasp and also makes it possible. We confront that horizon or limit as our own death, Sophocles' chorus tells us (*Ant.* 441–445). However, this essential limitation or finitude does *not* merely stand at the end or the edge of human life. Rather, our basic relation to the world is shot through with finitude, such that "Possessing a machinating *technē*, something wise beyond all hope, [the human] moves sometimes toward the bad, other times toward the good" (*Ant.* 365–367). Thus, the immense power of human technological mastery is *both* wondrously good and horribly bad, insofar as it tends to lose sight of its own constitutive limitation, falling prey to *hubris* (*Ant.* 370–375).

31. Heidegger's translation of *deinos* accomplishes the same, but with a different German word. In his extensive commentary on the choral ode in *Einführung in die Metaphysik*, Heidegger translates the first lines as "Vielfältig das Unheimliche, nichts doch / über den Menschen hinaus Unheimlicheres ragend sich regt" (1953, 112). 'Unheimlich' often rendered into English as 'un-canny,' literally means 'un-homely.' It thus conveys very much the same sense of a dynamic disruption or an exceeding of the familiar, the everyday world in which we dwell for the most part. Heidegger writes, "Das Un-heimliche verstehen wir als jenes, das aus dem »Heimlichen«, d.h. Heimischen, Gewohnten, Geläufigen, Ungefährdeten herauswirft. Das Unheimische läßt uns nicht einheimisch sein. Darin liegt das Über-wältigende" (116–117). See also Heidegger's discussion of Antigone in his lecture course *Hölderlins Hymne "Der Ister"* (1984), along with William McNeill's fine discussion thereof in relation to Sophocles' play and Aristotle's *Poetics* (2006, 153–197, esp. 192–197).
32. Meyer (1962, 25). Thomas Meyer supports this claim with multiple examples of legal rhetoric in Lysias, Demosthenes, and Isocrates.
33. Ibid. (26). Although such a claim is uncommon in rhetorical or law-court discourse, it does seem to have a precedent in Homeric poetry. See Campbell (1992, 32–33) for a discussion of the phrase *pasan alētheian* or the 'whole truth,' the telling of which does not entail making an exhaustively correct statement of fact, but rather giving a fulsome and deep accounting of a given phenomenon or event. He specifically discusses Homer's use of the phrase in the *Iliad* and *Odyssey* (see specifically *Il.* 23.361 and the *Od.* 13.254).
34. Ibid. According to Meyer's formulation of the project of Socratic discourse in the defense speech, the Socratic proto-phenomenological project we set out in search of would seem to be a proto-hermeneutic project as well, but a hermeneutic that is, as Gadamer puts it in *Wahrheit und Methode*, preemptively "von den ontologischer Hemmungen des Objektivitätsbegriff der Wissenschaft einmal befreit" (1960, 250). That Socrates' proto-phenomenology would entail a certain notion of proto-hermeneutics is to be expected. The tradition of hermeneutics, encompassing both the theory and practice of interpretation, was radicalized in the same way Husserlian phenomenology was radicalized with the ontological turn taken in Heidegger's *Sein und Zeit*. For the earlier Heidegger, the phenomenological project goes hand in hand with the hermeneutic project, insofar as both address themselves no longer to objective reality, but to Being as it presents itself in immediate, pre-philosophical appearances to human beings. Thus, hermeneutic thinking is

no longer limited to the interpretation of texts, but is now expanded to describe the very way in which human Dasein exists in an understanding of its world, the *Sache* of interpretation as that which *is already presenting itself to us to be interpreted.* Since Socratic proto-phenomenology would no doubt be ontological in character, it would also be proto-hermeneutic in the Heideggerian sense of the term. See Heidegger (1927, 34–39).

35. In actuality, it should be said that Heidegger capitalized on and interpreted a long-standing tendency to find in *alētheia* this relation. In his essay, "*Alētheia* in Greek Thought until Aristotle," Wolenski writes, "*Alētheia* is the most important Greek counterpart of our 'truth'; *alēthēs* (true), *alēthōs* (truly) and *alēthein* (to speak the truth) are related words. However, the Greek 'truth-family' is much more comprehensive and consists of 14 words, among others (adjectives): *atrekēs, nemertēs, adolos, ortos, apseudos, etymos and etetymos*. It is characteristic that several words, including *alētheia* also, belonging to this variety begin with '*a*.' The most common interpretation of this lexical phenomenon is to consider '*a*' as a sign of *privativum*, that is, as a negative noun or adjective. This understanding of *aletheia* was proposed by Sextus Empiricus, Plutarch, Olympiodoros and the so-called *Lexicon Guidianum* in antiquity. In our times, it was recalled by Leo Myers in his influential *Handbuch der griechischen Etymologie* (1901) and popularized by Rudolf Bultmann: '*alētheia* etymologisch das Nicht(s)-verheimlichen bedeutet.' According to this interpretation, we should consider such words as complexes of the following structure: *a-letheia, a-trekes, a-dolos or a-pseudos*; *nemertes* can be understood in a similar way, because '*ne*' functions as '*a*', that is, as an indicator of a privative character. As far as the matter concerns *alētheia*, its etymology is derived as *a* + *lethe* + suffix" (2005, 345). See also Luther (1935, 12–13) and Bultmann (1933). And Campbell articulates the widespread opinion that the relation between *alētheia* and *lēthē* can be found in Homer, writing, "Given this use in Homer, it appears that Aletheia is a matter of being truthful and open in one person's dealings with another, so that what is said can be taken by hearers as reliable and trustworthy. That being so, the meaning discernible in its use coincides with the etymology of the word given by most scholars, both ancient and modern. The word is generally taken to be derived from a root meaning 'to escape notice, detection'. The same root, with much the same meaning, underlies the Latin *lateo*, 'am hidden', 'remain unnoticed', from which English derives 'latent'. The word *lethe* in Greek means 'forgetfulness'. How prominent the nuance of not forgetting is

taken to be in Aletheia is debatable. But from the evidence it does appear that in Homer the nuance of not hiding is strong. People speak the truth if they hide or conceal nothing from their hearers" (1992, 33).

36. Gaisford (1848, 62, 51). This reference is supplied in the entry for the adjective *alēthes*, defined as "*unconcealed*, so *true*, *real*, opp. *false*, *apparent*," in Liddell and Scott et al. (1843, 64).
37. Detienne (1967, 24).
38. Ibid. For Detienne's at least partly critical remarks on Heidegger's etymological speculations (concerning the term *polis*, however, not *alētheia*), see his preface to the American edition of *Les maîtres de vérité dans la grèce archaïque*. Indeed, Detienne's central point in the book is that, prior to Parmenides' philosophical innovation, the archaic understanding of truth does not require the overcoming of obscurity or distance in one's relation to the subject matter in question, but rather in a sense includes these. As Detienne says later, "il n'y a pas d' *Alētheia* sans relation complémentaire à *Léthé*" (1967, 51).
39. Heidegger (1940, 98–134).
40. Friedländer (1964, 221–229). For discussion of this conception of truth as unconcealment, see especially Heidegger (1943, 73–97) and (1954b).
41. Indeed, in order to avoid the paradox of investigation or learning in the *Meno* Socrates seems to articulate quite directly an understanding of truth as 'unforgetting.' Socrates summarizes, "One cannot seek to know anything, neither if one knows, for there is no need to seek it, nor if one does not know, for one would not know what to seek" (*Men.* 80e). In response to the paradox, Socrates suggests that coming to know proceeds fundamentally by way of *anamnēsis* or a 'being reminded of' that which one already knew. The subsequent elements in Socrates' account, such as prenatal experience "of beings (τῶν ὄντων)" (*Men.* 86b) and the soul's disembodied existence (*Men.* 85b–86c), are introduced as explicitly speculative in character. They are introduced not because they are necessarily correct, but because they are beneficial for human life in circumventing the skeptical malaise that the paradox produces (*Men.* 86b). In any case, Socrates' resolution to the paradox clearly capitalizes on a notion of truth as 'un-forgetting.' See also the further development of the theme of *anamnēsis* in relation to the Ideas in the argument for the soul's immortality at *Phd.* 72e–77a and in the discussion of *erōs* in Socrates' Palinode, esp. at *Phdr.* 250a–b.
42. This compels me to both agree and disagree with Günter Figal (1998, 130), when he writes of "was in der *Apologie* schon zu verstehen gegeben

wurde: Philosophie ist ein gedanklicher Überstieg zu jenem, was im Denken nicht sicher faßbar ist. Philosophie hat keinen letzten Grund, in den sie, sich selber begründend, zurückgehen kann. Sie erweist sich als abgründig, wenn man nach letzten Begründungen fragt, und darum muß sie, dort, wo es um ihre eigene Möglichkeit geht, auf ihre Weise rhetorisch sein: Ihr Logos muß als stärkster vertreten werden, und das geschieht am besten mit der Überzeugungskraft eines philosophischen Lebens." As will be clear, I give full-throated endorsement to Figal's observation of the *abgründig* or 'abyssal' character of Socratic philosophizing (and this is true of all philosophical thinking in its most essential moments, in my opinion). I also endorse the groundbreaking work of Pierre Hadot, to whom Figal must be gesturing, who lays out the profound difference between ancient philosophy on the one hand, which is first of all a "mode de vie" out of which an understanding of one's world and oneself arises, and modern philosophy on the other hand, which demands a prior systematic metaphysical conception of the world, on which an ethics or politics must be grounded. See Hadot (1995, esp. 17–20). However, I believe that, more than inspiring emulation, more than relying on the "Überzeugungskraft eines philosophischen Lebens," Socrates hopes rather to encourage philosophizing by troubling his interlocutors (and in this case his jurors) through his elenctic questioning and thereby to expose them to that very same Abgrund that Figal recognizes at the base of Socrates' own thinking.

43. Cf. Reeve (1989, 9).

CHAPTER 4. THE SHELTERING OF *TECHNĒ* VERSUS THE EXPOSURE OF HUMAN WISDOM

1. Socrates explicitly denies this eristic *philonikia* as his motivation in the *Gorgias* (see, e.g., *Grg.* 515b). And Socrates contrasts himself to those who put on eristic displays, saying that they are "desiring of victory (φιλονοῦντας) rather than searching out the thing lying before them in the *logos* (τὸ προκείμενον ἐν τῷ λόγῳ). . . . And what sort of person am I? One of those who are pleased in being refuted (τῶν . . . ἐλεγχθέντων) if I say something not true (μὴ ἀληθές), but pleased also to refute (ἐλεγξάντων) if someone else should say something not true (μὴ ἀληθές)" (*Grg.* 457d–458a). Socrates states here as well that his only aim in speaking is "to have our subject matter become clear (τὸ πρᾶγμα . . . καταφανὲς γενέσθαι)" (*Grg.* 458a).

2. Jill Gordon identifies just such a basic human longing, arguing that the dialogues (and in particular the *Phaedo*) portray philosophy as a radical means of coping with (not overcoming) the "human anxiety suffered when our epistemological limitations confront our desire to know and to live by knowledge" (1999, 144).
3. In these two passages from the *Charmides*, Socrates emphasizes that his entire philosophical activity, his searching and questioning of opinions, arises only *dia* or 'through, on account of' his own acknowledged non-knowing. This is a formulation that resonates perfectly with Aristotle's general assessment in the *Sophistici Elenchi*—"Socrates questioned but did not answer, for he did not assert that he knew (ὡμολόγει γὰρ οὐκ εἰδέναι)" (*SE* 183b6–8). Not only is it true that Socrates does not have knowledge with respect to what he investigates in his philosophical activity (human virtue), but importantly his investigations are *motivated or necessitated by and arise out of this non-knowing*. This formulation foreshadows the results of this chapter's discussion, for what Socrates says here seems to resist any account by which Socratic philosophizing would, despite disavowing a strong or certain form of knowledge, nonetheless succeed in arriving at a weaker or less certain form of knowledge or at a form of true opinion. If this were the case, could Socrates say that his whole philosophical project is "on account of my own non-knowing (διὰ τὸ μὴ αὐτὸς εἰδέναι)" (*Chrm.* 165c)? That is, rather than being necessitated by epistemic failure and its distress, would not Socratic philosophizing under this view be motivated more by its (even if modest) epistemic success? Would Socratic philosophizing not arise "on account of" the modest positive ethical knowledge Socrates (on this view) presumes to arrive at and possess? See Vlastos (1985), Reeve (1989, 37–52), Brickhouse and Smith (1994, 30–72), and Irwin (1995a, 17–30), for the most prominent examples of this view, to which the rest of the chapter will present an alternative.
4. Recall that, in Socrates' critique of rhetoric in the *Apology* we found reason to suspect that, since rhetorical discourse produces the self-forgetting of epistemic confidence, Socratic discourse might as such bring about a certain self-knowledge. There is an indication of precisely that here. Socratic self-knowledge would seem to entail knowing where one stands with respect to virtue—one is distant from it and not able to grasp it.
5. This is an atypical elenchus insofar as Callicles has become so frustrated and recalcitrant that Socrates himself must carry the *logos* to its logical conclusion, the refutation of Callicles' position. However, by securing the

explicit or implicit agreement of his interlocutor at each step, Socrates nevertheless ensures that this continues to proceed like a normal elenctic conversation, where it is the interlocutor's earnest *doxa* and, thereby, his way of life and himself that are being examined, refuted, and exposed.

6. To name just a few of the most influential recent scholars, Vlastos (1985, 35), Penner (1992, 139–147), Brickhouse and Smith (1994, 31–32), Irwin (1995a, 17–18), and Matthews (2009, 103–118) all use the term "Socratic ignorance."

7. Kierkegaard (1841, XIII.260). Kierkegaard's brilliant description of the Socratic endeavor goes on: "[H]e placed individuals under his dialectical vacuum pump, pumped away the atmospheric air they were accustomed to breathing, and left them standing there. For them, everything was now lost, except to the extent that they were able to breathe ethereal air. Socrates, however, had nothing more to do with them but hastened on to new ventures" (1841, XIII.260).

8. We might mention here the myth of postmortem judgment recounted at the end of the *Gorgias*, which suggests that, just like the body, the human soul persists after death and bears the traces of what kind of life the individual has led. What leaves the soul of an individual scarred and deformed is a life of injustice, luxury, arrogance, hubris, and incontinence in *praxis*. What Socrates emphasizes here, when he summarizes, is that such a life leaves "everything warped by falsity and imposture (ὑπο ψεύδους καὶ ἀλζοντείας) and nothing straight from being nurtured without truth (διὰ τὸ ἄνευ ἀληθείας τεθράφθαι)" (*Grg.* 525a). Here, it is not strictly speaking knowledge that the soul needs in order to be well-formed, but just some *truth* that leads to good *praxis*, and this could well be the *deinos* truth in relation to which one is maintained in the "examined life" of Socratic elenctic philosophizing.

9. For important articulations of this opinion, see Arnim (1914, 141–154), Gould (1955, 7), Guthrie (1975, 130), Brickhouse and Smith (1989, 92–93), Reeve (1989, 132–142), and Irwin (1995a, 68–70, 72–73).

10. Aristophanes' *Clouds*, as good satire must, deploys and then outrageously exaggerates what are already generally held opinions about Socrates. Performed some twenty-five years prior to his trial, the comedy depicts Socrates as operating the "Thinkery," a school the curriculum of which is comprised partly of ludicrous cosmological theories and partly of relativistic sophistic and rhetorical instruction (*Cl.* 95). As to the former, the flamboyant character of Socrates states that belief in the gods is old-fashioned and that Zeus has been "dethroned" by the Swirl or the

vortex-motion, a likeness of which has been erected at the school as a statuary monument to its new god (*Cl.* 378–383). The traditional deities have no more currency with Aristophanes' Socrates, for he worships a pantheon of "deities of his own coinage," including the Clouds for whom the play is named (*Cl.* 248–249). It is this perceived iconoclasm of natural science from which Socrates attempts to distance himself first. And as to the latter, Aristophanes' association of Socrates with the sophists is no less overt. The main character of the comedy, Strepsiades, a father driven into debt by his spendthrift son, enrolls in Socrates' Thinkery (and then commands his son to enroll when he proves too slow for the sophisticated instruction). Strepsiades does so in order to escape from debts he rightly owes, asking Socrates to teach him the *adikon logon* or 'unjust argument' (*Cl.* 112), that skill in reasoning and speaking whereby he will be able to persuade an audience to believe what is not true and win out over his justifiably nagging creditors. In comically attributing this kind of instruction to Socrates, Aristophanes gives voice to the general failure to distinguish him from the sophists.

11. Socrates' accusers are capitalizing on the widespread belief that natural philosophy was iconoclastic, a belief that was not entirely false. The Pre-Socratic thinkers certainly do seem to have engaged, after a fashion, in a radical redefinition of the terms *theos* and *theios*, 'divinity' and 'divine.' This seems to begin already with the very first philosopher, Thales. According to Aristotle, Thales saw "everything to be full of gods (πάντα πλήρη θεῶν εἶναι)" (*De An.* I.411a7). This seems related to Thale's belief that everything was somehow constituted by a perhaps infinite and all-determining *archē*, water, which would consequently have taken on a quasi-divine status (*Met.* I.983b20). Anaximander proposed the *apeiron* or 'unlimited' as his answer to the Ionian question of what single, unifying, and all-determining substance was at base responsible for the various phenomena with which the world presents us. Of this, Aristotle writes, "[T]here is no origin for it, but it appears to be the origin of other things and to encompass all things and direct all things . . . and this is the divine (τὸ θεῖον), for it is immortal and imperishable, as Anaximander and most of the natural scientists assert" (*Phys.* 203b6–16). Aristotle's accuracy might well be doubted when he is recounting the finer points of his predecessors' theories, but there is little reason for suspicion here. It is quite likely that Anaximander referred to the *apeiron* as *theion*, due to its absence of any temporal or ontological limitation or boundary (*peras*) and due to its all-encompassing and all-determining

character. To the other side of the Greek mainland, no less a redefinition of the divine had taken place. The all-ordering, ontological power they attributed to numbers led the Pythagoreans to grant them a quasi-divine status. Hippolytus reports, "Pythagoras showed the monad to be a god" (*Ref.* I.2.2). Thus, the abovementioned popular assumption that "those who investigate these things [natural phenomena] do not acknowledge the gods" (*Ap.* 18c) has some reason to it. Guthrie observes, concerning the Pre-Socratics, "In their attempts to satisfy this intellectual craving for knowledge, they by no means excluded the possibility of divine agency, but they reached a conception of it very different from the polytheism current in contemporary Greek society. They believed that the world arose out of a primal unity, and that this one substance was still the permanent base of all its being, though now appearing in different forms and manifestations. The changes were rendered possible by an everlasting motion of the primary stuff due, not to an external agent, but to its own essential animation. The distinction between a material and an efficient principle had not yet been felt, and the primary entity, since it lived forever and was the author of its own movement and change, and of all the ordered world of earth, sky and sea, was naturally thought to merit the epithet 'divine'" (Guthrie 1962, 4). And cf. Burkert (1985, 307), on the redefinition of the terms for divinity. It seems clear then that when Socrates is charged with not acknowledging the gods of the *polis*, but introducing "other new daimonic entities" (*Ap.* 24c), his accusers are banking on a long-standing confusion of Socrates with the natural scientists and the consequent presumption of irreligion.

12. It is Protagoras in particular who was associated with the ability "to make the weaker argument the stronger" and to teach this to others (*Rhet.*, 1402a23ff). This is exactly the power Socrates sees as essential to rhetoric, in opposition to which he placed his own way of discourse in his *prooimion* in the *Apology*. That is, this is the power to make one's subject matter appear however one desires it to appear before an audience, even when this entails the subject matter appearing as it is not. In the words of Aeschylus, in the right (or wrong) hands, *Peithō*, the goddess of persuasion, is "a charmer to whom nothing is ultimately denied (οὐδὲν ἄπαρνον τελέθει θέλκτορι Πειθοῖ)" (*Suppl.* 1039–1040). Given that life for a citizen of Athens was always political life, implying participation in public and private discussions concerning the affairs of the city, rhetorical skill was an essential component of the fifth-century understanding of human *aretē*. In its full sense, to be an excellent human being was to

possess the ability to manage *both* one's own *and* the city's affairs, and managing the city's affairs required rhetorical skill in order to persuade the assembly to vote in accordance with one's recommendations.

This consonance of rhetoric and virtue in sophistic instruction is the subject of Plato's *Protagoras* (and the *Gorgias* as well). Before Socrates takes the young Hippocrates to meet with the renowned sophist, Socrates asks Hippocrates if he has any idea what a sophist would promise to teach him. Hippocrates responds that a sophist is "an expert in making one clever at speaking (δεινὸν λέγειν)" (*Prt.* 312d), the expression Socrates radicalizes in the *Apology*, as we saw in the last chapter (*Ap.* 17b). When they meet Protagoras, Socrates asks the great man what his students learn from him. Protagoras responds, eventually, "What is learned is good deliberation (εὐβουλία) concerning one's household affairs, how one might best manage one's household, and concerning the affairs of the *polis*, how one might be most powerful in action and speech concerning these" (*Prt.* 318e–319a). Protagoras claims here to teach a single thoughtful comportment, good deliberation, the possession of which will make one excellent and successful personally and politically. Rhetoric would be a direct expression of this comportment. Indeed, private and political excellence were so unified that Socrates can summarize, "You seem to me to be speaking of the political skill (τὴν πολιτικὴν τέχνην), and to promise to make men good citizens" (*Prt.* 319a), to which Protagoras enthusiastically agrees. The point of all this is simply that the sophists' instruction in making the weaker argument the stronger, of which Socrates has long been suspected by the many, was an essential element in their instruction of human virtue.

And the notion of virtue associated with the instruction of such a rhetorical power was grounded by a radical relativism of value, which itself was often grounded in an ontological relativism. This is clear in the famous opening line from Protagoras' treatise, *Alētheia*: "Of all things the human being is the measure, of those that are, how they are, of those that are not, how they are not" (Diogenes Laertius, *Lives* 9.51, cf. also *Tht.* 161c and Sextus Empiricus, *Adv. Math.* 7.60). Accordingly, convincing an audience of the weaker argument over the stronger was not at all to persuade them toward an *untruth* and, thus, to commit an injustice, for that would imply a measure independent of human perception and thought. Given this, there is no possibility of appealing to 'what is' beyond its appearance to the perceiver or perceivers, which theoretically removes any obstacles that stand in the way of using the powerful tool of rhetoric for whatever purpose one desires. The virtue of a human is his or her power to bring about a change in appearances, which is indistinguishable from a change in 'what *is*,' in such a way that is advantageous for him or her. In the *Theaetetus*, Socrates, in the name of Protagoras, generously defends Protagorean relativism against the charge that it leaves no criterion for judging one opinion to be better than another (*Tht.* 165e–168c).

Finally, although Protagoras provides the paradigm, this position was not at all limited to him. As Guthrie writes, despite the fact that the sophists in no way formed a school and were indeed characterized by complex and fundamental differences, there was "one art which all the Sophists taught, namely rhetoric, and one epistemological standpoint which all shared, namely a skepticism according to which knowledge could only be relative to the perceiving subject" (1971a, 50). All sophists, as teachers of rhetoric, are thus teachers of human excellence, insofar as rhetoric is a means to living well, to being excellent as a human being, which would initially mean nothing other than acquiring wealth, honor, power, and having the ability to meet all of one's needs and satisfy one's desires. Indeed, every sophist but Gorgias would have admitted openly to being, as primarily a teacher of rhetoric, also a teacher of human excellence or virtue. And Gorgias's expressed limitation of what he teaches seems to be merely strategic. It is an attempt to avoid responsibility for the expertise of virtue, a position that Plato depicts him as being ultimately shamed into abandoning by Socrates' questioning (*Grg.* 460a ff.). Furthermore, his student Meno summarizes the position he has presumably arrived at under Gorgias's instruction, saying that the single unifying human virtue or excellence is the power "to rule over human beings" (*Men.* 73c), which is precisely what the sophist himself even at the outset of the *Gorgias* claims to impart to his students (*Grg.* 452d).

13. This is surely the concern to which Protagoras's diplomatic presentation of the sophist's claim to superiority answers. In the dialogue named for him, even as he seeks to acknowledge that all citizens everywhere have a share in "the political art," Protagoras wishes to suggest that sophists are those who have refined and crystallized this general civic possession (*Prt.* 319a–328d).

14. See Gordon's illuminating refinement of Vlastos's "complex irony" (1999, 117–133), as well as her notion of "dramatic incongruity" (1999, 15), from which my discussion here benefited considerably.

15. Callias was well known for hosting sophists. For instance, Xenophon's

Symposium takes place at Callias's home (*XSmp.* 1–4) and, in the spurious *Axiochus*, the sophist Prodicus is said to have performed an *epideixis* or 'demonstration' there as well (*Ax.* 366c). Callias is also the host of the grand meeting of the sophists depicted in Plato's *Protagoras*. There, when Socrates becomes fed up with Protagoras's grandstanding, Callias is depicted imploring Socrates to stay, saying he would like nothing better than to hear Protagoras and Socrates "in discussion (διαλεγομένων)" with one another. Socrates responds that he has always admired Callias's "love of wisdom (τὴν φιλοσοφίαν)" (*Prt.* 335d–e), but this praise is clearly ironic, as this love expresses itself only insofar as Callias patronizes the sophists. Callias also comes up in the *Theaetetus*. There, when Socrates attempts to coerce Theodorus into defending Protagoras by painting Theodorus as a follower, Theodorus responds that it is not he, but Callias who can properly be called the guardian of Protagoras's thought (*Tht.* 165a). Finally, see the *Cratylus*, where Socrates makes reference to Callias's reputation for wisdom, saying that he purchased it from the sophists for a fortune (*Cra.* 391b–c). It seems that the association between Callias and the sophists would have been a strong one in the Athenian mind.

We might also note that, in his brief appearance in the *Protagoras*, Callias does more than implore Socrates to stay. He twice states frankly that he will not allow Socrates to leave (*Prt.* 335d, 338b), perhaps indicating a tendency toward willful self-assertion and a lack of *sōphrosunē*. These passages might be compared to the ominous final scene of the *Charmides*, where the later tyranny of Critias and Charmides seems to be foreshadowed by their readiness to use force in compelling Socrates to do their will (*Chrm.* 176c–d).

16. Nails (2002, 68).
17. Having first identified this questionable character as the spokesperson for the sophistic *technē* of virtue, Socrates' aside, "he has two sons" (*Ap.* 20a), seems calculated to recall a recent trial and scandal involving Callias and thereby to cast an even less positive light on his ethical education. Around a year before Socrates' trial, it seems that Callias himself had brought a man, Andocides, before the court on a charge of impiety. This charge was widely recognized as bogus, purely an attempt to distract Andocides from a dispute between the two men over an inheritance issue. In addition to associating Callias with his own accusers and vice versa, Socrates makes a point of introducing Callias's extremely unorthodox familial situation. By Andocides' account, which although strategic

is also corroborated by other material, Callias had married his second wife and then took her mother, Chrysilla, on as his mistress. He had a son with his wife and an illegitimate son with his mother-in-law, whom he later married after his second wife's death. During the inheritance dispute with Andocides, Callias was forced to recognize his bastard son in order to place him in position to inherit some wealth that Callias, having burned through the considerable sum he himself had inherited from his parents, would administer until the boy came of age. Thus, Socrates' remark, "he has two sons," is by no means innocent, but brings with it an air of immorality and intrigue that should attach itself to the sophists by way of their star pupil. See Nails's entry for Callias III (2002, 68–74).

18. See *Smp.* 216b–c, for Alcibiades' characterization of Socrates in opposition to the many, a characterization that the latter endorses by his silence.
19. Gonzalez (1998, 19–61) interprets both the *Laches* and the *Charmides* as situating Socrates between the sophisticated, formalized pseudo-knowledge of Nicias and Critias (on the one hand) and the simple, unreflective everyday opinions of Laches and Charmides (on the other hand). For Gonzalez, Socratic philosophizing reveals the unsatisfactory character of both of these modes.
20. *Contra*, e.g., Irwin (1977, 7), who claims that the Socrates of Plato's early dialogues "argues that virtue is simply craft-knowledge." Socrates never argues *for* any position "simply," but attempts to secure the agreement of his interlocutors in ways that do not necessarily express his own views, if indeed he has any he would be willing to defend on any important subject (i.e., anything relevant to human virtue). In Irwin's later work, although he suggests that more interpretive effort is required on this issue than he had earlier indicated, he puts forward the same basic thesis (1995a, 68–70).
21. Guthrie (1950a, 183–204). See also Parke and Wormell (1956, I.178–392) and Giebel (2001, 48–49).
22. There is a distinction in meaning between the differently accented adverbs ἀτεχνῶς and ἀτέχνως. The former is derived from the adjective ἀτεχνής and usually means something like 'simply, literally, truly,' while the latter, derived from ἄτεχνος, means 'without *technē*.' Although the former is what we have in our text, reflecting our editor's informed decision, we should first realize that these texts were meant to be read aloud and, although a distinction in accentuation could have been heard, it would have been less distinct even than in the written text, and in any

case this would by no means eliminate the other association. Indeed, David Roochnik, in his fine book on Plato's understanding of *technē*, devotes an appendix to the study of the seventy-five appearances (in Burnet's Plato) of ἀτεχνῶς, and he shows quite convincingly that Plato is often "punning" on its relation to *technē* and using the term ambiguously. That is precisely what we find in our passage from the *Euthydemus*, I believe, and I have translated it accordingly. See Roochnik (1999, 265–270), as well as the four occurrences of the adverb that Roochnik discusses in the *Apology* (*Ap.* 17d, 18d, 30e, 35d).
23. We address the interchangeability of these terms later in this chapter.
24. See Kirkland (2007) on the etymology of the 'Hermes' in Plato's *Cratylus* (*Cra.* 407e–408d), and for a discussion of this figure and the essentially problematic character of divine communication with mortals.
25. *Contra* Benson (2000, 180–185), who states concerning the disavowal of *technē* in the *Apology*, "I doubt that Socrates believes that the knowledge he professes not to have is beyond human reach" (180). This is perplexing, but Benson seems compelled to argue this in order to conclude that the radically skeptical project he sees as Socratic elenchus might serve in making progress toward the attainable ideal of a *technē*-like grasp of virtue. We are arguing here for an altogether different interpretation of the elenchus's benefit.
26. The vocabulary of *thaumazein* or 'wondering' is also employed at the end of the *Euthydemus* to invoke the specter of hubris. However, it is there tempered by Socrates' now qualified ironic praise. Here Socrates repeats his earlier assessment, saying that the *sophia* of these two men is "of a wondrous nature (τῆς θαυμαστῆς φύσεως)" (*Euthd.* 303c), particularly in that it is so "skillfully (τεχνικῶς)" contrived that it is masterable by anyone very quickly (*Euthd.* 303e). Socrates makes clear here that his praise for the men is contingent upon the fact that he sees their practice as entailing the elenctic refutation not only of their interlocutors, but of Euthydemus and Dionysodorus themselves, thereby rendering their eristic activity not (as it surely seems) hostile to others, but rather "wholly charming and the offense of their *logoi* is removed" (*Euthd.* 303e). Surely, if they understood the praise, the two eristic practitioners would not accept it, in that it strips them of wisdom as it is traditionally understood and grants them only Socratic human wisdom.
27. If Socratic human wisdom, as what is provoked and sustained by Socratic elenctic discussion, is indeed a wisdom that operates within this basic condition of insufficiency, then this points us toward a certain

interpretation of the *aporia*, literally the 'waylessness, being without means,' with which all the discussions of human virtue in the early dialogues end. We will turn to the phenomenon of *aporia* in the next chapter.

28. Pokorny (1959–1969, II.1058). In his etymological dictionary, Partridge states that the relations between these Greek and Latin terms and the semantic core of 'building, weaving' "can hardly be doubted." He also adds to the evidence for this original meaning the Sanskrit *táksan*, 'carpenter, builder,' and the Hitite *takkss-*, 'to join, build.' See Partridge (1958, 697–699).

29. Aeschylus's *Prometheus Bound* gestures to this original meaning of *technē*. When Prometheus recounts how he came to be punished, he presents a list of what he explicitly refers to as the various *technai* he bestowed on humankind—"All the arts (τέχναι) that belong to mortals are from Prometheus" (*Prom.* 506). Prometheus finds human beings, not just suffering, but without anything like a world—"Their eyes first saw in vain, their ears did not hear. But like figures in dreams, they bore their long life, all things without purpose" (*Prom.* 447–450). In this condition, the first *technai* that Prometheus finds humans lacking, and presumably the first that his gifts provided, were that of building "brick-woven houses (πλινθυφεῖς δόμους)" and "woodworking (ξυλουργίαν)" (*Prom.* 450–451).

30. Kube (1969, 9–40, esp. 28–29). Jorg Kube also argues that Plato's eventual association of *technē* with *aretē* was grounded in a general association of virtue with a kind of understanding (1969, 40–47). I certainly do not disagree with Kube's broader claim, although I will put forward a different interpretation of Socrates' employment of the *technē*-model of virtue.

31. Kube (1969, 17).

32. Nussbaum (1986, 94).

33. Ibid. (89).

34. In her reading of Plato's *Protagoras*, Martha Nussbaum's Socrates is after just such an ethical *technē*. By contrast, for us he is a late inhabitant of what Nussbaum would see as the tragic world, with its insistence on the irremediable human condition of exposure.

35. Employing terminology similar to that of Nussbaum, Gonzales emphasizes precisely this aspect of *technē* in his summary statement. He writes, "It is indeed the very purpose of *technē* to predict, to give one some control over what is going to happen. This kind of knowledge is therefore

the best armor against danger. By eliminating contingency as much as possible, it reduces vulnerability" (1998, 30).
36. For a discussion of the general Pre-Platonic conception of *technē*, which is consistent with but much more developed than the interpretation offered here, see Roochnik (1999, 17–88).
37. See also Aristotle's definition of *technē* in book six of the *Nicomachean Ethics* (*EN* 1140a1–24). Although *technē* is strongly associated here with making or production, as Heidegger (1992, 82) has emphasized, it is still understood as a state of the soul "in which the soul grasps the truth" (*EN* 1139b16), that is, as a mode of knowing or revealing the world.
38. The term τὰ δοκοῦντα is routinely translated in this passage as 'the things believed,' and then combined with πᾶσιν et al. as though these are to be understood as the agents of this participial form of δοκεῖν. However, the dative of personal agent appears only with passive verbs in the perfect or pluperfect tenses, while δοκοῦντα is a present active participle. Thus, the dative of πᾶσιν etc. must be taken not to indicate the subject of the verb, but as its indirect object—"the things that appear TO all," etc. For a discussion of this passage and its significance for understanding Aristotelian philosophical method as proto-phenomenological, see Kirkland (2009).
39. Nussbaum (1986, 95–96) lists four features of the fifth- and fourth-century understanding of *technē*: 1) universality, 2) teachability, 3) precision, and 4) concern with explanation. Reeve (1989, 39–45) argues that both Socrates and his contemporaries understood *technē* as 1) explanatory, 2) teachable, and 3) luck-independent, then adding later 4) certain or infallible, and finally (for Socrates), 5) elenchus-proof. The intimate connection between explanation and teaching seems to me self-evident, so I group these together. The certainty or infallibility, universality, and precision that are included in these lists seem to me to be grounded in the immediate grasp of 'what "x" is,' a usually implicit understanding that is made explicit by Plato's Socrates and Aristotle. In this, the technician would grasp what belongs to all x's, making his or her knowledge universal, would do so in a way that overcomes mediation or distance, and thus obscurity, in his or her relation to the being of x, that knowledge therefore being certain or infallible and precise. I emphasize the immediacy of the grasp because I believe it does better justice to the description of *technē* we find in Aristotle and in the early dialogues, and it does so precisely because it operates within phenomenality. That is, *technē*'s superiority arises not from its securing a relation to an objective

universal, but because it grasps directly that to which we relate only indirectly and at a distance via its obscure or indirect initial appearances (*doxai, phenomena*) to us.

40. In the Hippocratic treatise *Peri Technēs*, attempting to argue for medicine's status as a *technē*, knowledge of the *aitia* or 'causes' is presented as necessary for providing proper medical care (*PT* 11), and the very same point is made in *On Ancient Medicine* (*OAM* 23). Moreover, the latter text argues that a certain depth and sophistication of causal explanation is requisite for the possession of any *technē* (*OAM* 23).

41. With Aristotle, *epistēmē* becomes technically defined as that mode in which we know things that cannot be otherwise, arrived at through *apodeixis* or 'demonstration' by arguing from manifest, indemonstrable 'first principles' or *archai*. However, because *technē* as such is directed by an immediate grasp of the *eidos*, which is necessary with respect to the thing in question (the *eidos* of 'health' cannot be something else and still be health), Aristotle will sometimes refer to the understanding *technē* has as *epistēmē*. See *Met.* I.981a5–12.

42. See Schaerer (1930). In his study, *Epistēmē et Technē*, René Schaerer undertakes a broad study of these terms from Homer to Plato. He argues that during this period these two terms refer to the identical understanding condition in the soul, although *technē* additionally considers the practical application of that understanding. He writes, "les Grecs appellent ἐπιστήμη la connaissance claire et assurée d'un objet et τεχνή *cette connaissance* conçue dans ses possibilités de réalisation pratique" (1930, 189, emphasis mine). Schaerer also determines that both terms can refer either to the subject matter known or to the condition of the knower's soul, and he observes that *epistēmē* in its usage leans more toward the latter than does *technē*. Nonetheless, the knowing condition for which these two terms are used seems the same, at least up to Aristotle's systematic distinctions (see *EN* 1139b15–1140a24, also 1112b1–9).

43. See Lyons (1963) for a discussion of Plato's usage of *epistēmē, technē*, and *gnōsis*, and their related verbs. Indeed, Lyons observes that *technē* is often combined with the verb *epistasthai*, 'to know, understand,' as we saw earlier in the *Apology* (*Ap.* 20c). Ultimately, Lyons argues that *epistēmē* is slightly broader in meaning than *technē*, insofar as it can function to mean 'familiarity with someone or interpersonal knowing,' as can *gnōsis*, but *technē* cannot. In any case, for all intents and purposes, *technē* means no more than *epistēmē* for Plato and, it seems, for all Greek writers before him as well.

44. Knowing that Oedipus, that limit case in human suffering, counts himself the "son of *tuchē*" (*OT* 1080), it is easy to imagine that freedom from chance or luck would seem to the Greek mind a powerfully compelling notion. It is, nonetheless, emphatically not the promise of Socrates' philosophizing—that promise is a more abidingly tragic one.
45. Socrates' entire argument in the *Protagoras* hinges on the claim that if virtue is a form of *technē* or *epistēmē*, then it is teachable, whereas if it is not teachable, then it surely cannot qualify as such (see especially *Prt.* 361b).
46. See also *MM* 1198a10–11, as well as Aristotle's rejection of the claim that "courage is knowledge (ἐπιστήμην εἶναι τὴν ἀνδρείαν)," an extremely paradoxical aspect of what he sees as Socrates' equation of virtue with *technē* or *epistēmē* (*EN* 1116b4–5, also *MM* 1190b28).
47. See Kirkland (2009), on the tragic mediation and distance that characterize even fully virtuous individual's relation to the Good in Aristotelian ethics.
48. This is the point that Nussbaum fails to notice, in her otherwise subtle reading of the *Protagoras* (1986, 89–121). I agree wholly with her persuasive critique of Irwin (1977), specifically of his insistence on reading *technē* as narrowly referring only to arts or crafts that generate some product other than themselves, and I agree with her consequently broader understanding of what *technē* here denotes. I also find extremely illuminating her opposition throughout the book of *technē* and *tuchē*, as a defining tension in Greek experience and thought, as indicated previously. However, Plato does not here, *pace* Nussbaum (1986, 94), pit the sophistic *technē* of Protagoras against the Socratic *technē* of philosophy, as these two vie for the souls of Athenian citizens. Rather, Socrates proposes a way of life of perpetual inquiry, which, as will be shown, would order human souls and human lives for the better (*Ap.* 30a), but not by way of a *technē* of "human and political virtue" (*Ap.* 20a–21a). Indeed, as we shall see, Socrates does advocate the employment of a measure, but this measure is itself excessive and essentially distant, not the *ousia* grasped immediately by *technē*. Nussbaum might argue that I rely too much on the *Apology* in my presentation of Socratic philosophizing as non-craft-like (she cites it only twice in her book), thereby relegating my interpretation to a speculation on the nature of philosophizing for the historical Socrates. I can respond that what I derive from the *Apology* is wholly consistent with the other early dialogues, insofar as Socrates there as well denies having or teaching any *technē* of human

virtue, but nonetheless considers his life of philosophical inquiry (and especially the condition of non-knowing that it provokes) of supreme benefit for human beings. I would also note that the characterization of Socratic philosophical method that emerges here from the *Apology* is far more consistent with that of other early dialogues than the one on which Nussbaum focuses in the *Protagoras*, with its highly atypical emphasis on the saving power of a *technē* for quantifiably measuring pleasure.

49. Once again, scholars who put forth a more or less explicit version of this claim include Goldschmidt (1947, 74–75), Guthrie (1975, 132), Vlastos (1983b) and (1985), Reeve (1989, 37–53), Penner (1992), and Brickhouse and Smith (1994, 3–72).
50. Benson (2000, 170). On this tendency, Benson cites Vlastos (1994, 61–63) and Irwin (1986, 408) and (1992, 248).
51. Ibid. (169).
52. Ibid. (168).
53. Although he does observe at one point a regrettable scholarly tendency to apply improper and anachronistic epistemological models to Socrates' project, Benson's sensitivity on this issue does not extend to this particular presupposition. See esp. Benson (2000, 189–190). Benson notices that "many of Socrates' epistemological commitments are unlike the commitments of contemporary epistemologists," and therefore that "we need to be careful about foisting a contemporary justified true belief conception of knowledge back upon Socrates." However, when Benson lists three *non-anachronistic* conceptions of knowledge that others have suggested, aspects of which he himself will incorporate, he lists Woodruff's (1990) and Reeve's (1989) emphasis on a craft-like form of knowledge, Nehamas's (1985) and Brickhouse and Smith's (1994) insistence on understanding (rather than knowledge of facts or information), and Vlastos's (1983b) suggestion that Socrates is after "Cartesian indubitable certainty" (Benson, 190). How the identification of *Cartesian* certainty with Socrates' philosophical aim would qualify as non-anachronistic is beyond this reader.
54. Benson (2000, 190).
55. Ibid. (210, emphasis mine).
56. Kraut (1984, 247).
57. Callias provides a notorious example of a sophistic pupil, as we have seen (*Ap*. 19d–20c). Protagoras and Hippias were two of the most esteemed (and reviled) educators of their day, and we find Socrates in conversation with them in the dialogues that bear their names. Dionysodorus and

Euthydemus display their eristic rhetorical skills in the *Euthydemus*, and we find Socrates discussing the supposed *technē* of rhetoric with Gorgias and his pupils, Polus and Callicles, in the dialogue named for the former. In the *Euthyphro*, the eponymous character proclaims himself to know divine things with precision (*Euthphr.* 4e–5d), and Ion the rhapsode, in reciting wise Homer, lays claim under Socratic compulsion to having mastery of many subjects (*Ion* 536d–537a). Finally, Critias and Nicias, in the *Charmides* and *Laches*, respectively, prove to possess studied perspectives on temperance and courage. And Socrates' unsophisticated interlocutors are numerous as well. Often Socrates undertakes the task of finding a teacher for certain young men, as with the Hippocrates who wakes Socrates in childlike excitation over the sophist's visit in the *Protagoras*, the Clinias whom Socrates hopes the eristic experts will exhort to love wisdom in the *Euthydemus*, and the all-but silent sons of Lysimachus and Melesias (except for *La.* 181a) whom Socrates agrees to advise on the boys' education in the *Laches*. Charmides, Lysis, and Menexenes are also young men looking for guidance, as is the youthful Alcibiades in the dialogue named for him. Finally, even Laches and Crito, although both older, seem to strike a rather naïve and commonsensical, if decent, pose in their respective dialogues. Meno represents a curious combination, for he comes to Socrates wanting to be instructed (*Men.* 70a) and proves rather susceptible to *aporia* (contrast the resiliently confident Euthyphro in this), but he has a head full of sophistic, specifically Gorgian, teachings (esp. *Men.* 71c–d).

58. Cf. *Alc. I* 109d–112d, for Socrates' related argument that Alcibiades did not arrive at his understanding of justice from some sophistic educator, but had it from early childhood.
59. We witness this expectation throughout the early dialogues, but two important examples are the following. When he is forced to come to Gorgias's defense, his student Polus admits that "some inconsistency crept into his [Gorgias's] statements" in his attempt to explain his understanding of 'what is just, fine and good,' or when forced to make good on his claim to possess a *technē* of human virtue. But Polus protests that Socrates' questioning was unfair insofar as it took advantage of a universal and undeniable assumption in order to apply pressure, "for who is there who would deny that he himself knows what things are just and that he teaches these to others?" (*Grg.* 461c). That is, Polus thinks it unfair of Socrates to push Gorgias into answering whether or not his students learn 'what is just, fine and good' from him, because of a universal

expectation that everyone knows what these things are and can instruct others. This is an expectation that *no one* would openly admit to disappointing . . . except Socrates.

And in the spectacular display that Plato places in the mouth of Protagoras in the dialogue named for him, the great sophist observes precisely this fact about the everyday presumption of virtue. He states, "All human beings think that all men participate (μετέχειν) in justice and in the rest of political virtue. . . . For with other *technai*, just as you [Socrates] say, if someone says he is a good flute-player, or whatever other *technē*, but he is not, they laugh at him or are angry with him, and his own people come to him and rebuke him as a madman. With justice or any other political virtue, even if they know someone to be unjust, if that person speaks the truth about himself before the many, what they called decency before, speaking the truth (τἀληθῆ λέγειν), now they will call this madness (μανίαν)" (*Prt.* 323a).

Again, as with the *Meno*, Plato has Socrates' interlocutor articulate and dismiss the Socratic position as absurd. In his case, this particular *mania*, this madness of speaking the truth about his lack of knowledge with regard to virtue, is mitigated by Socrates' belief that the non-knowing of 'what virtue is' is itself human wisdom. Socrates will seek to emphasize that this assumption of "participating (μετέχειν)" in virtue is an assumption of 'knowing what virtue *is*,' by the everyday attitude's own admission. As we have seen previously, when an interlocutor claims to be virtuous in any way, Socrates will easily lead him to the claim that he therefore knows what virtue *is*. Thus, Protagoras's observation amounts to the universal claim among the many that everyone knows *at the very least* what human and political virtue *is*.

Indeed, given the many's presumption and the animosity toward the sophists that this generates, Protagoras admits that there is good reason for discretion in openly declaring oneself to be a sophist (*Prt.* 316c–d). He even makes a concession to this attitude, declaring his educational skill as a sophist to be simply a refinement and an extension of the skill possessed by every citizen (*Prt.* 325 c–d).

60. Gonzalez distinguishes the two generals in similar terms, arguing that Laches favors naïve, unquestioned experience, while Nicias favors sophistic *technē* and its abstracted formulae. For Gonzalez, Socrates' refutation of both these characters shows that virtue requires Socrates' own non-technical form of wisdom, a "knowing how" rather than a "knowing what." There is a certain harmony between Gonzalez's position and my own, but I would emphasize not the positive accomplishment of

knowing how (even when distinguished from the *technē*-like grasp of 'what virtue is'), but rather the abiding non-knowing of the condition provoked by Socrates' philosophizing. See Gonzalez (1998, 7–9).
61. The reticence of Charmides in the dialogue named for him does not contradict this claim of the general presumptuousness of the everyday attitude (as embodied by Socrates' unsophisticated interlocutors). Charmides does refuse to proclaim himself *sōphrōn* or 'temperate' and is hesitant to state a definition of *sōphrosunē* when Socrates asks, but this is more out of a fear of *seeming* immodest than out of an earnest acknowledgment of his own non-knowing, as he himself says (*Chrm.* 158c–e).
62. Renaud (2002, 195).
63. In response to Protagoras's claim to possess and teach the *technē* of virtue, Socrates makes an observation and puts forward an argument that might seem to run contrary to the interpretation being laid out here. Namely, that Socrates invokes the *technē*-model of virtue only because this allows him to make explicit what is implicit in the everyday attitude. Here, Socrates observes that the Athenian assembly accepts advice from any citizen on matters of running the city, matters of the excellence of the city, whereas on a matter they consider "technical (ἐν τέχνῃ)" they do not do so, instead shouting down any non-expert who attempts to advise them. From this, Socrates deduces that the Athenians generally believe that virtue is not a *technē*, and is therefore not teachable. See *Prt.* 319b–e. This does not, appearances to the contrary, conflict with the position being argued for here. Even leaving aside the interpretive issue of to what extent and at what point Socrates is presenting his "own" views in the *Protagoras*'s discussion of an art of measuring pleasure, I am not arguing that the many already understand virtue to be analogous to the knowledge possessed by experts in *technē*, but rather only that they presume an immediate and sufficient grasp of 'what virtue is.' It is only Socrates who, for reasons that serve his elenctic project, confronts the everyday attitude with the fact that, if this were so, the presumed grasp should then be explainable and teachable in the manner of a *technē*.

CHAPTER 5. THE TRUTHFUL ELENCTIC
PATHOS OF PAINFUL CONCERN

1. This passage is cited by Heidegger in § 42 of *Sein und Zeit* (along with the creation story involving *Cura* in 220 of *The Fables of Hyginus*) as ancient support for Heidegger's claim there that the very being of human

beings is not the objective presence of things, but care (*Sorge*) itself, and thus unfolds according to the temporality of a care-structure, a past having-been-thrown into a given, finite set of future possibilities. Although there is no work to my knowledge that connects Heidegger's emphasis on *Sorge* with the early Plato's emphasis on uncovering something like *meletē* or 'concern' as the proper human mode of relating to the being of virtue, there has been some fine work in this vein on *erōs* in the middle Platonic works. See especially Rosen (1967) and Hyland (1997).

2. This verb is usually translated as 'to care for, attend to,' but as the following will show, it entails in Socrates' sense a deeper condition of 'being concerned,' and indeed painfully, distressingly so. I have translated it accordingly.

3. See Liddell and Scott et al. (1843, 372, 383). For further evidence of this same ambivalence, see the entry for the related term *deon*, which is defined as "that which is binding, needful, right" (379).

4. It is for precisely this reason that I would be loathe to speak, with Mark McPherran, of a Socratic "duty to philosophize." See McPherran (1986). The compulsion that Socrates indicates here does not take place within the subject; it is not an internal recognition of the requirements of reason or of a moral code, for instance. Rather, one is compelled *only* through painful exposure to that which is experienced as exceeding one's grasp.

5. The term *oneidizein*, translated here as 'reproach, shame, disgrace,' has already been employed to describe the effect of Socrates' elenctic examinations (*Ap.* 30a, 30e, 39d). It should be noted that this is no inconsequential reprimand, but almost invariably a profoundly shaming form of censure. For instance, at the end of Sophocles' *Oedipus Rex*, when Oedipus bemoans the life of exile and infamy to which his children will be subjected, a life in which others will cast in their face their father's horrific crimes of patricide and incest, these terrible accusations of fateful corruption are a form of *oneidizein* (*OT* 1500). And when Euripides' Medea, in her justified rage, catalogues Jason's acts of cowardice and thankless betrayal, it is this same term that is used to characterize her vitriolic discourse (*Med.* 547), her speaking the "very worst (μέγιστον . . . κακόν)" about his conduct (*Med.* 467). Here we have a sense that an *oneidos* is most often a 'censure' not of this or that aspect of one's personality or behavior, but of *who one is*, of *one's basic character or way of life*.

6. Readers have generally missed this point, seeing only arguments for

Socrates' innocence that some deem fallacious (West 1979, 135), and others find valid (Reeve 1989, 97; Brickhouse and Smith 1989, 117–124). Brickhouse and Smith (1989, 113n.9) do note Socrates' usage of terms related to *meletē* throughout, but are distracted by the word-play, in which Socrates is surely engaging, between *meletē* and Meletus's name (esp. in the vocative, *Ō Melēte*). They fail to connect the passage to Socrates' frequent use of various forms of the verb *melein* throughout the *Apology*, and they do not approach the passage as Socrates introduces it, i.e., as a display of nothing but Meletus's lack of *meletē* for virtue. Gonzalez (2002b, 1–26) makes the exposition of Meletus's lack of concern central to his interpretation of the *Apology*, wherein he finds that Socrates' entire philosophical aim resides in this exhortation to care for virtue, specifically to care by engaging in Socratic discussion. For more on *protrepein* or 'urging forward, exhorting, turning toward' in Socratic philosophizing, see Gonzalez (2002a).

7. See Euthyphro's remarks in the opening lines of the dialogue that bears his name, where he greets Socrates with, "What's new, Socrates, such that you have left your usual haunts in the Lyceum and are now spending time around the king-archon's court? For surely you are not prosecuting someone before the king-archon as I am?" (*Euthphr.* 2a). When Socrates clarifies that he is there for a *graphē* or an 'indictment,' Euthyphro repeats, "Someone must have indicted you Socrates, for I know well that you have not indicted another" (*Euthphr.* 2b). In no time at all, Plato has already introduced a clear contrast between the human wisdom of Socrates and the hubristic confidence of Euthyphro. The latter is so secure in his own judgment that he is pushing ahead untroubled in the prosecution of his father for the accidental death of a slave (and a murderer) who was in his custody, a case that is quite controversial and, at the very least, complicated. Indeed, Euthyphro is so self-assured that he never once manages to notice that he has been refuted over the course of the ensuing conversation.

8. See Roochnik (1999, 265–270), once again, on Plato's punning use of this term.

9. We should take a moment to note that, in Socratic elenctic conversation, there are as it were two registers of 'reproach.' Indeed, in the relation between these two registers we might even see some evidence for the transition among the Greeks from a culture of public shame toward a culture of guilt, to which E. R. Dodds first drew attention in his seminal work, *The Greeks and the Irrational* (1951, 28–63).

The verb *elenchein*, translated most often as 'to refute,' itself often means 'to disgrace, put to shame.' That is, to be subjected to the elenchus is to be shamed *before others* and, thus, according to the prevailing opinions of what is blameworthy. And as mentioned previously, Socrates' interlocutors often seem to experience shame in being refuted (e.g., *Ly.* 213d, *Chrm.* 158c, *Euthd.* 275d, *Prt.* 312 a). See McKim (1988) on the *essentially* shaming aspect of Socratic elenchus. For Socrates, however, coming to acknowledge one's non-knowing with respect to virtue is itself arriving at "human wisdom." It *should not*, therefore, be shameful or disgraceful for a human being, even if it is experienced as such. In this, a not entirely shame-based or communal relation to the measure by which one would find oneself insufficient is announced. This is a relation that is not reducible to prevailing opinion and, thus, we might see in it a Socratic precursor to the later notion of conscience. The elenctic refutation, according to Socrates, should indeed be painful, insofar as one should come to feel distressed and compelled by the being of virtue to incessantly question and investigate it. That is, it should be painful not because publicly shameful, but in and of itself. Bringing this condition to light in its inherent suffering and intolerability is the first-order 'reproach' in Socratic elenchus, for one comes to experience oneself as profoundly inadequate, insufficient (even if one is not then to overcome this essentially human insufficiency). According to Socrates, what *should* warrant a disgracing or shaming censure or a second-order 'reproach,' even if it does not commonly do so, is *not being properly concerned*, which is to say, not being pained after the manner of the first-order 'reproach.'

If we do find here an important foreshadowing of what will eventually emerge through Paul and Augustine as the medieval Christian concept of *conscienta*, or 'conscience,' we must proceed with caution, for the Socratic precursor need not and does not entail the interiority or enclosed self-relation that will subsequently develop from this medieval notion, once it becomes situated in the modern subject. Paul writes in Romans, "They show that what the law requires is written on their hearts, to which their conscience also bears witness" (Rom. 2:15). The *koinē* term employed by Paul here, *suneidēsis*, which is composed of the prefix *sun-* with a noun from *eidenai* or 'to have seen, know,' is very literally translated into Latin with *conscienta*, a term that comes into prominence already with Cicero, but then acquires its fundamental Christian significance as 'conscience' only with Augustine. However, even in the articulated Christian notion, we do not yet have the full-fledged interiority of the modern moral subject's conscience, given the external relation to the divine necessarily entailed there. For this, see Paul's remark a bit later on, "I am speaking the truth in Christ—I am not lying; my conscience confirms it by the Holy Spirit" (Rom. 9: 1–2). "By the Holy Spirit" seems to indicate an 'external' or 'externalizing' source for the call of conscience. In any case, even while noting the presence in Plato's works of something like a precursor to our notion of 'conscience,' it is crucial that we mark a fundamental discontinuity in this development. With Plato's Socrates we see something like an *ecstatic conscience*, where one is pained and called by the being of virtue as it somehow presents itself in exceeding its initial appearances (Socratic elenchus facilitating just that painful self-presentation of virtue). By contrast, with the familiar modern notion we have a policing force operative utterly within the subject, in accordance ultimately with one's own merely subjective moral sensibility. For an attempt to argue for the relevance and non-primitive character of shame-based morality, see Williams (1993).

10. As indicated previously, it is not the condition of being non-knowing with respect to 'what virtue is' that Socrates believes should be shameful or produce a feeling of guilt, but, quite to the contrary, the condition of not being painfully concerned about virtue. This is perfectly manifest in the *Meno*, where Plato places Socrates in a contentious conversation with Anytus, who will be his chief, because most well-known and respected, accuser at his trial. Anytus, who is hosting Meno in Athens, happens by and enters the discussion *in medias res*. The fiercely democratic Anytus claims here that it is not from the sophists, but from any member of the Athenian citizenry that Meno should learn what he agrees must be the teachable *technē* of human virtue. In response, Socrates (as he often does) lists many great, seemingly quite excellent men who have failed to educate or to have their sons educated in virtue, indicating not only that these men do not possess any such teachable *technē*, but also perhaps that human virtue should be conceived of as no such thing. Anytus misses the latter point completely, being simply scandalized by Socrates' suggestion that these men did not possess a *technē*-like grasp of virtue. He finally issues Socrates an ominous warning, saying that one should not so easily "speak ill (κακῶς λέγειν)" (*Men.* 94e) of people, and storms off. After, Socrates observes that Anytus wrongly perceived him to be "slandering (κακηγορεῖν)" good Athenian citizens like himself, but this is only because Anytus does not know what it truly is to speak ill of people (*Men.* 95a). Although Socrates is indeed here indicating that

good Athenians do not have an immediate *technē*-like grasp of 'what virtue *is*' and are therefore unable to teach it, this should not be shaming or disgracing, since human wisdom seems to Socrates to be nothing other than the acknowledgment of this lack. In the distinction between truly 'speaking ill of people' (suggesting that they are not painfully concerned by virtue) and only apparently 'speaking ill of people' (suggesting that they do not have a *technē*-like immediate grasp of the being of virtue), we see the two abovementioned levels of reproach in Socratic elenchus.

11. Among those dialogues usually categorized as early, the *Meno* might seem to suggest that the Socratic elenchus is merely propaedeutic. After being led into *aporia* concerning his own previously presumed grasp of the being of virtue, Meno raises what is often called the 'paradox of inquiry.' It seems that either one does not know one's object, in which case inquiry is impossible to begin and impossible to complete (or recognize as complete), or one knows one's object already, in which case inquiry is unnecessary. Socrates then introduces for the first time the notion that learning is *anamnēsis* or 'recollection,' being reminded of "the truth of beings [that is] always in our soul (ἀεὶ ἡ ἀλήθεια ἡμῖν τῶν ὄντων ... ἐν τῇ ψυχῇ)" (*Men.* 86b). Before we see Socrates as advocating this positive epistemic grasp as an ideal, we should note the following moments that seem intended to mitigate that very positivity: 1) Socrates introduces the notion of *anamnēsis* not as a theoretical claim but explicitly as the suggestion of priests and priestesses (*Men.* 81a–b). 2) Socrates' demonstration of *anamnēsis* is carried out with respect to geometric knowledge, *not ethical knowledge*. This must be understood in relation to Socrates' frequent tactic throughout the early dialogues, whereby he offers to define "many inconsequential things" (*Euthd.* 293b) or things of no ethical importance and does so successfully, then asking his interlocutor to define virtue or an aspect of virtue. In the *Laches* he successfully defines "quickness (ταχυτής)" and then leads his interlocutors into *aporia* with respect to courage and virtue (*La.* 192a–b) and, in the Hippias Major, before provoking *aporia* concerning fineness Socrates defines "what all large things are large by" in the *Hippias Major* (*Hp. Ma.* 294a–c). Indeed, the *Meno* contains an earlier example of just this tactic, as Socrates has defined "shape (σχῆμα)" (*Men.* 76a). The *anamnēsis* demonstration has this same function here, insofar as Socrates and the servant boy successfully arrive at geometrical knowledge before he and Meno come into *aporia* with respect to virtue and its teachability. 3) After the demonstration Socrates explicitly disavows its complete truth, defending

rather its efficacy in fending off Meno's paradox, *thereby* encouraging and sustaining inquiry, and *thereby* making us better, braver, and less idle (*Men.*86b–c). 4) Lastly, the *Meno* only passes through the promise of some positive epistemic gain by way of *anamnēsis*, but ends as all the early dialogues do in an explicitly *aporetic* relation to 'what virtue is.' Thus, we have good reason not to accept simply and at face value the *Meno*'s suggestion of a positive, extra-*aporetic* relation to virtue. However, this does not entail that Plato is presenting the *muthos* of *anamnēsis* as merely a healthy fiction. Rather, something about our human relation to 'what is' comes to light in the *muthos*—namely, that we enjoy an always prior relatedness to 'what is,' even if that relatedness does not take the form of a fully realized *epistēmē*. Also, it makes clear for us that, contrary to the message of Meno's paradox, 'what is' is questionworthy, worthy of our concerned investigating and searching (even if no end or resolution to that distressed condition is promised).

12. Although it would be possible, for instance, to say that something is important or of great consequence for the welfare of a given individual, even in the case that he or she does not perceive it to be so.
13. Even the grammar of *epimeleisthai*, as a secondary mode of being concerned, suggests a relationship other than that of a subject acting upon an object. That is, *epimeleisthai*, which would commonly be translated as 'to take care, attend to, or give heed to,' does not take a direct object in the accusative case, but rather a complementary genitive. For instance, when Socrates says to his imagined interlocutor in the passage cited previously, "you are neither concerned toward (ἐπιμελῇ) nor think about (φροντίζεις) wisdom or truth or how it is best for your soul to be" (*Ap.* 29e), wisdom, truth, and soul occur in the genitive. Given Socrates' emphasis on pain and necessitation or distress, we have seen this in reference to a more original condition of being concerned *by* something, in the sense of being affected by it in a way that makes one needful of it. I have translated it accordingly as 'being concerned toward.' There is at least some support for this if we consider the preposition *epi*, which is here serving as prefix for the verb. Although in its most literal sense, when combined with a noun in the genitive case, *epi* will mean something like 'upon,' in the context of human desiring and acting, it will often take on a sense of 'toward.' Consider Socrates' remark in the *Protagoras*, where he speaks of "all actions toward this, toward living painlessly and pleasantly (αἱ ἐπὶ τούτου πράξεις ἅπασαι, ἐπὶ τοῦ ἀλύπως ζῆν καὶ ἡδέως)" (*Prt.* 358b). And this *epi* becomes all-important here

and peppers the conversation later on when Socrates follows Protagoras's position to its logical conclusion, namely, that while courageous and cowardly people might *do* different things, they are always *epi* or 'toward' the same thing, the good/pleasant (*Prt.* 359c–e). Thus, the distinction between them (according to the position now deduced as Protagoras's own) must be one of wisdom and ignorance about that toward which they are both striving. In any case, we might try to think more generally and more deeply about the complementary genitive itself, which we find with *epimeleisthai*, and also with *phrontizein*, or 'to think.' Why does Greek render the "object" of this action in the genitive case? In what sense, in caring, attending, or heeding, and in thinking are we doing so *of something*? Are we possessed by it, in possession of it, partaking in it, located within it, or some other relation associated with the genitive case? These questions point to the condition of being concerned by and made needful of, which we are arguing is the initially underlying human condition Socrates aims to provoke and bring to light through his questioning.

14. Indeed, we might think of the *lupē* or 'pain' Socrates wishes to bring to light as fundamentally the pain of being exposed to the world, torn outside of oneself by the non-presence or non-availability of Being, specifically the being of virtue. That is, this more fundamental pain is precisely not what one experiences internally as a self-enclosed subject, which might then be thought to yank one out of one's relations to others and to things and draw one into oneself, thereby robbing one of the ability to take part in and concern oneself with the world. Instead, the pain at stake here would be the first and always underlying opening of one's relatedness to the world, and Socratic elenchus means to uncover and amplify just this. In his fine essay on Heidegger's reading of Trakl's poetry, Andrew J. Mitchell finds just such a "world-entering role of pain," which he opposes to the interiorized and psychologized conceptions of pain in the work of Freud and Elaine Scarry. See Mitchell (2010). My discussion of the issue here has benefited greatly from his analysis.

15. It is possible as well to bring someone to see that his or her pre-existing concern actually covers, so to speak, an object that he or she did not realize. For instance, an egoist understands his or her concern for living well as a concern for his or her own welfare specifically as distinct from and not connected with that of others. It might be possible by means of argument to show this individual that his or her own pre-existing aim, living well, is always already dependent upon or includes the welfare of

others, thereby expanding his or her concern for his or her own welfare to include theirs. In this case, the argument has not generated a concern, but has instead clarified an already existing concern.

16. The poetic or non-Attic version of *peras* is *peirar*, which would presumably be related to *peirein*.
17. Indeed, this strange double relation, that of being always already connected to the aim of one's striving and questioning while also crucially and painfully lacking that aim is just what Socrates' Diotima brings mythically to light when she introduces a new lineage for *Erōs*. Although Hesiod's *Theogony* has him as one of the oldest of gods along with Gaia and Tartarus (*Theog.* 116–122), Diotima has him born of *Poros* and *Penia* or 'way, resource' and 'poverty, lack,' and as thus representing a perplexing combination of having and not-having (*Smp.* 178b–d, and see *Cra.* 398b–e, which connects *erōs* to the essentially *daimonic* and intermediary character of the human condition). Although this occurs in what is most likely a middle-period Platonic dialogue, it seems true of Plato's Socrates from the early period on that he would "claim to know nothing other than things pertaining to *erōs* (οὐδέν φημι ἄλλο ἐπίστασθαι ἢ τὰ ἐρωτικά)" (*Smp.* 177d), insofar as *erōs* is nothing but this concerned relatedness at a distance that we have associated with *aporia*. Consider his remark at the outset of the *Lysis*: "I might well be of no worth and useless when it comes to other things, but this has been somehow given to me from the god—to recognize very quickly lover and beloved (γνῶναι ἐρῶντά τε καὶ ἐρώμενον)" (*Ly.* 204b–c).
18. Nehamas (1998, 85).
19. In the introduction, we took up Vlastos's articulation of "*the* problem of the Socratic elenchus," namely, that Socrates preaches the saving power of knowledge alone even as he seems to point relentlessly to its unattainability with his seemingly purely destructive, elenctic mode of philosophizing. In chapter 1, we used Aristotle's assessments of Socrates in order highlight what must present itself (according to certain constitutive presuppositions of the orthodox interpretive approach to the dialogues) as a paradoxical tension between the aims of Socratic philosophizing—between knowing the 'being of virtue' and knowing oneself, between knowing an object and knowing ourselves as subject. And the manifestation of Socrates' paradoxicality that has attracted most of our attention is the seeming incompatibility of, on the one hand, the clear and consistent failure of Socratic philosophizing to arrive at its expressed aim, a definition and thus a *technē*-like knowledge of virtue, with on the

other hand, Socrates' unreserved estimation of the benefit it nonetheless as such provides for human beings (*Ap.* 36c, 38a).
20. Vlastos (1985, 5) (italics are provided in Nehamas's own citation of this quote). Vlastos points to passages where Socrates professes to be content in his belief that he has never wronged anyone (*Ap.* 37b, *Grg.* 522d) and also to the fact that Socrates goes to his death remarkably at peace with the life he has lived (*Phd.* 117b–c). Vlastos concludes from such moments that Plato's Socrates enjoys an undisturbed *certainty* concerning whether he has lived virtuously or well.
21. Nehamas (1998, 86).
22. Zeller too seems to observe a serene self-certainty in Socrates' comportment when he writes, "Das Bild des sterbenden Sokrates musste seinen Schülern im höchsten Grade das leisten, was es uns selbst heute noch, nach Jahrtausenden, leistet: ein lautes Zeugniss abzulegen von der Grösse des menschlichen Geistes, von der Macht der Philosophie, von der Unüberwindlichkeit eines frommen, reinen, in seiner klaren Ueberzeugung beruhigten Sinnes" (1885, 232). Although he seems to be speaking here of Socrates' comportment in the *Phaedo* most directly, Zeller would likely agree that this exemplarity carries through all Plato's earlier portraits of Socrates as well and his description parallels that of Nehamas and Vlastos quite clearly.
23. Seneca looks back through a Stoic lens as well and not surprisingly finds the same Socrates: "If you desire an example, take Socrates, a perpetually suffering old man who had been buffeted about by every hardship, but was vanquished by neither poverty, made more grave still by domestic troubles, nor by labors, among these military service. How sorely he was exercised at home, whether we recall his wife, a woman of ferocious manners and petulant language, or of his intractable children, surely more resembling their mother than their father. If you think of it, he lived always under wartime conditions, under the rule of tyrants, or under free rule that was even crueler than war or tyranny. The [Peloponnesian] war lasted for twenty-seven years and after the end of the armed conflict the city then fell prey to the Thirty Tyrants, most of whom were enemies of Socrates. At the end a culminating damnation, he was accused of violating state religion and corrupting the youth, whom he incited against the gods, against their fathers, and against the whole state. Then followed incarceration and death by poison. But all of these things did not disturb the soul of Socrates, nor even his expression (*haec usque eo animum Socratis non moverant, ut ne vultum quidem moverent*). How wonderfully

praiseworthy and singular he was! To the very end (*ad extremum*) no one ever saw Socrates too cheerful or too sad. He remained even, through all the unevenness of fortune (*Aequalis fuit in tanta inaequalitate fortunae*)" (*Epist. Mor.* CIV, 27–28).

24. Nehamas (1998, 91). Indeed, by Nehamas's lights (87–91), this dilemma largely motivates Plato's development in the middle period and many of the central theories and positions usually associated with mature Platonic philosophy are generated in Plato's attempt to resolve the perplexity his own character had generated for him in the early period. For example, under this interpretation, Plato introduces the theory of learning as *anamnēsis* or 'recollection' (*Men.* 81c–85b, 85d, 98a, *Phd.* 72e–77b, *Phdr.* 250a–251a), because this always prior connectedness allows the Ideas to serve as a reliable moral compass even without perfect knowledge.

25. This may seem cold comfort indeed, but we find it echoed, unexpectedly and with centuries of distortion to be sure, by the Trappist monk and poet Thomas Merton. In his *Thoughts in Solitude*, he prays, "My Lord God, I have no idea where I am going. I do not see the road ahead of me. I cannot know for certain where it will end. Nor do I really know myself, and the fact that I think I am following your will does not mean that I am actually doing so. / But I believe that my desire to please you does in fact please you. And I hope that I have that desire in all that I am doing" (1956, 83). Of course, for Merton to illuminate our Socrates, it is necessary to set aside a number of foreign and anachronistic elements: the ultimate aim of pleasing an all-powerful, omniscient, and loving creator God, the sense that suffering might be *per se* good for us as *massa damnata*, the perhaps also latent Kantian emphasis on the intentions of the agent in evaluating the moral value of an action, and finally any sense that the knowledge we seek can and will be revealed to us in heaven. If we are able to look past all of this, however, we might hear Merton articulating a contentment or serenity that arises precisely from one's awareness that one is properly distressed, disturbed, and made needful by what is good or virtuous and by the requirement that we know what the good or what virtue is. Vital here is the fact that this *meta-serenity* does not in any sense eliminate or transcend the initial disturbance and the suffering of non-knowing, but in fact requires that these be suffered deeply and in earnest. This is a form of serenity that *eo ipso* includes distress and discomfort, because it arises only via one's own non-knowing what it is to live well. That is, only insofar as one is persistently and at

every moment properly distressed by the withdrawal and ungraspability of what one feels a need to know ('what virtue is' for Socrates and God's will for Merton). This would be the only kind of "serenity" that Socrates might claim for himself, for virtue is essentially questionworthy, excessive, and distant.

26. Kierkegaard (1841, XIII.258). Indeed, Kierkegaard's term for this negative or non-speculative relation to 'what is' (or to the Absolute or divine), so long as the relation avoids skepticism, is 'irony,' the central theme of the book. The sentence that follows this citation is: "In all this, however, that which makes [Socrates] into a personality is precisely irony."

27. With this we answer Vlastos's central worry about the elenchus, even if by means of a shift in our perspective that he surely did not anticipate. Of the elenctic method, he wonders "how Socrates can claim to have proved that the refutand is false, when all he has established is the inconsistency [of the interlocutor's original opinion] with premises whose truth he has not undertaken to establish in that argument?" (Vlastos 1983b, 30). Vlastos's explicit question here is how Socrates can claim that a certain proposition about virtue is false (much less claim that its opposite is true), if all he has done is to expose the inconsistency among his interlocutor's opinions. However, his deeper worry is that Socrates' method might leave him and his interlocutors trapped on the subjective side of the chasm that threatens to separate them from objective reality, for it seems to deal *only with opinions* and never secures any necessary connection through argument to objective reality. Our response is that, although Socrates' elenchus does not manage to establish certain propositions as corresponding accurately to the objective reality of 'what virtue is,' this is simply not his aim. His aim is to bring to light that which is always already given in and in a sense appears via our everyday *doxai*, which is the essentially excessive and questionworthy being of virtue that is truthfully experienced not in a *technē*-like grasp, but in one's being painfully concerned by it. Socrates and his interlocutors are not thereby relegated to subjective isolation, for the "subjective" is not yet severed from the "objective" for Socrates, nor for any other ancient Greek thinker (at the very least) prior to post-Aristotelian Academic and Pyrrhonian Skepticism.

28. On the separation of the Ideas in the middle dialogues, see Devereux (1994) and Fine (1984) and (1986). In general, I believe the manner of approaching the problem of the immanence or transcendence of the Ideas in the middle dialogues leans too far toward the logical and away

from the phenomenological. All participants in the debate acknowledge the undeniable fact that, in Plato's discussion of the Ideas, he is not consistent insofar as he employs different explicitly non-technical terms in different contexts to describe the relationship of the Ideas to their instantiations. Interpreters then attempt to either explain away the inconsistency, as Devereux does, or they accept it as evidence of a failure in achieving a systematic conception of reality. However, it seems to me truer to what we find in the dialogues to say that Plato is not attempting to arrive at a system, but is simply approaching the ways 'what is' shows itself obscurely and variously in its appearances. He employs different descriptive vocabularies (e.g., vocabularies of participation, imitation, causation, teleology, appearance, etc.), in order to bring out different aspects of phenomenality, in response to the contextual concerns of various discussions and to the specific questions that arise there. If we understand the discussions as phenomenologically descriptive, not merely deductive, our task as interpreters becomes not finding or declaring absent the implicit philosophical system, but bringing to light the phenomenon that is there being described through our own interpretive effort.

29. See Ross (1951, 228–231) and Mabbott (1926) on Aristotle's critique of the Platonic *chōrismos*. Other passages offer some clarification. Elsewhere he writes, "Plato believed this knowledge [of what is according to the whole (τὸ καθόλου)] must be not of sensible things, but of some other things (περὶ ἑτέρων). For he thought a definition of sensible things impossible, as they are undergoing transformation. Thus, beings of this sort he called Ideas, and all the perceived things are spoken of by means of these and according to these, such that many things are synonymous by participation (κατὰ μέθεξιν) in the same Idea" (*Met.* 987b4–10). And elsewhere, "At the same time, they [the Platonists] make Ideas, as essences, according to the whole or universal, both separate and individual (ἅμα γὰρ καθόλου τε [ὡς οὐσίας] ποιοῦσι τὰς ἰδέας καὶ πάλιν ὡς χωριστὰς καὶ τῶν καθ' ἕκαστον)" (*Met.* 1086a33–36, see 1086b2ff). Here Aristotle is referring to the influence of the Heraclitean Cratylus on Plato's conception of sensible things (*Met.* 987a32 and 1010a12). Because sensible things are always changing and never remaining the same, Plato believed that knowledge, insofar as it is possible, could not be *of* the objects of perception. Knowledge must be *peri heterōn* or 'about other things,' which are not sensible, but intelligible (*Met.* 1079a2–1080a11.). Further, Aristotle seems to be claiming that these intelligible

Ideas are separate insofar as they are numerically distinct. That is, an Idea and the sensible thing that participates in it are *two* distinct things. This seems to be the significance of his complaint elsewhere that Plato and his followers made 'the things according to the whole' or universals have the same character as 'the things according to each' or particulars (*Met.* 1086b11–12). That is, he made them individual, numerically distinct things, rather than formal causes, as in the *Metaphysics*, or *deutera ousia*, as in the *Categories*. We might note that, although a part is something in some sense "other than" the whole to which it belongs, they need not be "separated" in the sense of existing independently of one another. Aristotle seems to indicate that the relation of Idea to particular material thing cannot be understood as similar in any way to a part's participation in the whole, since particular material things only *are* by participation in the Ideas. That is, its being is borrowed and it must be borrowed from somewhere. Thus, the ontological priority that Aristotle sees in Plato's Ideas seems to argue in his eyes for its independent existence. In sum, according to Aristotle, Plato's proper Ideas are *chōristai* insofar as they are intelligible things, both numerically distinct from and existing independently of the sensible things that derive whatever existence they have by participation in the Ideas.

30. E.g., Reeve (1988, 101–110). See also Grube (1935, 9), who argues against the claim that there is a fully developed "theory of Ideas" present in the early dialogues and evident in the *Euthyphro* and the *Meno*, where Socrates makes use of the terms *idea* and *eidos* to describe his *definiendum*. Although one would have to grant some of Grube's claims here, I would not agree that, from the absence of such a fully developed theory, "it follows from all these expressions [uses of *idea* and *eidos*, as well as phrases such as 'the "x" itself,' 'what "x" is,' 'the being of "x",' '"x" itself by itself,' 'the one thing "x",' etc.], whatever hidden meaning they hold for Socrates, are taken by the other speaker as describing no more than the common characteristics of particular things . . . *not as transcendentally existing but as immanent in the particulars.*" Although we must disagree with this, we do so not in order to argue that Socrates' interlocutors held a theory of *transcendental* Ideas. Rather, we say that Socrates develops or articulates possibilities inherent in ordinary language, specifically in ordinary expressions of 'what something *is*' or of 'something's *being* a certain way,' in order to reveal a *distance* between 'what is' and its appearance to us. That is all. This does not entail a *transcendental element* in the attitude of Socrates, nor in that of his interlocutors, but it does indicate

that there is a pre-understanding of 'what is' or of what it means 'to be,' a pre-understanding that can be employed in order to show our everyday failure to grasp 'what is' adequately. Also *contra* Grube, cf. Allen (1970, 107–110), who writes that the "progress of dialectic involves a passage from the respondent's naïve existence assumption that 'there is such a thing as holiness' to his acceptance, if dialectic is successful, of the highly sophisticated existence assumption that there is an essence of holiness, and that it can be defined. But if the latter claim is true, the passage is continuous: for a commitment to essence is then latent in our ordinary use of words. The essence of holiness is what the word 'holiness' means; to the degree that we do not understand that essence, we do not understand the meaning of our words." Here we can agree with much of what Allen says. We need not agree, however, with his claim that Socrates believes in the early dialogues that the object of his search is definable. It is interesting that, when discussing the presuppositions of Socrates' interlocutors, Allen removes the otherwise prominent vocabulary of ontology and 'what is' from his discussion, opting exclusively for a vocabulary of meaning and essence. He seems unwilling to attribute explicitly any kind of ontological presuppositions to the everyday attitude of Socrates' interlocutors, although he is willing to argue for Socrates' "ontological commitment" even in the early dialogues and against the common "linguistic" reading of Socrates' position (1970, 110–113). This seems to me peculiar, given his strong statement, just quoted, concerning the *continuity* between Socrates' attitude towards his *definiendum* and the everyday attitude of his interlocutors.

31. Shorey (1933, 68–70, 75–76), Friedländer (1964, I. 59–64).
32. I.e. that which is sometimes named *idea* or *eidos*, but which is also called *ousia* (*Prt.* 349b, *Euthphr.* 11a, *Hp. Ma.* 301b, 302c) and *paradeigma* (*Euthphr.* 6e), and is described as well as a *pragma* (*La.* 192c, *Prt.* 349b) or as *hen ti* (*Prt.* 329c, *Hp. Ma.* 375d), *ti to auto* (*Hp. Ma.* 300a), *auto autō(i)* (*Euthphr.* 5d), *auto homoion* (*Euthphr.* 5d), and *to koinon touto* (*Hp. Ma.* 300a).
33. See Allen (1970). Although Allen does speak of a "theory of Ideas" in the title, he develops his interpretation on the basis of passages where neither *idea* nor *eidos* occur, which seems to indicate that he is broadening his scope as previously suggested.
34. Indeed, in light of the frequency of these terms and the actual work they do in the discussions of the middle and later dialogues, the dominant role of the so-called "theory of Ideas" in the transmission of and

scholarship on Plato's thought must appear exaggerated and misleading.
35. We will return specifically to Plato's employment of the terms *idea* and *eidos* in the conclusion, where we take up the implications of this study for the interpretation of the dialogues of the middle period.
36. Hyland introduces this term, arguing for its applicability even in the middle and later dialogues of Plato. For Hyland, Plato's Ideas are not simply transcendent entities, but that which present themselves only in withholding themselves ultimately from the immanent experience of sensible, material, particulars (1995, 6, also 87–110).
37. See Casey (1993, 9). Casey's term is used here although the "placial" character of our relation to 'what virtue is' does not imply the embodied experience of place that is fundamental to his original discussion of it (1993, 43–105). Furthermore, Casey would presumably prefer 'far-ness' to 'distance' (1993, 60), since for Casey 'distance' carries with it the connotation of objective, geometrical space. We have attempted to counter this by speaking of a 'distressing distance.'

CHAPTER 6. THE COURAGE OF VIRTUE AND THE DISTANT HORIZON OF THE WHOLE IN THE *LACHES*

1. The only real source of perplexity that the orthodox approach to the Socratic elenchus seems to find in interpreting the *Laches* concerns the uncommonly long framing discussion that precedes the refutation of the interlocutors. In considering Socratic method, many have been tempted to pass over this dramatic introduction and focus on the refutations that make up the dialogue's second half. However, interpretive generosity would seem to be the ethic proper to reading the Platonic dialogues in general, for every element and every aspect, even every word, appears to prove itself under scrutiny to be thoroughly considered and significant, indeed often profoundly illuminating within the whole of the Platonic text. It is thus best to approach the dialogues with the attitude that nothing is superfluous. As we shall see, the *Laches*' extended preamble rewards this attitude.
2. Other Platonic texts seem to corroborate that the sons of Lysimachus and Melesias did in fact spend time with Socrates, but with divergent results. Plato has Socrates comment on the failure of Aristides II, the son of Lysimachus, to persevere long enough with philosophy (*Tht.* 151a) and Socrates in the *Theages* tells a similar story (*Thg.* 130a–e). Indeed,

there, Socrates tells a story contrasting him with Thucydides II, son of Melesias, who seems to have continued to share in Socratic inquiry at least up to the dramatic date of this dialogue, 409 BC. Cf. Nails (2002, 292).

3. Indeed, after having fought for the position for many years, Hyland is able to write the following in 1995 about the position that "the dialogue form in which Plato presents his thinking has not merely literary but philosophical importance as well": "The number of authors and works that have adopted this standpoint is now, happily, so large as to make short summary impossible" (Hyland, 1995, 1). He then recommends, in addition to his own earlier efforts, Tigerstedt's historiographical observations in *Interpreting Plato* and a critical assessment thereof by Bowen. See Tigerstedt (1977) and Bowen (1988). There have been no fewer than seven collections of essays on Plato that champion precisely this same approach: *Platonic Writings / Platonic Readings* (ed. Griswold, 1988), *The Third Way: New Directions in Platonic Studies* (ed. Gonzalez, 1995), *Retracing the Platonic Text* (ed. Russon and Sallis, 1999), *Who Speaks for Plato?* (ed. Press, 2000), *Does Socrates Have a Method?* (ed. Scott, 2002), *Plato's Forms: Varieties of Interpretation* (ed. Welton, 2003), and *Philosophy in Dialogue* (ed. Scott, 2007).

4. For an interpretation that situates Plato's works among other Socratic dialogues, see Kahn (1996). Kahn shows very clearly that Plato is working within a literary genre, the Socratic dialogue, and thus always within a certain set of tropes and assumptions. However, this fact does nothing to diminish the significance of the fact that the great thinker *decided* that this genre fit his own philosophical purposes, something Kahn himself indicates even in the full title of his book: *Plato and the Socratic Dialogue: The Philosophical Use of a Literary Form*.

5. Hyland (1995, 14).
6. Ibid. (5).
7. Ibid. (7).
8. I thank Jill Gordon for bringing to my attention the special relevance on this point of *Alcibiades I*. Socrates opens this conversation by describing Alcibiades as one who thinks he is utterly self-sufficient (*Alc. I* 104a). Socrates goes on to insist that Alcibiades will only succeed in achieving what he desires if he accepts Socrates as his companion. Paradoxically, Socrates' peculiar *philia* or 'friendship,' the *koinē boulē* or 'common deliberation' (see *Alc. I* 105d–e, also 106d, 124b) he offers, promises nothing but a certain way of being *insufficient*, a self-conscious non-knowing

and lacking. Indeed, this would be concomitant with Delphic "self-knowledge" (*Alc. I* 124b), ultimately understood here as a knowledge of one's soul. However, this is the case only insofar as the soul is understood as the site where this insufficiency is suffered. One comes to know one's self, one's soul, as lacking a knowledge of 'what virtue is,' only when the presumed wisdom of one's unquestioned *doxai* about virtue come under suspicion in the elenctic conversation that is Socratic *sunousia* or 'being together.'

9. It seems that Stesilaus had at some point taken the trouble to invent a new weapon, a combination scythe and spear, which he was confident would give him a distinct advantage in combat. When, while serving on a ship with Laches, he attempted to deploy it, the overreaching weapon became tangled in the rigging of the enemy ship. As the ships passed one another in opposite directions, Stesilaus could neither pull the weapon free nor would he let it loose, with the result that he was dragged the entire length of the ship desperately clinging to his invention until he finally lost his grip on it. The sight of his "clever contrivance (σόφισμα)" (*La.* 183d) dangling helplessly in the enemy's ropes as they sailed off drew laughter from all present. Laches refers derisively to Stesilaus's scythe-spear here as a *sophisma*, which does indeed name an ingenious device or tool, but it also refers to any 'acquired skill' or 'method.' Laches' point is clear. What seemed in the abstract such a valuable and clever instrument proved in the vicissitudes and in the unpredictable specific circumstances of battle to be perfectly useless.

10. According to many scholars, Plato's Socrates holds the conviction that one cannot make good judgments about virtue (or a virtue) and cannot act virtuously (or courageously, for instance) unless one knows the definition of virtue (or the specific virtue in question)—the strong articulation of the principle of the epistemological priority of definition. These include Crombie (1962, I.57), Geach (1966), Guthrie (1969, 352), and Allen (1970). Other scholars have argued for weaker forms of the principle, still finding here a Socratic conviction, such as Vlastos (1985, 23–26), Irwin (1977, 37–41), and Brickhouse and Smith (1984 and 1989).

11. At first glance, given his explicit praise for and familiarity with Socrates, we might be tempted to see Nicias as in a sense nearer to Socrates than the crude-speaking man of action, Laches. However, we might then ask ourselves, why is this dialogue called the *Laches*, and not the *Nicias*, although they participate more or less equally in the discussion and find

their positions equally refuted? We should listen very closely when Nicias declares his fondness for Socratic philosophizing. He does indeed recognize that, when one engages in conversation on any topic with Socrates, one inevitably winds up answering questions about oneself and one's very way of life (*La.* 188a). True enough. However, Nicias reports the following of his earlier contact with Socratic elenctic questioning: "I for one am accustomed (συνήθης) to this man and I know that it is necessary to suffer these things from him (ἀνάγκη ὑπὸ τούτου πάσχειν ταῦτα) and I know well that I myself will suffer these things. For I enjoy (χαίρω) associating with the man.... For me, then, there is nothing unusual (ἄηθες) and nothing unpleasant (ἀηδὲς) in being put to the test (βασανίζεσθαι) by Socrates" (*La.* 188a–b). In this, Plato has Nicias betray with remarkable precision the fact that, despite his previous participation in discussions with Socrates, he has never in fact experienced the condition at which those discussions were ultimately aimed. As should be clear from our earlier considerations, it is simply not possible to become *sunēthēs* or 'accustomed, habituated' to Socrates if one experiences his elenctic discussion as intended. For this discussion aims precisely to disrupt one's *ethē*, which is to say, to call radically into question the habitual and customary opinions on which one relies to make sense of one's world, make decisions, and take action. Indeed, Socrates aims to tear one out of one's *ēthos*, in the sense of one's 'customary dwelling place' or 'haunts,' specifically by exposing that previously sheltered site to its own always already constitutive excess. In this disruption, the *deinos* truth that the Socratic elenchus would accomplish is, as we have seen, the suffering of this excess as monstrously unfamiliar, overwhelmingly and profoundly troubling. Thus, it is clear that Nicias has never inhabited this site with Socrates, he has never yet found himself in the radically displaced and exposed condition, the *atopia* in which Socrates aims to situate those who participate in the elenchus (see *Smp.* 215a, 221d). Moreover, Plato has Nicias articulate the requirement of Socratic questioning, "it is necessary to suffer (πάσχειν) these things." However, he has Nicias then go on to indicate explicitly that he has not *suffered* in the properly painful, distressed, and concerned way. To the contrary, he states that he enjoys (*chairein*) being subjected to the Socratic elenchus and that there is nothing at all unpleasant (*aēdes*) about it. This is clearly not a man who has truly experienced Socratic *aporia*'s terrible needfulness.

12. See Penner (1971) and (1992), who argues that Socrates himself holds the conviction that each of the individual virtues is identical to all the

others, and therefore to wisdom, as well as to virtue itself. Brickhouse and Smith argue against this that Socrates instead believes that all of the individual virtue-related terms "refer to the same psychic condition and still have different *erga* as part of their definitions" (1994, 67–72). I believe this entire debate gets off on the wrong foot by not attending to the explicitly phenomenological project of Socratic philosophizing, focusing instead on the logical and terminological implications. Socrates, in accord with his human wisdom, does not himself believe or hold as a conviction or claim to "know" in any sense either of these. Socrates remains rather at the site of appearing, never presuming to transcend it or to overcome appearances, and he asks after the being of each of the individual virtues in order to bring his interlocutors before the being of virtue itself, which withdraws behind them when we try to think these as its parts.

13. It is Vlastos who introduces this term, which Hugh Benson refers to as the "doxastic constraint," referring to the fact that Socrates insists in numerous dialogues that he will not discuss hypothetical or, better, unchampioned definitions, requiring rather that his interlocutors state their own earnest opinions or how the subject matter in question appears to them. This has been seen to ensure that Socrates' elenchus will have an existential impact, i.e., that it will show not just the proposed definition, but the interlocutor's very way of life to be incoherent, false. Without a doubt. However, the deeper significance of this requirement is that it provides Socrates' thinking with its ground, its connection to 'what is.' For a discussion of the requirement, see Vlastos (1983b, 32), and for the strengthened "doxastic constraint," see Benson (2000, 32–56) and (2002, 105).

14. Mitchell Miller, in his characteristically subtle reading of the *Crito*, finds at work in that dialogue a complex relationship between the attitude of the many and the philosophical view of Socrates. Indeed, Miller suggests that the position of the *Laws* is not Socrates' own, but represents instead a compromise between Crito's fallenness into the perspective of the many and Socrates' (only implicitly stated) pure philosophical view. Vital for us in Miller's analysis is the sophisticated and fluid relation he identifies as joining and differentiating the everyday from the Socratic philosophical attitudes. See Miller (1996).

15. See Liddell and Scott et al. (1843, 1033–1034), where the first meaning of *legein* is 'to gather, pick up,' and only then 'to recount, retell' and 'to say, speak,' which seems to point then to something like a gathering

together and setting out in language for an audience. Heidegger capitalizes on this original meaning throughout his thinking, but perhaps most directly in his interpretation of Heraclitus, "*Logos* (Heraklit, Fragment 50)" (1954c).
16. In addition to the passages referenced here from the *Meno* and the *Euthyphro*, we might note also the particularly clear presentation of this same shift in the *Hippias Major* (*Hp. Ma.* 287e–289c) and the *Charmides* (*Chrm.* 173a–176a). In the former, Socrates draws the famous sophist out of that context in which *to kalos* or 'the fine' appears as a beautiful young woman and he does so by bringing into view what appears fine in other contexts—the humble contexts of farming, cooking, or playing music in which a pot, a horse, or a lyre might appear even more fine than an attractive maiden. In the latter, just as in the *Laches*' discussion of courage, we find Socrates here discussing *sōphrosunē* or 'sound-mindedness' first with an unsophisticated interlocutor in the eponymous Charmides and then with a sophisticated interlocutor in Critias. And here the dialogue unfolds by precisely the same dynamic as the *Laches*. Socrates first draws the young Charmides from the specific instantiations or examples of how *sōphrosunē* appears in certain contexts (as slowness or quietness and then as humility or shame), and Socrates does so by drawing into view other everyday contexts in which it seems sound-minded to do something altogether different, even the opposite. In so doing, Socrates demands that his interlocutor consider them all together in the horizon of the whole and Charmides proves perplexed by this. The being of *sōphrosunē* withdraws behind these context-specific appearances. But then, Socrates shows Critias that the question of 'what *sōphrosunē* is' emerges only within the context of and is situated within the even more terrible question of 'what the good is' (*Chrm.* 174b–d). Socrates will sometimes substitute questions concerning 'what *to agathon* or *eudaimonia* are' for his more characteristic inquiry into 'what *aretē* or "virtue" is' (*Grg.* 499c, *Euthd.* 282a). All of these together make up a varied terminology for describing that which is always at stake in every situation, in every decision in human life.
17. The word of praise Socrates uses here, *pankalōs*, is a compound of the adverb *kalōs*, which means 'finely, beautifully,' with *pan*, the 'whole, everything, all.' In this text, the employment of this term at this point seems particularly significant. Given that Socrates uses the term *pan* earlier in his attempt to indicate the scope of his question (*Euthphr.* 5d), this term might here mark very precisely the fact that Euthyphro's attempt is no

longer limited to a specific contextual appearance of piety. Rather, although it will prove not to accomplish the immediate *technē*-like grasp that Euthyphro presumes to possess, it at least attempts to take in view all appearances thereof. To answer in such a way would be to answer 'beautifully,' in the specific sense of according with or as situated within the horizon of the 'whole,' even if it fails to comprehend that whole utterly. This is completely lost in the standard translations of this passage, and of the term in general. Grube translates it as "splendid" and Allen as "excellent." It should be noted that, although these are not counterintuitive, the translation offered in Liddell and Scott et al. (1843, 1284), "all or very beautiful, good or right," does seem to stress the aforementioned sense.

18. Burnet (1914, 32). See also Taylor (1926, 30), Crombie (1962, 44), Allen (1970, 67–79), Guthrie (1975, 108), and, with respect specifically to the *Euthyphro*, Geach (1966, 370–371).
19. Indeed, Robinson (1953, 58–59) complains about asking the 'What is "x"?' question in English as well as in Greek, writing, "it is, perhaps, when unsupported by a context, the vaguest of all forms of question except an inarticulate grunt. It indicates less determinately than any other the sort of information the questioner wants." One could ask whether a question would even constitute language if it occurs unsupported by any context whatsoever, but in any case Socrates' question is certainly not without narrative context when he poses it, for, as seen earlier, he unfolds it out of the interlocutors' practical questions and he often then provides extremely elaborate indications of what he is looking for.
20. Nehamas (1975, 159–175).
21. Benson (1992, 99–111) agrees with Nehamas and focuses on a problem that I have attempted to indicate earlier in my readings of the passages. He asks the question that Nehamas's interpretation begs, namely, the question of what Socrates means when he says that the first answers of his interlocutors are the wrong *kind* of answers and that their second or third attempts are at least the right *kind* or "formally adequate," even if they are still insufficient. Benson argues that, although the first answers *are* definitions of a class of actions, not ostensive indications of a particular, they are still not yet definitions of virtue or a virtue as *one* and as a *whole*. Gonzalez (1998, 285 n.2) takes Benson's contribution further, and in precisely the direction I am heading, when he writes, "I would add the explanation that the interlocutor's vision is focused on ordinary experience in which the virtue under examination is neither one nor complete."

22. Ibid. (171).
23. Ibid.
24. Vlastos (1974, 95).
25. Nehamas (1975, 172).
26. Ibid.
27. See Held (2000) on the "controversy concerning truth" as arising within the everyday attitude.
28. Field (1949, 28).
29. It is vital to recognize that these are not answers to questions, but always only refinements of the original question. We should not derive comfort from the elenchus, but precisely the opposite. As we have seen, scholars commonly presume that Socrates' elenctic conversations point to the "correct" answer to his questions in the course of showing the interlocutor's answers as "incorrect." One might presume for instance to find this at the point when Socrates nudges Nicias to affirm his earlier statement that courage is a part of virtue and virtue is the sum of this and other parts, this statement then leading to his refutation. We might be tempted to think that the correct answer is here indicated—virtue is *not* an aggregate of distinct parts but all these "parts" name a single condition in various ways—courage, temperance, justice, piety, and, most illuminatingly for Socrates, wisdom or knowledge concerning what is good and bad. However, this is to miss the point completely, even to defuse the truth of *aporia*. For what the elenchus leaves us with is the troubling unresolved tension between that position, all the virtues are one, and the nevertheless compelling appearance of their differences that was affirmed at the outset in declaring them *merē* or 'parts.'
30. Oftentimes, even in the early dialogues, the all-encompassing question of 'what virtue is' will give way to the question of *to agathon* or 'the good.' In so doing, Socrates seems to make even more emphatic the non-context-specific character of that to which his questioning ultimately refers. Although the notions of 'virtue or excellence' and 'goodness' can clearly encompass human life with equal generality, 'goodness' seems to bring this all-encompassing character even more to the fore. See *Chrm.* 174b–c and *Ly.* 220a–b.
31. In *Dialectic and Dialogue,* Gonzalez offers an excellent reading of the *Laches,* and of the Socratic elenctic project in general, wherein he sees Socrates as situated between the everyday attitude and the presumed sophistic *technē* of virtue, being critical of both. However, Gonzalez then argues that Plato intends to portray Socrates as having a different,

non-*technē*-like knowledge of virtue that distinguishes him from his interlocutors. Indeed, he says that "The knowledge sought by Socrates is the same as that involved in *being* courageous: an open-ended knowledge that does not presume to have eliminated ignorance" (1998, 38). With this understanding of Socrates' elenchus as not at all aiming at, but harshly critical of, the *technē*-model of virtue, I am in complete agreement. However, and this may be just a question of emphasis, I would be hesitant to state as Gonzalez does that "this paradoxical 'ignorant knowledge' or 'knowing ignorance' . . . is clearly displayed in what Socrates himself does" (1998, 40) in such a way that we should feel confident that Socrates 'knows how' to be virtuous even if he does not 'know what' virtue is. In my view, even Socrates' own wisdom and virtue must remain radically in question. Just as we saw in the *Apology*, Plato does not overcome the indefensibility of Socrates' project by changing the terms of the discussion so much as he does so by placing those terms painfully in question. What compels us to follow Socrates is his having 'displayed,' not his superior (if radically redefined) wisdom, virtue, and courage, but rather the utterly questionworthy character of 'what these are.'

32. One is suspicious as to whether Nicias has come to suffer, as Laches explicitly did, the *aporia* that Socrates here generously grants him. His emerging from previous encounters with Socrates confessedly undisturbed speaks against this, as does his promise at the dialogue's end to consult with the Damon from whom he had received one of his sophistic formulae, who will surely answer the questions they have left open (*La.* 200b–c). As indicated earlier, this provides us with a good explanation as to why the dialogue might be named for the man of action Laches rather than the sophisticated Nicias—the former is perhaps no wiser, more courageous, or more virtuous, but he is more susceptible to *aporia*.

33. Recall here the *oikos* indicated by the condition of being *oikeios* or 'kindred' to one another, which Socrates suggests in the *Lysis* might be the true essence of human *philia* or 'friendship.' As mentioned in the introduction, it seems that we come together and are truly friends to one another in a human sense not by being alike and not by being different (and useful to one another), but by being situated together in the same *oikos* or 'dwelling place,' a site both distant from and yet exposed and opened toward the all-important being of virtue.

34. Hyland (1995, 5). Compare Socrates' remark at the end of the *Protagoras*, where he and the eponymous sophist have arrived at *aporia* on

the specific issue of whether virtue is a teachable form of knowledge, a *technē*. Returning to Protagoras's earlier *muthos* of how all human beings came to share in political virtue (*Prt.* 322d), Socrates says that he prefers Prometheus (who surreptitiously gave fire and technical wisdom to human beings) over Epimetheus (who forgot to outfit humans with any powers at all). Playing here on the etymology of the god's name, *Promētheus* as related to *pro-mēthēs* or 'fore-thinking, pre-understanding,' Socrates says, "Of him I at least am often making use, for because I take forethought (προμηθούμενς) concerning my life as a whole (ὑπὲρ τοῦ βίου τοῦ ἐμαυτοῦ παντὸς) I busy myself with all these things. And if you are willing, just as I said at the outset, I would be pleased to look into these things thoroughly together (συνδιασκοποίην) with you (μετὰ σοῦ)" (*Prt.* 361d). Important is the sense that Socrates' practice of investigating "these things," i.e., virtue and its various aspects and appearances, arises as a result of his taking a view that encompasses his life as a whole. However, as we emphasized earlier, this is the whole opened up and left open by the Socratic question, 'What *is* "x"?' It is not a presumably grasped whole, but a distant horizon that gathers all the discrete contexts of everyday life and demands that we consider them together, whereby the various appearances of 'what virtue is' in those contexts conflict with one another and open us up to the being of virtue as distressingly excessive.

CONCLUSION: *APORIA* IN THE MIDDLE DIALOGUES

1. Jaeger (1934, 85).
2. In opposing, on the one hand, his own mode of causal explanation by way of Ideas to, on the other hand, the materialistic mode of explanation employed by the Pre-Socratic natural philosophers, Socrates refers to these paradigmatic causes as "those oft-murmured-about things (τὰ πολυθρύλητα)" and even as those things "I am always speaking about, both before and elsewhere, and about which I do not stop speaking" (*Phd.* 100b).
3. Grube (1935, 1).
4. Ibid. (3).
5. Heidegger's discussions of the Platonic *idea*/*eidos* and its role in the birth of metaphysical thinking are far too numerous to cite, but we might note as representative and as particularly lucid the few pages devoted to

the subject in *Einführung in die Metaphysik*. Here Heidegger specifically emphasizes the ambivalence of Plato's turn to the Ideas, which he sees as indicating both "daß und wie das Sein im Erscheinen *mit* sein Wesen hat," as well as marking a definitive step away from the belonging together of Being and appearance and toward a modern, subject-object framework. See Heidegger (1953, 78–82).

6. Sallis (1975) is an exception to this, for in his reading of the dialogues he takes very much to heart the notion of *idea/eidos* as 'look.' Also, Gordon (1999) argues very persuasively for the need to reevaluate the relationship between being and appearances or images in the Platonic dialogues, and her emphasis in this discussion on the essentially finite character of human knowledge places her interpretation in very close proximity to that which is offered here. Indeed, she speaks of philosophy for Plato as not an "escape from this embodied life," but a "way of coping from within it," not a "purely rational activity carried out beyond the human realm," but rather a "human activity carried out within—and because of—our limitations" (1999, 142).

7. A question might arise here as to how this bond between being and appearing in the middle Plato relates to what Aristotle criticizes as the main Platonic departure from the historical Socrates, the introduction of a *chōrismos* between the Ideas and their sensible, material instantiations. On the separation of the Ideas in the middle dialogues, see chapter 5, note 28.

8. Rachel Barney, in her excellent article on the *Cratylus*, argues against the common tendency to see Plato/Socrates as arguing for some kind of conventionalism, due to the quite decisive rejection of the Cratylean position. Indeed, she finds that "Socrates' whole project in the *Cratylus* is to search for a standard of correctness for names which is independent of our conventions and so can be used to evaluate them—just as in other dialogues he searches for a standard against which to judge constitutions or statesmen" (1997, 147). This seems quite correct, so long as we understand that the "standards" to which Socrates' points are excessive, and thus we relate to them truthfully only in that divine wandering that is constant, lifelong Socratic questioning.

9. On the theme of play in general and on its specific importance in the Platonic dialogues, see Hyland (1972).

10. The very same justification can be given for focusing attention on the etymology of the name Hermes, since he is understood as 'the one who contrived *logos* for mortals' (*Cra.* 407e–408b). And *logos* is there related

to the *tragikos* or 'goat-like, tragic' character of the son of Hermes, the god Pan, due to its always double nature, rough and goatlike on the bottom in its relation to the appearances it names and smooth and godlike on the top in relation to the Ideas it always also names (*Cra.* 408b–d). For an interpretation of the *Cratylus* that foregrounds this etymology, see Kirkland (2007b).

11. Hermogenes also asks Socrates here to address *pseudos* or 'false' and *on* or 'being,' but the etymologies simply reinforce the two with which we are more centrally concerned. *Pseudos* is understood as related to restraint and sleep and thus opposed to the divine motion to which Socrates gestures here in the etymology of *alētheia*, and *on* and *ousia* "say the same as *alētheia*" insofar as they are related to *ion* or 'going.' See *Cra.* 421b–c.
12. Liddell and Scott et al. (1843, 63).
13. Kierkegaard (1841, XII.195).
14. Socrates states that he takes the Delphic imperative "Know thyself [*Gnōthi sauton*]" as his philosophical directive. This is already proof of an attitude quite different from that of the natural scientist. Just as the disappearance of Orithuia could be explained by the wind, likewise with the whisper from the hole in the rock at Delphi, which was heard as the voice of the god by the Pythian there. For Socrates, taking the Delphic imperative seriously means asking how one should live in order to live well and happily, which is equivalent to asking about issues related to 'what our human virtue or excellence is.' But *Gnōthi sauton* had quite a different valence in Delphic religion. In the context of other Delphic inscriptions, such as 'Nothing in excess,' 'Observe the limit,' 'Curtail hubris,' and 'Bow down to the divine,' it seems clear that what it is most important to know about oneself are one's mortal limitations over against the immortal. Thus, following its traditional meaning, Socrates' adherence to this inscription indicates that, in his investigations, he is careful to acknowledge the limitation of his human grasp. But this is simply another way of saying that he acknowledges a *distance* in the world of human experience, into which what he seeks to know withdraws. There is thus good reason even here to suspect that Socratic philosophizing shares with the mythical attitude an attendance to monstrosity, i.e., to *distance* in the world in which we find ourselves.

Bibliography

Ackrill, J. L. 1997, 1999. "Language and Reality in Plato's *Cratylus*." In *Plato I: Metaphysics and Epistemology*, ed. G. Fine, 125–142. Oxford: Oxford University Press.
Allen, R. E. 1960. "The Socratic Paradox." *Journal of the History of Ideas* 21.2: 256–265.
———. 1970. *Plato's Euthyphro and the Earlier Theory of Forms*. New York: Humanities Press.
Annas, J. 1985. "Self-Knowledge in Early Plato." In *Platonic Investigations*, ed. D. O'Meara, 111–138. Washington, DC: Catholic University of America Press.
———. 1999. *Platonic Ethics Old and New*. Ithaca, NY: Cornell University Press.
Arnim, H. von. 1914. *Platos Jugenddialoge und die Entstehungszeit des Phaidros*. Berlin: Teubner.
Ballard, E. G. 1965. *Socratic Ignorance: An Essay on Platonic Self-Knowledge*. The Hague: Martinus Nijhoff.
Barney, R. 1997. "Plato on Conventionalism." *Phronesis* 42.2: 143–162.
Bassett, S. E. 1928. "Note on *Ainittesthai*: Plato's *Apology* 27A, 21B." *Classical Review* 42:58.
Benardete, S. 1984. *The Being of the Beautiful: Plato's* Theaetetus, Sophist, *and* Statesman. Chicago: University of Chicago Press.
Benson, H. 1990. "Meno, the Slave-boy, and the *Elenchos*." *Phronesis* 35: 128–158.
———. 1992. "Misunderstanding the 'What is F-ness?' Question." In *Essays on the Philosophy of Socrates*, ed. H. Benson, 123–136. New York: Oxford University Press.
———. 2000. *Socratic Wisdom*. Oxford: Oxford University Press.

———. 2002. "Problems with Socratic Method." In *Does Socrates Have a Method?: Rethinking the Elenchus in Plato's Dialogues and Beyond*, ed. G. Scott, 101–113. University Park: Pennsylvania State University Press.
Blanchot, M. 1969. *L'Entretien infini*. Paris: Éditions Gallimard.
Bowen, A. 1988. "On Interpreting Plato." In *Platonic Writings / Platonic Readings*, ed. C. Griswold, 49–65. New York: Routledge.
Bradley, F. H. 1914, 2011. *Essays on Truth and Reality*. Cambridge: Cambridge University Press.
Brandwood, L. 1976. *A Word Index to Plato*. Compendia 8. Leeds: Mahey.
———. 1990. *The Chronology of Plato's Dialogues*. Cambridge: Cambridge University Press.
———. 1992. "Stylometry and Chronology." In *The Cambridge Companion to Plato*, ed. R. Kraut, 90–120. Cambridge: Cambridge University Press.
Brann, E. 2004. *The Music of the Republic: Essays on Socrates' Conversations and Plato's Writings*. Philadelphia: Paul Dry Books.
Brickhouse, T., and N. D. Smith. 1984. "Vlastos on the Elenchus." *Oxford Studies in Ancient Philosophy* 2: 185–196.
———. 1989. *Socrates on Trial*. Princeton: Princeton University Press.
———. 1994. *Plato's Socrates*. Oxford: Oxford University Press.
Brisson, L. 1998. *Plato the Myth Maker*, tr. and ed. G. Naddaf. Chicago: University of Chicago Press.
Brumbaugh, R. 1964. *The Philosophers of Greece*. New York: Crowell.
Brun, J. 1960. *Socrate*. Paris: Presses universitaires de France.
Bultmann, R. 1933. "Der griechische und hellenistische Sprachgebrauch von ἀλήθεια." In *Theologisches Wörterbuch zum Neuen Testament*, ed. G. Kittel. Vol. 1. 239–248. Stuttgart: Kohlhammer.
Burckhardt, J. 1898–1902, 1971. *Griechische Kulturgeschichte*. I–IV. München: dtv.
Burkert, W. 1985. *Greek Religion*. Cambridge: Harvard University Press.
Burnet, J. 1914, 1978. *Early Greek Philosophy*. London: Macmillan.
———. 1924. "Commentary." In *Plato's* Euthyphro, Apology of Socrates, *and* Crito, ed. J. Burnet. Oxford: Clarendon Press.
Burnyeat, M. F. 1971. "Virtues in Action." In *The Philosophy of Socrates*, ed. G. Vlastos, 209–234. Garden City: Doubleday.
Campbell, R. 1992. *Truth and Historicity*. Oxford: Clarendon Press.
Casey, E. S. 1993. *Getting Back into Place: Toward a Renewed Understanding of the Place-World*. Indianapolis: Indiana University Press.
Cherniss, H. 1945, 1962. *The Riddle of the Early Academy*. New York: Russell and Russell.

Churchill, W. 1930. *My Early Life: A Roving Commission.* London: Thornton Butterworth.
Coppleston, F., S.J. 1946, 1962. *A History of Philosophy.* Vol. 1. Part 1. New York: Doubleday.
Cornford, F. M. 1932. *Before and After Socrates.* Cambridge: Cambridge University Press.
———. 1933. "The Athenian Philosophical Schools, I: The Philosophy of Socrates." In *Cambridge Ancient History,* ed. D. M. Lewis and J. Boardman, 302–309. Vol. VI. Cambridge: Cambridge University Press.
———. 1950. *The Unwritten Philosophy.* Cambridge: Cambridge University Press.
———. 1952. *Principium Sapientiae: A Study of the Origins of Greek Philosophical Thought.* Cambridge: Cambridge University Press.
Crombie, I. M. 1962. *An Examination of Plato's Doctrines.* London: Routledge.
Derrida, J. 1972. *La dissemination.* Paris: Editions du Seuil.
Descartes, R. 1641, 1983. *Oeuvres de Descartes.* VII. *Meditationes de prima philosophia.* Ed. C. Adam and P. Tannery. Paris: Librairie philosophique J. Vrin.
Detienne, M. 1967. *Les maîtres de vérité dans la grèce archaïque.* Paris: Maspero.
Devereux, D. 1994. "Separation and Immanence in Plato's Theory of the Forms." In *Plato 1: Metaphysics and Epistemology,* ed. G. Fine, 192–214. Oxford: Oxford University Press.
Diels, H., and W. Kranz, tr. and ed. 1952. *Die Fragmente der Vorsokratiker.* I–III. 6. Berlin: Weidmann.
Dodds, E. R. 1951. *The Greeks and the Irrational.* Berkeley: University of California Press.
Dover, K. J. 1974. *Greek Popular Morality in the Time of Plato and Aristotle.* Berkeley: University of California Press.
Field, G. C. 1931. *Plato and His Contemporaries: A Study in Fourth-Century Life and Thought.* New York: Dutton.
———. 1949. *The Philosophy of Plato.* Oxford: Oxford University Press.
Figal, G. 1998, 2006. *Sokrates.* München: Beck Verlag.
Fine, G. 1984. "Separation." *Oxford Studies in Ancient Philosophy* 2: 31–87.
———. 1986. "Immanence." *Oxford Studies in Ancient Philosophy* 4: 71–97.
Fontenrose, J. 1978. *The Delphic Oracle: Its Responses and Operations with a Catalogue of Responses.* Berkeley: University of California Press.
Friedländer, P. 1964. *Platon.* I–III. Berlin: Walter de Gruyter.

Gadamer, H.-G. 1931, 1985. *Platos dialogische Ethik. Gesammelte Werke.* Bd. V: *Griechische Philosophie* 1. Tübingen: Mohr/Siebeck.
———. 1960, 1990. *Wahrheit und Methode: Grundzüge einer philosophischen Hermeneutik.* Tübingen: Mohr/Siebeck.
Gaiser, K. 1959. *Protreptik und Paränese bei Platon.* Stuttgart: Kohlhammer.
———. 1968. *Platons Ungeschriebene Lehre.* Stuttgart: Klett.
Gaisford, T. 1848. *Etymologicum Magnum.* Oxford: Oxford University Press.
Geach, P. T. 1966. "Plato's *Euthyphro*: An Analysis and Commentary." *Monist* 50: 369–382.
Gentzler, J. 1996. "Recollection and the Problem of Socratic Elenchus." *Proceedings of the Boston Area Colloquium in Ancient Philosophy* 10: 357–395.
Giebel, M. 2001. *Das Orakel von Delphi: Geschichte und Texte.* Stuttgart: Reclam.
Goldschmidt, V. 1947. *Les dialogues de Platon: structure et méthode dialectique.* Paris: Presses universitaires de France.
Gonzalez, F. 1995. *The Third Way: New Directions in Platonic Studies.* Lanham, MD: Rowman and Littlefield.
———. 1998. *Dialectic and Dialogue: Plato's Practice of Philosophical Inquiry.* Evanston: Northwestern University Press.
———. 2002a. "The Socratic Elenchus as Constructive Protreptic." In *Does Socrates Have a Method? Rethinking Elenchus in Plato's Dialogues and Beyond,* ed. G. Scott, 161–182. University Park, PA: Penn State University Press.
———. 2002b. "Conversing About Virtue Everyday: The *Apology*'s Defense of Care and Dialogue." *Proceedings of the Ancient Philosophy Society* 2:1–26.
Gordon, J. 1999. *Turning Toward Philosophy: Literary Device and Dramatic Structure in Plato's Dialogues.* University Park, PA: Penn State University Press.
Gould, J. 1955. *The Development of Plato's Ethics.* New York: Russell and Russell.
Greene, W. C. 1918. "Plato's View of Poetry." *Harvard Studies in Classical Philology* 29: 1–75.
Griffin, J. 1980. *Homer on Life and Death.* Oxford: Clarendon Press.
Griswold, C. L. 1986. *Self-Knowledge in Plato's* Phaedrus. University Park: Penn State University Press.
———, ed. 1988. *Platonic Writings / Platonic Readings.* London: Routledge.
Grote, G. 1865. *Plato and the Other Companions of Socrates.* Tr. Murray. 3 vols. London: John Murray.
Grube, G. M. A. 1935, 1980. *Plato's Thought.* Indianapolis: Hackett.

Gulley, N. 1968. *The Philosophy of Socrates*. London: Macmillan.
Guthrie, W. K. C. 1950a, 1975. *The Greek Philosophers: From Thales to Aristotle*. London: Methuen.
———. 1950b, 1968. *The Greeks and Their Gods*. London: Methuen.
———. 1962. *A History of Greek Philosophy*. Vol. I: *The Earlier Presocratics and the Pythagoreans*. Cambridge: Cambridge University Press.
———. 1965. *A History of Greek Philosophy*. Vol. II: *The Presocratic Tradition from Parmenides to Democritus*. Cambridge: Cambridge University Press.
———. 1969. *A History of Greek Philosophy*. Vol. III: *The Fifth Century Enlightenment*. Cambridge: Cambridge University Press.
———. 1971a. *The Sophists*. Cambridge: Cambridge University Press.
———. 1971b. *Socrates*. Cambridge: Cambridge University Press.
———. 1975. *A History of Greek Philosophy*. Vol. IV: *Plato: The Man and His Dialogues, Earlier Period*. Cambridge: Cambridge University Press.
Hackforth, R. 1933. *The Composition of Plato's* Apology. Cambridge: Cambridge University Press.
Hadot, P. 1995. *Qu'est-ce que la philosophie antique?* Paris: Gallimard.
Hegel, G. W. F. 1832–1845, 1971. *Vorlesungen über die Geschichte der Philosophie*. Werke 18. Vol. I. Frankfurt a.M.: Suhrkamp.
Heidegger, M. 1927, 1993. *Sein und Zeit*. Tübingen: Max Niemeyer.
———. 1940, 1976. "Platons Lehre von der Wahrheit." In *Wegmarken*, 109–144. Frankfurt a.M.: Klostermann.
———. 1943, 1976. "Vom Wesen der Wahrheit." In *Wegmarken*, 73–97. Frankfurt a.M.: Klostermann.
———. 1953. *Einführung in die Metaphysik*. Tübingen: Niemeyer.
———. 1954a. "Die Frage nach der Technik." In *Vorträge und Aufsätze*, 13–44. Pfullingen: Neske.
———. 1954b. "*Alētheia* (Heraklit, Fragment 16)." In *Vorträge und Aufsätze*, 53–78. Pfullingen: Neske.
———. 1954c. "*Logos* (Heraklit, Fragment 50)." In *Vorträge und Aufsätze*, 3–25. Pfullingen: Neske.
———. 1984. *Hölderlins Hymne "Der Ister."* Gesamtausgabe. Bd. 53. Frankfurt a.M.: Klostermann.
———. 1992. *Platon: Sophistes*. Gesamtausgabe. Bd. 19. Frankfurt a.M.: Klostermann.
Held, K. 1980. *Heraklit, Parmenides und der Anfang von Philosophie und Wissenschaft: Eine phänomenologische Besinnung*. Berlin: de Gruyter.
———. 2000. "The Controversy Concerning Truth: Towards a Prehistory of Phenomenology." *Husserl Studies* 17.1: 35–48.

Hölderlin, F. 1994. *Sämtliche Werke und Briefe*. I–III. Frankfurt a.M.: Deutscher Klassiker Verlag.
Howland, J. 1991. "Re-Reading Plato: The Problem of Platonic Chronology." *Phoenix* 45.2: 189–214.
Hüni, H. 1997. "Die Erscheinung der Sprache in Platons Kratylos." *Phänomenologische Forschungen* 2.2: 296–307.
Husserl, E. 1913, 2009. *Ideen zu einer rheinen Phänomenologie und phänomenologischen Philosophie*. Leipzig: Felix Meiner.
———. 1936, 2007. *Die Krisis der europäischen Wissenschaften und die transzendentale Phänomenologie: Eine Einleitung in die phänomenologische Philosophie*. Hamburg: Meiner.
Hyland, D. 1972. "Athletics and Angst: Reflections on the Philosophic Relevance of Play." In *Sport and the Body: A Philosophical Symposium*, ed. E. Gerber. Philadelphia: Lea and Febiger.
———. 1981. *The Virtue of Philosophy: An Interpretation of Plato's Charmides*. Athens, OH: Ohio University Press.
———. 1995. *Finitude and Transcendence in the Platonic Dialogues*. Albany: State University of New York Press.
———. 1997. "Caring for Myth: Heidegger, Plato, and the Myth of Cura." *Research in Phenomenology* 27.1: 90–102.
———. 2004. *Questioning Platonism: Continental Interpretations of Platonism*. Albany: State University of New York Press.
Irwin, T. H. 1977. *Plato's Moral Theory*. Oxford: Clarendon Press.
———. 1986. "Coercion and Objectivity in Platonic Dialectic." *Revue Internationale de Philosophie* 40: 49–74.
———. 1992. "Socratic Puzzles: A Review of Gregory Vlastos's *Socrates, Ironist and Moral Philosopher*." *Oxford Studies in Ancient Philosophy* 10: 241–266.
———. 1995. *Plato's Ethics*. Oxford: Oxford University Press.
———. 1995, 1999. "The Theory of Forms." In *Plato I: Metaphysics and Epistemology*, ed. G. Fine, 143–170. Oxford: Oxford University Press.
Jaeger, W. 1934, 1947. *Paideia: Die Formung des griechischen Menschen*. I–III. Berlin: de Gruyter.
Jowett, B. 1874, 1953. "Introduction and Analysis: *Parmenides*." In *The Dialogues of Plato: Translated into English with Analyses and Introductions*. Vol. IV. Oxford: Clarendon Press.
Kahn, C. H. 1996. *Plato and the Socratic Dialogue: The Philosophical Use of a Literary Form*. Cambridge: Cambridge University Press.
Kidd, I. G. 1967. In *The Encyclopedia of Philosophy*, ed. P. Edwards, 481–482. New York: MacMillan.

Kierkegaard, S. 1841, 1989. *The Concept of Irony: With Continual Reference to Socrates*, ed. and tr. E. Hong. Princeton: Princeton University Press.
Kirkland, S. 2004. "Socrates *contra scientiam*." *Epoché* 8.2: 313–32.
———. 2007a. "Thinking in the Between with Heidegger and Plato." *Research in Phenomenology* 37.1: 95–111.
———. 2007b. "*Logos* as Message from the Gods: On the Etymology of '*Hermes*' in Plato's *Cratylus*." *Bochumer philosophisches Jahrbuch für Antike und Mittelalter* 12: 1–14.
———. 2009. "The Tragic Foundation of Aristotle's Ethics." *Graduate Faculty Philosophy Journal* 30.2: 1–23.
Kitto, H. D. F. 1952, 1991. *The Greeks*. New York: Penguin.
Klein, J. 1965. *A Commentary on Plato's Meno*. Chapel Hill: University of North Carolina Press.
Krämer, H. J. 1959. *Arete bei Platon und Aristoteles: Zum Wesen und zur Geschichte der platonischen Ontologie*. Heidelberg: Winter.
Kraut, R. 1984. *Socrates and the State*. Princeton: Princeton University Press.
Krentz, P. 1982. *The Thirty at Athens*. Ithaca: Cornell University Press.
Kube, J. 1969. *TEXNH und APETH: Sophistisches und platonisches Tugendwissen*. Berlin: de Gruyter.
Landmann, M. 1941. "Socrates as a Precursor of Phenomenology." *Philosophy and Phenomenological Research* 2.1: 15–42.
Lesher, J. H. 1987. "Socrates' Disavowal of Knowledge." *Journal of the History of Philosophy* 25: 275–288.
Levet, Jean-Pierre. 1976. *Le vrai et le faux dans la pensée grecque achaïque: Etude de vocabulaire*. Paris: Editions les Belles Lettres.
Lewis, C. T. 1996. *An Elementary Latin Dictionary*. Oxford: Oxford University Press.
Liddell, H. S., and R. Scott et al. 1843, 1996. *A Greek-English Lexicon*. Oxford: Clarendon Press.
———. 1891, 1997. *A Lexicon: Abridged from Liddell and Scott's* Greek-English Lexicon. Oxford: Clarendon Press.
Lowell, R. 1978. *The Oresteia of Aeschylus*. New York: Farrar, Straus, and Giroux.
Luther, W. 1935. *"Wahrheit" und "Lüge" im ältesten Griechentum*. Leipzig: Borna.
Lyons, J. 1963. *Structural Semantics: An Analysis of Part of the Vocabulary of Plato*. Oxford: Blackwell.
Mabbott, J. D. 1926. "Aristotle and the Χωρισμός of Plato." *Classical Quarterly* 20: 72–71.

MacKenzie, M. M. 1988. "The Virtues of Socratic Ignorance." *Classical Quarterly* 38: 331–350.

Manchester, P. 2005. *The Syntax of Time: The Phenomenology of Time in Greek Physics and Speculative Logic from Iamblichus to Anaximander*. Boston: Brill.

Marion, J.-L. 1991. "Réponses à quelques questions." *Revue de métaphysique et de morale* 96.1: 65–72.

———. 1997. *Etant donné: Essai d'une phenomenology de la donation*. Paris: Presses universitaires de France.

Matthews, G. B. 2009. "Socratic Ignorance." In *A Companion to Plato*, ed. H. Benson, 103–118. West Sussex: Wiley-Blackwell.

McKim, R. 1988. "Shame and Truth in Plato's *Gorgias*." In *Platonic Writings / Platonic Readings*, ed. C. L. Griswold. 34–48. London: Routledge.

McNeill, W. 2006. *The Time of Life: Heidegger and Ēthos*. Albany: State University of New York Press.

McPherran, M. 1986. "Socrates and the Duty to Philosophize." *Southern Journal of Philosophy* 24.4: 541–560.

———. 2002. "Elenctic Interpretation and the Delphic Oracle." In *Does Socrates Have a Method? Rethinking the Elenchus in Plato's Dialogues and Beyond*, ed. G. Scott, 114–144. University Park: Penn State University Press.

Merton, T. 1956. *Thoughts in Solitude*. New York: Farrar, Straus, and Giroux.

Meyer, T. 1962. *Platons Apologie*. Stuttgart: Kohlhammer.

Meyerus, L. 1901. *Handbuch der griechischen Etymologie*. Leipzig: Hirzel.

Miller, M. 1996. "The Arguments I Seem to Hear": Argument and Irony in the 'Crito.' *Phronesis* 41.2: 121–137.

Mitchell, A. 2010. "Entering the World of Pain: Heidegger's Reading of Trakl." *Telos* 150 (Spring): 83–96.

Montuori, M. 1981. *Socrates: Physiology of a Myth*. Amsterdam: Gieben.

Nails, D. 1992. "Platonic Chronology Reconsidered." *Bryn Mawr Classical Review* 3: 314–327.

———. 2002. *The People of Plato: A Prosopography of Plato and Other Socratics*. Indianapolis: Hackett.

Natorp, P. 1903, 1961. *Platos Ideenlehre: Eine Einführung in den Idealismus*. Darmstadt: Wissenschaftliche Buchgesellschaft.

Nehamas, A. 1975, 1999. "Confusing Universals and Particulars in Plato's Early Dialogues." In *Virtues of Authenticity*, 159–175. Princeton: Princeton University Press.

———. 1985, 1999. "Meno's Paradox and Socrates as Teacher." In *Virtues of Authenticity*, 3–26. Princeton: Princeton University Press.
———. 1998. *The Art of Living: Socratic Reflections from Plato to Foucault.* Berkeley: University of California Press.
Nietzsche, F. 1872, 1988. *Die Geburt der Tragödie aus dem Geist der Musik. Werke. Kritische Studienausgabe.* Bd. I. Ed. G. Colli and M. Montinari. Berlin: de Gruyter/dtv.
———. 1874, 1988. *Vom Nutzen und Nachtheil der Historie für das Leben. Werke. Kritische Studienausgabe.* Bd. I. Ed. G. Colli and M. Montinari. Berlin: de Gruyter/dtv.
———. 1967. *Werke. Kritische Gesamtausgabe.* Bd. IV:1. Ed. G. Colli and M. Montinari. Berlin: de Gruyter.
———. 1980. "Nachgelassene Fragmente." *Kritische Studienausgabe.* Bd. VIII. Ed. G. Colli and M. Montinari. Berlin: de Gruyter/dtv.
Nilsson, M. 1952. *A History of Greek Religion.* Oxford: Oxford University Press.
Nussbaum, M. C. 1985. "Commentary on Edmunds." *Proceedings of the Boston Area Colloquium in Ancient Philosophy* 1: 231–240.
———. 1986. *The Fragility of Goodness: Luck and Ethics in Greek Tragedy and Philosophy.* Cambridge: Cambridge University Press.
———. 2003. *Upheavals of Thought: The Intelligence of Emotions.* Cambridge: Cambridge University Press.
Parke, H. W., and D. E. W. Wormell. 1956. *The Delphic Oracle.* 2 vols. Oxford: Blackwell.
Partridge, E. 1958. *Origins: A Short Etymological Dictionary of Modern English.* New York: Macmillan.
Patocka, J. 2002. *Plato and Europe.* Tr. P. Lom. Stanford: Stanford University Press.
Penner, T. 1971, 1999. "The Unity of Virtue." In *Plato 2: Ethics, Politics, Religion, and the Soul,* ed. G. Fine, 78–104. Oxford: Oxford University Press.
———. 1992. "Socrates and the Early Dialogues." In *The Cambridge Companion to Plato,* ed. R. Kraut, 121–169. Cambridge: Cambridge University Press.
Pokorny, J. 1959–1969. *Indogermanisches etymologisches Wörterbuch.* 2 vols. Bern: Francke.
Polansky, R. 1985. "Professor Vlastos' Analysis of Socratic Elenchus." *Oxford Studies in Ancient Philosophy* 3: 247–260.

Press, G. 2000. *Who Speaks for Plato? Studies in Platonic Anonymity.* Lanham, MD: Rowman and Littlefield.
Prior, William J. 1985. *Unity and Development in Plato's Metaphysics.* La Salle: Open Court.
———. 2004. "Socrates Metaphysician." *Oxford Studies in Ancient Philosophy* 27: 1–14.
Rappe, S. L. 1995. "Socrates and Self-Knowledge." *Apeiron* 28.1: 1–24.
Reeve, C. D. C. 1988. *Philosopher Kings: The Argument of Plato's Republic.* Princeton: Princeton University Press.
———. 1989. *Socrates in the* Apology. Indianapolis: Hackett.
Renaud, F. 2002. "Humbling as Upbringing: The Ethical Dimension of the Elenchus in the *Lysis*. In *Does Socrates Have a Method? Rethinking the Elenchus in Plato's Dialogues and Beyond*, ed. G. Scott, 183–198. University Park, PA: Penn State University Press.
Rilke, R. M. 1976. *Sämtliche Werke in 12 Bänden*, ed. E. Zinn. Frankfurt a.M.: Insel Verlag.
Robin, L. 1957. *Les rapports de l'être et de la connaissance d'après Platon.* Paris: Presses universitaires de France.
Robinson, R. 1953, 1966. *Plato's Earlier Dialectic.* Oxford: Clarendon Press.
de Romilly, J. 1975. *Time in Greek Tragedy.* Ithaca, NY: Cornell University Press.
Roochnik, D. 1988. "Terence Irwin's Reading of Plato." In *Platonic Writings / Platonic Readings*, ed. C. L. Griswold, 183–193. London: Routledge.
———. 1999. *Of Art and Wisdom: Plato's Understanding of Techne.* State College, PA: Penn State University Press.
———. 2004. *Retrieving the Ancients: An Introduction to Greek Philosophy.* Oxford: Blackwell.
Rosen, Stanley. 1967. "Heidegger's Interpretation of Plato." *The Journal of Existentialism* 7.28: 477–504.
———. 1973. "ΣΩΦΡΟΣΥΝΗ and *Selbstbewusstsein*." *The Review of Metaphysics.* 26.104: 617–642.
———. 1974. "Self-Consciousness and Self-Knowledge in Plato and Hegel." *Hegel-Studien.* Bd. 9: 109–129.
Ross, W. D. 1951. *Plato's Theory of Ideas.* Oxford: Clarendon Press.
Russon, J. 1999. "We Sense That They Strive: How to Read (the Theory of the Forms)." In *Retracing the Platonic Text*, ed. J. Russon and J. Sallis, 70–84. Evanston: Northwestern University Press.
Russon, J., and J. Sallis, eds. 1999. *Retracing the Platonic Text.* Evanston: Northwestern University Press.

Ryle, G. 1966. *Plato's Progress*. Cambridge: Cambridge University Press.
Sallis, J. 1975, 1996. *Being and Logos*. Indianapolis: Indiana University Press.
———. 1994. *Double Truth*. Albany: State University of New York Press.
Schaerer, R. 1930. ΕΠΙΣΤΗΜΗ *et* ΤΕΧΝΗ*: Etudes sur les notions de connaissance et d'art d'Homère à Platon*. Macon: Protat.
Schleiermacher, F. D. E. 1839. *Geschichte der Philosophie: Aus Schleiermachers handschriftlichen Nachlasse*, ed. H. Ritter. *Sämtliche Werke*. Bd. III. Teil 4.1. Berlin: G. Reimer.
———. 1996. Über die Philosophie Platons: Geschichte der Philosophie (Vorlesungen über Sokrates und Platon, 1819–*1823* & *Die Einleitungen zur Übersetzung des Platon 1804–1828*, ed. P. Steiner. Hamburg: F. Meiner.
Scott, G., ed. 2002. *Does Socrates Have a Method? Rethinking the Elenchus in Plato's Dialogues and Beyond*. University Park, PA: Penn State University Press.
———, ed. 2007. *Philosophy in Dialogue: Plato's Many Devices*. Evanston: Northwestern University Press.
Scruton, R. 1994. *Modern Philosophy: An Introduction and Survey*. New York: Penguin Books.
Seeskin, K. 1987. *Dialogue and Discovery: A Study in Socratic Method*. Albany: State University of New York Press.
Shorey, P. 1903. *The Unity of Plato's Thought*. Chicago: University of Chicago Press.
———. 1933. *What Plato Said*. Chicago: University of Chicago Press.
———. 1980. "The Idea of the Good in Plato's *Republic*: A Study in the Logic of Speculative Ethics." In *Selected Papers*, 2:28–79. New York: Garland.
Slings, S. R., and E. de Strycker. 1994. *Plato's* Apology of Socrates*: A Literary and Philosophical Study with a Running Commentary*. Leiden: Brill.
Snell, B. 1978. *Der Weg zum Denken und zur Wahrheit. Hypomnemata 57*. Göttingen: Vandenhoeck & Ruprecht.
Sourvinou-Inwood, C. 1996, 1999. "Dephic Oracle." In *The Oxford Classical Dictionary*, ed. S. Hornblower and A. Spawforth, 445–446. Oxford: Oxford University Press.
Spawforth, A. 1996, 1999. "Artisans and Craftsmen." In *The Oxford Classical Dictionary*, ed. S. Hornblower and A. Spawforth, 185. Oxford: Oxford University Press.
Stallbaum, G. 1863. "Notes." In *The* Apology of Socrates, *the* Crito, *and Part of the* Phaedo, ed. W. Smith. London: Walton and Maberley.

Stemmer, P. 1992. *Platons Dialektik: Die früheren und mittleren Dialoge.* Berlin: de Gruyter.
Stevens, W. 1922, 2011. "The Emperor of Ice-Cream." In *Selected Poems*, ed. J. Serio. New York: Knopf.
Stokes, M. C. 1986. *Plato's Socratic Conversations: Drama and Dialectic in Three Dialogues.* Baltimore: Johns Hopkins University Press.
———. 1992. "Socrates' Mission." In *Socratic Questions*, ed. B. Gower and M. C. Stokes, 26–81. Oxford: Oxford University Press.
Strauss, L. 1966. *The City and Man.* Chicago: Rand McNally.
———. 1983. *Studies in Platonic Political Philosophy.* Chicago: University of Chicago Press.
Tate, J. 1928. "'Imitation' in Plato's *Republic*." *Classical Quarterly* 22: 16–23.
———. 1932. "Plato and 'Imitation'." *Classical Quarterly* 26: 161–169.
Taylor, A. E. 1911. *Varia Socratica.* Oxford: Parker.
———. 1926, 1937. *Plato: The Man and His Work.* London: Methuen.
———. 1932. *Socrates.* London: Peter Davies.
Teloh, H. 1981. *The Development of Plato's Metaphysics.* University Park: Penn State University Press.
Tigerstedt, E. N. 1977. *Interpreting Plato.* Uppsala: Almquist & Wicksell.
Trawny, P. 2001. "Die Tragödie der Philosophie: Platons Streit mit den Dichtern." In *Denkwege 2: Philosophische Aufsätze*, ed. D. Koch and D. Barbaric, 106–128. Tübingen: Attempto.
———. 2003. "Apollon und der Anfang der Philosophie: Eine Anmerkung zur Grundlegung der Theoria bei Aristoteles." In *Internationales Jahrbuch für Hermeneutik*, ed. G. Figal, 225–242. Tübingen: J. B. Mohr (Siebeck).
———. 2007. *Sokrates oder der Geburt der politischen Philosophie.* Würzburg: Königshausen und Neumann.
Tredennick, H., tr. 1954, 1961. *Apology, Crito,* and *Phaedo.* In *Plato: The Collected Dialogues*, ed. E. Hamilton and H. Cairns. Princeton: Bollingen.
Tuckey, G. T. 1968. *Plato's* Charmides. Amsterdam: A. M. Hakkert.
Vernant, J.-P. 1979. *Religions, histories, raisons.* Paris: Maspero.
Versenyi, L. 1982. *Holiness and Justice: An Interpretation of Plato's Euthyphro.* Lanham: University Press of America.
Vlastos, G. 1956. "Introduction to Plato's *Protagoras*." In Plato, *Protagoras*, tr. B. Jowett and M. Ostwald, vii–lvi. Indianapolis: Bobbs-Merrill.
———. 1957/58. "The Paradox of Socrates." *Queens Quarterly* 64: 496–516.
———. 1971. *The Philosophy of Socrates: A Collection of Critical Essays.* New York: Doubleday and Co.

———. 1974. "A Note on 'Pauline Predications' in Plato." *Phronesis* 14: 95–104.

———. 1983a. "The Historical Socrates and Athenian Democracy." *Political Theory* 2: 495–516.

———. 1983b. "The Socratic Elenchus." *Oxford Studies in Ancient Philosophy* 1:27–58.

———. 1985. "Socrates' Disavowal of Knowledge." *Philosophical Quarterly* 35: 1–31.

———. 1991. *Socrates, Ironist and Moral Philosopher*. Ithaca: Cornell University Press.

———. 1994. *Socratic Studies*. Cambridge: Cambridge University Press.

Waldenfels, B. 1961. *Das sokratische Fragen: Aporie, Elenchos, Anamnesis*. Meisenheim am Glan: Hain.

Weinsheimer, J., and D. G. Marshall. 1997. "Translators' Preface." In H.-G. Gadamer, *Truth and Method*. New York: Continuum Publishing.

Welton, W., ed. 2003. *Plato's Forms: Varieties of Interpretation*. Lanham, MD: Lexington Books.

West, T. G. 1979. *Plato's Apology of Socrates: An Interpretation, with a New Translation*. Ithaca: Cornell University Press.

White, N. P. 1976. *Plato on Knowledge and Reality*. Indianapolis: Hackett.

Whitman, W. 1855, 2011. "Song of Myself." *Leaves of Grass: The Complete 1855 and 1991–1992 Editions*, ed. J. Hollander. New York: Library of America.

Wild, J. 1942. "Review of *Plato's Earlier Dialectic* by Richard Robinson." *Philosophy and Phenomenological Research* 2.4: 546–551.

Williams, B. 1993. *Shame and Necessity*. Berkeley: University of California Press.

Wolenski, J. 2005. "*Alētheia* in Greek Thought until Aristotle." *Annals of Pure and Applied Logic* 127: 339–360.

Woodruff, P. 1990. "Plato's Early Theory of Knowledge." In *Epistemology*, ed. S. Everson, 60–84. Cambridge: Cambridge University Press.

Zeller, E. 1885, 1963. *Die Philosophie der Griechen in ihrer geschichtlichen Entwicklung*. II. Teil. 1. Abteilung: *Sokrates und die Sokratiker: Plato und die alte Akademie*. Hildesheim: Olms Verlagsbuchhandlung.

Index

Ackrill, J.L., 13, 184n. 28
Aeschylus
  Agamemnon, 40
  Prometheus Bound, 212n. 29
  Robert Lowell's translation of the *Oresteia,* 150
  Suppliants, 206 n. 12
Alcibiades I, 235n. 8
Allen, R.E., 15, 179n. 8, 184n. 36, 233nn. 30, 33, 236n. 10, 240nn. 17, 18
alêtheia (truth), 48–55, 59–65
  and *meletê/lupê,* 109–111
  as *aporia,* 144–150, 151,
  as divine wandering, 159–162
  as unconcealment/unforgetting, 51–55, 192n. 10, 200n. 35, 201n. 38
  Socrates' commitment to, 48–51, 61, 199nn. 33, 34
anthrôpinê sophia (human wisdom), 38, 42, 69–70, 72, 113, 131, 211n. 27
Apology, xxi–xxii, 10, 36–38, 41–57, 64–70, 72, 89, 93–94, 97–99, 107, 108, 111, 154, 178n. 11, 215n. 48
aporia, xxi, 8, 99, 103–105, 109, 130–131, 145–147, 151, 155, 170, 176n. 10, 241n. 29, 242n. 34
appearance(s)
  and *alêtheia,* 51–55, 113–115, 144–150
  and *aporia,* 105, 135–136
  and the *deinos,* 48–50
  in relation to 'what is', xviii, 18–19, 21, 110, 140–144, 163, 232n. 30
  and Socratic questioning, 6, 25–27, 47, 80–82, 86, 95–96, 113–115, 121–122, 131–132
  and *meletê,* 101–103
  See *doxa*
  See *phainesthai*
aretê (virtue, excellence), xxi, 66–67, 88–91, 126–130, 180n. 15, 210n. 20
Aristotle, 61, 186n. 43
  assessment of Socrates, 3–8, 64, 82–83, 112, 133–135, 182n. 20, 203n. 3, 215n. 46
  on the *phusiologoi,* 65, 205n. 11
  on *technê,* 76–78, 213n. 37, 213n. 39, 214n. 41
  on the Platonic *chôrismos,* 112, 231n. 29, 244n. 7
  on the chronology of the dialogues, 175n. 9

Benson, Hugh, 84–85, 178n. 10, 179nn. 10, 11, 180n. 14, 182nn. 16, 18, 19, 183n. 25, 211n. 25, 216nn. 50, 53, 54, 238n. 13, 240n. 21
Blanchot, Maurice, 93

Bradley, F.H., 101
Brickhouse, T. and Smith, N.D.
Brisson, Luc, 39, 193n. 12

Callias, 67–68, 95, 208n. 15, 209n. 17, 216n. 57
Charmides, 9, 60–62, 64, 88, 89, 203n. 3, 219n. 61, 239n. 16
chronology of the dialogues, xx–xxii, 175n. 9
Churchhill, Winston, xv
Cicero, 5, 107, 222n.9
constructivist vs. non-constructivist interpretations, 8–12
Cratylus, 159–162, 193n. 14, 208n. 15, 244n. 10, 245n. 11
Crito, 89, 191n. 46
Croesus, 40

dei, 95–96, 145
deinos, 48–50, 55, 56, 76, 109, 115, 151, 198nn. 29, 30, 199n. 31
Delphic oracle, 40–41, 70, 178n. 2, 191n. 6, 194n. 16, 195n. 18, 196n. 20, 245n. 14
Descartes, Renè, 18–19, 186nn. 43, 44, 216n. 53
Detienne, Marcel, 39–40, 52, 192n. 10, 194n. 15, 201nn. 37, 38
Diogenes Laertius, 35, 43, 207n. 12
distance, 105, 108, 109–111, 111–115, 145–147, 151, 162–166, 232n. 30, 234n. 37, 245n. 14
divinity, 38–41, 71–72, 192nn. 7, 8, 9, 194n. 16
  and Socratic philosophizing, 191n. 6, 193n. 13, 196n. 20
doxa, 19–20, 23–27, 105, 148–150, 187nn. 1, 6
doxastic constraint, 238n. 13

elenchus, xvi–xvii, 3–8, 20, 55–57, 87–91, 146–150, 173n. 5, 179n. 11, 230n. 27
  and Socrates' defense, 37, 131n. 4, 241n. 29
epideixis (demonstration), 120, 125–126
epistêmê, 7–8, 78–79, 123, 214nn. 41, 42
eudaimonia, 75, 239n. 16
Euripides
  Melanippe, 41
  Medea, 220n. 5
Euthydemus, 60, 70–71, 72, 78, 79, 88, 89, 211n. 26, 224n. 11
Euthyphro, 59, 89, 138–139, 221n. 7
everyday attitude, xviii, xxiii, 6, 16–17, 19, 27, 30
  and Socratic questioning, 56–60, 62, 87–91, 132–133, 148–150, 150–151
  and sophistry, 87–91, 125
excess, 15–17, 49–50, 54–55, 71–72, 109–111, 111–115, 145–147, 162–166

Field, G.C., 142–143, 241n. 28
Friedländer, Paul, 52–53, 153, 201n. 40, 233n. 31

Gorgias, 59–60, 62–64, 71, 79–80, 88, 89, 107, 190n. 2, 191nn. 4, 5, 195n. 19, 202n. 1, 204n. 8, 206n. 12, 217n. 59
Grube, G.M.A., 156–157, 193n. 13, 197n. 26, 232n. 30, 240n. 17, 243n. 3
Heidegger, Martin, 27–28, 51–53, 157, 187nn. 8, 9, 199nn. 31, 34, 200n. 35, 201nn. 38, 39, 40, 213n.

37, 219n. 1, 226n. 14, 239n. 15, 243n. 5
Hegel, G.W.F., 27–28, 184n. 26, 188n. 10
Heraclitus, 40–41, 238n. 15,
Herodotus, 40
Hippias Major, 72, 88, 100, 239n. 16
Hölderlin, Friedrich, 38, 49, 111, 199n. 31
Homer, 51, 52, 74, 88, 161, 199n. 33, 200n. 35, 214n. 42
hubris, 71–73, 91, 98–99
Husserl, Edmund, 27–29, 36, 186n. 51, 187n. 9, 188n. 10, 199n. 34
Hyland, Drew, 114, 121–122, 151, 178n. 12, 185n. 38, 220n. 1, 234n. 36, 235nn. 3, 5, 244n. 9

ideal eidos, 112–113, 143, 156–159, 230n. 28, 231n. 29, 232nn. 30, 32, 243n. 5, 244n. 6
and the Good in Plato, 162–166
immanence. *See* transcendence
Ion, 88, 149
irony, Socratic, 10–11, 50, 67–68, 137, 149, 174n. 6, 176n. 10, 190n. 3, 208n. 14, 211n. 26, 230n. 26
and *muthos,* 160
Irwin, T.H., 13, 174n. 6, 184n. 29, 203n. 3, 204nn. 6, 9, 210n. 20, 215n. 48, 216n. 50, 236n. 10,

Jaeger, Werner, 155, 243n. 1
Jowett, Benjamin, 19, 186n. 45, 193n. 13, 197n. 26,

katholou (according to or from the whole)
and definition in Aristotle, 133–136
in Socratic questioning, 136–140, 170

Kierkegaard, Soren, 62–63, 108, 168, 184n. 26, 193n. 11, 204n. 7, 230n. 26, 245n. 13
Kube, Jorge, 74, 212nn. 30, 31

Laches, 72, 79, 80, 90, 119–151, 224n. 11, 236n. 11
logos, 55–57, 103, 109
and *muthos,* 41–43, 195n. 19
in the *Cratylus,* 193n. 194, 244n. 10
Lowell, Robert, 150
lupê (pain), 93, 96, 105, 145–146, 226n. 14
Lysis, xxii, 90, 227n. 17

Marion, Jean-Luc, 29–30, 189n. 11
meletê (concern), 94–95, 96–99, 105, 109, 151, 219n. 1, 220nn. 2, 6, 225n. 13, 227n. 15
Meno, 72, 89, 90, 100, 136–138, 195n. 19, 201n. 41, 217n. 59, 223n. 10, 224n. 11
Merton, Thomas, 229n. 25
Meyer, Thomas, 50–51, 191n. 5, 199nn. 32, 34
muthos (story, myth), 38–41, 167–171, 193n. 12
and *logos,* 41–43, 195n. 19

Nehamas, Alexander, 105–109, 140–143, 216n. 53, 227n. 18, 228nn. 20, 21, 22, 229n. 24, 240nn. 20, 21, 241n. 25,
Nietzsche, Friedrich, 3, 174n. 8
non-knowing of virtue, Socratic, 9, 62, 72–73, 82–87, 94–96, 131, 174n. 6, 203n. 3, 225n. 10
Nussbaum, Martha, 74–75, 197n. 24, 212nn. 32, 34, 213n. 39, 215n. 48

objective vs. phenomenal being, 12–21, 54, 110, 114, 156–159, 184n. 27, 230n. 27
   and Descartes, 18–19, 186n. 43
   and Husserl, 230n. 27
oneidizein (reproach), 220n. 5
   and Socratic elenchus, 99, 221n. 9

the paradox of Socrates xvi–xvii, 7, 12, 20–21, 35, 63, 106–107, 154, 227n. 19
pathos (affect), 44–45, 48, 56–57, 94–95, 149–150, 150–151
Penner, Terry, 13, 182nn. 15, 17, 184n. 30, 204n. 6, 216n. 49, 237n. 12
peras, 104–105
Phaedo, 107, 108, 156, 201n. 41
Phaedrus, 166–171, 171n. 5, 201n. 41
phainesthai (to appear, come to light), 25–27, 59–61, 81, 105
phenomenology, xviii, 27–31, 101–105, 115, 186n. 151
   and *doxa*, 30
   and intentionality, 29, 187n. 9, 188n. 10
   and givenness, 29–30, 189n. 11
philia (friendship), xxi
phusiologoi (natural philosophers), 65–67, 205n. 11
Pindar, 51–52, 71, 196n. 19
hoi polloi (the many), xxii, 68–70, 80, 91, 110–111, 113, 125
Protagoras, 48, 78–79, 81, 88, 89, 100, 206n. 12, 207n. 13, 208n. 15, 217n. 59, 219n. 63, 242n. 34

Republic, 88, 162–166
rhetoric, 37, 43–45, 60, 79–81, 91, 125, 196n. 21, 206n. 12
   Socrates and "true rhetoric," 191n. 5
Rilke, Rainer Maria, 119, 144

Robinson, Richard, 5, 14–15, 20–21, 173n. 5, 176n. 10, 179n. 7, 182n. 19, 184nn. 33, 34, 35, 185n. 39, 186n. 50, 240n. 19
Sallis, John, 35, 178n. 12, 176n. 19, 235n. 3, 244n. 6,
say-what-you-believe requirement, 131–132, 238n. 13
self-knowledge, 4–7, 63–64, 96, 178n. 2, 179n. 4, 180n. 12, 203n. 4
serenity vs. Socratic meta-serenity, 105–109, 229n. 25
Seneca, 93, 228n. 23
Shorey, Paul, 13, 179n. 8, 182n. 19, 184n. 27, 186n. 45, 233n. 31
Solon, 71, 94
sophists, 60, 65–72, 83, 88, 91, 124–126, 206n. 12
Sophocles
   Antigone, 49, 198n. 30, 199n. 31
   Oedipus Rex, 198nn. 29, 220n. 5
Stevens, Wallace, 23
subject-object relation, xvii, 7–8, 62–63, 185n. 41
Symposium, 41, 227n 17

Taylor, A.E., 15–16, 19–20, 182n. 19, 184n. 37, 186nn. 46, 47, 48, 192n. 6, 240n. 18,
technê (craft, art), 7–8, 64–65, 73–82, 210n. 20, 212nn. 30, 34, 35, 213n. 39, 214nn. 40, 42, 43
   as a sophistic (not Socratic) aim, 67–68, 123–124, 217n. 59
   etymology of, 73–74, 212n. 29
   in Aristotle, 76–78, 214n. 41
Theaetetus, 206n. 12, 208n. 15, 234n. 2
transcendence vs. immanence, 111–115
tuchê (fortune, chance), 74–75, 215n. 44

Vlastos, Gregory, xvi–xvii, 8, 16–17, 106–108, 173nn. 2, 3, 4, 5, 174nn. 6, 7, 175n. 9, 176n. 10, 178n. 1, 179n. 6, 182n. 17, 19, 185n. 38, 203n. 3, 204n. 6, 208n. 14, 216nn. 49, 50, 53, 227n. 19, 228nn. 20, 22, 230n. 27, 236n. 10, 238n. 13, 241n. 24

'What is "x"?' question, xxi, 5–7, 80–81, 111–112, 140–144, 179nn. 9, 10, 240n. 19

Whitman, Walt, 59

www.ingramcontent.com/pod-product-compliance
Lightning Source LLC
Chambersburg PA
CBHW020641230426
43665CB00008B/269